# Shutting the Door to the Kingdom of God:

## How Watch Tower Stole Salvation from Jehovah's Witnesses

By Eric Michael Wilson

www.beroeans.net

© Copyright 2022. All rights reserved.

Published by:

Good News Association Inc.
2711 Centerville Road Suite 400,
Willington, DE 19808
USA

Copyright 2022 by Eric Michael Wilson

Email: meleti.vivlon@gmail.com
First Edition 2022

Errata: https://beroeans.net/errata/

All rights reserved.

No part of this publication may be reproduced in any form, or by any means, electronic or mechanical, including photocopying, recording, or any information browsing, storage, or retrieval system, without permission in writing from the author.

ISBN

978-1-0880389-0-1 (Hardcover with dust jacket)
978-1-7781430-4-5 (Hardcover)
978-1-7781430-5-2 (Softcover)
978-1-7781430-6-9 (eBook)

Categorize under:

1. Religion, Christianity, Jehovah's Witnesses

# Contents

**Acknowledgments** .................................................. ix

**Preface** ............................................................ xiii
    Some Personal Background ................................. xiv
    My Awakening ............................................... xvi
    The Snare of Putting Men Before God ...................... xx
    Ongoing Harassment ....................................... xxii
    One Last Attempt to Reason with the Alliston Elders ...... xxii
    My Research Deepens ...................................... xxiii
    Why I Wrote This Book ..................................... xxiv

**Introduction** ..................................................... xxix
    About This Book ........................................... xxx

**1. What Is the Good News?** ........................................ 1
    What Is the Good News According to JW.org? ............... 2
    What Is the Good News that Jesus Preached? ............... 2
    Is JW Good News Bait in a Deathly Trap? .................. 13
    Why All Truth-loving Jehovah's Witnesses Need to Read This Book .. 16
    Never Be Misled Again! .................................... 19

**2. Bible Study Done Right** ........................................ 21
    Eisegesis: Bible Study the Wrong Way ..................... 22
    Exegesis: Bible Study the Right Way ...................... 24
    Comparing Eisegesis with Exegesis ........................ 27
    Are We Guided by Spirit or by Ego? ....................... 29
    Exegesis: Listening to God Rather Than Men ............... 31
    Analysing Daniel 12:1 ..................................... 32
    Analysing Daniel 12:2 ..................................... 34
    Analysing Daniel 12:3 ..................................... 35
    Analysing Daniel 12:4 ..................................... 36
    Analysing Daniel 12:5-12 .................................. 37
    Analysing Daniel 12:13 .................................... 39
    In Summary ................................................ 39

3. **Watch Tower's "Generation": A Bewildering Litany of Interpretations** .................................... 41
   - I Ask New York Headquarters for Clarification ..................... 42
   - Finally, the Governing Body Abandons the "Generation" Doctrine ... 50
   - The Governing Body Resurrects the Generation Doctrine .......... 54
   - What Really Is the Generation of Matthew 24:34? ................ 63

4. **Debunking the False Good News of 1914** ............... 65
   - Explaining the Core 1914 Teaching ................................ 66
   - The Origin of the 1914 Doctrine .................................. 69
   - What Is Revealed by the Dishonesty of the Watch Tower Society? ... 75
   - The 1914 Antitype: A Foundation Built on Sand .................... 76
   - Failed Attempts to Explain Away Acts 1:7 ......................... 84
   - The Governing Body Attempts to Justify Its 1914 Interpretation ..... 90
   - Pulling the 1914 Doctrinal Lynchpin .............................. 93
   - The JW 1914 Doctrine Is a House of Cards ......................... 97
   - Summing Up the Evidence ......................................... 105

5. **What You Need to Know About 607 BCE** ............... 109
   - A Heavier Judgment: Consequences of the 607 Teaching ........... 111
   - The One Bible Verse That Disproves 607 BCE ..................... 111
   - A Desperate Effort to Defend The 607 Doctrine .................. 119
   - A Humble Sister Uncovers the Lie of 607 BCE .................... 120
   - The Record of Kings: The 20 Years that Never Existed ............ 122
   - The Astronomical Record: The Truth Really Is in the Stars! ...... 127

6. **Preaching the Wrong Salvation Hope** ................. 135
   - A Bridge Too Far ................................................ 140

7. **Who Are the "Other Sheep"?** ......................... 143
   - Examining the Other Sheep Doctrine for Ourselves ............... 147
   - Watch Tower's Two "Proofs" for the Other Sheep ................. 159
   - Making Sense of the Sheep and Goats Parable .................... 170

8. **The Salvation Hope of the 144,000 and the Great Crowd** ............................................ 183
   - Salvation Is Not About Location ................................. 184
   - 144,000 – Literal or Symbolic? .................................. 185
   - Identifying the Great Crowd ..................................... 191
   - Unifying the 144,000 with the Great Crowd ...................... 196

## 9. Is the Great Tribulation a Single Event? . . . . . . . . . . . . . 207
Hebrews Explains Why Christians Undergo Tribulation . . . . . . . . . . 214
Why Do the Churches and JW.org Teach that the Great
Tribulation Is a Final Test? . . . . . . . . . . . . . . . . . . . . . . . . . . . . . . . . . . . . 218

## 10. J. F. Rutherford Invents the Salvation Hope of the "Other Sheep" . . . . . . . . . . . . . . . . . . . . . . . . . . . . . . . . . . . 223
Rutherford Talks Directly to God . . . . . . . . . . . . . . . . . . . . . . . . . . . . . . 225
Rutherford's Gangrenous Teaching . . . . . . . . . . . . . . . . . . . . . . . . . . . 228
Angelic Messengers Talk to Rutherford . . . . . . . . . . . . . . . . . . . . . . . 230
Rutherford Creates a Clergy Class . . . . . . . . . . . . . . . . . . . . . . . . . . . . 232
Rewriting History . . . . . . . . . . . . . . . . . . . . . . . . . . . . . . . . . . . . . . . . . . . 246

## 11. Is the Governing Body a False Prophet? . . . . . . . . . . . . . 249
False Prophets: The Watch Tower Definition . . . . . . . . . . . . . . . . . . . 250
What the *Reasoning* Book Omits . . . . . . . . . . . . . . . . . . . . . . . . . . . . . 250
The Failed Prophecy of 1914 . . . . . . . . . . . . . . . . . . . . . . . . . . . . . . . . . 255
The Failed Prophecy of 1925 . . . . . . . . . . . . . . . . . . . . . . . . . . . . . . . . . 257
The Failed Prophecy of 1975 . . . . . . . . . . . . . . . . . . . . . . . . . . . . . . . . . 260
The Aftermath of the 1975 Prophetic Fiasco . . . . . . . . . . . . . . . . . . . 267
The Danger Persists . . . . . . . . . . . . . . . . . . . . . . . . . . . . . . . . . . . . . . . . . 274

## 12. Was There a First-Century Governing Body? . . . . . . . . . . 281
Was There Really a Governing Body in the First Century? . . . . . . . . 282
No Bible Proof of a First-Century Governing Body . . . . . . . . . . . . . . 284
Why a Governing Body Is a Bad Thing . . . . . . . . . . . . . . . . . . . . . . . . 289

## 13. Who Is the Faithful and Discreet Slave? . . . . . . . . . . . . . . 293
Why Does the Governing Body Ignore Luke's Account of
the Faithful Steward? . . . . . . . . . . . . . . . . . . . . . . . . . . . . . . . . . . . . . . . . 295
Examining Luke's Account Exegetically . . . . . . . . . . . . . . . . . . . . . . . 298
Identifying the Four Slaves . . . . . . . . . . . . . . . . . . . . . . . . . . . . . . . . . . . 300

## 14. Should I Partake of the Bread and Wine? . . . . . . . . . . . . . 305
"But I Don't Want to Go to Heaven!" . . . . . . . . . . . . . . . . . . . . . . . . . . 307
What It Means to Partake of the Bread and Wine . . . . . . . . . . . . . . . 313

## 15. How the Watch Tower Society Shuts Up the Kingdom of the Heavens . . . . . . . . . . . . . . . . . . . . . . . . . . . . . . . . . . . . . 319
How Has Watch Tower Stolen Salvation from Jehovah's Witnesses? 323
Preparing Yourself to Become a Child of God . . . . . . . . . . . . . . . . . . 324

16. Can I Worship God Without Religion? . . . . . . . . . . . . . . . . . 329
    Jesus Explains the Difference Between Religion and Worship . . . . . . 332
    Why Is Religion a Snare and a Racket? . . . . . . . . . . . . . . . . . . . . . . . . 335
    Learning to Worship Without Religion . . . . . . . . . . . . . . . . . . . . . . . . 340
    Walking on Water . . . . . . . . . . . . . . . . . . . . . . . . . . . . . . . . . . . . . . . . . . 343

17. "Where Do I Go from Here?" The Path Forward . . . . . . . . 345
    How I Rebuilt My Faith . . . . . . . . . . . . . . . . . . . . . . . . . . . . . . . . . . . . . 346
    Breaking Free from the Past . . . . . . . . . . . . . . . . . . . . . . . . . . . . . . . . 348
    No Regrets . . . . . . . . . . . . . . . . . . . . . . . . . . . . . . . . . . . . . . . . . . . . . . . . 349

Appendix A: My Letter to the Alliston Congregation . . . . .355

Appendix B: My Letter to Headquarters and Reply . . . . . . .360

Appendix C: *Life Everlasting* Book Inside Cover . . . . . . . . .362

Appendix D: *The Harp of God* Cover and
Canvassing Script . . . . . . . . . . . . . . . . . . . . . . . . . . . . . . . . . . . . . . . .363

Appendix E: Gerrit Lösch's Declaration . . . . . . . . . . . . . . . .365

Appendix F: When Was Satan Cast Down? . . . . . . . . . . . . . .368

Appendix G: A Legacy of Shifting Years . . . . . . . . . . . . . . . .371

Appendix H: The One Man Who Is Really
Responsible for 607 BCE . . . . . . . . . . . . . . . . . . . . . . . . . . . . . . . . . .374

Glossary . . . . . . . . . . . . . . . . . . . . . . . . . . . . . . . . . . . . . . . . . . . . . . .376
    List of Abbreviations . . . . . . . . . . . . . . . . . . . . . . . . . . . . . . . . . . . . . . . 376

*Woe to YOU, scribes and Pharisees, hypocrites! because YOU shut up the kingdom of the heavens before men; for YOU yourselves do not go in, neither do YOU permit those on their way in to go in.*
*(Matthew 23:13, NWT)*

# Acknowledgments

I love God, whether you call him Jehovah, Yehowah, Yahweh, or YHWH. To me, He is "Father." I love my Lord who is Jesus or Yeshua. I love truth and hate lies.

This book is a labor of love.

Given that, I want to acknowledge the people who first taught me to love God and his Son, and who instilled in me a love of truth and a hatred of falsehood: My parents, Donald and Thelma, both asleep (in death) and awaiting the wakeup call of our Lord.

My only sibling is my younger sister, Maureen Cole, who's always been a supporter of anything I've endeavored to do. A more balanced and together woman you would be hard pressed to find. I thank her for continuing to support the work of the Children of God who are emerging from the clutches of organized religion (forgive the tautology). Not to be overlooked is her husband and my friend, Lucky Cole. Thank you Lucky for keeping my sister safe and happy, and for being the kind of man I can always count on to have my back. While you may "fear nothing bad" as you "walk in the valley of deep shadow," if you're caught in a dark alley, you'll feel better with Lucky by your side (Psalm 23:4).

I'd like to be able to thank the many men and women whom I counted as dear and loyal friends during my decades within the Organization of Jehovah's Witnesses; but alas, true to the direction of their masters, they've all abandoned me. I do not blame them. They are just acting in the way they think Jehovah God expects them to act. They are right in that. He does expect them to act that way, but he doesn't want them to, nor does he approve of it. Jesus warns us at John 16:2 that "men will expel you from the synagogue [or Kingdom Hall]. In fact, the hour is coming when everyone who kills you will think he has offered a sacred service to God."

More than for anyone else, I write this book for those former friends in the hope they will read it and awaken to the truth.

I have abandoned falsehood, but I have not abandoned my old friends, and continue to pray for them.

From this point forward, I'm going to use first names and aliases because I don't want to cause anyone unnecessary suffering. Some are still associating to some degree with congregation members, and if their names were linked with mine, they would be shunned, cut off from their family and friends.

I'm proceeding in chronological order, as that seems to be the best way to thank everyone.

Next, I thank Pam who is my spiritual daughter. She's been there for me and for my late wife during our darkest times and has never wavered in her love for us.

I worked alongside Sean Garvey when I was an elder and he joined me in leaving our former religion and setting up the Good News Association ten years ago, which is a non-profit US Corporation which helps to fund this new ministry. I've always admired Sean's fearlessness. He is a good friend, the kind you can count on in tough times.

This book is the result of years of research, resulting in hundreds of articles published in English on beroeans.net and in Spanish on losbereanos.com. ApollosOfAlexandria (an alias) was instrumental in getting me off the ground by challenging my JW indoctrination, specifically with regard to 1914. He and his lovely wife have been my good friends for many years. Thanks to you both.

Thank you, Hannah, for your kindness and for helping me to manage the web sites.

Thank you, Sam, and She-who-must-not-be-named, for your unflagging support over many years, and especially for brightening my life during the dark days of the Pandemic.

A very special thank you to Filomena whose exhaustive research provided me with the basis for pretty much all of the work on 607 BCE.

A tip of the hat to Jose and Caroline for their kindness when I was down and for their support through the years.

I would like to thank the regular attendees to our online meetings, in English, Spanish, German, Italian, French, and Polish who continue to send me words of encouragement. Their weekly presence and spirit-led instruction at our meetings is a continual support for me in staying the course. Thank you, Manny, Marcelo, Jonathan, and Ezequiel for managing the Spanish meetings and

## Acknowledgments

lightening my load. (Should you wish to join us, our meeting schedule is open to all and available at https://beroeans.net/events/)

There are many who have offered to translate this book, and it is my hope that by the end of 2022, we'll see versions in Spanish, Portuguese, Italian, German, Greek, French, Romanian, and Polish. I thank all the translators collectively here and will do so again in the individual versions as they are published. A special thank you goes out to Christian who is not only working on translating my videos into German but is also hosting German online meetings for the Children of God.

And a second thank you to Ezequiel for the additional help he gives me in tirelessly working on translations and in producing the Spanish videos. Ezequiel is a real fighter for truth.

Thanks is definitely owed to Jim Penton and his wife Beth for their hospitality and support, and specifically to Jim for guiding me through the process of editing and publishing books, something he has done successfully for decades. He is an esteemed member of the exJW community.

Most recently, my sincere gratitude goes out to Alfred who lives on the other side of the pond for taking on the work of proofreading and transforming this manuscript into a publishable form. His unfaltering good humour is always uplifting, and a number of his scriptural insights have been included in this work. Then there is Craig, my countryman, who has been generous in so many ways, and whose creativity we have to thank for the cover of this book. Great work, Craig!

A very special thank you to Jeff Mezera for his very revealing research into Watch Tower history which you'll find in "Appendix G: A Legacy of Shifting Years" and "Appendix H: The One Man Who Is Really Responsible for 607 BCE". I'm confident in saying that Jeff knows Watch Tower history better than anyone inside the Organization of Jehovah's Witnesses does.

Check out his YouTube channel:
youtube.com/c/WatchtowerHistory

Last, but far from least, is Wendy Wiens who has contributed immense time and effort, not only in producing my videos and editing my transcripts over the past few years, but in tirelessly editing and revising the manuscript for this book. I frequently call on her when I want to find the location of a Scripture which eludes me. She continually pushes me toward excellence. A very special thank you, dear Wendy.

# Preface

*Now all the things that are being reproved are made manifest by the light, for everything that is being made manifest is light. Wherefore he says: "Awake, O sleeper, and arise from the dead, and the Christ will shine upon you."*
*(Ephesians 5:13, 14)*

"Are you willing to obey the direction of the Governing Body?"

There it was! The loaded question I had been expecting.

I was at what turned out to be my final elders' meeting. The date was June 4, 2013. At the table with me, sat the other eleven elders of my congregation. Sitting at the head of the table was our young circuit overseer, Dean Jenkins. The meeting had been convened at the direction of the Canada branch of the Watch Tower Society to address some concerns that three of the elders in our body had raised about my qualifications to continue to serve as the COBE (Coordinator Of the Body of Elders). Most of the concerns that were raised turned out to be trivial, and even petty. These were all incidental to what was really on the table. The branch office was concerned about my loyalty to the Governing Body.

When Dean Jenkins finally asked me that loaded question, I did my best to answer it truthfully. I told them that I'd always obeyed the direction of the Governing Body, remarking that every one of the elders at that table could bear witness to that fact. None disagreed.

Perhaps, if I had left it there, I might have avoided being removed, but I added the assurance: "And I will continue to do so, but of course, I will always 'obey God as ruler rather than men.'"

You might recognize this as a direct quote from Acts 5:29 where Peter said the same words to the Jewish leaders in the Sanhedrin. I naively thought my reference to this Bible principle was bulletproof. After all, is there any situation in which a Christian would be required to obey men over God? So, you can imagine my shock at hearing some of the elders gasp in reaction to what I'd said. They'd actually taken offense at my reference to this verse.

Up to this point in our meeting, the only question was whether I was qualified to serve as the COBE, but now they were questioning whether I was qualified to serve as an elder at all. After a brief discussion, the C.O. asked me to wait outside the meeting room in the Kingdom Hall lobby while they deliberated.

I was simply not prepared for what was about to happen!

## Some Personal Background

Before getting into what happened next, it would make sense for me to share some of my personal history with you.

I was born in 1949 and raised as one of Jehovah's Witnesses. We'd refer to our religion as "The Truth." To a fellow Witness, I'd say that I was raised in *The Truth*. When meeting for the first time, we would commonly ask each other: "When did you learn *The Truth*?" or "How long have you been in *The Truth*?" We believed we were in the only true religion on earth, because all the others taught false doctrines.

As a JW, I was unconcerned by the worrisome state of the world. I was taught that the end of the "wicked system of things" was at hand and that God's Kingdom would put everything right. It was that belief that motivated me to leave Canada when I was only 19 years old, and to move with my parents and younger sister to Colombia to serve where "the need was greater." Back then, we received constant reminders at our conventions and assemblies as well as from the publications of the Watch Tower Society that 1975 would likely be the year when Satan's *wicked system of things* would end at Armageddon.

We all know that the end didn't come in 1975, so you may wonder why I continued to serve as an elder after that year came and went. The answer is that I still believed I was in *The Truth*. I put the whole 1975 fiasco down to human imperfection. I believed that the men heading up the Organization were capable of making mistakes, but that they were well intentioned, and that they just got carried away by their own interpretation of things but meant no harm. I also continued to believe that the generation of 1914 would live to see the end. That was my opinion.

None of what happened regarding 1975 affected my belief that our core doctrines were solidly based in the Bible. With few exceptions, the religions of Christendom teach the false doctrines of the Trinity, hellfire, and the immortal soul. I couldn't associate with any religion that taught such things. I also accepted the Organization's position on neutrality, particularly as it related to participation in wars. Except for some isolationist groups like the Amish and Mennonites, most Christian denominations get involved in politics and support wars.

I had faith that any doctrinal misinterpretations we had were small and would be corrected in due time as Jehovah God revealed *new light* to his Organization through the faithful and discreet slave class comprised of an anointed remnant of Jehovah's Witnesses on earth.

I continued to serve as an elder for a total of 40 years in both Spanish and English-speaking congregations. I loved teaching. I loved giving public talks. I helped with various Kingdom Hall building projects. I wrote custom software programs for the Ecuador and Canada branches. In short, I was very active in "the theocratic ministry."

However, I wasn't oblivious to the shortcomings of the leadership of the Organization.

During the years I spent in Colombia, Ecuador, and Canada, I came into close contact with many missionaries, circuit and district overseers, Bethelites, and branch committee members. Some were good people who really tried to display a Christ-like personality, but others seemed much closer to the mold of the ancient Pharisees. As the years have gone by, many have noticed that the Christ-like personalities seem to be dwindling in number as the Pharisaical element gains strength.

There were a number of occasions when families moved into the congregation where I was serving because they were fleeing from an oppressive body of elders and were looking for a safe haven, a place where the elders weren't acting like spiritual policemen.

For the last eight years leading up to my removal, I served as the COBE of the Alliston congregation in Ontario, Canada. During that time, there were some who moved their publisher record cards to our congregation, even though it meant driving an hour each way to attend our meetings.

At times, I would receive damning letters of introduction denouncing these spiritual refugees and demanding we deal with them as their former elders saw fit. In one case, the previous elder body insisted that we send one brother back to be counselled by them directly. Of course, we didn't comply. In most cases, the only sin these ones had committed was the "sin" of not being willing to do what they were told. Of course, that was always phrased euphemistically as "not being willing to obey the direction of Jehovah's Organization."

That such a Pharisaical spirit should be so pervasive within the congregations of Jehovah's Witnesses should have alerted me to the fact that something was fundamentally wrong, but sadly, it didn't. Still, it did engender a growing disquiet in my soul. Why didn't I react to that sooner? I consoled myself by remembering that ancient Israel didn't stop being Jehovah's Organization even when there were bad kings on the throne. And again, where else was I to go? We had *The Truth*, didn't we? Just as Noah and his family were saved by staying in the Ark, I accepted the teaching that I had to remain in the Organization to survive Armageddon.[1]

## My Awakening

As I've just stated, I was able to weather doctrinal failures like the 1975 fiasco, because I believed the Governing Body were men of integrity. I never suspected for a moment that they were capable of *knowingly* making stuff up for their own purposes. That's why the 2010 introduction—or should I say, reintroduction—of the generation doctrine came as such a shock. The now-infamous interpretation called the *overlapping generation*, marking the time span from 1914 to Armageddon, was so obviously a badly contrived fabrication that it shook my world and caused me to take a serious look at all the other teachings I had always accepted as scriptural.

---

1. "Just as Noah and his God-fearing family were preserved in the ark, survival of individuals today depends on their faith and their loyal association with the earthly part of Jehovah's universal organization." (w06 5/15 p. 22 par. 8 Are You Prepared for Survival?)

Studying the Bible on my own was challenging. I'd always relied on Watch Tower publications to answer my questions and clear up any doubts. But if *The Watchtower* magazine and the other publications of the Organization were the source of my doubts, where was I to go to find the truth?

I was mindful of the Bible counsel at 1 Thessalonians 5:21 which instructs all Christ's disciples to "make sure of all things; hold fast to what is fine." There's also the exhortation found at 1 John 4:1 to "test the inspired expressions to see whether they originate with God." Armed with this authority, I examined all the fundamental teachings of the Organization from a purely scriptural basis. I was interested in collaborating with others who, like me, wanted to study Scripture free from the personal interpretations and opinions of men. This turned out to be more difficult than expected, because as a Jehovah's Witness, I had been taught a faulty method for Bible study called *eisegesis*. It wasn't until I learned the proper method called *exegesis* that I was able to make real progress. (See "Chapter 2 Bible Study Done Right.")

Of course, I knew that the Organization would take a harsh view of such a venture, so I chose an alias, "Meleti Vivlon," to disguise my identity, and I launched a web site called "Beroean Pickets."[2]

## Learning to Think Critically

In 2012, as a result of my research, I also came to question the scriptural validity for the 1914 invisible presence of Christ. At the regional convention later that year, there was a talk titled: "Avoid Testing Jehovah in Your Heart." It brought tears of sadness to my eyes, because they had taken the most precious thing in my life, my religion, and trampled it underfoot. What was so bad about this talk?

---

2. "Meleti Vivlon" is a transliteration of two Greek words meaning "Bible study." "Beroean" was chosen for its reference to Acts 17:11; and "Pickets" was selected because the word refers to someone taking point or posted as guard at a military encampment (Ephesians 6:11-13 speaks of Christian soldiers). It is also an anagram for "skeptic"—a critical thinker.

I'll start with the fact that the speaker told us that having an online Bible study group outside of organizational arrangements amounted to "testing Jehovah in your heart." How so? Because it meant we were disparaging the spiritual food Jehovah God was providing to us through his Organization. The speaker went so far as to teach that even silently doubting the validity of any teaching amounted to *testing Jehovah in your heart*. But how could I possibly reconcile the speaker's words with the knowledge that the overlapping generation is not scriptural? How could he be speaking truth given that we are told to "make sure of all things" and to "test the inspired expression to see if it originates from God"? Holding two conflicting and contrary ideas in your mind and heart can be mentally and emotionally devastating. This condition is known as *cognitive dissonance*.[3]

After the convention, I got hold of the actual talk outline to make sure that what I'd heard was indeed from the Teaching Committee and not just the opinion of the speaker. My worst fears were confirmed. According to the outline, those who doubted the teachings of the Governing Body were compared to Korah, the Israelite who challenged Moses' authority and was condemned by God for his rebellion. This seemed like a gross and self-serving misapplication of a Bible account. After all, Korah wanted to replace Moses! I just wanted to make sure that everything I was being taught was based in Scripture and did not originate from men. Through this convention talk, the Governing Body was exerting control over Jehovah's Witnesses, making it a sin to question their teachings!

This was no little hiccup in Organization policy. The Governing Body was intentionally seizing control of all our minds and hearts. As I write this in 2022, ten years later, I know of a sister in a congregation in Utah who was just disfellowshipped because she refused to stop attending an online Bible study group that had no affiliation with any religion whatsoever. She just wanted to study the Bible without using Watch Tower publications. This was viewed as apostasy, a grievous sin.

Of course, she is no apostate. An apostate is one who turns her back on God. This sister continues to have faith in Jehovah God and his Son, Jesus Christ. You can bear witness to this fact by

---

3. The state of holding as true, beliefs that are contradictory.

listening to her judicial committee hearing on my YouTube channel, Beroean Pickets.[4]

As troubling as all this was, I still clung to the hope that Jehovah would fix everything in his due time and so I continued to serve as an elder for a short time. Since I was the coordinator, it fell to me to assign Service Meeting parts. This allowed me to avoid any talks promoting JW teachings which I now felt conflicted with Scripture.

From time to time, the Watchtower Study conductor—a man I counted as a good friend—would ask me to take the study when he couldn't be there. When that happened, I'd first read the article before agreeing to conduct. On one occasion, he asked me to take the Study of May 20, 2012. Upon reading it, I found this in the second paragraph:

> The other sheep should never forget that **their salvation depends on their active support of Christ's anointed** "brothers" still on earth.[5]

Your salvation does not depend on supporting the "anointed brothers" of the Governing Body. Peter tells us at Acts 4:8-12 that the *only name* upon which your salvation depends is that of Christ Jesus. To suggest otherwise is to replace the Christ with mere imperfect men. Now, if you're looking for a situation within the Organization of Jehovah's Witnesses that parallels Korah's presumption to replace Moses, you've found it! Bear in mind that even *The Watchtower* teaches that Jesus is the "Greater Moses."[6]

Clearly, I couldn't conduct that *Watchtower* study in good conscience, so I told my "trusted" friend that I didn't feel comfortable taking it, and that he should schedule someone else. He wanted to know why and sent me an email asking for clarification. I never responded and forgot about the entire incident. A year later, it was he who accused me before the body of elders and demanded to know what exactly it was that made me uncomfortable. What I didn't know at the time was that instead of confronting me man-to-man, he had scurried off to the circuit overseer

---

4. https://beroeans.net/2022/06/09/shunned-for-studying-the-bible/
5. w12 3/15 p. 20 par. 2
6. "When you strive to imitate Jehovah and the Greater Moses, Jesus Christ, you will be both approachable and refreshing to others. (Matt. 11:28, 29)" (w18 September pp. 25-26 par. 10)

who had instructed him to spy on me to gather hard evidence to use against me.

## The Snare of Putting Men Before God

Returning to the night of June 4, 2013—as I sat outside the Kingdom Hall meeting room waiting for the elders to finish their deliberation about whether to remove me as an elder, I was struggling with a question of my own: Did I even want to continue as an elder? On the one hand, by stepping down I'd be free of any conflict of conscience. But on the other hand, I'd be abandoning my responsibility to protect the flock from the type of elders that had abused the Alliston congregation in years past.

Earlier that day, I had told my wife, Reta, that I intended to remain an elder for the present, and that I was confident I could avoid incriminating myself. I was thinking that Jesus' words at Matthew 10:19-21 applied to my situation:

> However, when they deliver YOU up, do not become anxious about how or what YOU are to speak; for what YOU are to speak will be given YOU in that hour; for the ones speaking are not just YOU, but it is the spirit of YOUR Father that speaks by YOU. Further, brother will deliver up brother to death, and a father his child, and children will rise up against parents and will have them put to death.

Throughout history, these words have applied to religious inquisitions far more often than political ones. We must not conclude that Jesus is telling us that the right words *to escape persecution* will be provided to us by the Holy Spirit. No. What he is saying is that the words that will accomplish *God's will* are provided not by human wisdom, but by Holy Spirit. Our Father doesn't desire any to be lost, but all to be saved, so the Spirit will provide the words needed to search out the heart condition of the inquisitors.[7]

What was about to happen to me was of little consequence to me personally. What was of far greater importance was the soul of the other 12 men seated around that table. They were all facing a choice that could well affect their salvation. Would they side with God, or would they obey the dictates of men? To whom would they belong? To Christ? Or to the Governing Body?

---

7. 2 Peter 3:9; Revelation 2:23; 1 Corinthians 2:7-10

Upon returning to the meeting room, I was told that the brothers needed me to clarify what I meant by "obeying God as ruler rather than men." The circuit overseer asked me to give an example.

This was the moment of truth! To remain an elder, as was my intention, all I had to do was say that I couldn't think of an instance where that would be necessary. Of course, that would have been a lie. Still, I could have reasoned that this was a moment for the Organization's *theocratic warfare tactic* of not telling someone in authority something they had no right to know.[8] Alternately, I could have suggested something so outlandish that they would have all been forced to see my point. For example, I could have said that I wouldn't obey the Governing Body if they wanted me to preach the Trinity or hellfire.

Any of that would have likely got me off the hook, but it wouldn't have tested the heart of the men before me. I had worked with these men for years and despite a number of silly, and at times, troubling incidents, I considered most of them to be good men. But one never truly knows the character of another until it is put to the test.

I believe the holy spirit guided me that day because I entered the meeting with the idea of answering their questions in such a way as to avoid being removed, but I seemed blocked from carrying out my plan.

In answer to their question asking for a specific example of how I would apply Acts 5:29, I came up with this:

> Imagine, brothers, that we were back in time in 1924 when Rutherford was predicting that the next year would see the resurrection of the "ancient worthies"—men like Abraham, Moses, and Daniel. Now imagine Rutherford were to come to me and ask me to give a talk at the convention of that year promoting the idea that 1925 would be the start of the resurrection and the beginning of the end. If I were there, and knew what we all know now, I could not have given that talk in good conscience, and so I would have declined the assignment.

---

8. For the Watch Tower view on theocratic warfare, see w60 6/1 pp. 351, 352.

I thought this was a bulletproof response. I was wrong. As it turned out, it was just what the circuit overseer was looking for in order to recommend my removal.

Of the twelve men there, only one had the courage to stand up for truth. Only one refused to agree to my removal. That was Pat O'Brien, who had himself been the brunt of several unwarranted attacks on his character by some of the others. He stood his ground and voted against their decision.

When the time came to hand down the final verdict, the reason for my removal was, in the words of circuit overseer, Dean Jenkins: "It's obvious that you're not fully committed to the Governing Body."

This accusation shocked me, though it really shouldn't have, since only a year earlier the eight men of the Governing Body had proclaimed themselves to be the Faithful and Discreet Slave of Matthew 24:45.

## Ongoing Harassment

Though the elders lacked any evidence that could be used to disfellowship me, I was watched and harassed from that point on.

Three times I was hauled before two elders for questioning on false charges. When I asked for the names of those making the allegations, the elders suddenly developed bad memories. That they would lie so easily and base such serious charges on hearsay and gossip further diminished my view of those men whom I had once counted as my friends.

In 2014, my wife and I moved to Burlington, Ontario, which put us in the Aldershot congregation. The elders there also wanted to meet with me. When I declined their "invitation" to meet, the COBE got upset and put more pressure on me. He told me that they had a 20-page file sent to them from the Alliston congregation and that we needed to meet and discuss it. I asked if he would show me what had been written about me, but he refused. So, I declined to meet.

## One Last Attempt to Reason with the Alliston Elders

Despite how I was treated by the Alliston elders, I still had affection for those men with whom I had worked for years. If I were to give way to hate, I would have become the very thing I deplored.

My worry was that the attitude of the elders toward me was the tip of the iceberg. I felt that they had become Pharisaical. So, a few months after they removed me as an elder, I drafted a letter of admonishment. (See "Appendix A: My Letter to the Alliston Congregation" on page 355 for the full text of the letter.)

I soon learned that their reaction to my letter wasn't what I'd hoped for, though sadly, very much what I'd expected. Pat O'Brien, the elder who had opposed their decision to remove me, confided to me that the Watchtower Study Conductor wanted to use my letter as the basis to disfellowship me. However, one of the more senior men on the Body told him it wasn't possible to do so because I hadn't shared the letter with the congregation, but only with the elders.

Their response was to order me to appear before them so they could read a reply to me. This seemed like a childish attempt to exert their authority over me, so I told them to act like men and just give me the letter to read, as I had done for them. They refused to do so and to this day I have no idea what their letter said. I'm sure that my letter and their reply was included within the "20 pages" that the Alliston elders sent to the Aldershot congregation elders after I moved there.

## My Research Deepens

If you're wondering why I stayed in the Organization despite all this abuse, I would never let men push me away from God. What I had to endure was nothing compared to what our Lord went through:

> Indeed, consider closely the one who has endured such hostile speech from sinners against their own interests, so that you may **not get tired and give up.** (Hebrews 12:3 NWT 2013)

If Jehovah's Witnesses had the truth, then no amount of "hostile speech" was going to drive me out. But what if the Organization wasn't the true religion? Immediately after my removal in 2013, I intensified the Bible research that I'd started in 2010.

Some have counselled me over the years that I should have simply "waited on Jehovah" to fix the things that are wrong, suggesting that I was running ahead of the Organization. This is a common fallback Witnesses cling to when facing contradictions and hypocrisy.

Using the powerful tools in the desktop version of *Watchtower Library*, I did a search in the *New World Translation of the Holy Scriptures* on the theme of "waiting on Jehovah." Would you be surprised to learn that the Bible never once applies the exhortation "to wait on Jehovah" in relation to fixing what is wrong with the leaders of His people? Rather, it refers to waiting patiently for salvation while enduring tribulation and persecution from ungodly and presumptuous leaders. With that lightning-like illumination, I dove into studying all the doctrines unique to the Watch Tower Society, including:

- The 1914 invisible presence of Christ.
- The 1918 resurrection of the anointed.
- The 1919 appointment of the faithful and discreet slave.
- The earthly resurrection hope of "righteous other sheep."
- The 144,000 anointed ones as a literal number.
- The Governing Body as the faithful and discreet slave.
- The prohibition against blood transfusions.
- The "composite sign" of the Last Days.
- The exile to Babylon in 607 BCE.
- The scriptural basis for disfellowshipping.
- The prohibition against partaking of the emblems.
- The requirement to preach from house to house.
- Baptism as a symbol of dedication to God.

Can you imagine how I felt to learn that not a single one of these fundamental Watch Tower doctrines can be supported in Scripture?

## Why I Wrote This Book

When Jesus began preaching, his purpose wasn't to attack the religious leaders of Israel. What concerned him was helping sinners to repentance. He said to the Pharisees, "I was not sent forth to any but to the lost sheep of the house of Israel."[9]

This infuriated them because they viewed themselves as righteous and above reproach. They were not going to listen to Jesus' message of the good news of the Kingdom of God. Instead, they

---

9.   Matthew 15:24

saw him as a troublemaker because he was threatening their authority and control over the people.

In writing this book, and through my work on my two web sites (beroeans.net and losbereanos.com) and the *Beroean Pickets* and *Los Bereanos* YouTube channels, I wish to help Christians in general and Jehovah's Witnesses in particular to learn how to think critically about the things they are being taught by their priests, ministers, pastors, or governing body.

Of course, it's impossible to demonstrate that someone is wrong without casting them in a bad light, especially if they fail to accept their errors, but instead persecute those who expose them. Jesus did not soft pedal the truth just to avoid offending the scribes and Pharisees. He did not fear them. Paul was likewise fearless in the face of opposition. He told the Ephesians:

> Now all the things that are being reproved are made manifest by the light, for everything that is being made manifest is light. Wherefore he says: "**Awake, O sleeper, and arise from the dead**, and the Christ will shine upon you." (Ephesians 5:13, 14)

## Yielding to the Guidance of the Holy Spirit

We are being called to wake up! We were sleeping spiritually, dead in our sins and ignorant of truth. Now we can "arise" or come to spiritual life, which means to obtain a righteous standing before God by means of Jesus Christ.[10]

Jesus told us that the truth would set us free.[11] But that doesn't apply to everyone. Jehovah hides truth from many, while revealing it to those He chooses.

> At that time Jesus said in response: "I publicly praise you, Father, Lord of heaven and earth, because you have hidden these things from the wise and intellectual ones and **have revealed them to babes**. Yes, O Father, because to do thus came to be the way approved by you." (Matthew 11:25, 26)

The marvel of this arrangement of God is that the wise and intellectual—those who presumptuously consider themselves to be faithful and discreet—are unaware that the truth is being

---

10. Isaiah 53:10, 11
11. John 8:32

hidden from them. They believe they have the truth, but they will learn otherwise, though only when it is too late.

How can you or I be sure that we will not end up in the same boat as those self-declared "wise men"? The Apostle John wrote:

> I write you these things about those who are trying to mislead you. And as for you, the anointing that you received from him remains in you, and **you do not need anyone to be teaching you**; but **the anointing from him is teaching you about all things** and is true and is no lie. (1 John 2:26, 27)

How do John's words apply to you if you are one of Jehovah's Witnesses? If you think of yourself as one of the JW Other Sheep, is it reasonable to consider that your loving Father, Jehovah God, would deprive you of the anointing John speaks of—an anointing which frees you from being misled by the teachings of men? Would a loving Father force you to trust in self-appointed men to tell you what is true and what is false, what is good and what is bad? Why would God make you dependent on men when the anointing of his Holy Spirit is all you need "to be teaching you about all things"?

I know it can be very disturbing to examine your faith. But think about Saul of Tarsus. He believed he was saved. He was trained in God's law by one of the finest teachers in Israel. Bear in mind that the nation of Israel was truly God's people. Outside of Israel, there were only pagan nations worshiping false gods. Despite all those credentials, Saul of Tarsus didn't have the approved standing before God that he thought he had. He didn't figure that out on his own either. Jesus had to appear to him in a blinding light. Looking back at all he had lost—all his friends, all the wealth he might have accumulated, all the prestige he could have enjoyed—yes, looking back at it all—he wrote:

> What is more, I consider everything a loss because of the surpassing worth of knowing Christ Jesus my Lord, for whose sake I have lost all things. **I consider them garbage,** that I may gain Christ. (Philippians 3:8 NIV)

I'm not aware of any today who have been called to the Kingdom by means of a blinding light and a voice from heaven. Still, John 6:44 tells us that "no one can come to Me unless the Father who sent Me draws him..."[12] If the holy spirit is calling you to open

---

12. Berean Study Bible

your heart to the truth, then you have a choice. Do you let it guide you, or do you fall back on men to tell you what to believe? Will you belong to Jesus, or to an organization or church? True Christians belong only to Christ.

> Hence **let no one be boasting in men**; for all things belong to YOU, whether Paul or Apollos or Cephas or the world or life or death or things now here or things to come, all things belong to YOU; in turn YOU **belong to Christ**; Christ, in turn, belongs to God. (1 Corinthians 3:21-23)

If your answer is that you would obey our Lord Jesus over any man, then the next question is: To what extent will you obey him? How much are you willing to give up for Christ? How much reproach and humiliating gossip are you willing to endure? Will you endure the shame heaped upon the righteous, as Jesus himself did?

> ...as we look intently at the Chief Agent and Perfecter of our faith, Jesus. For the joy that was set before him he endured a torture stake, **despising shame**... (Hebrews 12:2)
>
> Blessed are you when people insult you, persecute you, and falsely say all kinds of evil against you because of Me. Rejoice and be glad, because great is **your reward in heaven**; for in the same way they persecuted the prophets before you. (Matthew 5:11,12)

Keep in mind that turning toward Christ doesn't mean turning away from Jehovah. Indeed, the doorway to our Father is only through Jesus Christ.[13] In Eden, Jehovah set up the means by which his lost human children could be reconciled to him. Indeed, your heavenly Father isn't looking for friends. He wants His children back. What is being offered to you as good news is the opportunity to become a child of God.

> However, **to all** who did receive him, he gave authority to become **God's children**, because they were exercising faith in his name. And they were born, not from blood or from a fleshly will or from man's will, but from God. (John 1:12, 13)
>
> **For all** who are led by God's spirit are indeed **God's sons**. For you did not receive a spirit of slavery causing fear again, but you received a spirit of adoption as sons, by which spirit we cry out: "*Abba*, Father!" (Romans 8:14, 15)

---

13. John 10:1-5

It is my hope that through this book you will find the encouragement and scriptural support to become one of our heavenly Father's adopted children, a right which is offered to all who put faith in Jesus Christ.

May our "Father of tender mercies" comfort you![14]

Your brother in Christ,

Eric Michael Wilson aka Meleti Vivlon

---

14. 2 Corinthians 1:3-7

# Introduction

Unless otherwise stated, all Bible citations in this book are taken from the *New World Translation of the Holy Scriptures*, Reference Bible (1984). I prefer this version over the newer 2013 edition which isn't a new translation at all, but rather an editorial work.

All boldface and italics are mine unless otherwise stated. Also, square brackets [ ] are added to citations and Bible texts to provide remarks that I feel will help the reader better understand the meaning of difficult scriptural passages or explain specific terms.

When referring to the corporate entity that is the Watch Tower Bible & Tract Society of Pennsylvania, and its sister corporation, the Watchtower Bible and Tract Society of New York, I will use "Watch Tower" with a space separating the two words. When referring to the flagship magazine of the corporation, I'll use either *The Watchtower* or simply *Watchtower*.

I capitalize "Organization" throughout when referring to the entity that governs the lives of Jehovah's Witnesses, because, for all intents and purposes, it has become a proper noun—a named ruler.

While I have endeavored to be as gender neutral as possible, there are times when it becomes difficult due to the restrictions of English. Therefore, I capitalize Man and Mankind when the terms refer to humans of both sexes. To illustrate: "Paul, was like any of us, a common man," versus, "Jesus' words are meant for everyone, for the common Man."

In most instances, I have removed the superscript verse numbers and at times the paragraph indentations from Bible citations because those were not part of the original manuscripts. They were inserted centuries later as an aid to the Bible student. However, they are subject to the bias of the copyist and/or translator. At times, the verse divisions and paragraph breaks obscure or even change the meaning of scriptures. So, by removing them,

I hope to promote greater clarity as to what the Bible writer meant to convey to the reader.

I also want to avoid the trap of cherry-picking verses to support an agenda, something that organized religion is notorious for doing. Our goal is to achieve an unbiased understanding of Scripture. Admittedly, we are setting ourselves a very high bar given the centuries of clouding doctrinal teachings plaguing Bible students as well as the challenges of understanding languages and cultures two millennia in the past.

## About This Book

The primary purpose of this book is to provide Jehovah's Witnesses with a way to research Scripture on their own so as to learn the truth about the hope of the good news being offered to all humankind by Jehovah God through His Son, Jesus Christ.

I'll begin in Chapter 1 with a brief introduction that will compare the good news preached by Jehovah's Witnesses with that declared to us by Jesus.

Next, I'll deal with the concern that most readers will have: "How do I know that Eric is not just another man attempting to mislead me with false teachings?" The only way for me to do that is to provide you with the same Bible study method that has protected me from being deceived "by means of the trickery of men, by means of cunning in contriving error" since I left the Organization.[1]

To that end, I've provided Chapter 2 called "Bible Study Done Right" where you'll learn the difference between eisegetical and exegetical Bible study. Once you have that in your spiritual arsenal, you'll never again need to depend on others to tell you what is true and how to identify falsehood.

We'll then take what we've learned from Chapter 2 and put those techniques to use by examining the core teachings of the Organization that relate to the good news Witnesses preach. This won't be a dry academic exercise, but a journey of discovery in which many troubling questions will be answered.

For instance, Chapter 3 covers Matthew 24:34 "this generation." It will cover the bewildering litany of interpretations—virtually

---

1. Ephesians 4:14

one per decade—that the Governing Body came up with to keep this doctrine alive until finally fabricating the now-infamous "overlapping generation." The seven years it took to roll out this doctrine in its present form also reveals much about the motivation behind it.

In Chapter 4, you'll see overwhelming scriptural evidence that makes the doctrine of the 1914 invisible presence of Christ impossible to sustain. More than that, you'll also learn how the Governing Body has recently undermined its own teaching on 1914, not once, but twice!

Chapter 5, "What You Need to Know about 607 BCE", will provide archaeological and astronomical proof that 607 BCE can't be the date of the Jewish exile to Babylon. But of even greater importance will be the evidence that Watch Tower leadership has known that fact for decades yet continues to promote what it knows isn't true.

When we reach chapters 6 and 7, we show from Scripture just how the Governing Body has misled the flock about the true nature of Christian salvation, and in so doing, has blocked Jehovah's Witnesses from entering the Kingdom of God.

Chapter 8 tackles the question of whether the number 144,000 is symbolic or literal—with drastic consequences for the good news proclaimed by Witnesses. It also addresses the issue of who exactly comprise the "great crowd" of Revelation 7:9. It's not who you think it is.

In Chapter 9, we'll apply exegesis to demonstrate that the "great tribulation" of Revelation 7:15 is something that affects all Christians throughout time.

There's no easy way to prepare you for the stunning revelations of Chapter 10 where you'll learn the true origin of the "Other Sheep" doctrine of Jehovah's Witnesses.

Chapter 11 deals with how to identify false prophets and what to do with them. Watch Tower leadership has always claimed they are not false prophets, but merely men who have made honest mistakes. Do the facts of history back up that claim or are they hiding the truth to protect themselves? You'll be able to decide for yourself as you read the historical evidence taken from the Organization's own publications on the three major prophetic failures of the last century and a half, specifically, 1914, 1925, and 1975.

The next two chapters (12 and 13) cover the question of divine authority. Is the current Governing Body appointed by God or are they self-appointed? Part of their claim to authority is the belief that they had a first-century counterpart, a governing body situated in Jerusalem. Chapter 12 analyses scripture to show how that can't be the case.

Chapter 13 scrutinizes the teaching that in 1919 Jesus appointed top men in the Watch Tower Society to be his Faithful and Discreet Slave. If there is no evidence to support that, then the current Governing Body would be little more than usurpers. You'll have all the facts you'll need to decide that for yourself.

Chapter 14 deals with what it means to partake of the bread and wine, and what your relationship with Jesus Christ really signifies in terms of your salvation.

Now we come to the clincher in Chapter 15 of how the Society has stolen salvation from Jehovah's Witnesses.

By the time the reader gets to Chapter 16, the question in mind will be "Where do I go from here?" Is it possible to move forward with your faith without joining another religion? Is religion even necessary. Those questions are answered in this chapter.

While the bulk of this book is devoted to tearing down false teachings, I would be doing you, dear reader, little good if I left it at that. My goal is not to destroy but to build up. Realizing that one's belief system has failed can have devasting consequences. However, when Peter was disturbed by something Jesus said, his decision was to stick to Christ. He said at John 6:68, 69, "Lord, **whom shall we go away to?** You have sayings of everlasting life. We have believed and have come to know that you are the Holy One of God."

It is my firm hope that you will finish this book with a faith that is stronger and more sure than ever before founded in Scripture—rather than on the publications of men.

# 1

# What Is the Good News?

> *"However, even if we or an angel out of heaven were to declare to you as good news something beyond the good news we declared to you, let him be accursed. As we have said before, I now say again, Whoever is declaring to you as good news something beyond what you accepted, let him be accursed."*
> *(Galatians 1:8, 9)*

The apostle Paul's words to the Galatians are a powerful denunciation against any person or religion that perverts the holy message of the good news. That message was transmitted by Jesus Christ and was spread throughout the Roman world by his apostles and followers. It wasn't long, however, before Satan's "ministers of righteousness"[1] began to sow a counterfeit good news. Paul makes it very clear how he feels about such deceivers. Twice he tells the Galatians: "Let him be accursed."

Cursed by God! It is hard to imagine anything worse than that.

Have Jehovah's Witnesses been preaching the same message of good news that Paul and the other apostles preached? Or are they guilty of sowing a perverted salvation hope?

In the Bible, it is called "good news of the Kingdom," "good news about Jesus," "good news of God," "good news about your

---

1. 2 Corinthians 11:15; Matthew 13:25-30

salvation" or just simply, "good news."[2] Let's start by examining what Jehovah's Witnesses preach.

## What Is the Good News According to JW.org?

**Figure 1. The brochure** *Enjoy Life Forever!*

The good news that Jehovah's Witnesses preach from house to house is one of "eternal life in an earthly paradise."[3] Typical of this message is the current *Enjoy Life Forever!* brochure available on JW.org. Watch Tower publications hold out the hope of eternal youth, eternal health, and eternal happiness on a paradise earth. Additionally, they offer the prospect of being reunited with your dead loved ones through the resurrection hope, and of living together in peace and harmony. Who wouldn't want that?

Images like this one in Figure 2 are intended to assure Witnesses that they are favored to survive Armageddon as long as they remain loyal to the Organization with its Governing Body of Christ's anointed brothers.

But we must ask, is it really Jehovah God's intention to restore earth to a paradise, filled with righteous humans, living forever? I do believe that the Bible teaches that eventuality. But, and this is the real question, is the good news that Jesus preached, the hope of living forever in an earthly paradise? No, it is not!

## What Is the Good News that Jesus Preached?

It is my goal through this book to prove that the Organization of Jehovah's Witnesses, since its creation in 1931, has not been preaching the same good news that Jesus and the apostles preached. I will not need to venture outside of Watch Tower publications to achieve this.

---

2. Ephesians 1:13; Matthew 4:23, 9:35, 24:14; Mark 1:14, 15, Acts 17:18.
3. w97 9/15 p. 17 pars. 4 "Who Will Survive 'the Day of Jehovah'"?

# 1. What Is the Good News?

**Figure 2. Surviving Armageddon.**

It would be unfair of me to expect any less of my own writing than that which I demand of the Society's publications. Therefore, for purposes of comparison, let us start by examining what the Scriptures reveal about the good news of God's Kingdom.

To understand the good news, we have to go back to the beginning to see why it is needed.

When Adam and Eve sinned, Jehovah God did what any loving parent would do when faced with rebellious children. He didn't force them to do things His way, but instead allowed them the freedom to make their case. He knew it would all go bad, but only hard experience was going to convince them of that.

Sadly, things went so bad that Jehovah had to start over. Only in the fullness of time will we be able to comprehend His wisdom as it relates to the flood of Noah's day that was the culmination of about 1,600 years of human history. It appears from the sparse record we have in Genesis[4] that Jehovah allowed humans free reign to develop as they wished following the rebellion in Eden.

Whatever message of good news of salvation that preflood faithful ones might have received is lost to us. The only recorded message of good news they received is found at Genesis 3:15 which reads: "And I shall put enmity between you and the woman and between your seed and her seed. He will bruise you in the head and you will bruise him in the heel."

---

4. The entirety of this 1,600-year span of history is covered in only the first nine chapters of Genesis.

Following the flood, more elements were added to the good news, such as the Abrahamic covenant:

> I shall surely bless you and I shall surely multiply your seed like the stars of the heavens and like the grains of sand that are on the seashore; and your seed will take possession of the gate of his enemies. And **by means of your seed all nations of the earth will certainly bless themselves** due to the fact that you have listened to my voice. (Genesis 22:17, 18)

The message of salvation for Mankind was refined further when Jehovah made a covenant with Israel through his servant Moses:

> And now if YOU will strictly obey my voice and will indeed keep my covenant, then YOU will certainly become my special property out of all [other] peoples, because the whole earth belongs to me. And YOU **yourselves will become to me a kingdom of priests and a holy nation.**' (Exodus 19:5, 6)

You will notice that these scriptures of hope make no mention of living in an earthly paradise. They do, however, make mention of a *seed* that will become a kingdom of priests and a holy nation. The nation of Israel failed to keep that covenant. They didn't respond to the promise of the good news because they lacked faith. We can see this clearly expressed in Hebrews:

> For we have *also* had **the good news declared to us, just as they [Israelites] had**; but the word that they heard did not benefit them, because they were not united by faith with those who listened. (Hebrews 4:2)

So, the good news about becoming a holy nation and a kingdom of priests was taken from the nation of Israel due to their lack of faith and given to a nation producing its fruits, the Christian congregation which included Gentiles and Jews.

> Jesus said to them: "Did YOU never read in the Scriptures, 'The stone that the builders rejected is the one that has become the chief cornerstone. From Jehovah this has come to be, and it is marvelous in our eyes'? This is why I say to YOU, **The kingdom of God will be taken from YOU and be given to a nation producing its fruits.** (Matthew 21:42, 43)

This shows that the message of the good news has not changed. It has only been *progressively* revealed. The promise to become a kingdom of priests by which all the nations would be blessed was initially limited to Jews, but due to their lack of faith, that same promise is now being extended to non-Jews.

> YOU are all, in fact, sons of God through YOUR faith in Christ Jesus. For all of YOU who were baptized into Christ have put on Christ. There is neither **Jew nor Greek**, there is neither slave nor freeman, there is neither male nor female; for YOU **are all one** [person] in union with Christ Jesus. Moreover, if YOU belong to Christ, YOU **are really Abraham's seed, heirs with reference to a promise.** (Galatians 3:26-29)

Can you see how the thread of the good news goes from Genesis, on through the promise made to Abraham, then to the nation of Israel, and now finally into the Christian congregation? When the final chapters of the Bible were written, we learned from John's vision that the good news includes being part of the first resurrection—the resurrection to life—and that the role of those who are first to be called "Children of God" is to rule as kings and act as priests with Jesus Christ.

> And I saw thrones, and those who sat on them were given authority to judge. Yes, I saw the souls of those executed for the witness they gave about Jesus and for speaking about God, and those who had not worshipped the wild beast or its image and had not received the mark on their forehead and on their hand. And they came to life and ruled as kings with the Christ for 1,000 years.... Happy and holy is anyone having part in **the first resurrection**; over these the second death has no authority, but **they will be priests of God and of the Christ, and they will rule as kings with him for the 1,000 years.** (Revelation 20:4, 6 NWT 2013)

While many Christian denominations, including Jehovah's Witnesses, believe that the salvation hope of the Children of God is to go off to heaven, never to return, the Bible indicates something more for them. In Proverbs, we read that "a large population is a king's glory, but without subjects a prince is ruined."[5] How can a King rule over his people unless he has a people to rule over?

Over whom will these Kings rule for a thousand years, and from where will they rule? Can they rule if they are away, far removed from their subjects' day-to-day lives?

---

5.   Proverbs 14:28 NIV

When Jesus went to heaven, he left his followers, whom he referred to in parables as his slaves, to tend to the needs of his flock.[6] This shows that a King must be present if he is to rule in a way that benefits his people.

But the covenant that the Israelites lost as a nation, and which was then given to the Christian congregation, also speaks of priests. In Israel, a priest was there to receive offerings of atonement for sin. The priest officiated between the sinner and God. Essentially, the priest had a role in a ceremony of reconciliation between Jehovah and the sinner. Again, a priest has to be present to perform his priestly function of reconciliation. How could he officiate if absent? John reveals to us that the place where the Children of God will act with Christ as rulers and priests is *on* the earth.

> ...and to open its seals, because You were slain, and You purchased us to God in Your blood, out of every tribe, and tongue, and people, and nation, and **made them [to be] to our God kings and priests, and they will reign *on* the earth**." (Revelation 5:9, 10 LSV)

The word "on" in the phrase "reign on the earth is *epi* in Greek and means "upon" or "on" which indicates location. So here we see some of the evidence that the Children of God will not govern from afar, but their rulership and priestly functions will be hands on.

## What Hope Did First-Century Christians Preach?

The hope of the good news preached by the apostles was in line with all we've just read. Perhaps the best evidence that their message of good news pertained to the hope of ruling with Jesus in the Kingdom of God can be found in a rebuke that Paul gave to the congregation in Corinth.

> YOU men already have YOUR fill, do YOU? YOU are rich already, are YOU? **YOU have begun ruling as kings without us, have YOU?** And I wish indeed that YOU had begun ruling as kings, **that we also might rule with YOU as kings**. (1 Corinthians 4:8)

Obviously, Paul did not go from door to door preaching the hope of becoming *subjects* of the Kingdom of God on a paradise

---

6. Matthew 24:45-51

earth, as Witnesses do. He hoped to be a King, a co-ruler with Jesus. His message of good news was to enter the new covenant as one of God's adopted children, with Jesus as mediator, and to eventually rule with him.

But to rule over what? Paradise?

## What Does the Bible Say About Paradise?

The word "paradise" only appears three times in the Christian Scriptures. If the hope held out to Christians through the good news preached by Jesus and his apostles related in any way to living in *paradise*, you would expect a little more emphasis on the word than that, wouldn't you? After all, *paradise* appears over 10,000 times in the publications of the Watch Tower Society!

In the *New World Translation* 2013 edition, we find it first at Luke 23:43 where Jesus tells the evildoer, "you will be with me in Paradise." No explanation is given as to what he means by that.

Next, we find it at 2 Corinthians 12:4 where Paul tells us of a vision in which he "was caught away to the third heaven...into paradise" which connects *paradise* with *heaven* in some way.

Finally, we have the words of Jesus directed to the congregation of Ephesus where we read:

> Therefore remember from where you have fallen, and repent and do the deeds you did at first. If you do not, I will come to you, and I will remove your lampstand from its place, unless you repent. Still, you do have this in your favor: that you hate the deeds of the sect of Nicolaus, which I also hate. Let the one who has an ear hear what the spirit says to the congregations: **To the one who conquers I will grant to eat of the tree of life, which is in the paradise of God.** (Revelation 2:5-7)

The first century Ephesian congregation was made up of anointed Christians. Are the anointed going to be resurrected and directed to eat of a literal tree of life, or is Jesus speaking symbolically? I think we can agree that he's speaking symbolically. There is no mention in the Christian Scriptures of the type of paradise depicted by the many colorful and appealing illustrations we find in the pages of Watch Tower publications.[7]

## The Role of Jesus Christ in the Good News

To this point, my focus has been on the Children of God and our role as recipients of the benefits of the good news of our salvation.[8] However, none of this is possible without Jesus, for there can be no good news without the Christ, as demonstrated by the following expressions tied to the preaching work of the apostles:

- Acts 5:42 – "good news of the Christ, Jesus"
- Acts 8:4 – "good news of the word"
- Acts 8:12 – "good news of the kingdom of God"
- Acts 8:35 – "good news about Jesus"
- Acts 11:20 – "good news of the Lord Jesus"
- Acts 17:18 – "good news of Jesus and the resurrection"

The mystery or "sacred secret" of the good news was finally revealed through our Lord Jesus, as Paul relates:

> I became a minister of this congregation in accord with the stewardship from God that was given to me in your behalf to preach the word of God fully, **the sacred secret that was hidden** from the past systems of things and from the past generations. But now it has been revealed to his holy ones, to whom God has been pleased to make known among the nations the glorious riches of **this sacred secret, which is Christ** in union with you, the hope of his glory. (Colossians 1:25-27)

For thousands of years, faithful men and women desired to understand the great mystery of our salvation that is now known to us as Jesus reveals in Matthew:

> However, happy are YOUR eyes because they behold, and YOUR ears because they hear. For I truly say to YOU, Many prophets and righteous men desired to see the things YOU are beholding and **did not see them**, and to hear the things YOU are hearing and **did not hear them**. (Matthew 13:16, 17)

---

7. The Organization has co-opted restoration prophecies from the Hebrew Scriptures pointing to Israel's return from Babylon and applied them antitypically to the New World that they depict in their publications. These are not part of the Christian hope of salvation.
8. Ephesians 1:13

## 1. What Is the Good News?

How sad it is now to learn that with all this knowledge openly revealed to us, the overwhelming majority of Christians have been led astray from the true nature of the good news into believing fables told by men about what that hope involves.

If there is a single passage of Scripture that explains the nature of the good news declared by Jesus and the apostles, it is this one from the letter to the Ephesians:

> ⁵ For **he foreordained us to the adoption through Jesus Christ as sons to himself**, according to the good pleasure of his will, ⁶ in praise of his glorious undeserved kindness which he kindly conferred upon us by means of [his] loved one. ⁷ By means of him we have the release by ransom through the blood of that one, yes, the forgiveness of [our] trespasses, according to the riches of his undeserved kindness. ⁸ This he caused to abound toward us in all wisdom and good sense, ⁹ in that he made known to us **the sacred secret of his will**. It is according to his good pleasure which he purposed in himself ¹⁰ for an administration [**stewardship**, household management] at the full limit of the appointed times, namely, to gather all things together again in the Christ, the things in the heavens and the things on the earth. [Yes,] in him... (Ephesians 1:5-10)

**In verses 5 thru 8** we learn that our adoption as God's children was foreordained. This foreordaining happened right after the rebellion in Eden when Jehovah prophesied that the seed of the women would eventually crush the seed of the serpent. This was *the* good news! Nevertheless, the way it would work out was kept as a divine mystery or sacred secret for millennia.

But no more! Because of the loving kindness (grace, or as Witnesses say, "undeserved kindness") of our God, He is now "making know to us the sacred secret of his will."

**In verses 9 and 10** we are introduced to something new: "an administration." The word in Greek is *oikonomia* which is defined as "stewardship, administration." HELPS Word-studies give us this:

> **3622** *oikonomía* (from 3621 /*oikonoméō*, "a steward, managing a household") – properly, a stewardship, management (administration), i.e. **where a person looks after another's affairs** (resources).
>
> [A "dispensation" can also refer to **a special period of time** (management). But this is a secondary (not primary) meaning of 3622 (*oikonomía*).]

This usage of the word indicates that the reward of the good news involves more than simply being adopted as God's children. There is work to be done. We are being called to act as *stewards*, to administer or *manage the affairs of another*—Jehovah God. This stewardship will be accomplished over *a special period of time*, specifically, a thousand years. The reason the Children of God are being adopted now is to eventually "gather all things together in the Christ," which includes "the things in the heavens and the things on the earth." This will be accomplished "at the full limit of the appointed times."

When the first couple sinned, the appointed times for the resolution of the problem of human sin began, and the full limit of those appointed times will be attained when sin and death are finally eliminated. This is revealed by Paul in his letter to the Corinthians:

> However, now Christ has been raised up from the dead, the firstfruits of those who have fallen asleep [in death]. For since death is through a man, resurrection of the dead is also through a man. For just as in Adam all are dying, **so also in the Christ all will be made alive**. But each one in his own rank: Christ the firstfruits, afterward those who belong to the Christ during his presence. Next, **the end, when he hands over the kingdom to his God and Father, when he has brought to nothing all government and all authority and power**. For he must rule as king until [God] has put all enemies under his feet. **As the last enemy, death is to be brought to nothing.** For [God] "subjected all things under his feet." But when he says that 'all things have been subjected,' it is evident that it is with the exception of the one who subjected all things to him. But when all things will have been subjected to him, then the Son himself will also subject himself to the One who subjected all things to him, **that God may be all things to everyone**. (1 Corinthians 15:20-28)

Jesus and his anointed brothers,[9] the Children of God, will work to bring all things into submission to God. Jesus will abolish Adamic death, and all those who put their faith in him will be saved. When the work of the administration or *stewardship* we read about in Ephesians is complete, when the affairs of

---

9. "For both he who is sanctifying and those who are being sanctified all [stem] from one, and for this cause he is not ashamed to call them 'brothers'" (Hebrews 2:11)

## 1. What Is the Good News?

Jehovah have been managed to His satisfaction, Jesus and his co-rulers will submit themselves to the Father, so that God will be all things to everyone. This will return the human family to its original, intended state where every man and woman will be a child of God.

At the current time, God is not the Father of every human, but only of the adopted Children of God who are born again due to their faith in Jesus.

> However, to all who did receive him, he gave **authority to become God's children, because they were exercising faith in his name**. And they were born, not from blood or from a fleshly will or from man's will, but from God. (John 1:12, 13)

Unrighteous humans are alienated from Him due to inherited sin. The stewardship of Jesus and the anointed will bring about the return of willing humans into the family of God. For them, Jesus, as the last Adam, becomes their eternal father.[10]

### The Essence of the Good News Jesus Proclaimed

The good news that Jesus reveals to us concerns the gathering of the holy[11] chosen ones of God together.[12] The good news is that these—the Children of God—have the hope of being resurrected to life. Revelation 20:4-6 specifically speaks of those who "came to life and ruled as kings with the Christ for 1,000 years," stating in verse 5 that "this is the first resurrection."

While the Bible speaks of two resurrections, the second one is not to life, but to judgment, and is destined for all the unrighteous offspring of Adam and Eve. Jesus didn't go about preaching to the sinners of the world: "Don't worry. Keep doing what you're

---

10. 1 Corinthians 15:45 speaks of the "last Adam," referring to Jesus' human nature. Adam derives from *Adamah* (Hebrew) meaning "red clay" or "red ground" or simply, "earth," alluding to the fact the first man was "made from the dust of the ground." Jesus, as a man, had the right to produce offspring, a right he never exercised, but a right that could not be stolen from him by those who murdered him. He will exercise that right by adopting children from the dying family of the first Adam to become the everlasting father of Isaiah 9:6.
11. "Holy ones" renders the Greek *hagios* "sacred, holy." HELPS Word-studies adds, "has the 'technical' meaning 'different from the world' because 'like the Lord.'"
12. Matthew 24:31

doing. You're going to get resurrected as unrighteous ones in any case; so, no worries, boys and girls." That was not the good news he was preaching. Jesus was preaching for sinners to repent so as to have the hope of being part of the first resurrection to life!

We first learn of the two resurrections from Jesus himself:

> Do not be amazed at this, for the hour is coming in which all those in the memorial tombs will hear his voice and come out, those who did good things to **a resurrection of life**, and those who practiced vile things to **a resurrection of judgment**. (John 5:28, 29)

Paul repeats what Jesus prophesied:

> ...there is going to be **a resurrection of both the righteous and the unrighteous.** (Acts 24:15)

Of course, the good news doesn't stop with the resurrection to life. It also includes the work that the Children of God are called to perform, which is to serve in the administration or stewardship that is the Messianic Kingdom for the reconciliation of all people back into God's family.

Therefore, we can now see that the good news that Jesus preached is the call or invitation to become adopted children of God to serve in His Kingdom, which becomes the framework for the eventual salvation of all of humanity.

This helps us to understand Paul's words to the Romans:

> For the creation is waiting with eager expectation for the revealing of the sons of God. For the creation was subjected to futility, not by its own will, but through the one who subjected it, on the basis of hope that **the creation itself will also be set free from enslavement** to corruption and have the glorious freedom of the children of God. For we know that all creation keeps on groaning together and being in pain together until now. Not only that, but we ourselves also who have **the firstfruits, namely, the spirit**, yes, we ourselves groan within ourselves while we are earnestly waiting for adoption as sons, the release from our bodies by ransom. For we were saved in this hope... (Romans 8:19-24)

Here Paul is making a clear distinction between the "sons of God" who have "the firstfruits, namely, the spirit" and "the creation." By *creation*, he is not referring to plant and animal life, but to unrighteous humanity; in other words, all those who are not the Children of God. To understand that, consider this passage from Ecclesiastes:

# 1. What Is the Good News?

> I, even I, have said in my heart with regard to the sons of mankind that the [true] God is going to select them, that they may see that **they themselves are beasts**. For there is an eventuality as respects the sons of mankind and an eventuality as respects the beast, and **they have the same eventuality**. As the one dies, so the other dies; and they all have but one spirit, so that there is no superiority of the man over the beast, for everything is vanity. All are going to one place. They have all come to be from the dust, and they are all returning to the dust. (Ecclesiastes 3:18-20)

Ecclesiastes does not apply to the Children of God because they do not die as the beasts and the unrighteous do. This is because, though still sinners, they have passed over from death to life. John 5:24 says:

> Most truly I say to YOU, He that hears my word and believes him that sent me has everlasting life, and he does not come into judgment but has **passed over from death to life**. (John 5:24)

Having been born again with holy spirit,[13] these ones are not like the beasts. Though they will die, they are alive from God's viewpoint. They are not dead, but merely sleeping. Their eternal life is assured. They no longer have the same eventuality as beasts.

However, the rest of humanity continues to live outside of the family of God. Until they return to that family, they have no inheritance of everlasting life and so will die like the beasts. Therefore, Paul's reference to *the creation* in Romans 8:19, 22 applies to the unrighteous who are groaning and in pain and are "waiting with eager expectation for the revealing of the sons of God."

Now that we have a more accurate understanding of what the good news of Christ consists of, it's time for us to examine the Watch Tower Society's version of the good news.

## Is JW Good News Bait in a Deathly Trap?

The good news that Witnesses preach is not just about their hope of living forever on earth. There is much more to it than that. Witnesses claim that their teaching that Jesus' invisible presence began in 1914 is part of the good news. *The Watchtower* reads:

---

13. John 3:3-8 Greek *anōthen* literally, "born from above"; compare 1 John 3:9 "born from God."

> Let the honest-hearted person compare the kind of preaching of the gospel of the Kingdom done by the religious systems of Christendom during all the centuries with that done by Jehovah's Witnesses since the end of World War I in 1918. They are not one and the same kind. **That of Jehovah's Witnesses is really "gospel," or "good news," as of God's heavenly kingdom that was established by the enthronement of his Son Jesus Christ at the end of the Gentile Times in 1914.**[14]

This *Watchtower* article wants you to believe that the 1914 start of the Last Days is part and parcel of the good news that they preach from house to house. What if the 1914 teaching is false? Wouldn't it mean that for more than a century, JWs have been preaching a different good news from what the Apostles preached, and didn't Paul tell the Galatians that doing that would bring a curse from God? In fact, he emphasizes this curse by stating it twice.

> Not that there is another good news; but there are certain ones who are causing you trouble and wanting **to distort the good news about the Christ**. However, even if we or an angel out of heaven were to declare to you as good news something beyond the good news we declared to you, **let him be accursed**. As we have said before, I now say again, Whoever is declaring to you as good news something beyond what you accepted, **let him be accursed**. (Galatians 1:7-9)

Think of the ramifications! If 1914 is a false teaching, then it cannot be used to mark the start of the Last Days, nor the starting point for the generation countdown. Without a 1914 presence of Christ, there can be no basis for a 1918 resurrection of the anointed.[15] It is worth noting that Paul's former associates, Hymenaeus and Philetus, were condemned for proclaiming that the resurrection had already occurred.[16]

But there is more. If Jesus wasn't installed as King in 1914, then there is no basis for the claim that Jesus came to his temple in 1918 and cleansed the Bible Students.[17] Finally, and perhaps of greatest importance: If the 1914 teaching is bogus, then there is no basis to accept the Watch Tower teaching that Jesus appointed

---

14. w81 5/1 p. 17
15. w88 10/15 p. 12 par. 13
16. 2 Timothy 2:17, 18
17. w98 5/15 p. 15 par. 21

his faithful and discreet slave in 1919. Without that doctrine, the current Governing Body of Jehovah's Witnesses has no claim to the title of *Faithful and Discreet Slave*—a title which they acquired by self-appointment in 2012.

In short, if the 1914 doctrine is false, there is a chain reaction of doctrinal failures that destroys the very foundation of the religion of Jehovah's Witnesses and deprives the Governing Body of any legitimate claim to the authority it holds over the flock.[18]

As significant as all of that is, it is not the only issue calling into question the authenticity of the good news that Witnesses preach. The basis for the hope of eternal life on a paradise earth is founded on a very specific interpretation of who the "other sheep" of John 10:16 are. Witnesses believe that only 144,000 are selected to be the Children of God, while the rest—millions of Jehovah's Witnesses—can only aspire to being God's friends.[19] Thus, there are two distinct salvation hopes for righteous Christians according to the theology published by the Watch Tower Society: one for the anointed 144,000 and another for the millions of Other Sheep.

If this should turn out to be false, then the leadership of the Organization has been deceiving millions of people who were trusting in them for their salvation. With good reason, we can see why Paul was so vehement in condemning any who were preaching a different good news than that which he and the other apostles had preached to the Galatians.

Given the dire consequences of preaching a false good news, it would be most foolish to miss the opportunity before us of examining our beliefs in Scripture. Many Witnesses will refuse to plunge into a study of the Bible, perhaps fearing where it might lead. Will that exonerate them? If I am preaching a good news that differs from what Paul and the apostles preached, can I escape judgment because I'm doing so unwittingly? Not according to the parable of the faithful and discreet slave.

You may not realize it, but the parable of the faithful and discreet slave found at Matthew 24:45-51 is an incomplete account of what Jesus said. Luke's account includes two additional slaves:

---

18. w13 7/15 p. 23 par. 12
19. w12 7/15 p. 28 par. 7

> Then that slave who understood the will of his master but did not get ready or do what he asked will be beaten with many strokes. But the one who did not understand and yet did things deserving of strokes will be beaten with few. (Luke 12:47, 48a)

So, even if we are failing to do the will of the Lord because we are being misled and are ignorant of what his true will is, we still end up being punished. Wouldn't it be better to be blessed by our Lord?

It is my hope that through this book as well as through the *Beroean Pickets* web site and YouTube channel[20] I can help others to learn the wonderful hope that has been offered to sincere Christians since the time of Christ.

I have one last thought to consider before we get underway:

## Why All Truth-loving Jehovah's Witnesses Need to Read This Book

If you are one of Jehovah's Witnesses, you may feel guilty just holding this book in your hands. An outsider might find that statement strange. Why would anyone feel guilty for looking at a book that studies the Bible? The reason is indoctrination. Witnesses have been ingrained to think that anything that disagrees with the teachings of the Governing Body is apostasy. How strange it is that most JWs fail to recognize the hypocrisy of this position. Let me explain.

Years ago, when I was a pioneer,[21] I studied *The Truth that Leads to Everlasting Life* with all of my bible students. At the time, these were mostly Catholics. I wanted them to overcome fear and prejudice so that they could examine their beliefs in the light of Scripture. Chapter 14 of the book was excellent for helping them to think critically about their faith. Here are the key paragraphs:

> LOGICALLY there must be just one true religion. This is in harmony with the fact that the true God is a God, "not of disorder, but of peace." (1 Corinthians 14:33) Furthermore, **Jesus Christ spoke of those who practice** such religion as **worshiping God "with spirit and truth,"** and truth is never at disagreement with itself. (John 4:23, 24) But who are these true worshipers today? **How**

---

20. https://beroeans.net; https://www.youtube.com/c/BeroeanPickets/videos
21. A title given to a Witness engaging in full time preaching; 100+ hours a month in the late 1960s.

## 1. What Is the Good News?

**can you identify them** and know that their worship is indeed the one approved by God?

**This cannot be decided simply on the basis of what people and organizations claim to be.** In his Sermon on the Mount, Jesus pointed out that many would call him "Lord, Lord," claiming to have done notable things in his name. Yet he would say to them: "I never knew you! Get away from me, you workers of lawlessness." Not only words but also appearances can be deceptive. Jesus said that false prophets would come in sheep's covering, while inside they would be like devouring wolves. However, he gave us a rule by which we can distinguish between the true servants of God and the false ones, saying: "By their fruits you will recognize them." **He showed that what really determines whether we are true worshipers of God is not merely our claims or even our apparently commendable works, but our actually doing the will of the heavenly Father.**—Matthew 7:15-23.

A faithful follower of Jesus, the apostle Paul, also showed the need for caution. He warned that some men would appear to be ministers of righteousness and yet would be false Christians. Outwardly they may not seem bad. But **when measured in the light of God's Word, the Bible, they are shown to be ministers of God's enemy, Satan, for their works are actually in opposition to God's will.** (2 Corinthians 11:13-15) Our following the lead of such false Christians could only result in our losing out on life eternal.[22]

So, as far back as 1968, the Organization rightly claimed that there was a right way to identify those who were worshiping God "with spirit and truth." It stated that "this cannot be decided simply on the basis of what people and organizations *claim to be*." Therefore, by its own criteria, the Organization's claim to being the one true religion as well as the channel Jehovah is using *cannot be used to establish* that they are the true religion. That would be circular reasoning. Furthermore, the *Truth* book teaches that Jesus "showed that what really determines whether we are true worshipers of God is not merely our claims or even our apparently commendable works, but our actually doing the will of the heavenly Father."

Preaching falsehoods—especially, a false good news—would clearly not be "doing the will of the heavenly Father." So, how can

---

22. tr chap. 14 pp. 122-123 pars. 1-3

you know if the Organization of Jehovah's Witnesses is "actually doing the will of the heavenly Father"?

Again, the *Truth* book answers the question: The ministers of any religion—including the religion of Jehovah's Witnesses—must be *"measured in the light of God's Word, the Bible."*

I couldn't agree more. The Bible provides the only reliable criteria for determining whether the works of any religion are righteous or not.

## Pay No Attention to the Man Behind the Curtain

If someone tells you to not even listen to what others have to say, alarm bells should be going off in your head. A person armed with the truth has no reason to fear others whose only weapons are lies.

When I used to preach from house to house, I never knew who would greet me when the door opened. It might be a Mormon, or an evangelical, or an atheist. Was I going to be challenged on my belief in creation, or that there is no hellfire, or that Jesus is not God Almighty? I wasn't afraid to talk about these things, because I had the truth and could defend my beliefs from Scripture. If you are armed with the truth, you have nothing to fear from lies and falsehood.

So, what is the Governing Body afraid of? Why do they label anyone who challenges them as apostates? Why don't they want you to look behind the curtain? And why is it when they condemn these so-called "apostates," they never state what the "apostates" are saying? Surely, if these are truly "lying apostates," then the best way to expose them would be to reveal the lies they claim they are spreading. They never do that. All we get from the Governing Body is slander and character assassination, but never specifics about what these so-called "opposers" have actually said. Usually, when someone resorts to *ad hominem*[23] attacks, it indicates they are in the wrong and have no recourse other than to slander the other person's character.

Jesus was attacked constantly by the religious leaders of his day, the governing body (Sanhedrin) of Israel. Those men were truly apostates, because they murdered the Son of God. Yet he

---

23. (of an argument or reaction) directed against a person rather than the position they are maintaining.

listened to their lies and defeated them easily using the truth. If these "opposers" and "apostates" that the Governing Body complains about so much are truly liars, why doesn't the Governing Body follow the example of our Lord Jesus and expose their lies publicly?

## Never Be Misled Again!

My overriding concern when I started my own Bible study is likely the same as yours: How to avoid ever being misled by men again!

Jesus assures us at John 8:31b, 32 that *"if you remain in my word, you are really my disciples, and you will know the truth, and the truth will set you free."*

Did you pick up on Jesus' warning? The truth will only set you free *if you remain in Jesus' word*. Not my word, not the Governing Body's word, not the word of some internet pundit, but only Jesus' word. But how do you make sure that it is *his* word you are listening to? How can you protect yourself from being misled by the subtle, contrived reasoning of those who clothe themselves in righteous garb, but inside are ravenous wolves?

> For such men are false apostles, deceitful workers, **disguising themselves as apostles of Christ**. And no wonder, for Satan himself keeps disguising himself as an angel of light. It is therefore nothing extraordinary if his ministers also keep disguising themselves as ministers of righteousness. But their end will be according to their works. (2 Corinthians 11:13-15)

Does that mean we should mistrust all teachers of God's word? Not necessarily. The Bible gives us this assurance:

> And he [Jesus] gave some as apostles, some as prophets, some as evangelizers, **some as shepherds and teachers**, with a view to the readjustment of the holy ones, for ministerial work, to build up the body of the Christ, until we all attain to the oneness of the faith and of the accurate knowledge of the Son of God, to being a full-grown man, attaining the measure of stature that belongs to the fullness of the Christ. So we should no longer be children, tossed about as by waves and carried here and there by every wind of teaching by means of the trickery of men, by means of cunning in deceptive schemes. (Ephesians 4:11-14)

This indicates that Jesus gives us some who are to be *shepherds and teachers* for the purpose of training the Children of God so that we can stand on our own feet and not be misled by the cunning and trickery of men. Still, how do we distinguish the real *shepherds and teachers* from the legion of false ones that surround us?

To answer that, let's use an illustration. Say you are travelling to a place you have never been and stop to ask for directions. How can you know that the person directing you is not leading you astray? You need an authoritative source, don't you? Like a map. But that only works if you know how to read a map. So, you need someone to teach you how to read a map, any map. Once you are armed with that knowledge and ability, you can avoid being misled.

The Bible is our map to truth, but we have to learn how to read it, like we would read any map. As one of Jehovah's Witnesses, I thought I knew how to study the Bible. I figured I could read the map, so to speak. I rejected all outside teaching sources, including WT publications, and based my study exclusively on Scripture, but I kept running into roadblocks.

I didn't realize it at the time, but I was still using the method for Bible study I had been brought up with. That study method is called *eisegesis* (pronounced *ahy-si-jee-seez*). It wasn't until I learned a different method (I didn't even know there was more than one up to that point) that I began to make real progress. Once I learned how to read the map for myself—how to study the Bible in a way to allow it to reveal itself—only then did I lose all fear of being misled by men.

As you go through this book, I want you to be sure that what you are reading does not originate from men but is truth which you have been able to confirm for yourself. I don't want to be just one more man who carries you "hither and thither by every wind of teaching by means of the trickery [and] cunning in contriving error."[24]

To that end, I need to share with you the Bible study method that has allowed me to read Scripture, like you might read a map, so that you can get to your destination, from falsehood to truth and ultimately to your salvation hope.

---

24. Ibid

# 2

# Bible Study Done Right

---

*"At this they said to him: 'We each had a dream, but there is no interpreter with us.' Joseph said to them: 'Do not interpretations belong to God?'" (Genesis 40:8)*

---

There are literally thousands of denominations within Christendom, each with its own unique doctrinal framework. Yet, all of them claim their teachings are Bible-based. So, how is it possible that while using the same book, there can be so many different beliefs? Is the Bible really that cryptic? Is it so vague and mysterious that it's impossible to draw absolute truth from its pages? Many believe that to be the case. They believe there is no such thing as absolute truth. That seems to have been the opinion of Pontius Pilate when he was judging Jesus:

> Therefore Pilate said to him: "Well, then, are you a king?" Jesus answered: "You yourself are saying that I am a king. For this I have been born, and for this I have come into the world, that I should **bear witness to the truth**. Everyone that is on the side of the truth listens to my voice." **Pilate said to him: "What is truth?** (John 18:37, 38)

Pilate's cynical comment echoes the sentiment of many today who believe all truth is relative, dependent only on the perception of the observer. Jesus was under no such delusion. He was the word of God and God's word is truth.

> **Sanctify them by means of the truth; your word is truth**. Just as you sent me forth into the world, I also sent them forth into the

world. And I am sanctifying myself in their behalf, that they also may be **sanctified by means of truth**. (John 17:17-19)

When I first started to have doubts about the reliability of the Organization's teachings, I resolved to study the Bible for myself free from the influence of Watch Tower publications. I just wanted to learn the truth. However, there was a problem. I was hampered by using the study method I had learned from the Watch Tower Society.

Since its inception in 1879, when the first issue of *Zion's Watch Tower and Herald of Christ's Presence* was published by C. T. Russell, the Organization has interpreted Scripture in very much the same way, using the same research method as the churches of Christendom. This research method is called *eisegesis* (pronounced ahy-si-jee-seez).

## Eisegesis: Bible Study the Wrong Way

*Eisegesis* is a Greek word that has been adopted into English and means "to lead into." This occurs when we start with a preconceived idea, and then cherry-pick a Bible verse to support it. In this way, we are 'leading our idea into' Scripture. This makes us vulnerable to *confirmation bias*. That is a common danger for any sincere Bible student because we all tend to see what we want to see and ignore anything that might conflict with our preferences.

The Bible actually warns us of this dangerous tendency. Peter wrote:

> For, **according to their wish**, this fact escapes their notice, that there were heavens from of old and an earth standing compactly out of water and in the midst of water by the word of God; and by those [means] the world of that time suffered destruction when it was deluged with water. But by the same word the heavens and the earth that are now are stored up for fire and are being reserved to the day of judgment and of destruction of the ungodly men. (2 Peter 3:5-7)

Peter tells us that ridiculers in his day were ignoring the warning message contained in the flood account "according to their wish," or to rephrase it, because "they wanted to." They only accepted what they wanted to believe and ignored all evidence to the contrary.

The only sure way to protect ourselves from falling into this confirmation bias trap is for us to determine in our heart to love

## 2. Bible Study Done Right

truth. Wherever it may lead and no matter how inconvenient or uncomfortable it may make us feel, we will find it. Remember that opposers are condemned by Jesus, not for failing to have the truth, but for failing to love it.

> But the lawless one's presence is according to the operation of Satan with every powerful work and lying signs and portents and with every unrighteous deception for those who are perishing, as a retribution because **they did not accept the love of the truth** that they might be saved. (2 Thessalonians 2:9, 10)

If we are going to succeed in our Bible study, we must start on this singular premise: We must *love* truth.

Jesus warns us at Matthew 15:9 that "it is in vain that they [religious leaders] keep worshiping me, because they teach commands of men as doctrines." Heeding this warning, let's look at an example of a doctrine constructed entirely on cherry-picked verses that are interpreted eisegetically.

The doctrine of the "great crowd of other sheep" is the product of splicing together two scriptures, "the great crowd" from Revelation 7:9 and the "other sheep" from John 10:16. Watch Tower publications refer to "the great crowd of other sheep" often, with this exact phrase appearing more than 300 times in their pages. It will likely surprise the average JW to learn that not only does the phrase "great crowd of other sheep" *never occur* in the Bible, but that there is no scriptural basis for uniting the *great crowd* with the *other sheep*. The relationship is entirely an eisegetical construct of the Organization. They had to create this artificial link between these verses for the purpose of creating a secondary, lower class of JWs that will survive Armageddon.[1]

Therefore, by misinterpreting and splicing together two small verses, they've established a false premise upon which they have built an entire salvation hope for millions.

When trusted religious leaders do this, that false premise becomes gospel for all church or congregation members. Once a false premise is accepted as fact, an entire doctrinal interpretation can be built upon it. As more and more teachings are built upon the false premise, the Bible student is moved further and further from the truth. It only takes a small deviation at the start

---

1. For a through discussion of this teaching, see "Chapter 7 Who Are the Other Sheep?"

of a long journey to end up way off course by the end. The farther down the wrong doctrinal road that we travel, the harder it is for us to find our way back.

While all this is discouraging, take heart. I'm about to show you the way to break free from any dependence on the interpretations of men—a sure way to defend yourself from false teachings and false teachers.

## Exegesis: Bible Study the Right Way

*Exegesis* (pronounced *ek·suh·jee·suhs*) is the opposite of eisegesis. It also comes from Greek and means "to lead out of." This involves drawing the meaning out of the Bible text rather than imposing a meaning onto it. Essentially, exegesis allows the Bible to interpret itself.

But how can an inanimate object interpret itself? First, we must not consider the Bible to be just dead words on a page.

> For **the word of God is alive** and exerts power and is sharper than any two-edged sword and pierces even to the dividing of soul and spirit, and of joints and [their] marrow, and [is] able to discern thoughts and intentions of [the] heart. (Hebrews 4:12)

According to John 1:1, the word or *logos* of God is Jesus. His words are recorded in the pages of the Bible. Since he is alive, they are alive. His words exert power. That power doesn't just come off the printed page, however. When Jesus was about to depart, he told his disciples:

> I have many things yet to say to YOU, but YOU are not able to bear them at present. However, when that one arrives, **the spirit of the truth, he will guide YOU into all the truth**, for he will not speak of his own impulse, but what things he hears he will speak, and he will declare to YOU the things coming. (John 16:12, 13)

Let us start by acknowledging that we are never going to understand "all the truth" if we are not led by God's holy spirit. To get that spirit, the scriptures show we have to do two things.

The first is to adjust our attitude. We have to be humble, divesting ourselves of egoistical tendencies. Bible knowledge is not going to be granted to us if we want to use it to lord ourselves over others. It's not for the wise and intellectual, but for childlike ones. Jesus rejoiced at this fact:

> At that time Jesus said in response: "I publicly praise you, Father, Lord of heaven and earth, because you have **hidden these things**

**from the wise and intellectual ones and have revealed them to young children.** Yes, O Father, because this is the way you approved. (Matthew 11:25, 26)

Second, we must pray continually for the holy spirit, "not doubting at all."

> So if any one of you is lacking in wisdom, **let him keep asking God, for he gives generously to all and without reproaching**, and it will be given him. But let him **keep asking in faith, not doubting at all**, for the one who doubts is like a wave of the sea driven by the wind and blown about. In fact, that man should not expect to receive anything from Jehovah; he is an indecisive man, unsteady in all his ways. (James 1:5-8)

> Accordingly I say to YOU, Keep on asking, and it will be given YOU; keep on seeking, and YOU will find; keep on knocking, and it will be opened to YOU. For everyone asking receives, and everyone seeking finds, and to everyone knocking it will be opened. Indeed, which father is there among YOU who, if his son asks for a fish, will perhaps hand him a serpent instead of a fish? Or if he also asks for an egg, will hand him a scorpion? Therefore, if YOU, although being wicked, know how to give good gifts to YOUR children, **how much more so will the Father in heaven give holy spirit to those asking him!** (Luke 11:9-13)

Okay, we're almost ready to begin our study of exegesis, but there's still one more thing to do; and in my experience, this can be the hardest thing of all. Before examining any scripture, we must clear our mind of all previous ideas, beliefs, and preconceptions. Why do I say that this can be the hardest thing to do? Because often these previous ideas, beliefs, and preconceptions are so deeply embedded in our mind that we're not even aware they're influencing our thinking. Let's illustrate this with an example.

When I first started my independent research, I wanted to understand how the generation of Matthew 24:34 could be applied to the Last Days. I knew that David Splane's *Overlapping Generation* interpretation was deeply flawed because it didn't fit with any secular or scriptural definition of the word, "generation." Still, there had to be an interpretation that fit with the events of our day. I say that because I was working on the premise—inherited from my time as a JW—that Matthew 24 had two fulfillments, the secondary or major fulfillment being counted from 1914. I tried various lines of reasoning, but never felt satisfied with the results. You can see my attempts for yourself by accessing this link to my web site:

beroeans.net/category/this-generation/

The reason I was having problems figuring this out was that I was working on a false premise or preconception—specifically, that Matthew 24:34 applied to our day. This premise had become embedded in my mind through decades of indoctrination studying Watch Tower publications at five weekly meeting! It was buried so deep that it had become a given, a fundamental truth. I never even thought to question it, until one day, I did. The moment I chose to examine that premise, I was able to apply the principles of exegesis and the meaning of Jesus' assurance regarding "this generation" became clear.

What do I mean by "the principles of exegesis"? In exegetical Bible study, we consider the textual, historical, and cultural context as well as who is speaking, and who is being addressed. Additionally, beyond the immediate context, there's the need to preserve overall Scriptural harmony, since any interpretation that contradicts other parts of Scripture must be considered as false. At times, we may need to use research tools, like Greek and Hebrew lexicons that explain the meaning of the original words. But even there, great care must be exercised since all such works are written by uninspired men who may unwittingly allow their own theological bias to color what they write.

The Bible tells us at Genesis 40:8 that "interpretations belong to God." Exegesis is how we let God speak to us through his inspired word, the Bible. It's how we allow the spirit to "guide us into all the truth."[2]

Letting the Bible speak to us is how we eradicate personal prejudice and ego from our study of Scripture. It's how we keep ourselves from falling into the trap of making personal interpretations that bring praise to ourselves rather than to our Lord Jesus, or our Heavenly Father, Jehovah.[3]

---

2. John 16:13
3. One example of this would be when a committee of men presume to appoint themselves as Christ's faithful and discreet slave by imposing this idea onto Matthew 24:45.

## Comparing Eisegesis with Exegesis

Let's put the principles of exegesis to work in a side-by-side comparison with eisegesis. This is the best way to judge the benefits of one and the dangers of the other.

I have chosen chapters 11 and 12 of the book of Daniel because they offer an excellent opportunity to compare these two opposing methodologies since those chapters figure prominently in the Last Days theology of Jehovah's Witnesses.

I would first recommend that you put down this book and read the entirety of Daniel chapters 11 and 12. Once you're done, have a look at Daniel 12:1 which reads:

> During that time Michael will stand up, the great prince who is standing in behalf of **your people**. And there will occur a time of distress such as has not occurred since there came to be a nation until that time. And during that time your people will escape, everyone who is found written down in the book. (NWT 2013 edition)

When the angel speaking to Daniel referred to "your people," about whom was he speaking? Do you think he was referring to Jehovah's Witnesses? That would seem to be a ridiculous conclusion to draw given that Jehovah's Witnesses wouldn't appear on the world scene for another 2,500 years.

Daniel was a Jew. His *people* would be the Jews exiled with him in Babylon, wouldn't they? Exegesis—allowing the truth to be *led out* of Scripture—would naturally bring us to that conclusion. With that as our starting point, everything else within the account that the angel says would happen to "your people" must be understood to happen to the Jews.

When I was passively allowing the publications of the Watch Tower to teach me, I missed that obvious conclusion. I'd been trained by years of weekly *Watchtower* studies not to think critically, but to just believe whatever I was taught. So, I believed that Daniel's people were Jehovah's Witnesses during the last days starting in 1914.[4] This is an example of eisegetical thinking.

By accepting this interpretation of the timing of Daniel 12:1, Jehovah's Witnesses are forced to consider that the last part of chapter 11 and all of chapter 12 applies to our day. Thus, when

---

4. w15 5/15 p. 30 par. 3

they get to Daniel 12:11, 12, they have to come up with a modern-day fulfillment for the two time periods of 1,290 days and 1,335 days.

> And from the time that the constant feature has been removed and the **disgusting thing that causes desolation** has been put in place, there will be **1,290 days**. "Happy is the **one who keeps in expectation and arrives at the 1335 days!**" (Daniel 12:11, 12)

Here is the prophetic fulfillment which the Organization of Jehovah's Witnesses claims for these two verses:

> Unquestionably that Cedar Point convention (September 5-13, 1922) was an impressive marker of the climax of the 1,290 days for the sanctuary class. But inspiriting as it was, Jehovah God foresaw something still further that deserved timing in his prophecy, because of what it would mean to his consecrated people. To put them in further expectation, he inspired his angel to say to Daniel: "Happy is he who waits till he reaches the thousand three hundred and thirty-five days!" (Dan. 12:12, AT) This period would be in addition to the 1,290 days and would be forty-five days or a month and a half longer in prophetic time. It would equal three years eight months and fifteen days. This time period would count from the end of the previous 1,290 days, **which had culminated at the second Cedar Point convention in September, 1922. The following period of 1,335 days would therefore end in the month of May, 1926.**[5]

I can't read this without thinking of that Monty Python sketch where the colonel says something like, "This started out as a nice little idea, but now it's got silly."

From this we can see how eisegesis is like lying. An initial lie may seem very plausible, but as time goes by, the liar is forced to create an elaborate fabric of lies to support the first lie, and eventually that fabric is stretched so thin that one can't help but see through it to the initial lie.

The Organization's interpretation of Daniel 12:11, 12 is an example of the failure of eisegesis as a viable Bible study method. So, why would anyone still use it. Indeed, why is it the most widely employed method of Bible study among Christian religions?

---

5. w60 5/1 p. 282 par. 21 "Part 37—'Your Will Be Done on Earth'"

## Are We Guided by Spirit or by Ego?

Jesus said that the spirit of truth would guide us into all the truth.[6] A guide leads, but it is up to us to be willing to follow that lead. If we are driven by ego—the spirit of the world,[7] rather than the spirit of truth—we will not follow the gentle leading of the spirit, but rather we will be driven by our own ego.

The application that the Governing Body of Jehovah's Witnesses imposes on Daniel 12:1 offers us an excellent example of how spiritually destructive ego-driven eisegetical interpretation can prove to be. It can even cause someone to add or subtract from Scripture to better support their interpretation.[8] Compare these two renderings from different editions of the *New World Translation*:

> "And during that time Michael will stand up, the great prince who is standing in behalf of **the sons of your people**." (Daniel 12:1 **NWT 1984 edition**)

> "During that time Michael will stand up, the great prince who is standing in behalf of **your people**...." (Daniel 12:1 **NWT 2013 edition**)

Why would the translators of the *New World Translation* 2013 edition remove the words "the sons of" from the 1984 edition which reads, "the sons of your people," when those words are clearly found in the original manuscript as the Hebrew interlinear confirms?[9] It appears that the translation committee felt compelled to support the theology of the Watch Tower Corporation over fidelity to Scripture. What could have possibly motivated them to do this?

This may sound incredible, but unless Daniel 12:4 can be made to apply to our day, the entire doctrine of 1914 becomes invalid and any claim to authority that the Governing Body assumes for itself evaporates like water on a hot day. (For a detailed analysis of how Daniel 12:4 has been pressed into service by the Governing Body to support the 1914 doctrine of the invisible

---

6. John 16:13
7. Ephesians 2:2
8. Revelation 22:18, 19
9. https://biblehub.com/interlinear/daniel/12-1.htm

presence of Christ, see "Failed Attempts to Explain Away Acts 1:7" on page 84.)

Can you see the difficulty? If *your people* in Daniel 12:1 (NWT 2013 edition) is supposed to apply to Jehovah's Witnesses, who are *the sons of your people* (NWT 1984 Edition)? Who are the sons of Jehovah's Witnesses? It is hard enough to make the words "your people" apply to Jehovah's Witnesses, but it become ludicrous if we now must explain who the "sons" would be.

If you were to read this without any need to support an established theology, would you or anyone else arrive as such a blatantly self-serving interpretation?

Daniel was a Jew in exile in ancient Babylon. To whom would he have understood the angel's words to apply? His people were the Israelites. So, *the sons of his people* would obviously be the descendants of those Israelites.

Because the Governing Body continues to support the interpretation that Daniel 12:1 refers to the Last Days, which they claim began in 1914, they've been forced to explain how two unbroken royal lineages—the Kings of the South and the North—can extend from ancient Babylon right down to our day—a 2,500-year span of time. Why? Because, right after speaking of the King of the North, the next verse (remember, there were no chapter, verse, or paragraph breaks in the original) starts off saying "During that time...." So, by applying Daniel 12 to modern times, the Organization is forced to make the closing verses of Daniel 11 all about Jehovah's Witnesses.

There is just not enough material in Daniel chapter 11 to account for all the Kings and rulers throughout history from Daniel's day down to the present. Not even close. So, the Organization has to make stuff up. To illustrate that, turn to chapters 13 and 14 of the *Pay Attention to Daniel's Prophecy!* book published by the Watch Tower Society. Over the course of 60 paragraphs, a span of 32 pages, the book details the twin royal lineages from one king to the next from Daniel's day down to the time of Christ, covering about six centuries of history. Then in the closing six paragraphs of chapter 14, they leapfrog over 20 centuries of history, 2,000 years, leaving enormous unexplained gaps in these two royal lines.

This is inevitably what happens when you try to understand Scripture by going into it with a preconceived idea, instead of letting the Bible explain itself.

Eisegesis is the bane of Christianity! It turns sincere Christians into followers of men.

## Exegesis: Listening to God Rather Than Men

Now let us re-examine Daniel chapter 12, but this time with an exegetical approach.

The first thing we must understand is that the modern chapter and verse divisions we utilize to quickly locate a Bible passage were introduced *many centuries* after the Bible Canon was completed. So, while the prophetic words of the angel speaking to Daniel span two chapters and are divided into many verses with paragraph breaks and modern punctuation, none of that existed in the original writing. It was up to the translators and scribes to make those divisions. You and I will see a chapter division in a book as the start of a new thought, but the words of Daniel 12:1 follow seamlessly from the words of Daniel 11:44, 45. Let's read it again, but without any modern division marks:

> "And in **the time of [the] end** the king of the south will engage with him in a pushing, and against him the king of the north will storm with chariots and with horsemen and with many ships; and he will certainly enter into the lands and flood over and pass through. He will also actually enter into the land of the Decoration, and there will be many [lands] that will be made to stumble. But these are the ones that will escape out of his hand, Edom and Moab and the main part of the sons of Ammon. And he will keep thrusting out his hand against the lands; and as regards the land of Egypt, she will not prove to be an escapee. And he will actually rule over the hidden treasures of the gold and the silver and over all the desirable things of Egypt. And the Libyans and the Ethiopians will be at his steps. But there will be reports that will disturb him, out of the sunrising and out of the north, and he will certainly go forth in a great rage in order to annihilate and to devote many to destruction. And he will plant his palatial tents between [the] grand sea and the holy mountain of Decoration; and he will have to come all the way to his end, and there will be no helper for him. And **during that time Michael will stand up, the great prince who is standing in behalf of the sons of your people**. And there will certainly occur a time of distress such as has not been made to occur since there came to be a nation until that time. And during that time your people will escape, every one who is found written down in the book. And there will be many of those asleep in the ground of dust who will wake up,

these to indefinitely lasting life and those to reproaches [and] to indefinitely lasting abhorrence. And the ones having insight will shine like the brightness of the expanse; and those who are bringing the many to righteousness, like the stars to time indefinite, even forever. And as for you, O Daniel, make secret the words and seal up the book, **until the time of [the] end**. Many will rove about, and the [true] knowledge will become abundant." (Daniel 11:40-12:4)

Can you see how even the insertion of artificial chapter and verse divisions can cloud our understanding of a Bible account?

In researching the Bible, we must try to put ourselves into the mind of the writer. In this case, Daniel is getting a revelation from God via a messenger, an angel. The angel is telling Daniel that during the end of the royal lineage of the King of the North, Michael will stand up. He further states that this will be a time of great distress and he refers to it as the "time of the end."

What *time of the end* is the angel referring to?

## Analysing Daniel 12:1

We've already established that Daniel would naturally take the angel's reference to "the sons of your people" to refer to the descendants of the Israelites who were his contemporaries. Still, it would be nice to have some scriptural confirmation for that conclusion outside of this immediate contextual setting. Fortunately, we find just that at Daniel 9:20 which reads: "While I was still speaking and praying and confessing my sin and the sin of *my people Israel*...."

Daniel refers to his people in 9:20 and 12:1. So it follows that when he speaks of a "time of the end," it must also refer to his people in some way, right?

> In **the time of the end** the king of the south will engage with him in a pushing, and against him the king of the north will storm with chariots and horsemen and many ships; and he will enter into the lands and sweep through like a flood. (Daniel 11:40)

> As for you, Daniel, keep the words secret, and seal up the book **until the time of the end**. Many will rove about, and the true knowledge will become abundant." (Daniel 12:4)

This is an example of how we let the Bible interpret itself. The *time of the end* referred to at Daniel 11:40 and 12:4 must refer in

## 2. Bible Study Done Right

some way to the sons of Daniel's people, that is, to future Israel, to the Jewish nation. Could it be otherwise?

Are there other clues to further validate this understanding?

Chapter 12:1 continues: "And there will occur **a time of distress** such as has not occurred since there came to be a nation until that time."

With exegesis, we look for scriptural harmony. Both Matthew and Luke record Jesus speaking about a "great tribulation" or "a time of distress" that would come upon Daniel's people, Israel.

> ...for then there will be **great tribulation** such as has not occurred since the world's beginning until now, no, nor will occur again. (Matthew 24:21)

> For there will be **great distress on the land and wrath against this people**. (Luke 21:23)

Jesus is here predicting the end of the Jewish nation. It would be the end of their system of things, or as it is rendered in Greek, "the end of the age."[10] Notice how closely Jesus' words parallel those of the angel speaking to Daniel. Further evidence that the Gospel accounts and Daniel's prophecy are linked and are referring to the same *time of the end* is found at Matthew 24:15 where Jesus tells his disciples to search into the prophecy of Daniel:

> Therefore, when you catch sight of the **disgusting thing** that causes desolation, **as spoken about by Daniel the prophet**, standing in a holy place (**let the reader use discernment**) (Matthew 24:15)

Three times, at Daniel 9:27, 11:31, and 12:11, the prophet refers to "the disgusting thing," each time in relation *to the end of the nation of Israel*.

From this, it becomes clear that *the time of the end* in which Michael stands up on behalf of Daniel's people, the Israelites, is *the end of their nation*. Jesus prophesied that end would come within a single generation,[11] and which did come to pass in 70 CE with the destruction of both the temple and the city.

All of this illustrates how allowing the Bible to interpret itself protects us from falling prey to the opinions of men. Such opinions cause us to draw conclusions from a Bible passage that

---

10. *Strong's Concordance* #4930
11. Matthew 24:34

will only end up leading us into deeper and more convoluted falsehoods.

Now that we have established that this prophecy is about *the time of the end of the nation of Israel*, we can see that the two royal lineages referred to in chapter 11 start during Daniel's time (circa 539 BCE) and end around the first century. Because Jehovah's Witnesses want to apply Daniel 12 to our day, they must stretch credulity to the breaking point by forcing the lineage of the kings of chapter 11 to continue to apply down to modern times.

Currently, the Governing Body claims that the King of the North (Daniel 11:44, 45) applies to Russia, and the "holy mountain of Decoration" applies to Jehovah's Witnesses because they are now being persecuted in that country. Nevertheless, they still claim the King of the North was Nazi Germany. So the disgusting thing in the land of decoration applies both to Witnesses in the Second World War and again in modern Russia!?

Let us continue our analysis of Daniel 12 to see if the remaining part of the verse fits with a first-century fulfillment. The third part of Daniel 12:1 reads: "And during that time your people will escape, everyone who is found written down in the book."

Is there a first-century fulfillment? Indeed, there is. At Luke 10:20, Jesus tells his disciples to "rejoice because your names have been written in the heavens." He also foretold that there would be an escape—as Daniel predicted—for the chosen ones during that time of distress.

> In fact, unless those days were cut short, no flesh would be saved; but on account of **the chosen ones** those days will be cut short. (Matthew 24:22)

To this point, we have found a direct relationship between what the angel predicted would happen to "the sons of your people" and what Jesus confirmed was going to happen to the nation of Israel.

## Analysing Daniel 12:2

Do the rest of the verses of this chapter fit with a first-century application? Let us continue our analysis:

> And many of those asleep in the dust of the earth will **wake up**, some to everlasting life and others to reproach and to everlasting contempt. (Daniel 12:2)

Reading this verse will make many of us think that this is speaking of judgment day and the resurrection of both the righteous and unrighteous.[12] But are we jumping to a conclusion and letting eisegesis slip into our research?

Doing a word search on "life" and "death" in the *New World Translation of the Holy Scriptures* brings us to an interesting and revealing verse:

> Most truly I say to YOU, He that hears my word and believes him that sent me **has everlasting life**, and he does not come into judgment but **has passed over from death to life**. (John 5:24)

All those to whom Jesus spoke were considered dead by God due to their sinful state, but some became alive by putting faith in the Son of God. Paul tells us at Ephesians 2:1 that "God made you alive, though you were dead in your trespasses and sins...."

This provides us with an alternate understanding of what Daniel is referring to by being "asleep in the dust of the earth" and by "waking up," one that is consistent with the context of that prophecy. Instead of referring to a literal resurrection of the dead, it is a spiritual one as shown by these words of Paul to the Ephesians:

> Therefore, it is said: "Awake, O sleeper, and **arise from the dead**, and the Christ will shine upon you." (Ephesians 5:14)

But what about those of whom Daniel says will awaken "to reproach and to everlasting contempt"? These would likely be the religious leaders who opposed Jesus and his followers. They thought they were righteous men, but their status changed during the birth of Christianity. To this day, those men are held in contempt for their sin of killing the holy Son of God. The feeling of contempt we will have for such men will be everlasting, because we will be everlasting.

## Analysing Daniel 12:3

The next verse continues the thought expressed in verse 2 by referring to what the "awakened sleepers" will do.

---

12. John 5:28, 29

> And those having insight will shine as brightly as the expanse of heaven, and those bringing the many to righteousness like the stars, forever and ever. (Daniel 12:3)

Jesus brought light into the world and that light was not extinguished when he died but continued to shine forth through his disciples.

> ...by means of him was life, and the life was the light of men. And **the light is shining in the darkness**, but the darkness has not overpowered it. (John 1:4, 5)

> YOU **are the light of the world**. A city cannot be hid when situated upon a mountain. People light a lamp and set it, not under the measuring basket, but upon the lampstand, and it shines upon all those in the house. Likewise **let** YOUR **light shine before men**, that they may see YOUR fine works and give glory to YOUR Father who is in the heavens. (Matthew 5:14-16)

Jesus' righteous followers have preached the world over and have brought "many to righteousness." Like the stars in the heavens, they bring light into darkness, and since they will live eternally, that light will shine "forever and ever" as Daniel 12:3 says.

## Analysing Daniel 12:4

The Israelites of Daniel's day couldn't have foreseen how all the events described in chapter 11 regarding the Kings of the North and South would be fulfilled. The same can be said about what is being foretold in chapter 12. These words were sealed and were to remain secret for hundreds of years until *the time of the end of the Jewish nation.*

> As for you, Daniel, keep the words secret, and seal up the book until **the time of the end**. Many will rove about, and **the true knowledge will become abundant**. (Daniel 12:4)

While the words of Daniel's prophesy were known throughout the centuries leading up to Christ, the words were not secret but the meaning or application of them was. The prophecy's fulfillment was sealed, as it were, waiting for someone to reveal the meaning. When that time came, many would understand and would spread that knowledge widely. Who would these ones turn out to be?

From Daniel's day down to the moment Jesus was baptized by John, the Kingdom of God was a mystery, a divine (or sacred) secret. It took the arrival of the Son of God to reveal that secret and unravel that mystery. That sacred secret was the "true knowledge" of which Daniel spoke. The true knowledge is essentially the message of the good news.

Through Jesus and after him, the apostles, the true knowledge became abundant, and many evangelizers roved about the world shining like stars, illuminating the darkness in the minds of men and women.

Paul was one of those who made the "true knowledge abundant," that is, the good news would be preached far and wide.

> **In other generations this [secret] was not made known** to the sons of men as it has now been revealed to his holy apostles and prophets by spirit, namely, that people of the nations should be joint heirs and fellow members of the body and partakers with us of the promise in union with Christ Jesus through the good news. (Ephesians 3:5, 6)

> ...provided, of course, that you continue in the faith, established on the foundation and steadfast, not being shifted away from the hope of that good news that you heard and **that was preached in all creation under heaven**. Of this good news I, Paul, became a minister." (Colossians 1:23)

## Analysing Daniel 12:5-12

From this point forward, we get into the area of speculation. Being raised as one of Jehovah's Witnesses, I was indoctrinated with the idea that we had the answer to every Bible question. This Organizational hubris led to many silly, farfetched interpretations, several huge prophetic fiascos, and at times, great embarrassment. All of these are the inevitable outcome of eisegetical interpretation.

A sincere Bible student learns to differentiate between that which can be known for sure and that which can only be guessed at for the present. It was important for first-century Christians to accurately understand the fulfillment of Daniel's prophecy in chapter 12 since it applied to the destruction of their nation. While this prophecy doesn't apply to our day, there's still a lesson for us. As Paul says at Romans 15:4, "All the things that were written aforetime were written for our instruction."

Returning to our analysis of Daniel 12, let's focus on verse 7:

> Then I heard the man clothed in linen, who was up above the waters of the stream, as he raised his right hand and his left hand

to the heavens and swore by the One who is alive forever: "It will be for an **appointed time, appointed times, and half a time**. [3½ times] As soon as the **dashing to pieces of the power of the holy people** comes to an end, all these things will come to their finish. (Daniel 12:7)

Do the 3½ times of verse 7 apply to the 3½ year period between the first siege of Jerusalem in 66 C.E. by General Cestius Gallus and the final siege in 70 C.E. by General Titus? Quite possibly, but we can't say for sure.

As for the "dashing to pieces of the power of the holy people," Daniel recognized that the Israelites were called God's holy people.[13] Indeed, when Christ walked the earth, there had been no other people or nation which God called his own for the previous 1,500 years. The Israelites were truly "God's holy people." Yet, their power was clearly "dashed to pieces" when their city was razed to the ground in fulfillment of Jesus' words.[14]

We now come to a verse that demonstrates the absurd extremes to which JWs are pushed in the Governing Body's need to sustain an eisegetical interpretation.

And from the time that the constant feature has been removed and the **disgusting thing that causes desolation** has been put in place, there will be **1,290 days**. Happy is the one who keeps in expectation and who arrives at the **1,335 days!**" (Daniel 12:11, 12)

Exegetically, it is easy to see that "the disgusting thing that causes desolation" was very likely the Roman Army. That army of unclean gentiles put tar on the temple gate in order to burn it and enter Jerusalem through the temple grounds—the Jews most holy place.

This would allow us to apply the 1,290 days (about 3 ½ years) to the period between the first and second sieges. Did the 1,335 days count concurrently with the 1,290 days? Or did they only start to count once the 1,290 days had ended? If the latter, that would amount to a period of just over 7 years, which might apply to the final defeat of Jewish forces by Rome at the Jewish fortifications at Masada in 73 CE. Admittedly, all of this is just speculation. The point is that the fulfillment of this prophecy was intended for first-century Jews, not for twenty-first-century Gentiles! We are

---

13. Exodus 22:31; Deuteronomy 7:6
14. Matthew 24:2

about 2,000 years removed from those events and many details have been lost to the stream of time. While these events may appeal to academics, they don't affect us directly. We don't need to know exactly how they were fulfilled. It is enough that those going through the events of that time period understood their application.

## Analysing Daniel 12:13

The chapter concludes with the angel promising Daniel that he would rest (die) but receive his reward "at the end of the days." When would that be? We've already established through exegesis that Daniel 12 was fulfilled during the last days of the nation of Israel in the first century. Since Daniel wasn't resurrected during that time, the phrase "at the end of the days" must refer to a different time.

The publications of the Organization teach us that Daniel will come back as an imperfect sinful human in the "earthly resurrection of the righteous" *during* the thousand-year reign of Christ. That would mean that he would be resurrected *not* at the end of the days, but *after* the end of the days of human rule, and *before* the end of the Messianic rule when Jesus hands back all authority to Jehovah God.[15]

That doesn't quite fit, does it?

There is an explanation that does fit very nicely, one that allows us to have Daniel resurrected at the very end of the days when Jesus returns. We will get into that later in this book in the chapters discussing the hope of the Other Sheep.

## In Summary

It is hard to explain the feeling of relief one gets when finally freed of doctrinal preconceptions and the pressure to support the theology of JW.org. To be able to simply study the Bible and let the holy spirit lead you into all the truth, to just allow the Bible to speak for itself—well, it is a wondrous sensation. If you can attain it, you will fully understand the meaning of Jesus' words at John 8:31, 32 where he says, "if YOU remain in my word,

---

15. 1 Corinthians 15:24

YOU are really my disciples, and YOU will know the truth, and the truth will set YOU free."

When I studied the Bible as one of Jehovah's Witnesses, I was not remaining in the word of Jesus Christ. The word that guided me was not from Jesus, but from the men of the Governing Body. While many of their teachings are based on the Bible, others are not—as you'll see in the following chapter. Trying to reconcile those teachings of men with God's Word in the Bible often felt like I was forcing a round peg into a square hole. It was so liberating when I stopped doing that, when I finally learned to let the Bible speak for itself and let the holy spirit guide me, as it will guide you.

With exegesis, and guided by the holy spirit, you have the tools you will need to examine everything we discuss here to ensure you are learning the truth and will never again be misled by the contrivances and trickery of men.[16]

---

16. Ephesians 4:14

# 3

# Watch Tower's "Generation": A Bewildering Litany of Interpretations

---

*"Truly I say to you that this generation will by no means pass away until all these things happen." (Matthew 24:34)*

---

I don't think there's a single verse in the Bible that influenced my life course more than Matthew 24:34. Every major decision I made as one of Jehovah's Witnesses was strongly influenced by my belief in the Organization's interpretation of this verse.

Throughout my life during the last half of the twentieth century, Watch Tower publications have defined the "generation" Jesus refers to as representing people who were alive to see the events of 1914 and would still be alive to see the end at Armageddon.[1] With that understanding in mind, there was every reason to believe the prediction made by the Society concerning 1975. It seemed logical and consistent with our understanding of Matthew 24:34 to believe that the 6,000 years of man's existence was calculated

---

1.   w08 7/1 p. 13

to end in 1975, and would also coincide with the start of the millennial rule of God's Kingdom under Christ.[2]

Even after that year came and went, none of us true believers doubted that the end would come before the twentieth century ended. Obviously, we'd been wrong about 1975, but having accepted the logic behind the 1914 teaching, no other application of Matthew 24:34 seemed possible.[3]

Nevertheless, there is no arguing with hard reality, is there? Here we are in the third decade of the twenty-first century and still there's no end in sight. Yet little has changed in the Organization. The men of the Governing Body are still declaring that the end is *imminent.* How can they continue to sell the flock on that notion after so many false alarms?[4]

To understand what is really going on, we have to look at the history of this teaching within the context of JW theology and expectations. Are we dealing with a group of learned Bible scholars, or are these just ordinary men made wise by the leading of God's spirit, or...is something else at work here? Let's consider the evidence.

## I Ask New York Headquarters for Clarification

In "Appendix B: My Letter to Headquarters and Reply" on page 360, you will find scans of correspondence between myself—a young 25-year-old elder writing from Bogotá, Colombia—and the Service Desk at Brooklyn Headquarters. The study article in question was from the November 15, 1974 issue of *The Watchtower*[5] explaining Matthew 24:22 which reads:

> In fact, unless those days were cut short, no flesh would be saved; but **on account of the chosen ones those days will be cut short**. (Matthew 24:22)

---

2. The 6,000-years calculation was based on sequential generations listed in the Masoretic text which is the basis for the Hebrew Scriptures translation in the *New World Translation of the Holy Scriptures* published by the Watch Tower, Bible & Tract Society. There is evidence that the ages listed for these generations are not altogether reliable, since they vary from those recorded in the Septuagint.
3. w14 7/15 p. 30 par. 9
4. I am in no way saying that the end is far off. I believe what Jesus tells us, that it will come when we least expect it.
5. w74 11/15 p. 683, col. 2, par. 1

For ease of reading, I've reproduced the relevant text from my letter below:

> In the November 15, 1974 issue of "The Watchtower" on page 683, column 2, first paragraph, the statement is made that 'because Jehovah's "chosen ones" had fled the doomed city, He did not have to prolong the time of distress and could thereby spare some "flesh". Applying the rules of logic, if we put this in the conditional negative, we get: 'If Jehovah's "chosen ones" had not fled from the doomed city, He would have to have prolonged the time of distress and thereby some "flesh" would not have been saved.'
>
> I do not understand how the fleeing of Jehovah's chosen ones allowed for the days to be cut short—as if their remaining in Jerusalem would conversely require the lengthening of those days. Also, I do not understand why Jehovah would cut those days short on account of his chosen ones. They were far away in the mountains and would not be affected by those days whether they were short or long—leaving 97,000 alive or killing all the jews (sic) in the city. I would truly appreciate any help you can give me in clearing up these doubts.

At the time, I didn't understand that the Organization was bound by eisegetical thinking. (I never learned about eisegesis until I started studying the Bible on my own.) You see, back then, the official JW application of verse 22 was that the "flesh" that was saved referred not to the Christians escaping from the city in 66 CE, but to the approximately 97,000 Jews who survived the destruction of the city of Jerusalem in 70 CE and were subsequently taken into slavery in Rome. The writer of the article was compelled to bend the meaning of the Bible phrase "on account of the chosen ones" to fit that official interpretation. It would be over twenty years before they came up with a more reasonable understanding.[6]

The reply to my letter arrived two weeks later (See "Appendix B: My Letter to Headquarters and Reply" on page 360). Here are key excerpts from it with commentary:

> We have received your letter with regard to the application of Jesus' words at Matthew 24:21, 22.
>
> To a considerable extent **we have to be guided by the way things actually worked out**.

---

6. w96 8/15 pp. 17-18 pars. 9-14

What that last sentence means is that 'our interpretation is right, so we have to work everything else to fit it.' Continuing with their letter:

> When the tribulation on ancient Jerusalem began in 70 C.E., the Christian chosen ones were out of the city, so they were not in danger. When the tribulation began, it came swift and hard. It was not protracted over a very long period of time.

Here, the letter writer (all correspondence from the Service Desk is anonymous) is explaining how the days were cut short, but I had already got that information from the original *Watchtower* article. So, this was irrelevant to my question, which was essentially: "Why cut the days short on account of people who are not there to benefit?" He continues:

> You bring up a possible question for consideration: What would have happened if the Jewish Christians were not in the city, whether the tribulation would not have been cut short, so to speak. But that is contrary to how things actually worked out and it would seem to be pointless to consider hypothetical cases that are contrary to fact and thus are contrary to the prophecy, for what Jesus prophesied was in accord with what occurred.

The purpose of my "hypothetical" case was to demonstrate the flaw in the article's logic, but the writer is so sure that the interpretation is correct that he fails to see that flaw. I'm giving him the benefit of the doubt here because it is also possible that he did see the flaw in his reasoning, but that his hands were tied since he had to provide an answer that supported official doctrine.

Unfortunately, I was too young and inexperienced to recognize the evidence that was before me. Still, the effect of the next paragraph destroyed any illusion I might have had that the men in charge at Headquarters had some special insight into Scripture. What follows is, at least for me, an early indication of the Organization's penchant for playing with the meaning of words, twisting them to fit their official interpretation of Scripture. (We'll see this again in a moment when we examine their latest definition of "this generation.")

> Dealing with the fact of the matter, that the Jewish Christians were already out of the city, having fled when they saw the signal Jesus mentioned, the tribulation was not being cut short **for their sake**, as if they were going to benefit in some way because of its being cut short. Hence, its being cut short must have been **on account of the chosen ones**, on account of the fact that they

## 3. Watch Tower's "Generation"

were not there and would not be directly affected when Jehovah brought the destructive tribulation.

So, the days were not cut short **for their sake**, but they were cut short **on their account**? Those are synonymous phrases! We could just as easily say that "the days were not cut short on their account, but they were cut short for their sake," and still come away with the exact same nonsensical reasoning. That one piece of correspondence was the beginning of a growing awareness that those taking the lead didn't know what they were doing. How could I remain a Witness after that? Simple, I believed that such things were the result of human imperfection, of men running ahead with personal interpretations, but that in the end, Jehovah would put things right and would reveal the truth when it came time for us to know it.

I'll ignore the rest of that paragraph, since it deals with an antitypical interpretation which is not valid.[7] But I think the final paragraph of the reply letter deserves your attention:

> We join with you in looking forward to the outworking of matters, knowing that the understanding of Bible prophecy is always the best **after prophesied events have taken place**.

One would think that almost two thousand years would be long enough *after prophesied events have taken place* to arrive at a proper understanding, but apparently not.

Again, I should have realized then that something was very wrong, but I was only 25, and I hadn't been fed solid spiritual food up to that point in my life, so my perceptive powers were not yet "trained to distinguish both right and wrong."[8] With hindsight born of long years of experience, I can now see that what is important to the leadership of the Organization isn't truth, but the preservation of their authority which they always justify in the name of "unity." I believe that it's that very motivation—the need to hold on to their position of authority—that drove them to come up with a new interpretation of Matthew 24:34 concerning "this generation" in the twenty-first century after all the previous interpretations had been abandoned.

---

7. See "No More Antitypes!" on page 77.
8. Hebrews 5:14

### Jesus Provides His Disciples with a Guarantee

While sitting on the Mount of Olives, some of Jesus' disciples asked him for a sign that would alert them of his arrival as the King of Israel. They were influenced by the common Jewish belief that the Messiah would ascend to power and the nation of Israel would again dominate all the other kingdoms of the world.

Of course, the fact that they asked for a sign didn't mean they were going to get one. Anything we ask for will be given to us *as long as* it's in accord with Jehovah's will, as John explains:

> And this is the confidence that we have toward him, that no matter what we ask **according to his will**, he hears us. (1 John 5:14)

Was it God's will that they have a sign to calculate how close they were to the start of the Messianic Kingdom? No, it was not. Even Jesus admitted that not even he had any idea when the Kingdom would start. As part of his answer to them, he said:

> Keep on the watch, therefore, because **you do not know on what day your Lord is coming**. (Matthew 24:42)

> On this account, you too prove yourselves ready, because the Son of man is **coming at an hour that you do not think to be it**. (Matthew 24:44)

Do these two verses, delivered within the context of his answer to his disciples' question, leave us with any uncertainty about why we shouldn't be searching for signs? In fact, Jesus begins his response to their question with a very strong warning:

> **"Look out that nobody misleads you, for many will come on the basis of my name, saying, 'I am the Christ,' [Greek *cristos*, anointed one] and will mislead many.** You are going to hear of wars and reports of wars. See that you are not alarmed, for these things must take place, **but the end is not yet.** "For nation will rise against nation and kingdom against kingdom, and there will be food shortages and earthquakes in one place after another. **All these things are a beginning of pangs of distress**. (Matthew 24:4-8)[9]

---

9. The NWT inserts a paragraph break at verse 7 to promote the idea that "warring nations" refers to World War I in 1914, and not to the wars that occurred leading to the destruction of Jerusalem in 70 CE. But there were no paragraph breaks in the original manuscript, which is why most Bible versions, not burdened with promoting JW 1914 theology, do not add this break. (See biblehub.com for comparisons.)

## 3. Watch Tower's "Generation"

So, his first words to his disciples were that many would come on the basis of his name—claiming to be representatives of Jesus—and saying, "I am the anointed one." In other words, I am the one Jesus has anointed to lead his people. (Does that ring a bell?)

Jesus then says that when we experience catastrophic events like wars, famines, pandemics, and earthquakes, **we shouldn't accept them as signs** which these false anointed ones might use to mislead us.

*The Watchtower* disagrees with this conclusion. It claims that these verses constitute a *composite sign* for identifying Christ's presence. You may be struggling with this due to years of Watch Tower indoctrination.

One way to determine the true understanding of any prophetic interpretation is to see if everything fits with the actual events of history; or to borrow the phrase that Watch Tower Headquarters used in their 1974 correspondence with me: "To a considerable extent, we have to be guided by the way things actually worked out."[10]

### Applying "This Generation" to 1914

We might start by asking why it is that the Organization has always taught that there is a single generation of people who live from 1914 to Armageddon? To answer that, let's start by reading the relevant verses in Matthew:

> Likewise also YOU, when YOU **see all these things**, know that he is near at the doors. Truly I say to YOU that **this generation will by no means pass away until all these things occur.** Heaven and earth will pass away, but my words will by no means pass away. (Matthew 24:33-35)

The phrase, "all these things," occurs twice in those three verses. What are *all these things*?

If we were to examine Matthew chapters 23 and 24 exegetically, looking for the meaning of *all these things*, we would surely settle on verses using the same phrase. For example:

> Serpents, offspring of vipers, how are YOU to flee from the judgment of Gehenna? For this reason, here I am sending forth to YOU

---

10. "Appendix B: My Letter to Headquarters and Reply" on page 360

> prophets and wise men and public instructors. Some of them YOU will kill and impale, and some of them YOU will scourge in YOUR synagogues and persecute from city to city; that there may come upon YOU all the righteous blood spilled on earth, from the blood of righteous Abel to the blood of Zechariah son of Barachiah, whom YOU murdered between the sanctuary and the altar. Truly I say to YOU, **All these things** will come upon **this generation**. (Matthew 23:33-36)
>
> Departing now, Jesus was on his way from the temple, but his disciples approached to show him the buildings of the temple. In response he said to them: "Do YOU not behold **all these things**? Truly I say to YOU, By no means will a stone be left here upon a stone and not be thrown down." (Matthew 24:1, 2)
>
> For nation will rise against nation and kingdom against kingdom, and there will be food shortages and earthquakes in one place after another. **All these things** are a beginning of pangs of distress. (Matthew 24:7, 8)
>
> Likewise also YOU, when YOU **see all these things**, know that he is near at the doors. Truly I say to YOU that **this generation** will by no means pass away until **all these things** occur. (Matthew 24:33, 34)

A sound argument can be made that "all these things" refer to the things Jesus predicted which were not limited to wars, famines, etc., but also to the persecution that Jewish Christians were to suffer at the hands of opposers as well as the punishment of God upon the Jewish religious leaders and their nation by the destruction of the city with its temple.

For the Organization, *all these things* refer to wars, famines, pestilences and earthquakes, and exclude the other things Jesus refers to here. This myopic focus of the WT Society causes them to look to people who witnessed World War I, the 1918 Spanish Influenza pandemic, and the famines that resulted following the war—not to mention any earthquakes that might have happened around that time. They claimed that these people would not die off before all the other things Jesus spoke of had also occurred. The trouble is that **all** the other things Jesus spoke of include events that only occurred in the first century: the destruction of the city and temple.

This is where eisegesis again comes into play. What do the things that happened to Jerusalem from 66 to 70 CE have to do with our day? Nothing, unless we can accept the idea that the

Watch Tower Society has promoted since the time of Russell, which is that this prophecy has two fulfillments.

The Organization calls the first fulfillment, a minor fulfillment (the type) which deals with the destruction of Jerusalem. They call the second fulfillment, a major fulfillment (the antitype), which they apply to events of our day.

Are you still with me?

If so, then you can see how, throughout the twentieth century, they could use a generation to calculate how close they thought the end must be. According to the Bible, a normal lifespan is between 70 and 80 years:

> In themselves the days of our years are **seventy years**; And if because of special mightiness they are **eighty years**, Yet their insistence is on trouble and hurtful things; For it must quickly pass by, and away we fly. (Psalm 90:10)

If people old enough to witness World War I in 1914 were still going to be alive to see the end of the system of things, it was child's play for Watch Tower to work out how close Armageddon would have to be.

### Adjusting "This Generation"

When I graduated from high school in 1967, the belief was that those making up the generation of 1914 had to be old enough to understand the significance of the events of 1914. This reasoning continued to work even as late as 1985. For instance:

> Thus before the 1914 generation completely dies out, God's judgment must be executed. This generation still exists in goodly numbers. For example, in 1980 there were still 1,597,700 persons alive in the Federal Republic of Germany **who were born in 1900 or before**.[11]

However, just four years later, a subtle adjustment was made to buy more time. It was no longer necessary for members of *this generation* to have been old enough to bear witness to the events of 1914. Now, even babies born in that year would be considered part of *this generation*.

> For over **seven decades** now, the people of this 20th-century generation **living since 1914** have experienced the fulfillment of

---

11. w85 5/1 p. 4 "Is God Delaying His Judgment?"

events listed in Jesus' prophecy found in Matthew chapter 24. Therefore, this period of time is nearing its end, with the restoration of Paradise on earth close at hand.—Matthew 24:32-35; compare Psalm 90:10.[12]

Toward the end of the twentieth century, people were living longer because of advances in medicine. This allowed the Organization to look beyond the 80-year limit, so by the 1990s, Psalm 90:10 was dropped as hope rose that the original interpretation, that a single generation would live to see Armageddon, might still hold water.

> Today, a small percentage of mankind can still recall the dramatic events of 1914. Will that elderly generation pass away before God saves the earth from ruin? Not according to Bible prophecy. "When you see all these things," Jesus promised, "know that he is near at the doors. Truly I say to you that this generation will by no means pass away until all these things occur."—Matthew 24:33, 34.[13]

As the years continued with no end in sight, further *adjustments* had to be made. The generation was no longer anchored to the year 1914 but was cut loose to allow the Governing Body to salvage its key doctrine for instilling the flock with an artificial sense of urgency, as this 1994 *Watchtower* shows:

> Many now living were eyewitnesses to World War I when this modern fulfillment began. But **even if you were born after 1914**, you have witnessed Jesus' prophecy coming to pass.[14]

## Finally, the Governing Body Abandons the "Generation" Doctrine

Nevertheless, as time marched inexorably onward and there was no end, the Organization was forced to abandon its interpretation of Matthew 24:34 altogether. Did they admit they were wrong? Did they confess to misleading the flock with false hope based on a speculative interpretation? Was there any apology at all, some grand *mea culpa*?

---

12. w89 8/15 p. 14 par. 18
13. w92 5/1 p. 3 1914—The Year That Shocked the World
14. w94 4/15 p. 10 par. 11

## 3. Watch Tower's "Generation"

No! Instead, they fell back on a tactic they have used repeatedly to dodge the bullet of responsibility: They blamed someone else. The following comes from the June 1, 1997 issue of *The Watchtower* "Questions from Readers."

> So the recent information in The Watchtower about "this generation" did not change our understanding of what occurred in 1914. But it did give us a clearer grasp of Jesus' use of the term "generation," helping us to see that **his usage was no basis for calculating—counting from 1914—how close to the end we are**.[15]

A person reading this with no background in the history and doctrines of Jehovah's Witnesses would likely take the tone of this paragraph to be one of admonishment. That reader could not be blamed for assuming that the writer is correcting a faulty perception on the part of *Watchtower* **readers**, and perhaps mildly chastising them for getting carried away with unscriptural time calculations.

There is nothing in this *Watchtower* article to indicate that the publishers of the magazine are at fault for getting people's hopes up. Instead of following the example of Bible characters, like King David and the Apostle Paul, who candidly admitted their sins and repented, the Governing Body chose to whitewash an interpretation that had adversely altered the lives of millions, passively putting the blame on others. In the same article, they write:

> It must be acknowledged that we have not always taken Jesus' words in that sense. There is a tendency for **imperfect humans** to want to be specific about the date when the end will come. Recall that even the apostles sought more specifics, asking: **"Lord, are you restoring the kingdom to Israel at this time?"—Acts 1:6**.

With similar sincere intentions, **God's servants** in modern times have tried to derive from what Jesus said about "generation" some clear time element calculated from 1914. For instance, **one line of reasoning** has been that a generation can be 70 or 80 years, made up of people old enough to grasp the significance of the first world war and other developments; thus we can calculate more or less how near the end is.

However **well-meaning such thinking was, did it comply with the advice Jesus went on to give?** Jesus said: "Concerning that

---

15. w97 6/1 p. 28

day and hour nobody knows, neither the angels of the heavens nor the Son, but only the Father.... Keep on the watch, therefore, because you do not know on what day your Lord is coming."—Matthew 24:36-42.[16]

Let's analyse these three paragraphs carefully.

**"There is a tendency for imperfect humans..."** Whenever you question a Witness about failed predictions, they will respond with "Well, that was just because of human imperfection." In other words, "Let's not get excited. Everybody makes mistakes."

Quite right. Everybody makes mistakes. But how do you feel when someone makes a mistake that causes you pain and suffering, and yet refuses to take ownership of their mistake? How do you feel when that someone fails to acknowledge that the problem was their fault, and refuses to say, "I'm sorry!" How do you feel when you have been misguided—sometimes at great personal cost—and the person who misled you is unwilling to make amends?

In a situation like that, are you going to excuse them because, well, "nobody's perfect," or are you enabling people to carry on in conduct that is simply unacceptable, even sinful?

Continuing with our breakdown of the above three paragraphs, we have this: **"With similar sincere intentions, God's servants...have tried to derive...some clear time element calculated from 1914..."**

One of the problems I had with the leadership of the Organization even when I was a young man in the 1970s was their unwillingness to own up to their mistakes. At times, doctrinal changes were introduced using the passive verb tense. They would write, "it was thought," but rarely would you read, "we thought," unless that "we" could include all Jehovah's Witnesses, such as is the case with the change we are currently examining.

Who precisely are "God's servants" in the above disclaimer? The average Jehovah's Witness didn't try "to derive some clear time element calculated from 1914." Rank-and-file Jehovah's Witnesses believe what the publications tell them to believe. If they don't, they risk being disfellowshipped for causing "division"!

---

16. w97 6/1 p. 28 "Questions From Readers."

The evocative 1984 *Watchtower* cover (Figure 3) is an example of how Jehovah's Witnesses are conditioned to unquestioningly believe what they are taught.

Trying to soft-pedal what they had done by making it appear as equivalent to the question posed at Acts 1:6 ("Lord, are you restoring the kingdom to Israel at this time?") is further evidence that they were unwilling to own up to their incredible failure and the incumbent responsibility it entailed in disrupting the lives and hopes of millions of sincere Christians.

The apostles asked a simple question and got a clear answer. They didn't then go forth and for decades proclaim a false belief used to measure just how close the end was. They stuck to what Jesus said, which was that knowing the times and the seasons of God was *none of their business*.

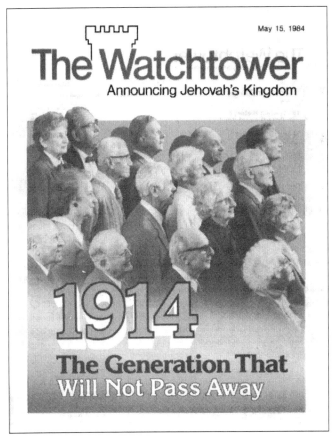

Figure 3. *The Watchtower*, May 15, 1984.

The "Question From Readers" in the June 1, 1997 *Watchtower* ends with a final admonition to *God's servants* that they should have heeded Jesus' warning that no one can know the day or the hour. This is particularly patronizing—and frankly, quite dishonest—given that just nine years earlier, they had counselled *God's servants* to do the very opposite—to ignore Jesus' words about knowing the time of the end. Notice what they said in this 1968 *Watchtower*:

> This is not the time to be **toying with the words of Jesus** that "concerning that day and hour nobody knows, neither the angels of the heavens nor the Son, but only the Father." (Matt. 24:36) To the contrary, it is a time when one should be keenly aware that the end of this system of things is rapidly coming to its violent end. Make no mistake, it is sufficient that the Father himself knows both the "day and hour"![17]

## The Governing Body Resurrects the Generation Doctrine

In spite of all the foregoing, I have to admit to feeling a sense of relief at reading the announcement in the 1997 *Watchtower* that we were no longer going to use *this generation* as a means to calculate how close the end was. At last, we could do away with false hope and the disillusionment that comes with it. Instead, we could concentrate on developing our Christian personalities. Whether Jesus returns in our lifetime, or whether we must die before we can meet him, either way, we have a finite amount of time in which to build a relationship with Jehovah God that results in everlasting life. I felt that was what we should have been concentrating on, not an artificial sense of urgency generated from an erroneous and wrong-headed interpretation.

The relief I then felt ended eleven years later with the publication of an article in *The Watchtower* issue of February 15, 2008[18] which introduced a change in the understanding of who comprised *this generation*. At the time, it seemed very strange to devote an entire study article to making a single, seemingly irrelevant point: That the generation of Matthew 24:34 was

---

17. w68 8/15 pp. 500-501
18. w08 2/15 "Christ's Presence—What Does It Mean to You?" page 21.

Figure 4. Its caption reads: "This generation will be no means pass away until all these things occur".

not comprised of all the people alive in 1914, but only of Jesus' anointed followers. Since his followers live, on average, the same length of time as everybody else, it seemed like the publishers were making a meaningless distinction and devoting an entire *Watchtower* study article to do it. How strange!

For that reason, I sensed there was something important going on that they weren't telling us about. For instance, I was troubled by this footnote from page 24:

> The time period during which "this generation" lives seems to correspond to the period covered by the first vision in the book of Revelation (Rev. 1:10-3:22) This feature of the Lord's day extends from 1914 until the last of **the faithful anointed ones dies** and is resurrected.—See *Revelation—Its Grand Climax At Hand! Page 24, paragraph 4.*

Jesus clearly says that "this generation would by no means pass away." Since all the anointed alive in 1914 had passed away in 2008, I couldn't see what the writer of the article was driving at. Adding to my consternation was the picture also from page 24, shown in Figure 4.

Were they trying to suggest that the anointed of 1914 had not passed away? Was there to be a redefinition of the term "passed away"? The answer lay hidden in the box on page 25 of the *Watchtower* article (See Figure 5) which reads:

### Can We Calculate the Length of "This Generation"?

The word "generation" usually refers to people of various ages whose lives overlap during a particular time period or event. For example, Exodus 1:6 tells us: "Eventually Joseph died, and also all his brothers and all that generation." Joseph and his brothers varied in age, but they shared a common experience during the same time period. Included in "that generation" were some of Joseph's brothers who were born before him. Some of these outlived Joseph. (Gen. 50:24) Others of "that generation," such as Benjamin, were born after Joseph was born and may have lived on after he died.

So when the term "generation" is used with reference to people living at a particular time, the exact length of that time cannot be stated except that it does have an end and would not be excessively long. Therefore, by using the term "this generation," as recorded at Matthew 24:34, Jesus did not give his disciples a formula to enable them to determine when "the last days" would end. Rather, Jesus went on to emphasize that they would not know "that day and hour." –2 Tim. 3:1; Matt. 24:36.

Reading this in hindsight reveals an enormous duplicity on the part of the Governing Body. For instance, it lays the foundation for what would come just two years later in 2010—the infamous "overlapping generation"—when it says "the word "generation" usually refers to people of various ages whose lives **overlap**..." It then says that "the term 'generation' is used with reference to people living at a particular time, the exact length of that time cannot be stated except that it does have an end and would not be excessively long."

This box lays the foundation for a premeditated, seven-year-long doctrinal rollout to resurrect the generation doctrine. Yet the box, in itself, seems innocuous, reassuring Jehovah's Witnesses that the Governing Body has no intention of doing that at all. It states: **"Jesus did not give his disciples a formula to enable them to determine when "the last days" would end."** This is not a lie, but it is misleading. It is true that Jesus *did not* give us a formula for calculating the length of the last days. But the Governing Body is about to, and they will inevitably claim it comes from Jesus!

We now move to phase two of the Governing Body's plan: In the April 15, 2010 issue of *The Watchtower*, Witnesses were presented with a new definition for the word "generation," one not found in

## 3. Watch Tower's "Generation"

### Can We Calculate the Length of "This Generation"?

The word "generation" usually refers to people of various ages whose lives overlap during a particular time period or event. For example, Exodus 1:6 tells us: "Eventually Joseph died, and also all his brothers and *all that generation.*" Joseph and his brothers varied in age, but they shared a common experience during the same time period. Included in *"that* generation" were some of Joseph's brothers who were born *before* him. Some of these outlived Joseph. (Gen. 50:24) Others of "that generation," such as Benjamin, were born after Joseph was born and may have lived on *after* he died.

So when the term "generation" is used with reference to people living at a particular time, the exact length of that time cannot be stated except that it does have an end and would not be excessively long. Therefore, by using the term "this generation," as recorded at Matthew 24:34, Jesus did not give his disciples a formula to enable them to determine when "the last days" would end. Rather, Jesus went on to emphasize that they would not know "that day and hour."—2 Tim. 3:1; Matt. 24:36.

Figure 5. Can We Calculate the Length of "This Generation"?

the Bible, nor in any dictionary nor secular work. Tying back to the 2008 article, we have this:

> Third, holy spirit is at work in bringing Bible truths to light. (Prov. 4:18) **This magazine has long been used by "the faithful and discreet slave" as the primary channel for dispensing increased light.** (Matt. 24:45) For example, consider our understanding of those who make up "this generation" mentioned by Jesus. (Read Matthew 24:32-34.) **To what generation did Jesus refer?** The article "Christ's Presence—What Does It Mean to You?" explained that Jesus was referring, not to the wicked, but to **his disciples, who were soon to be anointed** with holy spirit. Jesus' anointed followers, both in the first century and in our day, would be the ones who would not only see the sign but also discern its meaning—that Jesus "is near at the doors."
>
> What does this explanation mean to us? Although we cannot measure the exact length of "this generation," we do well to keep in mind several things about the word "generation": It usually refers to people of varying ages whose lives overlap during a particular time period; it is not excessively long; and it has an end. (Ex. 1:6) How, then, are we to understand Jesus' words about "this generation"? **He *evidently* meant that the lives of the anointed who were on hand when the sign began to become evident in 1914 would overlap with the lives of other anointed ones who would see the start of the great tribulation.** That generation had a beginning, and it surely will have an end. The fulfillment of the various features of the sign clearly indicates that **the tribulation must be near**. By maintaining your sense of urgency and keeping on the watch, you show that you are keeping up with

advancing light and following the leadings of holy spirit.—Mark 13:37.[19]

I remember how my heart sank as I read this. I couldn't excuse this as just the result of human imperfection. Here they were actually making stuff up, and stupid stuff at that. This was a fabrication, plain and simple. The reference to Exodus 1:6, first introduced in the box on page 25 of the 2008 article, does not support this new definition of a generation. Let's read the context:

> Now these are the names of Israel's sons **who came into Egypt with Jacob**, each man who came with his household: Reuben, Simeon, Levi, and Judah; Issachar, Zebulun, and Benjamin; Dan and Naphtali; Gad and Asher. And **all those who were born to Jacob were 70 people**, but Joseph was already in Egypt. **Joseph eventually died, and also all his brothers and all that generation**. (Exodus 1:1-6)

The Organization uses this verse in Exodus to support the idea of an overlapping generation, but the verse doesn't say that at all. That generation which came into Egypt numbered 70 people. What defined them as a generation? The fact that *they came into Egypt together*. They were the 70 people—the generation—that came into Egypt. They were of different ages—some were children, some were elderly—but the common element binding them into a single generation was the shared experience of *coming into Egypt together*. Any child born after they arrived in Egypt wouldn't be part of the generation, because that child was not part of the 70 that emigrated to Egypt. So even though there would be people born to them decades later whose lives would overlap to some degree with the 70, those would not be considered part of the generation because they didn't come into Egypt with Jacob.

I was in high school when President John F. Kennedy was assassinated. I remember the event clearly. It is etched in my brain. Millennials born long after that event would have no memory of it and would be laughed at were they to claim that they were part of the generation of President Kennedy. Yet, according to the Organization's definition, those Millennials are part of that generation because their lives overlap with mine. Ridiculous!

---

19.  w10 4/15 pp. 10-11 pars. 13-14 "Holy Spirit's Role in the Outworking of Jehovah's Purpose"

I was born after World War II, but my father and mother lived through it. My grandmother lived through World War I. I was 19 when she died. Does that mean that I'm part of the generation that fought in both world wars? Claiming that would make me a laughingstock. Yet, with all this simple logic at hand, the Governing Body expects Witnesses to abandon reason and just accept an outrageous teaching by taking a great leap of faith. Not faith in God, mind you, but faith in men.

Returning to the key scripture—indeed, the only scripture—that the Governing Body uses to support this teaching, what would correspond to the "entry into Egypt" in our day? Would it not be the single event of the war that began in 1914? Like the 70 that entered Egypt, the lives of those witnessing World War I would overlap, some being mere children at the time, while others were old and near death. Still, they were all part of a single generation. My grandmother was one of them, but while my life overlapped with hers by 19 years, I was not around for that single event that defined that generation. Both Exodus 1:6 and the JW doctrine of the start of the last days share one thing in common: They speak of a single point in time, an event that defines those living through it. Those coming after it cannot be considered as part of that generation.

It is also worth noting that in the 2010 article, the Governing Body, which now declares itself to be the Faithful and Discreet Slave, claims to be God's primary channel for dispensing increased light.

So, this new understanding is "light from Jehovah God." However, the previous understanding—also supposedly *light from Jehovah*—is dismissed as the result of the imperfection of God's servants.

Unfortunately for the Governing Body, quite a number of *God's servants* weren't buying into this new interpretation. It just didn't make sense to them, and many wondered what was behind it all.

Why would the Governing Body attempt to perpetrate such a ridiculous doctrinal teaching?

## Creating an Artificial Urgency

Since 1879, *The Watchtower* magazine[20] has been preaching the impending return of Jesus at Armageddon. The early Bible Students and the Jehovah's Witnesses that arose from the few groups that remained loyal to J. F. Rutherford in 1931 lived with the expectation that Jesus' coming was imminent. Over the decades, the various adjustments to the interpretation of the Matthew 24:34 *generation* fed that hope.

In 1997, the Organization abandoned the *generation* doctrine as a yardstick to measure the length of the Last Days. This had the effect of robbing the rank-and-file of the all-important sense of urgency that had been driving the Organization since Russell's day. If the Governing Body was going to maintain its control and position, they needed to restore that sense of urgency.

It now seems that a plan was hatched and rolled out slowly over a seven-year period. It began in 2008 by redefining the generation of Matthew 24:34. No longer was it made up of all the people alive in 1914 but instead referred only to anointed Christians living then. The next step, introduced two years later, allowed for another generation of anointed not alive in 1914 to become part of the 1914 generation: an *overlapping generation*. But that still didn't shorten the time period enough to engender the urgency needed to keep the flock in fear of missing out and dying at Armageddon, if they didn't remain faithful to the Organization. Something more was needed, and it came five years later in 2015.

## David Splane Shortens the Span of the Generation

There were still many "anointed" Jehovah's Witnesses alive in the 1980s who had witnessed the events of 1914. As I write this, there are about 20,000 Jehovah's Witnesses claiming to be of the anointed. Anyone born in the 1980s who is in this group would now be in their 40s. So, the *generation* could easily run for another 40 or 50 years. It's hard to feel anxious about Armageddon if it's still half a century away.

---

20. First published in July 1879 as *Zion's Watch Tower and Herald of Christ's Presence*.

Figure 6. David Splane with his "overlapping generation" chart.

Thus, step three of the plan was rolled out in the September 2015 video on JW Broadcasting[21] by Governing Body member, David Splane. He introduced a further "refinement" to the understanding of *this generation* that greatly shortened the time span and brought the end of this system of things forward to the imminent future. No longer was the overlap based on the lifespan of the anointed. Instead, it was based on the time of their anointing.

To illustrate this, Splane used the lifespan of Fred Franz, a former president of the Watch Tower Society. David explained that Fred Franz was anointed in 1913 and died in 1992. He then showed how someone born in 1990 would not be part of the 1914 generation even though his lifespan overlapped with that of Fred Franz. To be part of *this generation*, an individual would need to be *anointed with holy spirit* while Fred Franz was still alive. Since Witnesses believe that those rare individuals who receive the anointing of holy spirit are chosen by God from among long-time faithful servants, it follows that to have been anointed while Fred Franz was still alive, the person would have been born 40 or 50 years earlier. In other words, the anointed who make up the

---

21. https://www.jw.org/en/library/videos/#en/mediaitems/StudioMonthlyPrograms/pub-jwb_201509_1_VIDEO

second part of the overlapping generation are now in their 70s or older. Thus, the end must be "imminent."

Why did I find this latest refinement to be distressing? Simply put, because it proves there was premeditation to this whole doctrinal change. They knew where they were going with it back in 2008.

Let's assume the 2008 *refinement* limiting the makeup of *this generation* to only anointed Christians had never been published. Would that have made any difference to the understanding of the overlapping generation introduced in 2010? Obviously not. Whether we are speaking of anointed Christians only or everyone on earth, they could still have explained that the lives of people alive in 1914 would overlap with the lives of people still alive when Armageddon arrives. So why, in 2008, did they choose to limit the generation to only anointed Christians? A revelation from God? Does Jehovah engage in piecemeal prophetic revelation, adding a piece to the puzzle every few years? I see no evidence of that in Scripture, do you?

So here we have a new doctrine that took seven years to fully deploy! Why would the Governing Body do that? It obviously wasn't a revelation from God. What then?

The answer lies embedded in the warning that Jehovah gave to the Israelites as recorded in the book of Deuteronomy:

> If any prophet presumptuously speaks a word in my name that I did not command him to speak or speaks in the name of other gods, that prophet must die. [21] However, you may say in your heart: "How will we know that Jehovah has not spoken the word?" [22] When the prophet speaks in the name of Jehovah and the word is not fulfilled or does not come true, then Jehovah did not speak that word. **The prophet spoke it presumptuously. You should not fear him.** (Deuteronomy 18:20-22)

The goal of a false prophet is to instill fear in his listeners. If they are fearful, they will believe him; and if they believe him, he gains control over their hearts and minds. It is for that reason that Jehovah specifically tells us *not to fear the false prophet*!

With the 1997 abandonment of the original interpretation of *this generation*, the Governing Body lost a valuable tool for ensuring loyalty from the flock. Again, they needed to restore the sense of urgency that drove the average Witness to remain compliant. It is important for us to see the significance of the timing of these morsels of *new light*:

- 2008: *This generation* is limited to anointed Christians.
- 2010: *This generation* is made up of overlapping lifespans.
- 2015: *This generation* is made up of overlapping anointings.

## "There Is Something Rotten in Denmark"

If you are going to introduce truth, you simply speak it and those who love truth will eat it up. However, a fabrication, especially one as farfetched as the *overlapping generation*, needs to be introduced slowly and subtly. The seed planted in 2008 would not bear fruit for seven years until the final element in their doctrine was introduced, yet they must have known it would be needed right from the start. If this doctrine were firmly based in Scripture, they could have given it to us all at once, back in 2008. But it is not based in Scripture. So, they had to feed it to us piecemeal, getting us to buy into it slowly.

## What Really Is the Generation of Matthew 24:34?

It is only natural to wonder what Jesus was referring to when he said that "this generation will not pass away." The context of his words shows that he is giving his disciples the strongest of assurances that something was going to happen within a specific timeframe. He went so far as to say that "heaven and earth will pass away, but my words will by no means pass away" (vs. 35). You can't get a better guarantee than that. Yet, applying his words to 1914 as Witnesses continue to do has been a total fiasco. Obviously, there has to be another application, and indeed there is.

I plan to do an exegetical analysis of the whole of Matthew 24 in a forthcoming book. For now, why not exercise what you have learned of exegesis and put it to work for yourself? Start with chapter 23 of Matthew. Consider the cultural context. Consider the viewpoint of his disciples. How often did Jesus use the word "generation," and to whom was he referring in each instance? Is there any evidence that Matthew 24:34 was intended to have a minor and major fulfillment as Witnesses contend? Now there's a nice little research project for all of us to work at.

# 4

# Debunking the False Good News of 1914

> *"Then if anyone says to YOU, 'Look! Here is the Christ,' or, 'There!' do not believe it. For false Christs and false prophets will arise and will give great signs and wonders so as to mislead, if possible, even the chosen ones. Look! I have forewarned YOU. Therefore, if people say to YOU, 'Look! He is in the wilderness,' do not go out; 'Look! He is in the inner chambers,' do not believe it." (Matthew 24:23-26)*

As I stated in the previous chapter, I was very distressed by the realization that the men I had trusted to provide me with "food at the proper time"[1] were actually capable of knowingly fabricating a false teaching. However, since I now knew that at least one doctrinal interpretation was false—*the overlapping generation*—I decided to look deeper into the beliefs that had been the bedrock of my faith.

The first of these was the teaching that in October of 1914, Jesus Christ was installed in heaven as the Messianic King who sits on the throne of David. That invisible enthronement was supposed to be marked by events on earth that made up a visible sign.

An outsider benefitting from 21st century hindsight might think that I and my fellow Witnesses were incredibly naïve to believe such a teaching, but that judgment would be unfair given the facts of history. What I was taught and believed was that

---

1. Matthew 24:45

*The Watchtower*, since its initial publication in 1879, had been foretelling that momentous events would occur in 1914. To me, this fit perfectly with the time calculation derived from Daniel chapter 4 which we'll discuss shortly. Additionally, the outbreak of World War I, followed by famines and the pandemic of the Spanish Influenza, seemed to fulfill my JW understanding of the "beginning of pangs of distress" that Jesus spoke of, and which I thought comprised a *composite sign* of his invisible presence. In short, everything seemed to fit nicely.

## Explaining the Core 1914 Teaching

The teaching of a 1914 invisible presence is crucial to the theology of Jehovah's Witnesses because, without it, the Governing Body can't claim they have been divinely appointed to lead the Organization. To explain why this is the case, consider that Witnesses are taught that Jesus came to inspect his spiritual temple as the *messenger of the covenant* referred to at Malachi 3:1 shortly after 1914. According to official JW doctrine, this inspection took a few years to complete.[2] Then, by 1919, Jesus "had concluded" that all Christian denominations had failed to live up to his standard except for Jehovah's Witnesses.[3]

Prior to 2012, Witnesses were taught that a living remnant of the 144,000[4] anointed ones made up the faithful and discreet slave that Jesus refers to at Matthew 24:45-51. It was widely held, though never official, that members of this anointed remnant living in various parts of the world contributed *new light* on the doctrinal beliefs of the Organization. This turned out to be false. Changes only come from the leadership within headquarters.

Then came a radical change to the understanding that all anointed made up the faithful and discreet slave. In 2012, the Governing Body of Jehovah's Witnesses suddenly proclaimed

---

2. w16 November p. 30 par. 14
3. The name, "Jehovah's Witnesses," was coined by Rutherford in 1931. It should be noted that only about a quarter of the Bible Student groups associated with the Watchtower, Bible & Tract Society in 1919 remained to accept the 1931 name change. This can be seen by the decline in partakers between 1925 and 1928 from about 90,000 to under 18,000. (See jv chap. 22 p. 424 and *Jehovah's Witnesses in the Divine Purpose* pp. 313, 314).
4. Witnesses believe that Revelation 7:4 refers to a literal number.

itself to be the exclusive holder of the title Faithful and Discreet Slave.[1]

This doctrinal change—called *new light* in JW nomenclature—transformed the Governing Body into "Jehovah's sole channel of communication" with the flock. As such, they were now in charge of the Lord's *domestics*—the worldwide community of Jehovah's Witnesses—together with the financial assets of all Watch Tower corporations around the world.[2] Besides liquid assets, there are vast real estate holdings including tens of thousands of Kingdom Hall properties worth billions of dollars. In 2014, the ownership of all kingdom halls and assembly halls built and paid for by local congregations was seized by the Organization through an official decree of the Governing Body. This enabled them to direct that any Kingdom Hall could be sold without the approval of the local congregation and the funds sent in to headquarters.[3] Additionally, any excess funds held in the bank account of the local congregations were to be sent to headquarters. About the same time, the circuit overseers were given greater authority over the elders and could delete any they felt didn't meet organizational requirements. There were occasions when the local elders opposed the transfer of funds or the sale of a hall, but they were told they had to comply or face removal by the circuit overseer.

Given all the foregoing, it is almost impossible to overstate how vital the teaching of 1914 is to the faith of Jehovah's Witnesses. Without an invisible presence in 1914, there could be *no* appointment in 1919 from Jesus as the "messenger of the covenant" naming prominent men at Watch Tower headquarters as his faithful and discreet slave. Without that 1919 appointment, there would be *no* scriptural basis for the Governing Body to own billions of dollars worth of property, nor for them to exercise control over the lives of millions of adherents.

Yet, all of that is nothing when compared to the impact that the belief in a 1914 invisible presence of Christ has had on the life decisions of individual Jehovah's Witnesses. Millions of

---

1. A change in doctrine was released at the October 2012 Annual Meeting.
2. w13 7/15 p. 20 "Who Really Is the Faithful and Discreet Slave?"
3. See *Letter to Bodies of Elders*, March 29, 2014: "Re: Adjustment to financing Kingdom Hall and Assembly Hall construction worldwide."

congregation publishers—as members of the community are known—have staked their life course and salvation hope on the belief that the Last Days began in 1914 and would end before they died. Consequently, they saw themselves as surviving Armageddon to live forever in God's New World as subjects of the Messianic Kingdom.

Because they were taught to believe that the end was always just a few years away, some devoted men and women chose to remain celibate. Others married, but didn't have children, reasoning that it would be better to raise a family in the New World. Countless Jehovah's Witnesses, including myself, followed the counsel of the Governing Body to forsake higher education and to be content with a simple life. Many ended up working at menial jobs such as late-night janitors or window cleaners, so that they could "put the Kingdom first".[4]

The effect of this teaching can be demonstrated by the chart in Figure 7 that shows Jehovah's Witnesses at the very bottom of an income/education scale. Their low educational and economic status is not the result of outside cultural pressures, but due to coercion effected by the Governing Body through its publications and convention programs.

Of course, all these sacrifices would be justified if the good news that Witnesses preach were true. That good news includes the belief that the Last Days started in 1914 and would end within a single generation. However, over a century has passed since the supposed start of the Last Days with no end in sight. Are Jehovah's Witnesses wrong in focusing their attention on chronological calculations? Is the whole 1914 invisible presence of Christ just an elaborate hoax, or has the Watch Tower Society deciphered some divine mystery allowing JWs to see things others can't? The answer to those questions will only be found in the Bible.

While it may seem daunting to put such a fundamental doctrine under a scriptural microscope, if we love truth, we have nothing to fear, because Jesus assures us all that "the truth will set [us] free."[5]

---

4. Based on the Governing Body's interpretation of Matthew 6:33.
5. John 8:31, 32

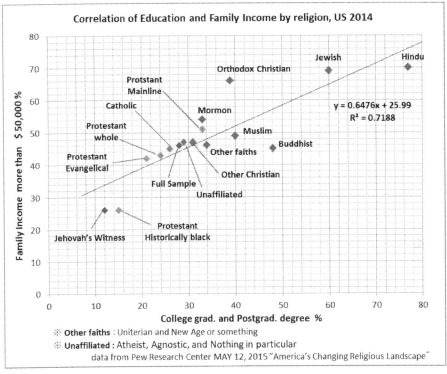

Figure 7. *Correlation of Education and Family Income by religion, US 2014.*

## The Origin of the 1914 Doctrine

It will surprise the average Jehovah's Witness to learn that the calculation that led to 1914 as a year of prophetic importance *predates* the birth of Charles Taze Russell in 1852. In the first half of the 19th century, an American Baptist preacher named William Miller concluded that a prophetic pattern with a secondary, modern-day application was to be found concealed within Daniel chapter 4 where the prophet interprets the Babylonian King's dream.[6] Miller was not the first to come up with this idea, but he refined it to the point of actually predicting the return of Christ Jesus. He thought the Lord would return in 1843. The dream which troubled King Nebuchadnezzar was of a great tree that was cut down and bound with iron and copper bands for a

---

6. https://en.wikipedia.org/wiki/William_Miller_(preacher)

period of seven times.[7] The dream, its interpretation by Daniel, and its eventual fulfillment are all described in that one chapter. There is no other reference to the dream anywhere else in Scripture. It is a single, self-contained prophetic interpretation with its accompanying fulfillment all wrapped up in a nice little package contained in the fourth chapter of the book of Daniel.

Nevertheless, Miller claimed there was indeed a secondary or antitypical fulfillment. Was he being guided to a deeper truth by the holy spirit? Jesus assures us that the holy spirit will guide us into all the truth.[8] On the other hand, the apostle Paul warns us that there is also an evil spirit that can mislead us.

> ...in which you at one time walked according to the system of things of this world, according to the ruler of the authority of the air, **the spirit that is now at work in the sons of disobedience**. (Ephesians 2:2)

That is why John instructs us:

> Beloved, **do not believe every spirit**, but test the spirits to see whether they are from God. For many false prophets have gone out into the world. (1 John 4:1 BSB)

One way to determine whether a prophet or teacher is being led by a foreign spirit or by God's spirit is to recognize that the holy spirit leads us to truth. It will not lead us to a belief that ends in failure, embarrassment, and disillusionment. We are assured of this by our Lord Jesus:

> Keep on asking, and it will be given you; keep on seeking, and you will find; keep on knocking, and it will be opened to you; for everyone asking receives, and everyone seeking finds, and to everyone knocking, it will be opened. Indeed, which one of you, if his son asks for bread, will hand him a stone? Or if he asks for a fish, he will not hand him a serpent, will he? Therefore, if you, although being wicked, know how to give good gifts to your children, **how much more so will your Father who is in the heavens give good things to those asking him!** (Matthew 7:7-11)

Miller was obviously not led by holy spirit, for his prediction failed and his followers left in disillusionment. Why didn't his prophetic interpretation die then and there? Evidently, the spirit

---

7. Daniel 4:13-17
8. John 16:13

# 4. Debunking the False Good News of 1914

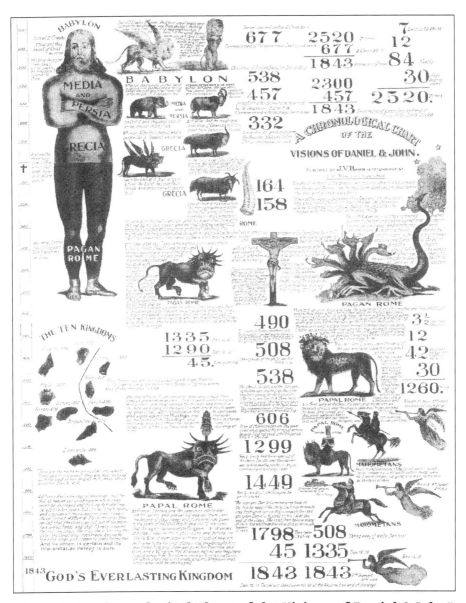

Figure 8. "A Chronological Chart of the Visions of Daniel & John" by William Miller.

that inspired it didn't want to let a good thing go. There was more work to be done, more people to mislead, as we shall now see.

The core elements of Miller's interpretation are still alive and well within the theology of Jehovah's Witnesses. The Governing Body continues to accept Miller's idea that the seven times mentioned in Daniel 4:16 correspond to seven prophetic years measuring 360 days each. That gives them a sum of 2,520 years. They also believe, as Miller did, that those years make up a time period called "the times of the Gentiles" or "the appointed times of the nations." They base this on what Jesus said in Luke when referring to the destruction of Jerusalem in the first century.

> And they will fall by the edge of the sword and be led captive into all the nations; and **Jerusalem will be trampled on by the nations until the appointed times of the nations are fulfilled.** (Luke 21:24)

They believe that the trampling will stop when Jesus returns. All that is missing is a starting point to run the calculation. Miller concluded that the gentile times or "appointed times of the nations" started when King Manasseh was captured by the Assyrians in 677 BCE. Counting from that year is what gave Miller his failed 1843 prediction.

Just how did Miller's prediction end up in the hands of Jehovah's Witnesses? For the answer, we turn to another Adventist[9] preacher, Nelson Barbour. Barbour believed Miller's antitypical application of Daniel chapter 4. He just needed a better starting year to run it.

Barbour used 606 BCE, the year he believed Israel was taken into exile by the king of Babylon. This led him to the year 1914,[10] a year he believed would mark the start of the great tribulation.[11]

---

9. Not to be confused with Seventh Day Adventist. Barbour was an adventist in the generic sense. He was affiliated with the Advent Christian Church which published the periodical *The World's Crisis and Second Advent Messenger*.
10. Barbour erroneously thought there was a year Zero, which is why he didn't use 607 BCE.
11. Most Christian denominations, JWs included, believe that the great tribulation referred to in Revelation 7:14 represents the final war of God with the nations. There is an alternate understanding worth considering under the subheading, "Is the Great Tribulation a Single Event?" on page 207.

## 4. Debunking the False Good News of 1914

Barbour believed that Christ's presence would precede the great tribulation by forty years; thus, his presence was to occur in 1874. When Christ didn't manifest himself in the heavens in 1874, Barbour could have simply admitted he'd made a mistake, but historically, false prophets find it almost impossible to admit when they're wrong, preferring to recraft their lies to hide their failures. So, Barbour redefined his prophecy by making Christ's presence an invisible one. An invisible presence in the year 1874.

Doesn't that just ring a bell?

This also allowed him to continue to support his prediction that 1914 would mark the start of the great tribulation.

In 1876, Barbour met Charles Taze Russell and shared this chronology with him. Russell was so convinced by it that he sold his share of his father's clothing store business and began his preaching and publishing campaign. Russell, and after him, J. F. Rutherford, continued to teach this Adventist doctrine, claiming that Christ's invisible presence occurred in 1874. It wasn't until 1934 that the Watch Tower Society changed its timing of Christ's alleged invisible presence moving it from 1874 to 1914.[12] It is noteworthy that the Organization continued to teach that 1914 was also the start of the great tribulation right up until 1969 when *new light* came out claiming that the great tribulation is still to come.[13]

### Questionable Implications

Notably, the publications of the Watchtower Bible & Tract Society have been less than forthright about all these changes. They continue teaching that Jehovah's Witnesses have *always understood* these prophetic events of Adventist origins as they do today. For example:

> Well, a monumental development was **the enthronement of Jesus in heaven, which marked the beginning of his presence** in Kingdom power. Bible prophecy shows that **this took place in 1914**. (Daniel 4:13-17) **Anticipation of this event** also caused some religious people in modern times to be filled with expectation. **Expectation was evident** also among the sincere Bible

---

12. Golden Age of March 14, 1934 "The Nobleman's Return"
13. w99 5/1 16

Students who began to publish this magazine **in 1879** as Zion's Watch Tower and Herald of Christ's Presence.[14]

Notice with each sentence that *The Watchtower* writer accurately conveys JW doctrine, but when read together, they lead the reader to believe the falsehood that *The Watchtower* always claimed 1914 as the start of Christ's presence, when in fact it taught that 1874 was the year and continued to do so for 20 more years after 1914.[15] Follow their logic: They write that 1914 was the start of Christ's presence, then they claim this was an event which religious people in modern times expected, and then they claim that Bible students were also in expectation in 1879, leading the reader to incorrectly assume they were in expectation of a 1914 presence, when in fact they were expecting Armageddon in 1914.

Anyone without prior knowledge who read this paragraph would naturally conclude that in 1879, the Bible Students believed Christ's presence began in 1914, but they didn't.

The writer depends on the ignorance of Watch Tower history on the part of his readers, correctly assuming they will infer the falsehood he wishes to perpetuate. This is one of the reasons why the Organization strongly discourages Witnesses from examining past publications, and why an edict went out years ago directing the elder bodies around the world to remove all publications prior to 1950 from Kingdom Hall libraries.

The fact that the article is so carefully worded in a way to avoid actually lying, while still giving a false impression, reveals that the writer knew exactly what he was doing.

However, it is not always possible for them to avoid actually lying, as this next quote demonstrates:

> Russell and his associates **quickly understood that Christ's presence would be invisible**. They disassociated themselves from other groups and, in 1879, began publishing spiritual food in *Zion's Watch Tower and Herald of Christ's Presence*. **From its first year of publication, this magazine pointed forward, by sound Scriptural reckoning, to the date 1914 as an epoch-making date in Bible chronology. So when Christ's invisible presence**

---

14. w99 8/15 p. 21 par. 10 "Jehovah Prepares the Way"
15. Golden Age of March 14, 1934 "The Nobleman's Return"

**began in 1914**, happy were these Christians to have been found watching!¹⁶

This is a very revealing quote because it starts off with a lie. In 1879, "Russell and his associates" did not quickly understand that Christ's presence in 1914 would be invisible. How could they when they already believed in an invisible presence starting in 1874, five years earlier? And what "sound scriptural reckoning" is the writer referring to that pointed forward to 1914, when Russell and associates had already used "sound scriptural reckoning" to settle on 1874 as the date of his presence? And why exactly were they "happy" to have been found watching, when they were not watching for a 1914 presence, but for a 1914 start to the great tribulation?

## What Is Revealed by the Dishonesty of the Watch Tower Society?

The fact that these publication references demonstrate a lack of candor and honesty regarding the true nature of historical Watch Tower Society teachings should not be brushed off as of little consequence. Their own words condemn them as hypocrites as this 1982 *Watchtower* article reveals:

> Something else that identifies the Bible as coming from God is the candor of its writers. Why? For one thing, it is contrary to fallen human nature to admit one's mistakes, especially in writing. In this, the Bible is distinguished from other ancient books. But, more than that, **the candor of its writers assures us of their overall honesty**. Reveal their weaknesses and then make false claims about other things, would they? **If they were going to falsify anything, would it not be unfavorable information about themselves?** So, then, the candor of the Bible writers adds weight to their claim that God guided them in what they wrote down.—2 Timothy 3:16.¹⁷

If you consider yourself to be a critical thinker, then you are obliged to ask why the Organization would mislead millions of Witnesses to believe that the early Bible Students foreknew 1914 would be the year of Christ's enthronement and the start of

---

16. w84 12/1 p. 14 par. 20 "Happy Are Those Found Watching!"
17. w82 12/15 p. 5-6

the Last Days, when in fact, they did not know that at all! What they "knew," based on Russell's published works, was that the Last Days began in 1799[18] and Jesus' presence began in 1874.[19] It would be three decades after 1914 when, in hindsight, Jehovah's Witnesses would finally be informed by their leadership that the Last Days and Christ's presence began in 1914.

If the "candor of [Bible] writers assures us of their overall honesty," then what does the lack of candor on the part of *Watchtower* writers assure us of?

## The 1914 Antitype: A Foundation Built on Sand

For the doctrine of 1914 to work, one has to accept the concept of an antitypical application. What does that mean? Let's start by understanding what an *antitype* is.

> **Antitype**, noun. A person or thing that is foreshadowed or represented by a type or symbol, esp. a character or event in the New Testament prefigured in the Old Testament, an opposite type.[20]

According to the Organization, the *type* in this case is Nebuchadnezzar's dream of the great tree recorded in Daniel chapter 4. Its primary (typical) fulfillment was the madness of the king that persisted for seven times, after which he regained his sanity and was restored to the throne. Often, the publications refer to a primary or typical fulfillment as a *minor fulfillment*.

The Governing Body doesn't accept that this is a stand-alone prophecy with a single fulfillment, even though there's nothing in the fourth chapter of Daniel's book to suggest any application beyond his day. Despite that lack of evidence, Witnesses are taught that there is indeed a secondary (antitypical) fulfillment—*a major fulfillment*—wherein the king of Babylon represents God's kingdom over Israel; his removal as king due to his madness typifies the removal of God's rulership over Israel, when the line of kings descending from King David was broken in 607 BCE;[21]

---

18. Russell believed a complex eschatology based on the 19th century Adventist movement that pointed to 1799 as the start of the last days – *Zion's Watch Tower* 1879 July 1, page 1.
19. jv chap. 5 p. 47 Proclaiming the Lord's Return
20. Dictionary.com
21. 607 BCE is a disputed date, but for purposes of discussion, we are tacitly accepting it here. It will be fully discussed in the next chapter.

## 4. Debunking the False Good News of 1914

and his return to sanity and reinstatement as King of Babylon corresponds to the 1914 presence of Jesus as the Messianic King. Finally, they believe that the precise timing of that invisible enthronement can be calculated by accepting that the seven literal times of Nebuchadnezzar's madness represent seven prophetic times that equate to 2,520 calendar years.[22]

It is worth repeating that the *entire premise* of the JW doctrine of a 1914 invisible presence of Christ *depends on the belief that there is an antitypical or secondary fulfillment to that prophecy*, even though there's nothing in the fourth chapter of Daniel to apply that prophecy antitypically.

Why is it so important to Jehovah's Witnesses that there be an *antitypical or secondary fulfillment* to Daniel chapter 4? It's important—in fact, vital—because the good news that Witnesses preach, and the authority over them that the Governing Body assumes, all rests on 1914 being the start of Christ's presence.

Given the importance of the 1914 doctrine and the fact that it depends on an antitypical application *not applied nor found* in Scripture, it is remarkable that the Governing Body should abandon antitypes as it did in 2014—an astonishing development that few seem to have noticed.

### No More Antitypes!

In a talk at the 2014 annual meeting delivered by Governing Body member David Splane, the audience was told of a new understanding regarding the use of antitypes:

> Who is to decide if a person or an event is a type, if the word of God doesn't say anything about it? Who is qualified to do that? Our answer? We can do no better than to quote our beloved brother Albert Schroeder who said, "We need to exercise great care when applying accounts in the Hebrew Scriptures as prophetic patterns or types **if these accounts are not applied in the Scriptures themselves**." Wasn't that a beautiful statement? We agree with it.
>
> In recent times, the trend in our publications has been to look for the practical application of events and not for types **where the**

---

22. w84 4/1 p. 6 "1914 a Marked Year—Why?"

**Scriptures themselves do not clearly identify them as such. We simply cannot go beyond what is written.**[23]

I'm sure you would agree that it's a very serious thing "to go beyond what is written" in God's word. Yet, by continuing to promote the antitypical application of Nebuchadnezzar's dream, that's precisely what the Governing Body is doing.

A careful reading of the fourth chapter of Daniel will reveal that no prophetic pattern nor antitypical fulfillment is, to use David Splane's own words, "applied in the Scriptures themselves." Any such application can be found only in the publications of the Watchtower, Bible & Tract Society. Thus—again using Splane's own words—to make such application is "to go beyond what is written."[24]

Based on their own *new light*, and for no other reason, the Governing Body should have renounced the entire 1914 doctrine in 2014. Why didn't they? Because doing so would have torn apart the very fabric of JW.org theology! Preserving their theology is evidently more important to them than upholding Bible truth and providing the flock with a theology that doesn't contradict itself.

As we've stated earlier in this chapter, they presume to have been authorized by Jesus in 1919 as his faithful and discreet slave and appointed over all his belongings. Therefore, to admit they were wrong about 1914 would take away any basis for that so-called 1919 appointment, stripping them of all the divine authority they claim to hold over the flock of God.

It follows that since the entire 1914 doctrine is based on an *antitypical or secondary fulfillment* of Daniel 4, they must find a basis in Scripture to support their application of it; otherwise, they would be, by their own admission, "going beyond what is written."

Let us examine how they attempt to do this, so we can determine whether their claim is valid, or is, in fact, just a desperate attempt to hold on to their power.

---

23. Transcribed from the 2:13:00 minute mark of the video on JW.org: https://www.jw.org/en/library/videos/#en/mediaitems/VODPgmEvtAnnMtg/pub-jwbam_201410_1_VIDEO
24. 1 Corinthians 4:6

## 4. Debunking the False Good News of 1914

### Scrounging Around for Proof

My earliest memories of the 1914 doctrine of the invisible presence of Christ go back to the book study arrangement when we were studying the book, *Babylon the Great Has Fallen! God's Kingdom Rules!* (1963).

I was just an adolescent but it seemed to me to be a well-researched book. I didn't yet possess the ability to see through the flaws in its reasoning—flaws that predate the book by years. Let me give you an example dating back to a 1952 *Watchtower* that tries to create an antitypical fulfillment out of Daniel chapter 4:

Figure 9. *Babylon the Great Has Fallen! God's Kingdom Rules!*

> **Clearly** this pictures the suspension of the office of righteous heavenly rulership through which God will exercise his sovereignty again over the earth. It would be kept in abeyance until He should come who would prove his right thereto. The dream shows that the Most High will give this kingdom right to the "lowest of mankind" or a son of man.—Dan. 4:17, Mo.[25]

Notice the blatant assertion that Daniel 4:17 "*clearly*...pictures the suspension of the office of righteous heavenly rulership through which God will exercise his sovereignty again over the earth." *Clearly* is one of those JW buzzwords we must be watchful for. Others are "evidently," "undoubtedly," and "doubtless." These are often used to introduce a piece of speculative interpretation as if it is a self-evident truth. What Daniel 4:17 actually says is:

> This is by **the decree of watchers** [angels], and the request is by the word of the holy ones, **so that people living** may know that the Most High is Ruler in the kingdom of mankind and that he gives it to whomever he wants, and he sets up over it even the lowliest of men. (Daniel 4:17)

What we can see here is that there were angels assigned to watch over Israel, and they were calling on God to do something

---

25. w52 5/1 p. 270 par. 16 "Determining the Year by Fact and Bible"

about the arrogance of the King who was bragging and exalting himself due to his conquest of Jehovah's people. The King, and by extension, the Babylonian people ("people living") had to be taught a lesson. There is nothing here linking this prophetic dream to the establishment of the Messianic Kingdom. The Organization is trying to make bricks without straw.

Daniel 4:17 concludes by saying that Jehovah can set up anyone he wishes as king, even the lowliest of men. The Hebrew word rendered "men" in Daniel 4:17 is *enash* which according to *Strong's Concordance* means simply "man, mankind." It doesn't mean "a son of man" as the *Watchtower* quote implies—an obvious reference to Jesus Christ. This is a blatant, unscriptural attempt to create a link where none exists between Nebuchadnezzar's restoration to the throne and the enthronement of Jesus—a link that is needed to establish their prophetic antitype.

This is completely inconsistent with the content of Daniel chapter 4. How can they claim, as they do in the above Watchtower quote, that Daniel 4:17 "clearly...pictures the *suspension of the office of righteous heavenly rulership*," when Daniel chapter 4 states that his rulership *has never ceased and cannot ever be suspended*? It states this not once, not twice, but three times.

First, Daniel tells the King:

> ...seven times will pass over you, until **you know** that the Most High is Ruler in the kingdom of mankind and that he grants it to whomever he wants. (Daniel 4:25)

Then a voice from heaven tells the king:

> ...seven times will pass over you, until **you know** that the Most High is Ruler in the kingdom of mankind and that he grants it to whomever he wants. (Daniel 4:32)

Then finally the King himself is inspired to proclaim to his people:

> At the end of that time I, Nebuchadnezzar, looked up to the heavens, and my understanding returned to me; and I praised the Most High, and to the One living forever I gave praise and glory, because **his rulership is an everlasting rulership** and **his kingdom is for generation after generation**. All the inhabitants of the earth are regarded as nothing, and he does according to his own will among the army of the heavens and the inhabitants of the earth.
>
> Now I, Nebuchadnezzar, am praising and exalting and glorifying the King of the heavens, because all his works are truth and

his ways are just, and because **he is able to humiliate those who are walking in pride.** (Daniel 4:34, 35, 37)

What Daniel 4:17 is referring to by the statement, "he sets up over it even the lowliest of men," is Nebuchadnezzar himself. Here was the most powerful man in the ancient world, who suddenly became a crazy wild man, eating grass like an animal. Why didn't anyone steal his throne from him during the seven times of his divinely inflicted madness? They didn't because God wouldn't allow it. There were caretakers on the throne, but it was held for him because that was the will of God. Jehovah had a point to make, and he made it so strongly that the king's declaration praising the "Most High" was sent out to the farthest outpost of the Babylonian empire. The King was moved to do this so that all would know that Jehovah's "rulership is an *everlasting rulership* and his kingdom is for *generation after generation.*"[26]

The publications might try to get around this by claiming that it's not God's universal rulership that was suspended for 2,520 years, but only his kingship over Israel. But how can that be considering the words "his kingdom is for *generation after generation*"? Whose generations are being referred to here? This is an obvious reference to God's rulership over Israel, generations of people.

In light of those powerful words, it's quite remarkable and more than a little presumptuous—even blasphemous—to suggest that God lost his kingdom and rulership for 2,520 years before reclaiming it invisibly in 1914 by enthroning Christ Jesus in that year.

## Jesus' Words Prove a 1914 Presence Can't Be True

When I first started to look into the 1914 teaching, I began to discuss it with a friend, a fellow JW elder, who believed the doctrine was wrong. So, I took the opposite position trying to prove its validity.

He began our discussion by asking me to explain how the 1914 teaching could be true in light of what is recorded at Acts 1:6, 7?

> So when they had assembled, they asked him: "Lord, are you restoring the kingdom to Israel at this time?" He said to them: "It

---

26. Daniel 4:34-37

**does not belong to you to know the times or seasons** that the Father has placed in his own jurisdiction." (Acts 1:6, 7)

If Jesus' handpicked apostles couldn't know the *times and seasons* concerning Jesus' enthronement, how could Jehovah's Witnesses know that to the point of predicting the year and month: October 1914?

The official position of the Watch Tower Society is that Jesus restored the spiritual kingdom of Israel when he sat on the Davidic throne in heaven in 1914. The *Insight on the Scriptures* explains this:

> In a similar prophecy, the references to David as being the king of this cleansed people and their "one shepherd" and "chieftain to time indefinite" clearly point to a greater fulfillment on the **nation of spiritual Israel**, the Christian congregation, under the anointed **Heir to David's throne**, Christ Jesus.[27]

So, the presence of Christ and his being placed on the throne of David to rule over spiritual Israel are all one and the same according to the Organization.[28] The disciples also thought that way initially. Jesus' apostles didn't yet have the holy spirit to lead them into a proper understanding of what it would mean for Christ to restore the kingdom of Israel. They likely shared the common belief among Jews of that time that when Messiah came, he'd restore the nation to its former status by taking his place on the throne of King David and making the gentile nations subservient to Israel.

What the disciples would eventually realize was that the Kingdom under Christ was much more than they imagined. Jesus would indeed sit on the throne of David in a spiritual sense, and spiritual Israel—the Christian Congregation—would replace the literal nation of Israel, and the whole of humanity would

---

27. it-1 p. 634
28. In ancient times, the time or era that marked "the presence" of a ruler was different from time of his enthronement. Emperor Hadrian was already on the throne when he visited Corinth. Yet, coins were minted in Corinth marking the date of his visit as "the presence of the Emperor" because when he was *physically* present, things changed and laws were enacted. So, by the same logic, Jesus could be enthroned as King upon his return to heaven following his resurrection, but his *presence* on earth would be later; in fact, it is still in our future.

## 4. Debunking the False Good News of 1914

be blessed as a result.[29] However, the "when" of all that was the mystery.

As Acts 1:6 indicates, when Jesus was about to ascend to heaven, his disciples thought he was going to restore the earthly kingdom of Israel to what they thought was its rightful place. He told them in no uncertain terms that the "when" or fulfillment of the restoration prophecy was the sole domain of his Father.

Can you see the problem that Acts 1:7 creates for the Watch Tower doctrine of a 1914 kingly presence of Christ? Though Jesus told his disciples that they couldn't know the *times or seasons* pertaining to his presence, Jehovah's Witnesses are taught that they can know it. They have a nifty formula for calculating the specific *times or seasons* pertaining to the presence of Christ. This formula, they believe, has been encoded into a prophecy of Daniel, meaning it had been around for over six centuries before ever the disciples asked their question.

Why wouldn't Jesus just tell them to look at Daniel's prophecy to get the answer to their question? It would have been child's play for them to consult the temple records and run the calculation that would tell them the year and even the month of his return to sit on the Davidic throne.[30]

Why would Jesus intentionally hide that truth from his chosen apostles? Indeed, wouldn't telling them it didn't "belong to them to know" such things amount to a lie, given that the formula was already in their possession, clearly spelled out in the book of Daniel? Jesus even mentions Daniel in Matthew 24:15 in the context of the Last Days prophecy, telling his disciples to read his prophecy and use discernment. So, if they weren't allowed to understand the *times and seasons* pertaining to his return to rule over the Kingdom of Israel—Spiritual Israel, as it turns out—how come Jehovah's Witnesses are not also denied that knowledge? How could men like Baptist preacher, William Miller, Adventist Pastor, Nelson Barbour, and C. T. Russell have been given knowledge that the inspired Bible writers were denied?

---

29. Genesis 18:18; Galatians 3:29
30. it-1 pp. 132-133; w14 7/15 p. 30 par. 9.

## Failed Attempts to Explain Away Acts 1:7

Obviously, the Organization can't deny that the first-century Christians were prohibited from knowing the *times and seasons* of the Lord's presence because that is clearly stated in Scripture. On the other hand, the Governing Body claims to know those *times and seasons* down to the month: October 1914. What justification can they provide to explain away that contradiction?

They attempt to do so by misapplying yet another Bible verse from the book of Daniel:

> As for you, Daniel, keep the words secret, and seal up the book until **the time of the end**. Many will rove about, and **the true knowledge will become abundant**. (Daniel 12:4)

The Governing Body has claimed that "the time of the end" referred to here applies to our day.[31] This has allowed them to say that the knowledge that was hidden from Jesus' handpicked apostles was revealed to C. T. Russell and his associates.[32]

There is a problem with this line of reasoning. When Jesus revealed truth to his apostles, they never got it wrong. There was no such thing as *new light* in the first century. Yet, to date, all the men connected to the 1914 doctrine, from Miller, through Barbour, on to Russell, Rutherford, Nathan Knorr, Fred Franz, and ending with the current Governing Body, have issued revision after revision to their doctrinal interpretations.

Is Jesus not capable of communicating the *true knowledge* accurately and abundantly all at one time? Jesus isn't some bumbling communicator incapable of getting it right the first time, is he?

As shown in chapter 2 of this book, the entirety of Daniel chapter 12 was fulfilled in the first century. The *time of the end* mentioned at Daniel 12:4 refers to the end of the Jewish system of things, not to our modern day.[33] So the premise for the Organization's workaround of Acts 1:7 is invalid. It wasn't meant to apply to the 19th and 20th centuries, but only to the first century.

---

31. w09 8/15 p. 14 par. 12; w01 7/1 p. 9 par. 9
32. This has now changed. In the September 2022 Watchtower, the Organization has revised its application of the timing of Daniel 12, moving it forward to Armageddon and into the New World.
33. See "Analysing Daniel 12:1" on page 32.

## 4. Debunking the False Good News of 1914

Of course, there is an even greater problem which Jehovah's Witnesses face when they claim they knew in advance when Christ would return: It flies in the face of Jesus' clear statement that nobody could know it, including himself:

> Concerning that day and hour **nobody knows, neither the angels of the heavens nor the Son**, but only the Father. (Matthew 24:36)

### The Governing Body Undermines Its Own Teaching!

However, we can put all the foregoing reasoning aside. We don't need it to prove the Governing Body is wrong in claiming that the *special knowledge* of Daniel 12:4 applies only to Jehovah's Witnesses. In a truly hapless move, they have done that job for us.

At the 2021 annual meeting of the Watch Tower Bible & Tract Society, Governing Body member Geoffrey Jackson undertook to explain some *new light* to his audience.[34]

> All of this also helps us to understand an amazing prophecy in the book of Daniel. Let's turn there. It's Daniel 12, verses one through three. There it says, "**During that time**, Michael, [who is Jesus Christ] will stand up **[that is at Armageddon]**, the great prince who is standing [since 1914] in behalf of your people. And there will occur a time of distress [that is the great tribulation] such as has not occurred since there came to be a nation until that time. And during that time your people will escape, everyone who is found written down in the book [and this refers to the great crowd]."[35] (Jackson's comments in square brackets.)

So, verses 1 thru 3 of Daniel 12 are now being applied not to Russell's day, nor to our day, but to Armageddon and into the New World!? Jackson then goes on to explain verse 2 which reads: "And there will be many of those asleep in the ground of dust who will wake up, these to indefinitely lasting life and those to reproaches [and] to indefinitely lasting abhorrence." Geoffrey then explains:

> So, looking at Daniel chapter 12 and verse two, it seems appropriate too, that we **adjust our understanding** of this verse. Notice

---

34. For a full analysis, see beroeans.net/2022/02/14/gj_1914/. Also, see w22 09 p. 21 pars. 4-20
35. Ibid

> there, it speaks about **people waking up in the form of a resurrection**, and **this occurs** after what's mentioned in verse one, **after the great crowd survives the great tribulation**. So, this obviously is talking about **a literal resurrection** of the righteous and unrighteous.[36]

The resurrection that Jackson refers to is the JW teaching that both righteous and unrighteous humans will be resurrected on earth during the thousand-year reign of Christ. He then moves on to explain Daniel 12:3.

> Now, let's finally read verse three: "And those having insight will shine as brightly as the expanse of heaven, and those bringing the many to righteousness like the stars, forever and ever." **This is speaking about the massive education work that will be done in the New World.** The glorified anointed ones will shine brightly as they worked closely with Jesus to direct the education work that will bring the many to righteousness.[37]

Geoffrey has taken a prophecy that they used to apply to the Last Days—even prior to the Last Days to include the time of Russell—and reapplied the whole thing to a future fulfillment after Armageddon! Can you see how that undermines their 1914 doctrine?

Again, for the Organization to have predicted 1914 years in advance, as they claim they did, they would have needed some exemption from the injunction of Acts 1:7 prohibiting the disciples from knowing "the times and seasons that the Father has put in his own jurisdiction." Remember, they had specifically asked Jesus when he would restore the Kingdom of Israel—a clear reference to his kingly presence that Witnesses claim occurred in 1914. The Governing Body claimed that Daniel 12:4 granted them that exemption. They claimed that in the Last Days, "many will rove about, and the [true] knowledge will become abundant," meaning that the knowledge hidden from the 12 apostles was revealed to Jehovah's modern servants through the publications of the Watch Tower Society.

But Daniel 12:4 starts out by saying, "and as for you, O Daniel, make secret the words and seal up the book, until the time of [the] end." Now, according to Geoffrey's *new light*, the time of the

---

36. Ibid
37. Ibid

end is Armageddon and Daniel 12:1-3 all apply from Armageddon on into the New World, and no longer to the Last Days.

Once again, the Governing Body has knocked the legs out from under its own core doctrine of a 1914 invisible presence of Christ.

First, they tell us that they will no longer use antitypes unless explicitly applied in the Scriptures themselves. Since there is no explicit antitypical application of Nebuchadnezzar's dream, that kills their so-called secondary fulfillment.

Second, they claim that Daniel 12 applies from Armageddon onward, and that the true knowledge becoming abundant would fit with the global education work in the New World which they believe Witnesses will engage in.

(There is no support in scripture for their speculation that Witnesses will be engaged in a *global education work*. They are making stuff up to tickle the ears of their flock. Paul foretold this at 2 Timothy 4:3, 4 which reads: "For there will be a period of time when they will not put up with the healthful teaching, but, in accord with their own desires, they will accumulate teachers for themselves to have their ears tickled; and they will turn their ears away from the truth, whereas they will be turned aside to false stories.")

Since they now apply Daniel 12 to the future, there is no basis for them to claim that the injunction found at Acts 1:7 isn't still in force. We can say with confidence that "it does not belong to [Jehovah's Witnesses] to know the times or seasons that the Father has placed in his own jurisdiction."

Finally, there is a certain irony in connecting "**times** and seasons" of Acts 1:7 with the "seven **times**" of Daniel 4:16. Jehovah established the start and duration of the seven *times* that applied to Nebuchadnezzar but doesn't tell us when they started nor how long they lasted. Then Jesus, also referring to *times* tells us that knowledge of them belongs to Jehovah, not to us. So why do we presume to steal what belongs to God?

The publications of the Watch Tower Society often point to Proverbs 4:18 to justify what they call doctrinal refinements and adjustments, or *new light* from God. It reads: "But the path of the righteous ones is like the bright light that is getting lighter and lighter until the day is firmly established." However, this theological bumbling around is more in keeping with the next verse:

> But the way of the wicked is like total darkness. They have no idea what they are stumbling over. (Proverbs 4:19 NLT)

## A Brief Word About *New Light*

Whenever the men of the Governing Body change their interpretation of a doctrine, they claim it as *new light* revealed to them by Jehovah God. Notably, though, anyone who disagrees with the current understanding [*present truth*] of the Organization on any point of Scripture will be accused of independent thinking and even of apostasy. However, when the Organization releases an *adjustment* to a previous truth, calling it *new light*, it becomes apostasy to stick to the old doctrine. Essentially, if you want to be one of Jehovah's Witnesses, you have to believe what you're told to believe. You may be surprised to learn that the founder of the Watch Tower Society, Charles Taze Russell, condemned the very concept of *new light*. He wrote the following in 1881:

> If we were following a man undoubtedly it would be different with us; undoubtedly one human idea would contradict another and that which was light one or two or six years ago would be regarded as darkness now: But with God there is no variableness, neither shadow of turning, and so it is with truth; any knowledge or light coming from God must be like its author. **A new view of truth never can contradict a former truth. "New light" never extinguishes older "light," but adds to it.** If you were lighting up a building containing seven gas jets you would not extinguish one every time you lighted another, but would add one light to another and they would be in harmony and thus give increase of light: So is it with the light of truth; **the true increase is by adding to, not by substituting one for another.**[38]

Russell makes perfect sense, doesn't he?

Of course, Jehovah God never lies.[39] He may not reveal all the truth at one time, but anything he does reveal is truth. So, any *new light* would simply add to the truth he's already revealed. *New light* would never replace old light, it would simply add to it, wouldn't it? If the Governing Body is truly acting as God's channel, and Jehovah God is truly speaking to His flock through them, then anything they say would have to be truth, right?

If any so-called *new light* were to end up replacing a previous understanding, rendering the old understanding false, that

---

38. *Zion's Watchtower*, February 1881, p. 3, par. 3
39. Titus 1:2

## 4. Debunking the False Good News of 1914

would mean that the old understanding didn't come from the God who cannot lie. Of course, there is a god who can lie.[40]

Now, you or I may teach something only to find out later that we made a mistake and spoke in error. But I don't present myself as God's channel of communication. Do you? But the Governing Body does! And if you disagree with them, they'll have the local elders accuse you of apostasy and kill you socially by forcing all your family and friends to shun you and treat you as dead.

Let's be clear on this. If any man or woman presumes to tell others that they are God's appointed channel, then they take upon themselves the role of a prophet. You don't have to foretell the future to be a prophet. The word in Greek is *prophétēs* and refers to "an interpreter...of the divine will"[41] and is used about someone who "declares the mind (message) of God, which sometimes predicts the future (foretelling) – and more commonly, *speaks forth* His message for a particular situation."[42]

You can't say you aren't inspired, as the Governing Body alleges for itself, and still claim to be God's channel of communication.[43] If you aren't inspired, then you're not God's channel. However, if you're speaking as and claiming to be God's channel, then you *are*, by definition, inspired. What the Governing Body wants is to have its cake and eat it too.

If the Governing Body truly wants to be called the channel of God for communicating to his flock on earth today, then their *new light* had better be new revelations from God that enhance the current light, and not replace it. If it is replaced, then the old light wasn't from God after all. It was the utterance of a false prophet. If old teachings are replaced, then how can we have confidence that the new teachings aren't just more falsehood? If someone lies once, if someone deceives you once, if someone misleads you once, why would you think they couldn't do it again? Why would you think they *wouldn't* do it again?

---

40. 2 Corinthians 4:3, 4
41. *Strong's Concordance* #4396
42. *HELPS Word-studies* #4396
43. w12 9/15 p. 26 par. 13

## The Governing Body Attempts to Justify Its 1914 Interpretation

For the sake of argument and for those who are still not convinced, let's overlook all the foregoing. Let's assume that maybe, *just maybe*, there is a secondary fulfillment possible in the seven times of Nebuchadnezzar's madness. The Organization certainly wants us to believe that is the case, and the reasons they give are listed below taken from *Insight on the Scriptures*:[44]

1) The time element is everywhere in the book of Daniel.
2) The book repeatedly points toward the establishment of the Kingdom.
3) It is distinctive in its references to the time of the end.

All three of these points are correct but the flaw in their reasoning is their premise. They assume Daniel is referring to the last days of our current system of things when in fact he is pointing repeatedly to the last days of the Jewish nation in 70 CE.

Let's consider the abundant evidence for that as we look at the various prophecies of Daniel. We'll see that the *Insight* book is correct in saying that "the time element is everywhere in the book of Daniel," but it's always pointing to the last days of the nation of Israel in the first century. Consider:

**When** Jesus speaks of the end of the nation of Israel, he tells his listeners to use discernment and turn to the book of Daniel.

> Therefore, when you catch sight of **the disgusting thing** that causes desolation, as spoken about by **Daniel the prophet**, standing in a holy place (let the reader use discernment) (Matthew 24:15)

That disgusting thing was the Roman Army that brought the nation of Israel to its end. That was a first-century fulfillment.

**When** Peter speaks to the crowd at Pentecost, he references Joel's words to tell the crowd of Jews in Jerusalem that the nation had entered its *last days*, he clearly isn't referring to the 20th and 21st centuries.

> On the contrary, this is what was said through the prophet Joel, "'**And in the last days**," God says, "I shall pour out some of my spirit upon every sort of flesh, and YOUR sons and YOUR daughters

---

44. it-1 p. 133 "Related to 'appointed times of the nations'"

will prophesy and YOUR young men will see visions and YOUR old men will dream dreams; and even upon my men slaves and upon my women slaves I will pour out some of my spirit in those days, and they will prophesy. And I will give portents in heaven above and signs on earth below, blood and fire and smoke mist; the sun will be turned into darkness and the moon into blood before the great and illustrious day of Jehovah arrives. (Acts 2:16-20)

All of these things occurred to the nation of Israel. We have proof of that from the Bible record and from secular history. There were Christian prophets foretelling the future. There were young Christian men seeing visions and old Christian men dreaming prophetic dreams. The words about "portents in heaven" involving the sun, moon and stars are Hebraic poetic imagery that was used to foretell doom and gloom upon Babylon and Egypt.[45]

**When** the King of Babylon had a dream of a great statue, Daniel reveals the interpretation and the *time element*.[46] Did it apply to our day? No. Observe: The statue is made of gold (Babylon), silver (Medo-Persia), copper (Greece) and iron (Rome).

Daniel says that:

> **In the days of those kings** the God of heaven will set up a kingdom that will never be destroyed. And this kingdom will not be passed on to any other people. It will crush and put an end to all these kingdoms, and it alone will stand forever. (Daniel 2:44 NWT 2013)

Since Rome, not Britain nor the United States, is the last king depicted in that vision, the *Kingdom must have been set up* while Rome was still a world power and the other three (Babylon, Medo-Persia, and Greece) were still around. Did that happen? It did, as revealed by these four scriptures:

> ...nor will people say, 'See here!' or, 'There!' For look! the **Kingdom of God is in your midst.** (Luke 17:21)

> He rescued us from the authority of the darkness and **transferred us [present tense] into the kingdom of his beloved Son**... (Colossians 1:13)

---

45. Isaiah 13:1, 9, 10; Ezekiel 32:1-8
46. Daniel 2:28-45

> But he, being full of holy spirit, gazed into heaven and caught sight of God's glory and of **Jesus standing at God's right hand**... (Acts 7:55)

> Jehovah declared to my Lord: "**Sit at my right hand** Until I place your enemies as a stool for your feet." Jehovah will extend the scepter of your power out of Zion, saying: "Go subduing in the midst of your enemies." (Psalm 110:1, 2)

When Daniel reveals the prophecy of the 70 weeks,[47] the time element is also abundant, but notice that God provides the reader with a clear time span: 70 weeks. We all know what a week is and how many days it contains. Jehovah also provides an event to mark the start of the countdown: The command to rebuild Jerusalem. And finally, we are told what to expect when the 70 weeks are up: The arrival of Messiah.

If the seven times of Nebuchadnezzar were also a means to calculate the enthronement of Messiah, specifically his invisible presence as king, then wouldn't Jehovah have followed the pattern of the 70-weeks prophecy? We'd have no doubt about how to measure the length of seven times. We'd also have a clear indication of the event that would mark the start of the countdown, and finally Jehovah would have told us what to expect when the seven times were completed. We have none of that in Daniel chapter 4. In fact, the starting time of the seven times turned out to be a complete surprise because the madness of the king came upon him without warning.

As for what "a time" represents, the word in Hebrew, *iddan*, simply means time and its precise meaning is unclear. The seven times could easily be seven seasons, not seven years. The Organization claims "a time" represents 360 days by using Revelation 12:6, 14. They refer to it as a *prophetic year*, a term *not* found anywhere in Scripture. But there's nothing in Scripture linking Daniel 4:16 with Revelation 12:6, 14. The two passages were written 700 years apart in distinct languages.[48] It's pure speculation to link them up and assume that the seven times of Nebuchadnezzar's madness measures 2,520 days. And even if they did, there is still nothing supporting the idea that we can

---

47. Daniel 9:24-27
48. Revelation was written in Greek, while parts of Daniel were in Hebrew and other parts in Aramaic.

## 4. Debunking the False Good News of 1914

Figure 10. A lynchpin.

now apply the so-called "day for a year" rule to run a secondary calculation to arrive at the presence of Christ.

The assumptions are starting to pile up and we haven't even begun to scratch the surface of the problems facing us if we're to accept the interpretations of Miller, Barbour, Russell, Rutherford, and Fred Franz about 1914 being the year marking the invisible presence of Christ.

## Pulling the 1914 Doctrinal Lynchpin

A lynchpin is a pin or rod made of wood or metal which is used to hold a wheel on an axle. Take out the lynchpin, and the wheel falls off, rendering the entire vehicle useless.

The lynchpin of the 1914 doctrine is the event marking the start year. Obviously, if the Organization can't fix on something to mark the start of the 2,520-year span, they won't have a way of arriving at an end year, such as 1914.

If there were to be some indication of a starting point for the seven times of the king's madness, we would expect to find it within the prophecy of Daniel chapter 4. However, there is nothing there. The king was boasting about his achievements when suddenly, and without warning, he was struck with a madness that lasted for seven times.[49]

Since what Witnesses call the minor fulfillment had no prophesied event to mark the start of the King's madness, there is no type. Therefore, there can be no antitype—nothing in the chapter even hints at anything constituting an event to mark the start of the 2,520 years. So now we are expected to break with the principle of a typical/antitypical relationship. We have no *type* in Daniel 4 marking the starting point, so how can there be an *antitype* making the start of our 2,520-year countdown?

Does the Governing Body give us this antitype? Actually, no, they don't. William Miller does. (Remember him?) Miller[50] chose Luke 21:24 for this, and the Governing Body continues to support the conclusion of this Baptist Preacher down to this day:

> And they will fall by the edge of the sword and be led captive into all the nations; and **Jerusalem will be trampled on by the nations until the appointed times of the nations are fulfilled**. (Luke 21:24)

Here is the application of that verse according to *Insight on the Scriptures*.[51]

> **The 'trampling' on that kingdom of the dynasty of Davidic rulers** did not begin with the Roman devastation of the city of Jerusalem in 70 C.E. It **began** centuries earlier with the Babylonian overthrow of that dynasty **in 607 B.C.E.** when Nebuchadnezzar destroyed Jerusalem and took captive the dethroned king Zedekiah and the land was left desolate.

Notice they're making a bald assertion by claiming that *the 'trampling' on that kingdom of the dynasty of Davidic rulers began in 607 BCE*. Where is the scriptural support for this? There is none!

This is an example of a logical fallacy known as an *appeal to authority*. The Organization expects its readers to accept this interpretation simply because they say so. Not good enough! We want

---

49. Daniel 4:28-33
50. https://en.wikipedia.org/wiki/William_Miller_(preacher)
51. it-1 p. 133 "Appointed Times of the Nations"

to know where in the Bible it says that the "appointed times of the nations" began when the Babylonians destroyed Jerusalem.

The reason the publications never provide that little piece of proof is that Luke 21:24 contains the *only* mention of the "appointed times of the nations" or the "gentile times" in the entire Bible! The phrase appears nowhere else. How odd that a prophecy in Daniel that *hinges* on this phrase would make no mention of it.

Rather than follow the misguided path of eisegesis and try to impose our own theology on a Bible verse, let's use exegesis and have the Bible speak for itself? What does the context of Luke 21:24 tell us?

The phrase in question in Greek is καιροὶ ἐθνῶν ("times of Gentiles"). For an Israelite of that era, the world was divided into two factions: Jews and Gentiles. In the case of Luke 21:24, the Gentiles in question were specifically the Roman legions that destroyed the city of Jerusalem.

Now let's look at the context of Jesus' words.

> Furthermore, when YOU see **Jerusalem** surrounded by encamped armies, then know that the desolating of her has drawn near. Then let those in **Judea** begin fleeing to the mountains, and let those in the midst of **her** withdraw, and let those in the **country places** not enter into her; because these are days for meting out justice, that all the things written may be fulfilled. Woe to the pregnant women and the ones suckling a baby in those days! For there will be great necessity upon **the land** and wrath on **this people**; and they will fall by the edge of the sword and be led captive into all the nations; and **Jerusalem** will be trampled on by the nations, until the appointed times of the nations are fulfilled. (Luke 21:20-24)

In Luke 21:20, Jesus says that *Jerusalem* will be surrounded by encamped armies. In the next verse, he tells those in *Judea—the province where Jerusalem* was located—to flee to the mountains. In verse 23, he speaks about great distress on the land, meaning *Judea with Jerusalem* as its capital. He speaks about wrath against "this people" meaning the Israelites living in *Judea and Jerusalem*. Then he speaks of them falling by the sword and being led captive into all the nations (vs. 24).

Would anyone reading this suddenly jump to the conclusion that Jesus is speaking metaphorically? That he is not referring to the literal city of Jerusalem, the literal province of Judea, the literal land of Israel, and the literal inhabitants of the city?

If you were to read this account *without* the bias of needing to find support for a 1914 start year, would you assume, in the midst of all this literality, that Jesus suddenly turns to metaphor in verse 24? That he isn't talking about the literal city, but of the everlasting kingdom of God?

Our Lord is not one given to sloppy speech. If Jesus, speaking here under inspiration and foretelling events of which he alone knew, wanted to give us the crucial start year for another prophecy, then why not use the correct verb tense? Why mislead us by using the future tense? He speaks of events that have not yet happened when he says, "and Jerusalem *will be* trampled on by the nations..." If the trampling in question had been ongoing for over 600 years—as the Governing Body contends—the accurate and truthful expression would have been, "and Jerusalem *will continue to be* trampled on by the nations." This would indicate a past event that continues to the present and on into the future. But Jesus didn't say that!

To "trample" means "to crush something under foot." If you razed a city to the ground, as the Romans did with Jerusalem in 70 CE, leaving no "stone upon a stone" in fulfillment of Jesus' words at Matthew 24;2, you definitely would have engaged in a *trampling*.

Since the Jews that survived the destruction were led into all the nations, and since the gentile nation of Rome was used to trample the city, and since Jesus is referring to the literal city and region throughout, we are left to conclude that the trampling began in 70 CE and ended when the city had been completely flattened. There is absolutely no scriptural reason to go beyond what is written here.[52] What the Organization does in this instance is a textbook case of *eisegesis*—of imposing their preconceived ideas onto a verse of Scripture.

Removing Luke 21:24 from their equation is devastating to the 1914 teaching. With nothing to mark the start, there can be no calculation and therefore no end year. The lynchpin has been pulled. The wheel falls off. The 1914 vehicle can't go anywhere.

---

52. 1 Corinthians 4:6

# The JW 1914 Doctrine Is a House of Cards

Building a house of cards requires a steady hand and a light touch, but some pretty complex structures can be achieved if you have the skill and dedication to persist at the task. Yet, no matter how impressive the result may appear, all it takes to bring the whole thing crashing down is the removal of a single card.

The doctrine of the 1914 invisible presence of Jesus Christ is such a house of cards, and the cards making up its precarious structure are all doctrinal assumptions! Let's now consider each and every one of these assumptions, bearing in mind that even if only one proves false, the entire doctrinal structure will collapse.

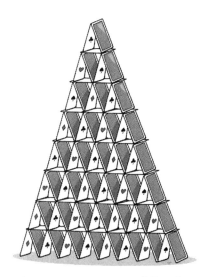

**Figure 11. House of Cards.**

## Assumption 1: Christ's Presence Will Be Invisible

There is nothing in Scripture to suggest that Christ's presence will be invisible. In fact, Jesus warns against it quite specifically:

> Look! I have forewarned you. Therefore, if people say to you, '**Look! He is in the wilderness,**' [far away in heaven] do not go out; '**Look! He is in the inner rooms,**' [hidden from sight] do not believe it. For just as the lightning comes out of the east and shines over to the west, so the **presence of the Son of man** will be. (Matthew 24:25-27)

The publications teach Jehovah's Witnesses that Jesus' presence is hidden from the rest of the world and revealed only to them. He is hidden in *the inner rooms* of heaven. He is far off from view *in the wilderness*. But that contradicts the metaphor Jesus gives us of lightning flashing across the sky. Even if your eyes are shut, you can still know that a lightning bolt has flashed across the sky, so bright is the light produced. You don't need special knowledge to see lightning and recognize it for what it is, nor do you need someone else to tell you that lightning has flashed. You witness it for yourself.

By comparing his presence to lightning, Jesus tells us that it will be visible to everybody, and that he will come suddenly and without warning.

Revelation 1:7 uses similar imagery when it refers to the visible evidence that Christ has returned as King:

> Look! He is coming with the clouds, and **every eye will see him**, and those who pierced him; and **all the tribes of the earth will beat themselves in grief** because of him. (Revelation 1:7)

The Organization says that Jesus came invisibly in 1914, but the Bible tells us that when he comes, "every eye will see him" and "all the tribes of the earth will beat themselves in grief." How does the Watch Tower Society get around this glaring contradiction between what they teach and what the Bible clearly states? Observe: They attempt to do so by making a scripturally unfounded, categorical assertion. For example, take this so-called proof from *Insight on the Scriptures*:

> **In past cases** clouds represented invisible presence; but observers could "see" the meaning with their mental "eyes." In this case the physical occurrences that are visible would cause the one looking to "see" or realize that Christ is invisibly present.—See also Mt 24; Mr 13; Re 14:14.[53]

Did you notice that no references to these "past cases" are given? It would be ridiculous to believe that the tribes of the earth will "beat themselves in grief" when Jesus returns if he is hidden from sight inside a cloud. If they can't see him, why would they be beating themselves in grief? However, according to the *Insight* book, that is how Jesus arrived in 1914: In the clouds, invisibly. If that is the case, then Revelation 1:7 was fulfilled in October 1914. So, where is the news footage of people from all the tribes and nations beating themselves in grief?

### Assumption 2: Daniel 12:4 Negates Acts 1:7

We've already discussed this in detail, but I've included it here to be thorough. We have to assume that Daniel 12:4 applies to the 19th century granting the early Bible Students knowledge that was denied the apostles of Christ. If it doesn't apply to Russell and associates, then they couldn't have known about the *times*

---

53. it-1 p. 484 "Cloud"

*and seasons* that Jehovah has put within his own jurisdiction. What is now laughable is that accepting this assumption would make a Jehovah's Witness guilty of apostasy because he would be rejecting the *new light* that Geoffrey Jackson released at the 2021 annual meeting which placed the fulfillment of Daniel 12:4 in the New World and no longer in the time of Russell![54]

## Assumption 3: Daniel 4 Has a Secondary Fulfillment

Neither Daniel nor any other Bible writer even hints at the possibility that Nebuchadnezzar's dream has some secondary or antitypical fulfillment. At Matthew 24:15, Jesus refers to Daniel chapters 9 and 12 when he speaks about the destruction of Jerusalem, but he makes no application of the events detailed in Daniel chapter 4. As we've already seen, this also violates the Organization's own policy of not applying an antitypical or secondary fulfillment to a Bible account unless the Scriptures specifically do so.[55]

## Assumption 4: God's Kingdom Has Been Trampled

*The Watchtower* states:

> So, in harmony with this, Jesus' words at Luke 21:24 referred to the treading or trampling down of the typical kingdom of God."[56]

But, the context of Luke 21:20-24 is *very clearly* referring to the literal city, not the whole of God's Kingdom throughout history. By 70 CE, the nation of Israel already had been rejected by God. It no longer represented God's Kingdom. Jesus said at Matthew 21:43, "this is why I say to you, **the Kingdom of God will be taken from you** and be given to a nation producing its fruits."

Daniel's prophecy of the 70 weeks foretold that the covenant would end just after the Messiah had died, and that the result would be the trampling (desolation) of the city of Jerusalem.[57] So how can the Jerusalem of 70 CE continue to represent God's

---

54. See "The Governing Body Undermines Its Own Teaching!" on page 85.
55. See the 2:13:00 minute mark of the video: https://www.jw.org/en/library/videos/#en/mediaitems/VODPgmEvtAnnMtg/pub-jwbam_201410_1_VIDEO
56. w83 1/1 p. 10 par. 1
57. Daniel 9:24-27

Kingdom since that status was taken from the Jewish nation and given to the Christian Congregation?

The covenant with the Jews ended in 36 CE when Peter baptized the first Gentiles—Cornelius and his family.[58] From that point onward, the nation of Israel with Jerusalem as its capital and the temple as the place where God resided ceased to represent the Kingdom of God. Now Christians, as God's children, were in God's Kingdom under the Jerusalem above, and they constituted his temple where his spirit resides.[59] Each of those elements from the Jewish system is represented now within the Christian congregation.

## Assumption 5: The Trampling Began with The Babylonian Exile

*The Watchtower* of 1985 claims:

> From that time onward [607], the Gentile trampling upon what represented God's Kingdom began, and the Gentile Times really started.[60]

Under the heading, "Pulling the 1914 Doctrinal Lynchpin," we saw that Jesus was speaking about the literal city of Jerusalem and not figuratively about God's Kingdom. Additionally, his words were all expressed in the future tense, so he couldn't have been looking to an event 600 years in his past. At Luke 21:24, he foretold that "Jerusalem **will be** trampled on by the nations," not that it was already being trampled on. Without any other reference in Scripture to a trampling of Jerusalem, reassigning the fulfillment of Jesus' words to an event that occurred six centuries before his day is the work of desperate human speculation.

## Assumption 6: The Exile Occurred in 607 BCE

All the archeological and astronomical evidence points to 587 BCE for the time of the Jewish exile to Babylon. Historians and archeologists have no reason to fudge this date. They're not conspiring to foul the theology of Jehovah's Witnesses, nor confound the fulfillment of Bible prophecy. In fact, as Carl Olof Jonsson

---

58. Daniel 9:27a; Acts 10
59. Colossians 1:13; 1 Corinthians 3:16
60. w85 2/1 p. 11 par. 12

shows in his excellent book, *The Gentile Times Reconsidered*, all the prophecies involving the 70 years of servitude to Babylon still work even with a 587 BCE date for the full exile of Israel.[61]

One might ask, "Then why don't they use 587 BCE as a start year for the 2,520-year calculation which would give the year for Christ's invisible presence as 1934?"

The problem is that nothing happened in that year that could be made to seem significant scripturally. On the other hand, 1914 is just too good a year to pass up. It marked the start of World War I, and on the heels of that war, the world suffered through a pandemic called the Spanish influenza. Also, there were many war-related famines. These historical events dovetail too nicely with the incorrect interpretation of Jesus' words in Matthew 24:6, 7 (where he talks about wars, famines, and pestilences) to be left unexploited by an organization with a millennialist agenda.

Then why doesn't the Governing Body just keep 607 BCE, which they now say is the year that Jerusalem was destroyed, but re-apply it as the date that Babylon first conquered Jerusalem and took the youth and intelligentsia of the nation into exile, including Daniel and his three famous companions?

The problem with that interpretation is that there was still a king in the line of David on the throne. Nebuchadnezzar installed Zedekiah as a puppet-king over Judah. The Society's interpretation of the "trampling of Jerusalem" requires that *no king of the royal line of David* be sitting on the throne of Israel, even a vassal-king like Zedekiah.

So, to support 1914, we have to assume that the overwhelming historical and archeological evidence is all wrong.

### Assumption 7: The Trampling Ends in 1914

The publications teach that the "trampling of Jerusalem" ended in 1914, because that was the year when "the appointed times of the nations" mentioned at Luke 21:24 were fulfilled:

> The Kingdom, for which his disciples were taught to pray to God in the Lord's Prayer, was established in the heavens, **now that the Gentile Times, "the appointed times of the nations,"**

---

61. *The Gentile Times Reconsidered*, Fourth Edition, p. 191 (Available on Amazon)

for trampling upon God's Kingdom by his Messiah (Christ) **had ended**.[62]

What twentieth century historical evidence is there to support this? The way that the nations govern the earth hasn't changed since 1914. There is nothing to suggest their "times" have ended.

When Jesus is installed as King, he waits for God to subdue his enemies. Psalm 110:1 says, "The utterance of Jehovah to my Lord is: 'Sit at my right hand until I place your enemies as a stool for your feet.'"

Given the state of the world since 1914, there is no reasonable basis to claim that the Lord's enemies have now been placed as a footstool for his feet. Jesus is the King, but the time for him to assert kingly power—which is what would happen at his presence—is still in our future. There is absolutely no empirical evidence that this happened in 1914.

## Assumption 8: God's Kingdom Can Be Trampled

The assumption that God's Kingdom can be trampled upon in any sense is ludicrous, but this is what the Watch Tower Society requires its followers to believe. The 1983 *Watchtower* claims:

> Then **the trampling down of the Kingdom of Jehovah God** as once represented by the kingdom of Israel in Jerusalem in the royal line of King David ended.[63]

According to this, even after God's Kingdom was no longer represented by the Kingdom of Israel in Jerusalem, the nations continued to trample on it for over 1,800 years. We must bear in mind that the word "trample" means to "crush under foot". Witnesses are saying that since the time of Christ, the nations of the world have had their foot on the back of the neck of God's Messianic Kingdom. How is such a thing even possible and where is the scriptural and historical evidence showing that this has been taking place for the past two and a half millennia? What nonsense!

According to Witness theology, the first king to trample on the Kingdom of God was Nebuchadnezzar. Yet he himself had this to say:

---

62. w83 5/15 p. 25 par. 12
63. w83 5/15 p. 21 par. 1

> I am pleased to declare the signs and wonders that the Most High God has performed toward me. How great are his signs, and how mighty his wonders! **His kingdom is an everlasting kingdom, and his rulership is for generation after generation.** (Daniel 4:2, 3)

That hardly sounds like he was trampling upon God's Kingdom. Instead, Nebuchadnezzar was made to recognize that God's kingdom is everlasting and that there is no break in its rule, continuing from generation to generation. This is all unabashed speculation utterly lacking in any scriptural foundation.

## Assumption 9: Satan Was Cast Down in 1914

Imagine if nothing significant had happened in 1914? Baptist preacher William Miller predicted Jesus would come back in 1843, then again in 1844, but when nothing of importance happened in those years, his followers became disillusioned and left him.[64]

It would be hard to build enduring faith in a pivotal doctrine if all you had was a mathematical calculation that led to an uneventful year. However, something big did happen in 1914: World War I. Still, it would add great credibility to the interpretation if some Bible prophecy could be tied to the war so that there would be a reason to explain why it happened. The Organization found just such an event in Revelation:

> **Woe for the earth** and for the sea, because the Devil has come down to you, **having great anger**, knowing that he has a short period of time. (Revelation 12:12)

What was their interpretation of this verse? The April 1, 1990 *Watchtower* reads:

> **Why did World War I break out in 1914?** And why has our century seen worse wars than any other in history? Because the first act of the heavenly King was to banish Satan for all time from the heavens and cast him down to earth's vicinity. The result? The prophecy says: "Woe for the earth and for the sea, **because the Devil has come down to you, having great anger**, knowing he has a short period of time.[65]

---

64. https://en.wikipedia.org/wiki/William_Miller_(preacher)
65. w90 4/1 p. 8

This demonstrates the desperation that the Organization has displayed over the years to lend credibility to a failed doctrine—one they can't afford to abandon. Why would linking the ousting of Satan from heaven to the outbreak of World War I represent a desperate act on the part of the Governing Body? Look at the timing!

*The Watchtower* teaches us that Jesus took power in October of 1914.

> Then Jehovah would enthrone Jesus as King over the world of mankind. That happened in **October 1914**, marking the beginning of "the last days" of Satan's wicked system.[66]

Consider now that if Satan was thrown out of heaven right after Jesus assumed power in October 1914, and if Satan's anger at being ousted brought *woe to the earth*—specifically, the start of World War I as Witnesses suggest—then the old Devil must have access to a time machine. You see, war was declared on June 28, 1914, following the assassination of Archduke Ferdinand of Austria. In August of that year, battles were fought and thousands died. All this happened two months before Satan was supposedly chucked out of heaven.

Is it that no one at Headquarters takes the time to look up the dates of historical events, or do they just hope that no one will notice their lack of research? Probably the latter.

It is not even as if the war sprang into being out of nothing, as the publications seem to suggest. The nations in Europe had been engaged in the biggest arms race in history up to that point. Germany had amassed a million-man army! The factories had been building up their arsenals for the previous ten years. Everyone expected a war, though they were unprepared for its ferocity. They thought the whole thing would be over in a few weeks and they'd all be home in time for Christmas. For Satan's anger to have influenced the world, given that he isn't some puppet-master with absolute control over the minds of men, he must have been working for decades prior to 1914.

There is no predicted world event—no sign—that can be used to give 1914 empirical or historical credibility. (If you are wondering when Satan was cast out of heaven, see "Appendix F: When Was Satan Cast Down?" on page 368.)

---

66. w14 7/15 p. 30 par. 9

## Summing Up the Evidence

So, there you have it: Nine assumptions, not one of which has scriptural support, and every one of which must be true for the doctrine of 1914 to work.

If you pull out a single card from their house of cards, there is a cascade effect and the whole structure collapses. Even if one of these nine assumptions is false, the doctrinal structure comes crashing down.

**Figure 12. Pick a card to bring it all down.**

Are you willing to continue to base your salvation on doctrinal teachings founded entirely on human speculation?

Our Lord Jesus does not play games with us, nor does our heavenly Father say one thing, then do another. Jesus told us that his presence would be as obvious as lightning flashing in the sky. He warned us not to follow after men who try to convince us that his presence would be hidden, known only to a select few. Would he speak like this, knowing that his presence would be exactly that—invisible, hidden from view, and revealed to only a few select individuals? To again review his words of warning, Jesus tells us:

> Then if anyone says to YOU, 'Look! Here is the Christ,' or, 'There!' do not believe it. For **false Christs [*christos*, false anointed ones] and false prophets** will arise and will give great signs and wonders so as to mislead, if possible, even the chosen ones. Look! I have forewarned YOU. Therefore, if people say to YOU, 'Look! He is in the wilderness,' do not go out; 'Look! He is in the inner chambers,' do not believe it. For just as the lightning comes out of eastern parts and shines over to western parts, so the presence of the Son of man will be. (Matthew 24:23-27)

A false prophet is someone who claims to speak for God but keeps getting their predictions and interpretations wrong. A false christ is literally, a false anointed one. A false christ is someone claiming to be an anointed one of God when in fact he is not.

## The 1914 Doctrine Is Gangrenous

Let's consider the sobering parallel the 1914 doctrine creates between Jehovah's Witnesses and gangrenous elements within the early Christian congregation. We will begin by examining a necessary ramification of the 1914 teaching.

According to JW theology as expressed in this 1988 *Watchtower*, the resurrection of the anointed began in 1918:

> Those of the anointed who had already died faithful began to be resurrected to their promised place in the heavenly sanctuary starting in 1918.[67]

In a talk given at the 2020 annual meeting, Geoffrey Jackson claimed that C. T. Russell, who died on October 31, 1916, was alive in heaven to witness the 1919 appointment of the Governing Body as Jesus' Faithful and Discreet Slave. The Governing Body believes the following two scriptural prophecies were fulfilled in 1918.

> For this is what we tell YOU by Jehovah's word, that **we the living who survive to the presence of the Lord** shall in no way precede those who have fallen asleep [in death]; because the Lord himself will descend from heaven with a commanding call, with an archangel's voice and with God's trumpet, and those who are dead in union with Christ will rise first. Afterward we the living who are surviving **will, together with them, be caught away in clouds to meet the Lord in the air**; and thus we shall always be with [the] Lord. (1 Thessalonians 4:15-17)

> Look! I tell YOU a sacred secret: We shall not all fall asleep [in death], but we shall all be changed, in a moment, in the twinkling of an eye, during the last trumpet. For the trumpet will sound, and **the dead will be raised up incorruptible, and we shall be changed**. (1 Corinthians 15:51, 52)

The problem with this idea of a 1918 resurrection of the anointed is that it doesn't fit with Paul's words. He says that those surviving to the presence of the Lord are "caught away...to meet the Lord in the air" *together* with those who are resurrected" and that "the dead will be raised...and we shall be changed."

There were thousands of anointed Bible Students in 1918. Where is the historical evidence of the sudden mass disappearance of

---

67. w88 10/15 p. 12 par. 13

those faithful men and women, transformed in the "twinkling of an eye" and taken up to meet with the Lord?

Paul tells the Thessalonians that those "living who survive to the presence of the Lord...will, **together** with them [those sleeping in death] be caught away...to meet the Lord." The word rendered "together" is in Greek *hama*. According to *Strong's Concordance* it's defined as "at once." Its usage by *Strong's* is given as "at the same time, therewith, along with, together with."

This hardly fits with a process that would follow the resurrection of the anointed over a time span surpassing one hundred years. What the Organization has been forced to do to support their 1914 doctrine is to preach that the resurrection has already occurred and is now ongoing. Is this such a bad thing? Instead of us guessing at an answer, let's allow Paul to speak:

> Do your utmost to present yourself approved to God, a workman with nothing to be ashamed of, handling the word of the truth aright. But shun empty speeches that violate what is holy; for they will advance to more and more ungodliness, and ***their word will spread like gangrene.*** Hymenaeus and Philetus are of that number. These very [men] have deviated from the truth, **saying that the resurrection has already occurred; and they are subverting the faith of some.** (2 Timothy 2:15-18)

What a powerful condemnation Paul makes! He compares the teachings of these men who were preaching that the resurrection had already occurred to gangrene. When gangrene sets in, you have to start amputating if you want to save the body. We are now speaking of the body of Christ. If gangrene sets into the Body of Christ, the Christian Congregation made up of the Children of God, what parts will you have to amputate to save the whole? By preaching the resurrection occurred in 1918, the Governing Body is guilty of subverting the faith of Christians just as Hymenaeus and Philetus did. Doesn't that mean they have to be amputated? And since they were not, hasn't the Body of Christ been corrupted?

## How Supporting 1914 Mocks Scripture

According to Watch Tower theology, Christ's presence began over a century ago in 1914, and four years later, in 1918, the first resurrection came about. Revelation 20:4-6 tells us that those who make up the first resurrection will rule "as kings with Christ for 1,000 years." That means we have been in the thousand-year reign of Christ for more than a century already! Does that make any sense? Is there any evidence to bear that out?

Paul tells us that "the lawless one will be revealed, whom the Lord Jesus will do away with by the spirit of his mouth and bring to nothing by the **manifestation of his presence**."[68]

How was his presence made manifest in 1914, and how was "the lawless one" brought to nothing?

James tells us to "exercise patience, therefore, brothers, until the presence of the Lord..."[69] If his presence began over a century in our past, why are we still exercising patience? What are we waiting for? A third presence?

Are not Jehovah's Witnesses making a mockery of Scripture by continuing to perpetuate the falsehood that Jesus' presence began over a hundred years ago?

## Do They Know They Are Wrong?

When I first came to realize that 1914 was wrong, I wondered if the Governing Body was truly aware of the fact. It was hard to believe that men I had looked up to as spiritual leaders could be aware they were teaching falsehoods. Surely they were as much in the dark as I had been. I just couldn't bring myself to believe they were knowingly and willfully perpetrating a lie!

Based on what Revelation says, willfully lying carries a dreadful consequence:

> Outside are the dogs and those who practice spiritism and those who are sexually immoral and the murderers and the idolaters and **everyone who loves and practices lying**. (Revelation 22:15)

As it turns out, I was being hopelessly naïve. The Governing Body and their helper committees have known for decades that the date upon which their doctrine is based, 607 BCE, was wrong. Nevertheless, not only have they chosen to hide the fact, but they go out of their way to punish anyone who courageously attempts to shine the light of truth on it. The evidence for this will be revealed in the next chapter.

---

68. 2 Thessalonians 2:8
69. James 5:7

# 5

# What You Need to Know About 607 BCE

*"Outside are the dogs and those who practice spiritism and the fornicators and the murderers and the idolaters and everyone liking and carrying on a lie." (Revelation 22:15)*

At this stage of our research, it might seem like a moot point to investigate whether the year the Governing Body uses as the start date for their 2,520-year prophetic calculation is valid or not. In the previous chapter, we demonstrated that the entire doctrine of 1914 as the year of the so-called invisible presence of Christ is a fabrication with no foundation in Scripture. We saw how David Splane of the Governing Body, in a talk given at the 2014 annual meeting of the Watch Tower Society, unwittingly undercut the very foundation of the 1914 interpretation.[1] If all that were not enough to completely discredit the theology behind the 1914 presence of Christ, GB member Geoffrey Jackson put the final nail in the doctrine's coffin in his 2021 annual meeting talk revealing *new light* on Daniel chapter 12.[2]

One would think, given all the above, that any further discussion concerning the validity of 607 BCE as the supposed start of the gentile times might be the theological equivalent to beating a dead horse. For that reason, when drafting this book, I had

---

1. "The 1914 Antitype: A Foundation Built on Sand" on page 76.
2. "The Governing Body Undermines Its Own Teaching!" on page 85.

decided not to cover the topic of 607 BCE. What caused me to change my mind? These words of our Lord:

> Be on the watch for the false prophets that come to YOU in sheep's covering, but inside they are ravenous wolves. **By their fruits YOU will recognize them**. Never do people gather grapes from thorns or figs from thistles, do they? Likewise every good tree produces fine fruit, but every rotten tree produces worthless fruit; a good tree cannot bear worthless fruit, neither can a rotten tree produce fine fruit. Every tree not producing fine fruit gets cut down and thrown into the fire. **Really, then, by their fruits YOU will recognize those [men]**. (Matthew 7:15-20)

The Bible says that deceitful men will dress up in the guise of righteous teachers. If we're sincerely interested in learning the truth, and drawing close to God as our Father, it's important that we learn to identify false teachers dressed in disguise.

> But what I am doing I will continue to do, in order to eliminate the pretext of those who are wanting a basis for being found equal to us in the things about which they boast. For such men are false apostles, deceitful workers, **disguising themselves as apostles of Christ**. And no wonder, for Satan himself keeps disguising himself as an angel of light. It is therefore nothing extraordinary if **his ministers also keep disguising themselves as ministers of righteousness**. But **their end will be according to their works**. (2 Corinthians 11:12-15)

If the members of the Governing Body have erred innocently, and if upon being rebuked for their mistakes, they repent, then we have the scriptural basis to grant them forgiveness. Regarding forgiveness, Jesus tells us:

> If your brother commits a sin, rebuke him, and **if he repents, forgive him**. Even if he sins seven times a day against you and he comes back to you seven times, saying, 'I repent,' you must forgive him." (Luke 17:3, 4)

The condition for granting forgiveness is repentance. But what if there is no repentance? What if we point out the mistakes of the Governing Body—a rebuke—and instead of repenting, they reject the rebuke and go out of their way to silence us for pointing out their sin? What if they use intimidation and threaten us with being disfellowshipped to get us to shut up and toe the line? Then, we'd have no scriptural basis for granting them forgiveness, would we? Instead, other actions would be called for.

## A Heavier Judgment: Consequences of the 607 Teaching

Those who devote their time, energy, and resources—as the apostles did—to teaching the flock of God are worthy of double honor, just as the apostle Paul acknowledged at 1 Timothy 5:17. However, there is another side to that coin: With that double honor comes increased responsibility before God. James tells us that "not many of YOU should become teachers, my brothers, knowing that we shall receive heavier judgment."[3]

The Governing Body members now present themselves as the Guardians of Doctrine.[4] Any revelation—any *new light* as they call it—can only come through them as Jehovah's channel of communication. Jehovah's Witnesses have great faith that Jehovah is using the Governing Body to reveal truth to them and to prepare them for the great tribulation to come. The general feeling among Witnesses is that there are no finer Bible scholars in the world than the members of the Governing Body. It is therefore quite devastating for a Witness to learn that this is not the case at all.

How would you feel if you were to learn that with all the research invested in the 1914 teaching, with all the volumes of literature published to preach and teach this prophetic doctrine, that the whole thing can be disproven with a single Bible verse?

## The One Bible Verse That Disproves 607 BCE

As any Jehovah's Witness can tell you, the calculation that is used to arrive at October 1914 as the start of Christ's presence, begins at 607 BCE which supposedly was the date the nation of Israel was taken into exile. While Bible scholars generally accept that 587 BCE was the actual year of the exile based on archeological findings, Jehovah's Witnesses reject such evidence. Instead, they use their *interpretation* of Bible prophecy to fix the year at 607 BCE. The specific passage upon which this interpretation is based is found in the book of Daniel:

---

3. James 3:1
4. A term revealed by GB member Geoffrey Jackson under oath on August 14, 2015 as he testified before the *Australia Royal Commission into Institutional Responses to Child Sexual Abuse.*

In the first year of Darius the son of Ahasuerus of the seed of the Medes, who had been made king over the kingdom of the Chaldeans; in the first year of his reigning I myself, Daniel, discerned by the books the number of the years concerning which the word of Jehovah had occurred to Jeremiah the prophet, **for fulfilling the devastations of Jerusalem, [namely,] seventy years.** (Daniel 9:1, 2)

Jehovah's Witnesses are taught to believe that the phrase "devastations of Jerusalem" refers to the total desolation and depopulation of Israel following the diaspora that occurred at the hands of the army of Babylon under Nebuchadnezzar. While that interpretation can and has been challenged, let us accept it here for purposes of this discussion. Having arrived at a specific length of time—70 years—all one needs is a single end point to fixate that time period in history.

According to the book *Babylon the Great Has Fallen! God's Kingdom Rules!* (1963), that end point was 537 BCE. To arrive at that year, the writer of the *Babylon* book, having summarily rejected the archeological evidence supporting 587 BCE, now does an about-face and readily accepts the archeological evidence pointing to 539 BCE as the year in which Babylon fell to the forces of the Medes and Persians.

In calculating the "first year of Cyrus the king of Persia," we must faithfully proceed according to the inspired Word of Jehovah God. **We accept from secular historians the year 539 B.C. as a fixed date, marking the downfall of Babylon**, the Third World Power.[5]

The book then goes on to explain that two years later, in 537 BCE, the Jews were allowed to return to their homeland, thus ending the 70 years in which—according to JW theology—Jerusalem had to lie desolate and uninhabited.

But is that actually what the Bible says about the termination of the 70-year period? *Does it say that the 70 years end when the Jews returned to their homeland?*

If you look to the cross references for Daniel 9:2 that are placed in both the NWT Reference Bible (1984) and the more recent NWT 2013 edition, you will find a reference to Jeremiah's prophecy which reads:

---

5. *Babylon the Great Has Fallen! God's Kingdom Rules!* Ch. 18, p. 366

And all this land will be reduced to ruins and will become an object of horror, and these nations will have **to serve the king of Babylon for 70 years.** (Jeremiah 25:11)

What you won't find is a reference to the next verse:

But **when 70 years have been fulfilled, I will call to account the king of Babylon and that nation for their error**," declares Jehovah, "and I will make the land of the Chaldeans a desolate wasteland for all time." (Jeremiah 25:12)

When did Jehovah call "the king of Babylon and that nation" to account? According to the *Babylon* book, and all the other publications of the Watch Tower Society, that happened in 539 BCE. According to this one verse in Jeremiah, the 70 years ended in 539 BCE, not in 537 BCE. That means that by the reckoning of Jehovah's Witnesses, the start date for the calculation of the 2,520 prophetic years begins in 609 BCE and thus ends in 1912.

Let's restate that: **Based on the chronology accepted by the publications of Jehovah's Witnesses, the gentile times ended in 1912, not 1914.**

This may seem like a small miss, but in fact this miscalculation has huge ramifications. First, it calls into question the level of scholarship in a group of men claiming to be the channel God is using. How could 140 years go by without anyone noticing this mistake? If we accept that all this is just an oversight that has endured for a century and a half, how can we put trust in such men to lead us to salvation? Yet, they continue to claim that our salvation depends on them.[6]

The far more likely alternative is even worse: That they knew that this verse ruined their calculation and chose to cover it up.

The Organization claims that the findings and interpretations of secular investigators like historians and archeologists must take second place to what is clearly stated in Scripture. Does that rule not also apply to the findings and interpretations of the Watch Tower researchers? It is hypocritical to apply a rule to others which one is not willing to apply to oneself. The *Babylon* book lays out the rule that the Organization claims to follow:

---

6. "The other sheep should never forget that their salvation depends on their active support of Christ's anointed "brothers" still on earth." (w12 3/15 p. 20 par. 2)

Jehovah God is thus proved to be an accurate Timekeeper. **If we follow his system of counting time, according to his written Word, we shall make no mistakes in our calculations.** We cannot therefore go along with the chronologers of Christendom who date Jerusalem's destruction as occurring in 587 B.C. and who thereby limit the desolation of the land of Judah without man or domestic animal to merely fifty years. **Almighty God decreed that the land had to lie unworked, uninhabited for seventy years in order to enjoy a relatively perfect number of sabbaths**, that is to say, ten times seven sabbaths. Had the land enjoyed less than this perfect number of seventy years, it would not have enjoyed its full number of sabbaths. God's decree could not be broken or set aside, and, true to his decree, the land of Judah did rest uninhabited seventy years, from 607 to 537 B.C. In his own Word Almighty God, the perfect Time Measurer and Counter, says so. — 2 Chronicles 36:19-23[7]

The only scripture that is put forward to support the claim that "Almighty God decreed that the land had to lie **unworked, uninhabited for seventy years**" is 2 Chronicles 36:19-23 which says nothing of the sort:

> He burned down the house of the true God, tore down the wall of Jerusalem, burned all its fortified towers with fire, and destroyed everything of value. He carried off captive to Babylon those who escaped the sword, and they became servants to him and his sons **until the kingdom of Persia began to reign, to fulfill Jehovah's word spoken by Jeremiah, until the land had paid off its sabbaths. All the days it lay desolate it kept sabbath, to fulfill 70 years.** In the first year of King Cyrus of Persia, in order that Jehovah's word spoken by Jeremiah would be fulfilled, Jehovah stirred the spirit of King Cyrus of Persia to make a proclamation throughout his kingdom, which he also put in writing, saying: "This is what King Cyrus of Persia says, 'Jehovah the God of the heavens has given me all the kingdoms of the earth, and he has commissioned me to build him a house in Jerusalem, which is in Judah. Whoever there is among you of all his people, may Jehovah his God be with him, and let him go up.'"

Jeremiah 25:12 tells us that the 70 years end when the *King of Babylon is called to account* and 2 Chronicles 36:21 tells us that the 70 years end when the *King of Persia starts to reign*. The publications of the Watch Tower Society all agree that 539 BCE was

---

7. *Babylon the Great Has Fallen! God's Kingdom Rules!* Ch. 18, pp. 372-3.

## 5. What You Need to Know About 607 BCE

the year in which that occurred. So, even if we accept the idea that the nation had to be *totally desolate and uninhabited for 70 years,* we have to set the year for the exile to Babylon at 609 BCE. It's simple arithmetic.

Have we overlooked something? Is there some other scripture that would help us understand why the Organization has not made this alteration to its chronology? After all, the 1914 teaching is just about as fundamental a doctrine to JW theology as you can get. It marks the start of the Last Days, the starting point for the measurement of the *generation* of Matthew 24:34, the basis for the belief that the anointed were resurrected to heaven in 1918, and of utmost importance, the reason why the Governing Body claims their divine appointment as the Faithful and Discreet Slave came in 1919. It is inconceivable that the significance of Jeremiah 25:12 and 2 Chronicles 36:21 has gone unnoticed by the Bible scholars at Watch Tower Headquarters for the past 100 years. Surely there must be some overriding Scriptural reason that guided them away from 609 BCE and onto 607 BCE.

I happen to possess an almost complete library of Watch Tower publications going back to the beginning of the founding of the Society. Looking up Jeremiah 25:12 in the reference works of the JW Library program provided me with references going back to 1933—almost a century of published works! Scanning through all of these publications wherever Jeremiah 25:12 was mentioned produced one—yes, that's right, only one—explanation for why this verse is not used to establish 609 BCE as the start year for the 1914 calculation. Here it is from the book, *All Scripture Is Inspired of God and Beneficial*:

> The closing verses of Second Chronicles (36:17-23) **give conclusive proof** of the fulfillment of Jeremiah 25:12 and, in addition, show that a full 70 years must be counted from the complete desolation of the land **to the restoration of Jehovah's worship at Jerusalem in 537 B.C.E.** This desolation therefore begins in 607 B.C.E.—Jer. 29:10; 2 Ki. 25:1-26; Ezra 3:1-6.[8]

That's it! In almost 100 years of publishing information on 1914, **this is the only attempt** at explaining why Jeremiah 25:12 doesn't provide a basis for starting the count from 539 BCE. The claim is that 2 Chronicles 36:17-23 provides "conclusive proof,"

---

8.  si p. 84 par. 35 Bible Book Number 14—2 Chronicles

but notice that no effort is made to reveal what the *conclusive proof* is. We've just read 2 Chronicles and it says nothing about "the restoration of Jehovah's worship in Jerusalem in 537 B.C.E." However, it does clearly state that the 70 years end with the enthronement of the king of Persia which happened in 539 BCE. So, the only "conclusive proof" it provides is that the start of the 70 years should be 609 BCE, not 607 BCE.

### Why Would They Conceal This from You?

The Watch Tower Society inherited its interpretation of Daniel 4 from Nelson Barbour who got it from William Miller.[9] The outbreak of World War I, which came within months of the timing predicted by C. T. Russell in *Zion's Watchtower*, gave tremendous impetus to the fledgling Bible Students' movement—impetus which Rutherford was quick to exploit with his "Millions Now Living Will Never Die" campaign.[10]

Since that time down to this day, Jehovah's Witnesses have been one of the largest and most visible of all advent-style (apocalyptic) movements, owing much of their staying power to the coincidence of their 1914 prediction with the outbreak of World War I. To change that now, to suggest they got it wrong all along, even by a mere two years, would surely undermine not only this cornerstone doctrine of their belief system, but would also call into question the basis for the claim that the Governing Body was appointed in 1919 by Jesus Christ.

How serious is this failure to reveal the truth? How would our Lord Jesus view this willful act of concealment?

When Ananias and Sapphira concealed the truth about the amount of money they had received for the sale of a plot of land they owned, claiming they had donated the entire sum to the emerging Christian community of the time, God put them both to death. Though their sin actually harmed no one, the Lord showed just how he views liars.

In Revelation 22:15, we are told that liars and those who support them are denied life. What, therefore, can be said about a group of men who presume to lead millions of Christians and to teach

---

9. See "The Origin of the 1914 Doctrine" on page 69.
10. See "Appendix D: The Harp of God Cover and Canvassing Script" on page 363.

## 5. What You Need to Know About 607 BCE

them as God's channel of communication when we learn that they have been gaslighting their flock for more than a century?

As I said at the beginning of this chapter, the issue isn't that 607 BCE is the wrong date. The issue is that they knew it was wrong and hid that knowledge from Jehovah's Witnesses.

### Is the Governing Body Really Guilty of Lying?

In the November 2016 broadcast[11] on JW.org, Gerrit Lösch of the Governing Body explains to his audience just what constitutes a lie. Here are some key excerpts from that discourse:

> **A lie is a false statement deliberately presented as being true.** A falsehood. A lie is the opposite of the truth. **Lying involves saying something incorrect to a person who is entitled to know the truth about a matter.** But there is also something that is called a half-truth. The Bible tells Christians to be honest with each other.
>
> So, we need to speak openly and honestly with each other, **not withholding bits of information** that could change the perception of the listener or mislead him.
>
> Since Jehovah hates liars, **we should avoid all lies**, not just big or malicious lies.

I think we can all agree with his definition. Of course, for there to be a lie there must be previous knowledge that one is speaking a falsehood. It is one thing to be unknowingly wrong about a belief, and quite another to be aware one is wrong and nevertheless continue to teach the false doctrine. This is what Gerrit Lösch, in this same broadcast, says about religions that lie.

> Then there are religious lies. If Satan is called the father of the lie, then Babylon the great, the global empire of false religion, can be called the mother of the lie. **Individual false religions could be called daughters of the lie.**

Gerrit tells us that knowingly preaching a falsehood would make any religion into a false religion and *by his own words* constitute a religion as a "daughter of Babylon the great." He says all this without a hint of irony in his voice. Is he unaware that the Organization has done precisely that with regard to 607 BCE?

---

11. At about the 3:00 minute mark https://www.jw.org/en/library/videos/#en/mediaitems/StudioMonthlyPrograms/pub-jwb_201611_1_VIDEO

Please bear in mind that this is no trivial matter. Here is what one scholar has to say on the importance of 607 BCE to Watch Tower theology:

> An examination of the evidence demonstrates that **it constitutes the very foundation for the claims and message of this movement.**
>
> The Watch Tower Society claims to be God's "sole channel" and "mouthpiece" on earth. Summing up its most distinctive teachings: it asserts that the kingdom of God was established in heaven in 1914, that the "last days" began that year, that Christ returned invisibly at that time to "inspect" the Christian denominations, and that he finally rejected all of them except the Watch Tower Society and its associates, which he appointed in 1919 as his sole "instrument" on earth.
>
> *For about seventy years*, the Society employed Jesus' words at Matthew 24:34 about "this generation" to teach clearly and adamantly that the generation of 1914 would positively not pass away until the final end came at the "battle of Armageddon," when every human alive except active members of the Watch Tower Organization would be destroyed forever. **Thousands of Jehovah's Witnesses of the "1914 generation" fully expected to live to see and to survive that doomsday and then to live forever in paradise on earth.**[12]

This reference comes from a book written by a Swedish Jehovah's Witness named Carl Olof Jonsson who in 1968 was challenged while in the preaching work to provide proof for the Society's position on 607 BCE as the year of the Jewish exile to Babylon. Being a lover of truth and sure that the theology of the Organization was solid, he embarked on what would turn out to be many years of research—research which would eventually lead to the conclusion that the Watch Tower's position on 607 BCE was in error.

Carl was working under the same assumption that many of us had at the time, that the Organization was the one true religion, and that Jehovah's Witnesses were different from other religions in that they would willingly change any doctrinal understanding if it was found to be false and if Scripture revealed the correct understanding.

---

12. *The Gentile Times Reconsidered*, Fourth Edition, p. 2

The publications had often shown how other religions dealt with those who spoke truth to power. For instance, the Catholic Church had the Spanish Inquisition which lasted six centuries. But we believed that Witnesses, as lovers of truth, were different. Only wicked people promoting lies would attack those who speak truth, because they have no other defence. A prime example of this comes from the first century when the Pharisees and religious leaders had to attack and persecute Jesus Christ and his followers in an effort to silence them from speaking truth.

Alas, brother Carl Olof Jonsson learned that in this, as in many other things, the Organization of Jehovah's Witnesses was no different from the religions of Christendom it routinely condemned.

He presented his findings to the Governing Body in 1977. They required him to recant and deny his research, something he couldn't do. As a result, he was vilified and eventually disfellowshipped.

In 1983, Carl published his findings in his book *The Gentile Times Reconsidered* which is currently in its fourth edition, published by Hart Publishers and available on Amazon. If you're interested in understanding the facts concerning the 607 BCE controversy, I would highly recommend you obtain this publication.

Gerrit Lösch says that "we need to speak openly and honestly with each other, not withholding bits of information that could change the perception of the listener or mislead him." However, the Governing Body doesn't live by those words. Witnesses aren't allowed to read books that disagree with Witness theology. A Witness caught reading a book like *The Gentile Times Reconsidered* would be accused of associating with apostates, harassed by the elders, and threatened with being disfellowshipped.

By Gerrit Lösch's own definition, this conduct is that of a liar. The Governing Body he represents is deliberately presenting as true something they know to be false, and "withholding bits of information that could change the perception of the listener or mislead him."

## A Desperate Effort to Defend The 607 Doctrine

The final decade of the twentieth century saw the start of "the information age." With the creation of the World Wide Web in 1989, it has become possible for any individual to publish information that can be accessed instantaneously by millions. Not since the invention of the printing press has technology presented such a challenge to the powerful hold religious leaders have traditionally held over their flocks. (I recall sitting in the Kingdom Hall during a meeting and using my iPad to fact-check what was being taught in *The Watchtower* study.)

The Governing Body must have recognized this threat to their authority early on because we were getting constant reminders in the magazines and through Letters to the Body of Elders about "the dangers of the Internet." Such was the resistance to anything related to the internet that it came as a shock to many of us when we learned that the Governing Body had set up their own web site, now called JW.org. I'm sure they were only following the adage, "If you can't beat 'em, join 'em."

Still, the exhortation to avoid social media and any other sources of information outside of the Organization's official web site continued. Not surprisingly, such efforts failed. Brothers and sisters began to hear and read of challenges to long held beliefs such as the validity of 607 BCE.

Very likely, this would be the reason that the Organization published a two-part article in 2011 titled, "When Was Ancient Jerusalem Destroyed," starting with the October 1 public edition of *The Watchtower*.[13] I remember reading that series of articles and believing that it provided credible evidence in support of the Organization's claim that 607 BCE was the year in which Jerusalem was destroyed by the army of Babylon under King Nebuchadnezzar. I had no reason to doubt that date, and at that time, I still trusted in the integrity of the Society's leadership. Not long afterwards, my own examination of the 1914 doctrine began, but it focused on the scriptural basis for the doctrine, not the historical accuracy of the dating.

## A Humble Sister Uncovers the Lie of 607 BCE

While on vacation in 2016, my late wife, Reta, and I met up with a good friend[14] whom we hadn't seen in years. Naturally, we took the opportunity to share our newfound knowledge about

---

13. w11 10/1, pp. 26-31; w11 11/1, pp. 22-28
14. Our friend desires to remain anonymous because she is part of a large family of Jehovah's Witnesses and doesn't wish to be shunned for not sharing their beliefs anymore.

the falsehood of the 1914 teaching. This friend was understandably doubtful at first, but she has an open mind and so listened to what we had to say. I was afraid that our candor might have ended an enduring and valuable friendship, since my past efforts at sharing the truth with JW friends had almost always resulted in what might be called *soft shunning*. What I didn't know at the time is that our good friend possessed that quality which seems to be increasingly rare these days: A love of truth. Like the Beroeans of Paul's day, she put our words to the test.

For her, the dating of the 1914 calculation was a good starting point, so she decided to examine the most recent "evidence" presented by the publications.

Now before going further, I should clarify that this Christian woman is not a university graduate. She holds no scholarly degrees. Most Jehovah's Witnesses would look at her and see just your average congregation publisher. They would class her as a humble sister, nothing more. She is that, though her humility is of the type that God cherishes. But in addition to that, she has a keen intelligence, and the determination that drives a truth seeker to ferret out the facts. So, she chose to tackle the Watch Tower Society's reasoning by using the same references that the October and November 2011 issues of the public edition of *The Watchtower* use to defend the Organization's position on the dating of 607 BCE. If the year of the exile was actually 587 BCE as almost all the experts claim, then the Witnesses are off by 20 years and should be preaching 1934 as the year of Christ's invisible presence.

Rather than admit they were wrong, the Governing Body attempted to discredit the hard evidence of archeology. Did they do this unwittingly? I believe that after reviewing the evidence our friend uncovered, you would have to be very naïve not to realize that these two *Watchtower* articles were written with the direct intention of misleading the flock and protecting the authority of the Governing Body.

What our friend learned was that the October and November 2011 issues of *The Watchtower* attempt to undermine the evidence of the archeological record by calling into question the dating of the lineage of Babylon kings as well as by casting doubt on the integrity of the astronomical records from ancient Babylon, both of which establish 587 BCE as the date of the Jewish exile.

What follows is the result of her research.

## The Record of Kings: The 20 Years that Never Existed

For the 607 BCE interpretation to work, the Organization needs to find a way to add 20 years into the record of Babylonian Kings. Their claim is that those years exist but are missing from the record of archeological findings. To discredit what the researchers have found, *The Watchtower* claims:

> ...why do many authorities hold to the date 587 B.C.E.? They lean on 2 sources of information; the writings of classical historians and the Canon of Ptolemy.[15]

This is simply not true. Indeed, using the same resources *The Watchtower* article lists in its bibliography, our friend learned that researchers lean on literally **tens of thousands of Neo-Babylonian written documents preserved in clay**, located in the British Museum and many other museums around the world. These historical documents have been painstakingly translated by experts, then compared with each other, then combined like puzzle pieces to complete a chronological picture. The comprehensive study of these documents presents the *strongest evidence* because the data are from primary sources, *people who actually lived* during the Neo-Babylonian era. In other words, *they were eyewitnesses.*

The Babylonians were meticulous in recording mundane everyday activities such as marriages, purchases, land acquisitions, et cetera. They also dated these documents according to the regnal year and name of the current king. What the archeologists have discovered is that the Babylonian people kept an overwhelming abundance of business receipts and legal records, inadvertently recording a chronological trail for each reigning king during the Neo-Babylonian era.

There are so many of these documents accounted for that when they are placed in sequence, the average frequency is one for every few days. We are not talking about time spans in weeks, months, or years. So, for every week, experts have documents with the name of a Babylonian king inscribed on it, along with the numbered year of his reign. The complete Neo-Babylonian

---

15. w11 10/1 p. 20

## 5. What You Need to Know About 607 BCE

era has been accounted for by archeologists, and they consider this as *primary evidence*.

Given the weight of this chronologically sequenced *primary evidence*, it would be impossible for 20 years to just go missing!

Therefore, the above statement made in *The Watchtower* article is false. It requires us to accept without any proof that these archeologists ignore all the evidence they have worked so hard to compile in favor of "the writings of classical historians and the Canon of Ptolemy."

## A Strawman Argument

There is a classic logical fallacy known as a *strawman argument*. It consists of making a false claim about what your opponent really means so that you can be seen to defeat him. In other words, you misrepresent his argument completely, argue against something he doesn't mean at all, and so appear to come off the winner. Your goal isn't to convince your opponent that he's wrong. If that were your goal, you would not engage in the subterfuge of a strawman argument. No, your goal is to seem to be right while hiding the true nature of your opponent's argument from all onlookers. Essentially, you use a strawman argument to mislead others when you can't fall back on truth to support your teaching or belief.

How sad it is to see Watch Tower publications fall back on this dishonest technique. One instance of its use is found in this October 1, 2011 *Watchtower* article. On page 31, the writer uses a graphic (see Figure 13) to build just such a strawman argument.

This "Quick Summary" starts off by stating something that is true:

> Secular historians usually say that Jerusalem was destroyed in 587 B.C.E.

Speaking as a former long-time elder, I know that *secular* is a loaded term for Jehovah's Witnesses. It is synonymous with *worldly* and immediately conjures up the idea in the minds of Witnesses that the data is suspect since it comes from "Satan's world." This bias plays into their next statement which is false:

> Bible Chronology strongly indicates that the destruction occurred in 607 B.C.E.

No, it does not. In fact, the Bible gives us no dates at all. It only points to the 19th year of Nebuchadnezzar's reign and indicates

> **A QUICK SUMMARY**
>
> ■ Secular historians usually say that Jerusalem was destroyed in 587 B.C.E.
>
> ■ Bible chronology strongly indicates that the destruction occurred in 607 B.C.E.
>
> ■ Secular historians mainly base their conclusions on the writings of classical historians and on the canon of Ptolemy.
>
> ■ The writings of classical historians contain significant errors and are not always consistent with the records on clay tablets.

Figure 13. The "Quick Summary" box from the October 1, 2011, *Watchtower*.

that the period of servitude lasts 70 years. We must rely on secular research for our starting date, not the Bible.

We've already demonstrated that the third statement isn't true. Secular historians don't use the writings of classical historians, nor the canon of Ptolemy as their primary source of research. Instead, they draw conclusions based on hard data acquired from thousands of unearthed clay tablets. This is the essence of the Organization's strawman argument.

The Organization needs to find a reason to support their claim that some 20 years are missing from the historical record of Babylonian kings, but unfortunately, the thousands of clay tablets unearthed fail to provide the evidence they need to support their 607 BCE date.

Notice how the Organization first acknowledges this abundance of hard data that establishes the precise year of Jerusalem's destruction, then attempts to dismiss it all with an unsubstantiated assumption:

> Business tablets exist for all the years traditionally attributed to the Neo-Babylonian kings. When the years that these kings ruled are totaled and a calculation is made back from the last

## 5. What You Need to Know About 607 BCE

Neo-Babylonian king, Nabonidus, the date reached for the destruction of Jerusalem is 587 B.C.E. **However, this method of dating works only if each king followed the other in the same year, without any breaks in between.**"[16]

The highlighted sentence introduces doubt in the findings of the world's archeologists but produces *no evidence* to back it up. Are we to assume that the Organization of Jehovah's Witnesses has uncovered hitherto unknown overlaps and gaps in regnal years which countless dedicated researchers have missed?

These thousands of cuneiform tablets are primary sources. Despite occasional scribal or deciphering errors, irregularities, or missing pieces, as a combined set, they *overwhelmingly* present a cohesive and coherent picture. Primary documents present impartial evidence because they do not have an agenda of their own. They cannot be swayed or bribed. They merely exist as an unbiased witness who answers questions without uttering a word.

To make their doctrine work, the Organization's calculations require there to be a 20-year gap in the Neo-Babylonian era that simply cannot be accounted for.

Were you aware that Watchtower publications have actually published the accepted regnal years of the Neo-Babylonian kings without any challenge to them? This ambiguity seems to have been done unwittingly. You should draw your own conclusions from the data listed here.

Counting backwards from 539 BCE when Babylon was destroyed—a date that both archeologists and Jehovah's Witnesses agree upon—we have Nabonidus who ruled for 17 years from 556 to 539 B.C.E.[17]

Nabonidus followed Labashi-Marduk who only reigned for 9 months from 557 B.C.E. He was appointed by his father, Neriglissar who reigned for four years from 561 to 557 B.C.E. after murdering Evil-merodach who reigned for 2 years from 563 to 561 B.C.E.[18]

Nebuchadnezzar ruled for 43 years.[19]

---

16. w11 11/1 p. 24 "When Was Ancient Jerusalem Destroyed?—Part 2"
17. it-2 p. 457 "Nabonidus"; see also *Aid to Bible Understanding*, p. 1195
18. w65 1/1 p. 29
19. dp chap. 4 p. 50 par. 9; it-2 p. 480 par. 1

Adding these years together gives us a starting year for Nebuchadnezzar's rule as 606 BCE.

| King | Period of Reign | Length of Reign |
|---|---|---|
| Nabonidus | 556-539 BCE | 17 years |
| Labashi-Marduk | 557-556 BCE | 9 months |
| Neriglissar | 561-557 BCE | 4 years |
| Evil-merodach | 563-561 BCE | 2 years |
| Nebuchadnezzar | 563-606 BCE | 43 years |

All that data is taken *directly from Watch Tower publications.*

According to the Bible, Jerusalem's walls were breached in Nebuchadnezzar's *18th year and destroyed by the 19th year of his reign.*

> In the fifth month, on the seventh day of the month, that is, in the 19th year of King Nebuchadnezzar the king of Babylon, Nebuzaradan the chief of the guard, the servant of the king of Babylon, came to Jerusalem. He burned down the house of Jehovah, the king's house, and all the houses of Jerusalem; he also burned down the house of every prominent man. (2 Kings 25:8, 9)

Therefore, adding 19 years to the start of Nebuchadnezzar's reign which data taken from Watch Tower publications sets as 606 BCE gives us 587 BCE which is precisely what all the experts agree upon!

Using its own published data, the Organization has unwittingly contradicted its own teaching that 607 BCE is the date of Jerusalem's destruction.

Yet, never ones to let the facts get in the way of a good doctrine, they ignore the math and in the book, *Insight on the Scriptures*, arbitrarily change the years of Nebuchadnezzar's reign to start in 624 BCE:

> Second ruler of the Neo-Babylonian Empire; son of Nabopolassar and father of Awil-Marduk (Evil-merodach), who succeeded

him to the throne. Nebuchadnezzar ruled as king for 43 years (624-582 B.C.E.)[20]

Ignoring math and historical evidence in favor of one's personal interpretation of Scripture is not the path to truth.

How does the Organization get around this? Where do they find the missing 19 years to push back the start of Nebuchadnezzar's reign to 624 BCE to make their 607 BCE destruction of Jerusalem work?

They can't find the missing 19 years, so they simply imply that they must be there and rely on the trust of rank-and-file Jehovah's Witnesses not to look too deeply into the evidence.

## The Astronomical Record: The Truth Really Is in the Stars!

VAT 4956 is a number assigned to a particular clay tablet which describes astronomical data relating to the 37$^{th}$ year of Nebuchadnezzar's reign.

The Babylonians were experts in astronomy. Over many centuries, they recorded precise planetary, solar, and lunar movements as well as eclipses. The combination of these planetary positions locks them into an absolute timeline that we can trace back with precision.

Each combination is as unique as a human fingerprint or a lottery ticket number.

Exactly how accurate is the timing of planetary orbits? They are so accurate and so predictable that scientists have been able to create computer algorithms which will allow us to know exactly where each planet in the solar system was at any time in recorded history. In fact, there is an excellent app that you can download and run on your smartphone or tablet called *SkySafari 6 Plus*, which is available on the web or from the Apple and Android stores. With it, you can see precisely where a particular planet described on VAT 4956 was in the sky on a given date to see if the positions match. If they match, then the data on VAT 4956 are proven to be accurate.

I would recommend you download it yourself so you can do your own research. Make sure you get the *Plus* version of the

---

20. it-2 p. 480

Figure 14. VAT 4956.

app as the cheaper version does not allow calculations for years before Christ.

What we are about to see is so devastating to the doctrine of the Watch Tower Society concerning 607 BCE that it would seem they would have no choice but to readjust their doctrinal interpretation. The astronomical data proves conclusively that the 587 BCE date for the destruction of Jerusalem—the one all the archeologists agree on—is in fact, the true date, and 607 BCE is not.

As we've just seen, the men of the Governing Body are not willing to let hard evidence disrupt their neat little doctrinal framework. Nevertheless, it is hard to argue with facts that the average Witness is able to corroborate for themselves using just a smart phone. This is precisely what our *humble sister* did. Still, the November 2011 *Watchtower* (part 2 of the article) tries its best to get its readers to discount the evidence. Observe:

> In addition to the aforementioned eclipse, there are 13 sets of lunar observations on the tablet and **15 planetary observations**.

# 5. What You Need to Know About 607 BCE

Figure 15. The constellations.

These describe the position of the moon or planets in relation to certain stars or constellations.[21]

As we'll see, the planetary observations provide conclusive proof that 587 BCE was the date of the destruction of Jerusalem. Therefore, the Governing Body must discredit this proof somehow. They attempt to do so using footnote 18 which reads in part:

> Though the cuneiform sign for the moon is clear and unambiguous, **some of the signs for the names of the planets and their positions are unclear.**[22]

This vague statement is intended to sow doubt as to the reliability of the available data. Is it really relevant? The fact is that on the VAT 4956 tablet, the Babylonian sign for the planet Saturn *is known and is clear*. There is nothing ambiguous or doubtful about what that symbol represents. It represents the planet Saturn.

---

21.  w11 11/1 p. 26
22.  w11 11/1 p. 28

What does the location of the planet Saturn as described by Babylonian astronomers tell us about the timing of events on earth?

According to the translation of the VAT 4956 tablet, during Year 37, Month 1 of Nebuchadnezzar, King of Babylon, Saturn was in front of the Swallow. The Swallow is the region of the night sky we now call Pisces. The night sky is divided into 12 regions. Saturn passes through all of them on its 29.4 year-long orbit.

That means that Saturn takes 2.42 years to move through each of the 12 constellations. Once Saturn moves out of Pisces, it will not return there *for another 27 years*. According to Babylonian astronomers, Saturn was in Pisces in Nebuchadnezzar's 37th year which archeologists set at 568 BCE.

Running our *SkySafari Plus* program and setting the time and date to Friday, April 22, 568 BC, 1:00 AM, location: Baghdad, we get an image showing the planet Saturn within the Pisces (Fish) constellation (Figure 16).

Here we have astronomical data confirming that the 37th year of Nebuchadnezzar's reign was 568 BCE. Why does this matter? Because of what Jeremiah tells us about the destruction of Jerusalem.

Jeremiah 52:12 tells us that in the 19th year of Nebuchadnezzar the king of Babylon, Jerusalem was destroyed. In Jeremiah chapter 5 we learn that the siege lasted over a year. Jeremiah got a vision in the 18th year of Nebuchadnezzar's reign while the city was under siege.[23] So, if we can fix with precision the 37th year of Nebuchadnezzar, it is easy subtraction to arrive at the year of the siege and of Jerusalem's destruction which turns out to be 587 BCE.

If you were to type in 588 BCE into the *SkySafari* app as the 37th year of Nebuchadnezzar in line with what *The Watchtower* teaches, you would find Saturn in Cancer (Latin for Crab). To be where the Babylonian astronomers observed it to be, Saturn would have had to leave Cancer, pass through Leo, Virgo, Libra, Scorpius, Sagittarius, Capricornus, and Aquarius, before reaching Pisces or the Swallow to Babylonians. That's a 19-year journey. The missing years aren't missing at all. *The Watchtower* got the year wrong! It got the year wrong because Russell got it

---

23. Jeremiah 32:1, 2

5. What You Need to Know About 607 BCE 131

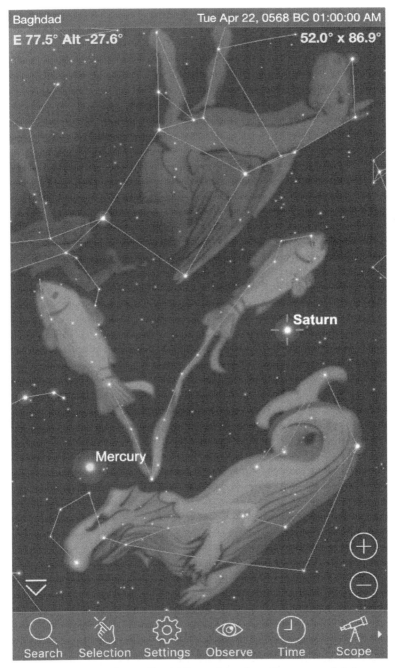

Figure 16. *SkySafari Plus* showing Saturn within Pisces on April 22, 568 BC.

wrong, and Russell got it wrong, because he accepted the chronology of Adventist Pastor Nelson Barbour, and Barbour got it wrong, because he rejected the research of others and made up his own. What we have here is a mistake made about 200 years ago that continues to confound Jehovah's Witnesses who trust in the teachings of men.

**The Real Issue We Face**

There is a great deal more evidence to consider. For those interested, I would again refer you to the very scholarly work of Carl Olof Jonsson, *The Gentile Times Reconsidered*.[24]

You will be missing the point if all you take away from this is that the Organization's position on 607 BCE as the date of the Babylonian Exile is wrong. We are all imperfect, and we all make mistakes, and so anyone can be wrong about something, even something as important as the 1914 doctrine. The point isn't that they are wrong. The point is that *they knew they were wrong and did nothing to fix it*. The point is that knowing it was wrong, they still continued to promote this false doctrine as God's truth; and by disfellowshipping anyone who tried to publish the real truth, as they did with Carl Olof Jonsson, they willingly sin.

If you still wish to believe that they didn't know and were merely acting with the best of intentions, consider the fact that to discover these facts did not take a Harvard scholar, but just your average Jehovah's Witness—a sister with a love for truth and the drive to verify the evidence. Well, perhaps not your average Jehovah's Witness, since the willingness to be noble-minded like the ancient inhabitants of Berea is sadly lacking in the majority of my former JW friends and associates.[25]

If my friend could find out the truth, why couldn't those men who so proudly claim to be God's special channel do the same? Would not the spirit of God have led them into all the truth?[26] Are they not supposed to be the Faithful and Discreet Slave that feeds the domestics their food at the proper time? Is that food not handed to them by Jesus by means of holy spirit?

---

24. On Amazon.com, ISBN-13: 978-1039110816
25. Acts 17:11
26. John 14:25, 26, 16:13

Clearly, they have failed miserably to feed the flock Bible truth. To this day, the leadership of the Organization continues to promote their interpretation of the *gentile times* and do all they can to deny the flock access to any other source of information. In addition, they intimidate anyone who tries to reveal the truth about this doctrine with threats of disfellowshipping on the fake charge of apostasy.

In a vision to the apostle John, our Lord Jesus warns us:

> Outside are the dogs and those who practice spiritism and those who are sexually immoral and the murderers and the idolaters and **everyone who loves and practices lying**. (Revelation 22:15 NWT 2013)

When we love something, we will defend it. The Organization continues to defend their 1914 teaching and continues to promote it in the worldwide preaching even though they have ample evidence to show that it is false. The question for us as individuals is whether or not we will participate in spreading this false teaching, this false good news, this lie!

# 6

# Preaching the Wrong Salvation Hope

*"However, even if we or an angel out of heaven were to declare to you as good news something beyond the good news we declared to you, let him be accursed." (Galatians 1:8)*

When Jehovah's Witnesses stand on the street by their literature carts or go from door to door in their ministry, what good news are they really offering the public? What salvation hope do Witnesses look forward to for themselves? Obviously, their hope is strong, for it motivates them to sacrifice so much of their lives and livelihood to engage in the preaching work as well as other time-consuming *theocratic*[1] activities. I can say this without fear of contradiction because I lived it, and my situation and motivation were all typical of the average Jehovah's Witness.

As a youth, I wanted to go to university, but decided against it because I was led to believe that Armageddon was just around the corner. Instead of pursuing a career, I spent seven of my formative adult years preaching in Colombia, South America. When I married at 27, my wife and I decided to forego having a family because the end was so near. We wanted to bring our children up in the New World.

---

1. *Theocratic* (rule by God) is a term Witnesses use to describe any labor offered on behalf of or in obedience to the Organization.

For more than forty years, I would get up virtually every Saturday morning, put on a suit and tie, and go out in the preaching work. I thought I was serving Jehovah God. I thought I was engaging in a lifesaving, never-to-be-repeated worldwide preaching campaign to proclaim the King and his Kingdom. I thought I was preaching the good news of salvation.

Of course, if I'd been actually preaching the true good news of the Kingdom of Christ, then all that sacrifice would have been justified. But I now know that was not the case, and not just because the 1914 presence of Christ is false. There is something far worse about the good news that Jehovah's Witnesses preach. They are preaching a false salvation hope.

## The Good News According to Jehovah's Witnesses

Witnesses preach a perversion of the good news of salvation that divides the salvation hope into two categories: The first hope is to immortal life in heaven. That is limited to a mere 144,000 anointed individuals, most of whom have already been selected. The second hope which is held by 99.9% of all Jehovah's Witnesses is to be declared righteous as friends of God to live on earth either by surviving Armageddon, or by being resurrected in the New World. Oddly enough, this declaration of righteousness by God is conditional. It doesn't guarantee them life as it does for the anointed. They will continue to be sinners and must work toward perfection by the end of the thousand-year reign of Christ.

As for the rest of humanity, traditionally there were two possibilities according to Watch Tower theology: If they are alive when Armageddon comes, they will be destroyed by God with no hope of a future resurrection. If they die before Armageddon, they likely will be resurrected during the millennial reign and have the opportunity of accepting the benefit of Christ's ransom sacrifice. If they do not, they will die for all eternity.

Recently, there appears to be some *new light* on the subject of who of the unrighteous gets resurrected. Of course, Jesus doesn't say, but the Governing Body feels the need to weigh in on the matter. In the May 2022 issue of *The Watchtower* Study Edition, we read:

> Does this mean that everyone will be resurrected to life on earth during the Thousand-Year Reign? No. Those who wickedly rejected the opportunity to serve Jehovah before their death will not be raised to life. **They had their chance and proved that**

**they were not worthy of life on the Paradise earth.** —Matt. 25:46; 2 Thess. 1:9; Rev. 17:8; 20:15.[2]

So, if you have an unbelieving (i.e., non-JW) mate or parent or child, they won't get a resurrection, because "they had their chance" and blew it!?

The arrogance of Watchtower "scholars" is matched only by their ineptitude at interpreting the Bible!

The proof texts they quote in this paragraph only prove that some people will die eternally, but there is no firm indication of when that happens. Worse is the statement that follows: "They... proved that they were not worthy..."

Exactly who of the unrighteous are worthy? Isn't it due to *undeserved kindness* (a JW expression) or grace that the unrighteous are granted a chance at eternal life?

Be that as it may, according to Jehovah's Witnesses, there are going to be three resurrections. At one end of the spectrum will be the resurrection of the righteous to life in heaven. At the other end will be the resurrection of the unrighteous to judgment. And in between these two is a resurrection of the righteous but not to life unless they are judged worthy after a thousand years; so technically, that makes it a resurrection of the righteous to judgment. What a strange concept!

Here's the doctrine in a nutshell:

> Jehovah has declared his **anointed ones righteous as sons** and the **other sheep righteous as friends** on the basis of Christ's ransom sacrifice...[3]

Of course, the Bible says nothing of a resurrection of Christians who are declared righteous by God *as friends* and who are subsequently judged for 1,000 years to make sure they stayed righteous. Is Jehovah hedging his bets? Can you see how ill-conceived eisegetical interpretations can make a mockery of God's mercy?

Of course, the Bible makes no mention of this middle or third resurrection of friends of God. In fact, it makes no mention of three types of resurrection, but only of two.

> I have hope toward God...that there is going to be **a resurrection of both the righteous and the unrighteous**. (Acts 24:15)

---

2. W22 05 p. 17, par. 17
3. w12 7/15 p. 28 par. 7

Do not marvel at this, because the hour is coming in which all those in the memorial tombs will hear his voice and come out, those who did good things to **a resurrection of life**, those who practiced vile things to **a resurrection of judgment**. (John 5:28, 29)

At Luke 12:32, Jesus refers to his Jewish disciples as a "little flock." Jehovah's Witnesses have appropriated this term and claim it refers to the 144,000 anointed with a heavenly hope. Jesus makes no mention of 144,000 when he refers to the little flock. It would be another 70 years or so before that number was revealed by Jesus in his Revelation to John.

At John 10:16, Jesus makes reference to the Gentiles who would later join with his Jewish disciples to become a single flock under him as "other sheep." The Governing Body have appropriated this term to refer to all Jehovah's Witnesses who are not of the anointed 144,000. These do not have a heavenly hope and are not resurrected to life.[4]

The following chart illustrates the fundamental differences between the two salvation hopes which Jehovah's Witnesses preach as part of the message of the Good News of the Kingdom.

---

4. it-2 p. 270; w84 2/15 15-20

## Chart of Differences between "Little Flock" & "Other Sheep"

| Little Flock | Other Sheep |
|---|---|
| Called Children of God. (Romans 8:14, 21) | Called Friends of God. (it-1 p. 606; w95 7/1 p. 15 par. 5) |
| In the New Covenant. (Luke 22:20) | Not in the New Covenant. (w09 1/15 p. 29 par. 16) |
| Have Jesus as their mediator. (1 Timothy 2:5, 6) | Do not have a mediator. (it-2 p. 362) |
| Are resurrected to immortal life. (Revelation 20:4-6) | Remain imperfect as sinners until the end of thousand years. (w85 10/15 p. 31; w51 5/15 p. 308) |
| Are born again. (John 3:3-5) | Are not born again. (w82 2/1 pp. 26-29; w86 2/15 p. 14 par. 16) |
| Partake of the emblems representing Christ's flesh and blood. (Luke 22:19; 1 Corinthians 11:24, 25) | Do not partake of the emblems representing Christ's flesh and blood. w09 1/15 p. 29 par. 16) |
| Rule with Jesus as kings and priests. (Revelation 5:10; 20:4-6; 1 Corinthians 4:8) | Will live as subjects under Jesus and the 144,000. (w12 3/15 p. 20 par. 2) |

You will notice that while there are scriptural references provided for each characteristic listed for the *Little Flock*, there are no scriptural references for those characteristics listed under the *Other Sheep* class as defined by Jehovah's Witnesses. This isn't an oversight. There simply are no clear scriptural references to support those elements which Witnesses are taught characterize the members of the Other Sheep.

Here is a question worth considering: What if the Other Sheep are actually part of the Little Flock? We'll get to that in a moment.

## A Bridge Too Far

Questioning doctrines like the overlapping generation or the 1914 invisible presence of Christ doesn't really affect the hopes and dreams of the average JW. Not so when you question the hope of the Other Sheep. For decades, the publications have presented Witnesses with beautiful graphics depicting an idyllic life in the New World with bountiful food and joyful gatherings. Children are shown frolicking safely with wild animals. Resurrected ones are portrayed returning to be with their families.

It's natural that people who have been fed with these powerful and moving images would balk at the thought that the good news is not about an earthly hope. They'll likewise balk at the thought of going to heaven, as Witnesses teach will happen to the anointed. They'll recoil at the idea of never seeing their loved ones again, because according to JW doctrine, the 144,000 go off to heaven never to return. And more than all that, the average Witness will resist the hope being offered by Jesus, because they've been trained by countless *Watchtower* study articles and Memorial talks to feel unworthy of being anointed with holy spirit, or born again.

If you're feeling any such trepidation, I'd ask you to put it aside for now and move forward with your investigation into what is the real hope being offered to you as a Christian. If the Governing Body can be wrong about who the Other Sheep are, then they can be wrong about everything else as well.

Here is where trust comes in. We must trust in the goodness of our heavenly Father. Consider this scripture:

> But just as it is written: "Eye has not seen and ear has not heard, neither have there been conceived in the heart of man the things that God has prepared for those who love him." For it is to us God

has revealed them through his spirit, for the spirit searches into all things, even the deep things of God. (1 Corinthians 2:9, 10)

For thousands of years, faithful servants like Abraham, Moses, and Daniel, looked forward to the things God had reserved for them, but these things were beyond their imaginings. Still, they trusted that anything they could imagine would be surpassed in wonder by the reality that Jehovah had stored up for them. Now, these realities have been revealed by Jesus through the holy spirit to those God counts as his Children. Let us never think that the reward the Watch Tower Corporation has presented to us could even come close to the wondrous nature of the salvation hope that "God has prepared for those who love him."

# 7

# Who Are the "Other Sheep"?

*"And I have other sheep, which are not of this fold; those also I must bring, and they will listen to my voice, and they will become one flock, one shepherd. (John 10:16)*

To my mind, there is no other topic in this entire book that is as important as this one, the Other Sheep[1] doctrine of Jehovah's Witnesses. I can say that with confidence because getting this understanding wrong will literally block your entry into the Kingdom of God.

To recap what we've learned so far, Jehovah's Witnesses preach that the hope now being held out to all humans is to be declared righteous by Jehovah God as one of his friends. In that state, you will survive Armageddon or, should you die before it comes, you will be resurrected into the New World. If you don't accept this offer, you will not survive Armageddon. However, if you die before Armageddon, you'll still be resurrected into the New World. So, what is the difference for the resurrected ones?

According to JW theology, the righteous friends of God will be resurrected first and have positions of oversight in the New World. That gives them first dibs on all homes, choice living locations, and goods left over from the battle of Armageddon. The JW Armageddon survivors will join with those that are part of the

---

1. I have capitalized "Other Sheep" throughout when referring specifically the JW interpretation of this term.

earthly resurrection of the righteous friends of God to educate the unrighteous resurrected ones about God. However, whether you are part of the earthly resurrection of the righteous or unrighteous, you will all still be living as imperfect (i.e., sinful) humans. That is, in a nutshell, JW theology as it pertains to the hope of the good news of salvation that they preach in their public ministry.

When I came to realize from my Bible research that the overlapping generation was false, and that the doctrine of the invisible presence of Christ in 1914 was also false, I began to look into the teaching of the Other Sheep. Since I was still serving as an elder of Jehovah's Witnesses, I started by using the *Watchtower Library*[2] program in the hope that some explanation based on Scripture could be found.

By typing "other sheep" (with double quotes) into the *Library* search field, I got over 2,000 hits in *The Watchtower* magazine alone. Yet, in the NWT Reference Bible, there was only a single occurrence of the term. How odd!

Think about it. According to the Watch Tower Society, God has two groups of faithful servants. The first group is made up of anointed Christians called the Children of God numerous times in Scripture. The second group far outnumbers the first by about 100 to 1. If the Watch Tower is right, then one would expect equal if not greater attention in Scripture to be given to this much larger group. Yet the only scripture that is provided in the publications is the following single, cryptic reference.

> And I have **other sheep**, which are not of this fold; those too I must bring in, and they will listen to my voice, and they will become one flock, one shepherd. (John 10:16)

I call this a cryptic reference because Jesus doesn't actually define who he is referring to by the terms: "this fold" and "other sheep."

I had trustingly believed the Organization's teaching concerning the salvation hope of the Other Sheep, but I had never actually

---

2. This program can be downloaded for free at https://www.jw.org/en/online-help/watchtower-library/install-watchtower-library/

## 7. Who Are the "Other Sheep"?   145

tried to prove it from Scripture. For that matter, I couldn't recall ever having studied the subject in depth in a *Watchtower* study article.

So, I turned to the publication indexes of the Society, of which there are two: *Publications Index 1986-2022* and *Publications Index 1930-1985*. All the important doctrines of Jehovah's Witnesses have been thoroughly explained in study articles that are considered in the congregations' weekly *Watchtower* study, and these are listed in the indexes under the subheading *Discussion*. For instance, if you look up topics like "Sons of God," "Anointed Christians," or "Resurrection," you'll find multiple references under the *Discussion* subheading. These always give the fullest and most detailed treatment of any topic.

The Other Sheep doctrine is a cornerstone of JW theology, so I expected to find a number of references under the Discussion subheading. You can just imagine my surprise when I discovered that there was no Discussion subheading at all in the index for the years 1986 to 2022. In over 35 years of Watch Tower publications, how could there not be a single discussion article on this most important of teachings? How very strange!

Undaunted, I switched to the older index covering the years 1930 to 1985. I knew from my years attending and also conducting the weekly *Watchtower* Study that the doctrine was introduced by J. F. Rutherford in the mid-1930s. For instance:

> **In 1935 the "great crowd" of Revelation 7:9-15 was understood to be made up of "other sheep,"** Christians with an earthly hope, who would appear on the world scene in "the last days" and who as a group would survive Armageddon. (John 10:16; 2 Timothy 3:1; Revelation 21:3, 4) After that year, the thrust of the disciple-making work turned to the gathering in of the great crowd. Hence, especially after 1966 it was believed that the heavenly call ceased in 1935. This seemed to be confirmed when almost all who were baptized after 1935 felt that they had the earthly hope. Thereafter, any called to the heavenly hope were believed to be replacements for anointed Christians who had proved unfaithful.[3]

So, when I consulted the older index which covers publications from 1930 to 1985, I expected some reference to that 1935 article. This time there was a Discussion subheading, but it only

---

3.  w07 5/1 pp. 30-31 "Questions From Readers"

contained a paltry three references to discussion articles, none of them earlier than 1980.[4]

Strange and stranger!

I looked up the three references given, hoping to find some scriptures that would prove the other sheep of John 10:16 refer to a class of unanointed Christians with an earthly hope. However, no support from the Bible was provided. Each article treated the Other Sheep as a given, something already established. Just as you don't have to prove the sky is blue, the Organization seemed to be of the opinion that they didn't have to prove the Other Sheep were who they said they are.

I then took the time to do a word search on every occurrence of "other sheep" in the publications. It was time consuming and painstaking, but I got through it and discovered that in every instance, the Other Sheep are treated as an established fact and no scriptural support is provided for the belief. This is therefore a scripturally unsubstantiated salvation doctrine. They categorically use the term to refer to a class of Jehovah's Witnesses with a different hope than that offered to the Children of God. This is like saying unabashedly that the sky is red, and just expecting everyone to accept it.

Still, I knew the article originated with Rutherford in the mid-1930s, so I scoured my copies of old *Watchtower* volumes for the article that first introduced the doctrine to the flock of Jehovah's Witnesses. Why was this article not represented in the Watch Tower *Publications Index 1930-1985*?

The answer to that question became clear when I finally discovered the article that explained the alleged scriptural basis for the teaching. It is broken into a two-part article series in the August 1 and 15, 1934 issues of *The Watchtower*. After reading it, I realized why the Organization did not include it in their index. The entire interpretation—remember, as a JW, you are pinning your salvation hope on this understanding—is based not on hard Bible fact, but on a series of fabricated antitypical applications that at times are so bizarre as to stretch credulity to its limits. So that you can make up your own mind about it, I have devoted an entire chapter to review the two articles in detail.[5]

---

4. w84 2/15 15-20; *Survival* (1984) 72-73; w80 7/15 22-28
5. See "Rutherford Creates a Clergy Class" on page 232.

But before we confuse the issue with the interpretations and speculations of men, let's allow the Bible to speak for itself. As we do that, we will also consult, by way of comparison, what the publications of the Watch Tower Society have to say on the subject of the Other Sheep. Our reason for doing this is that it will provide an excellent case study on the contrast between eisegesis (imposing one's own interpretation on Scripture) and exegesis (letting the Bible speak for itself).

## Examining the Other Sheep Doctrine for Ourselves

Let's begin by trying to define the two terms in John 10:16 upon which everything depends: "this fold" and "other sheep". If we are going to understand this, we must approach it without any preconception. The Watch Tower Society doesn't have this luxury having been burdened with Rutherford's interpretation since the 1930s. Let us compare:

### Watchtower Eisegesis

To explain who make up "this fold," *The Watchtower* has this to say:

> WITH the introduction of the new sheepfold of spiritual Israel on the day of Pentecost in 33 C.E., the former sheepfold for the natural Jews under the Mosaic Law covenant passed away as having served its purpose. Three and a half years later came the conversion, baptism and spirit anointing of the Roman centurion Cornelius and his believing family and friends at Caesarea. Thus the nonproselyted, uncircumcised Gentiles were brought into the sheepfold of which Jesus Christ is "the door." (Acts, chapter 10) This fold encloses "the Israel of God," Israelites according to the spirit, or spiritual Israelites. Could it be said of any of these—Jew or Gentile—that they "are not of this fold"—the fold gathered according to the new covenant arrangement? Surely not!—Galatians 6:16; John 10:16.[6]

If you look up all the scriptures cited in this paragraph, you will see that they provide *no support* for the idea that "this fold" refers to all anointed Christians, both Jew and Gentile. However,

---

6. w84 2/15 p. 15 par. 1 "The Recent Pen for 'Other Sheep'"

the article does make a telling admission. The Organization claims that at the time our Lord said the words at John 10:16, there were two sheepfolds: one of spiritual Israel and another of the natural Jews. But is that true? Spiritual Israel was formed only when the holy spirit was poured out at Pentecost, not before. So, at the time Jesus spoke those words, there was only one sheep fold, the nation of Israel.

## Christian Exegesis

Let's try this again, but this time we'll let the Bible speak for itself, and we'll refrain from drawing arbitrary conclusions that conform to some religious theology.

At John 10:16, Jesus only speaks of two sheepfolds or flocks: "this fold" and "other sheep." By saying "*this* fold," Jesus indicates that the fold or flock was then present. Before we venture outside the immediate context, let's ask ourselves: To whom was he speaking? The answer is given just three verses on:

> Again **a division resulted among the Jews** because of these words. Many of them were saying: "He has a demon and is mad. Why do YOU listen to him?" Others would say: "These are not the sayings of a demonized man. A demon cannot open blind people's eyes, can it?" (John 10:19-21)

Obviously, this wasn't a private discussion with his trusted disciples, but a public one in which his opposers were also present. It is important to bear that in mind.

How did Jesus view his countrymen, even those who opposed him? When sending his apostles out to preach, he gave them these instructions:

> Do not go off into the road of the nations, and do not enter any Samaritan city; but instead, go continually to **the lost sheep of the house of Israel**. (Matthew 10:5, 6)

On a different occasion when a Gentile woman asked Jesus for help, he told her:

> I was not sent to anyone except to **the lost sheep of the house of Israel**. (Matthew 15:24)

So, his mission was to find Jewish lost sheep and to bring them into his own flock.

The Governing Body make a comparison between the "little flock" of Luke 12:32 and the "other sheep" of John 10:16. But that is strictly a JW comparison. The Bible makes no such comparison.

## 7. Who Are the "Other Sheep"?

What then did Jesus mean by calling his immediate disciples a "little flock"?

Since the sheepfold of Israel was large—there were millions of Jews alive at the time—while his flock of disciples was tiny, it fits that he would give them the reassurance found at Luke 12:32: "Have no fear, little flock, because YOUR Father has approved of giving YOU the kingdom."

He was telling them that despite Israel's long history, despite its magnificent temple and established religious traditions, despite its Mosaic covenant for a kingdom, it was not to them but to his little flock of disciples that the Kingdom of God was to be given. He confirms this at Matthew 21:43, saying to his Jewish opposers: "This is why I say to YOU, the kingdom of God will be taken from YOU and be given to a nation producing its fruits."

With that in mind, we have the basis for understanding who the other sheep are.

Remember that Jesus was speaking to the Jews in general, including opposers looking for any opportunity to find fault with him. Jews despised Gentiles. Jesus knew that a major change was about to take place with his death. The exclusive covenant that Jehovah God had made with the Jews was about to become void because of the faithlessness and wickedness of the nation of Israel—wickedness which reached it zenith with the murder of God's Son.[7] Soon, a new covenant was to be made, one which included Gentiles. If he had revealed to those haughty Jewish leaders that they were about to be replaced by people of the gentile nations whom they despised, they would have tried to stone him then and there. So, he couched his words in cryptic language.

Therefore, a logical conclusion is that Jesus was referring to the Gentiles as his other sheep, who were not of the sheepfold of Israel, but who would eventually become part of the one flock under Christ.

Is there support in Scripture for such a conclusion? We are looking for sheep drawn from two sheepfolds to come under a single shepherd, becoming a single flock. Consider these three passages:

---

7. Matthew 21:33-22:14

> For I am not ashamed of the good news; it is, in fact, God's power for salvation to everyone having faith, **to the Jew first and also to the Greek**. (Romans 1:16)
>
> For there is **no distinction between Jew and Greek**. There is the same Lord over all, who is rich toward all those calling on him. (Romans 10:12)
>
> There is **neither Jew nor Greek**, there is neither slave nor freeman, there is neither male nor female, for you are all one in union with Christ Jesus. Moreover, if you belong to Christ, you are really Abraham's offspring, heirs with reference to a promise. (Galatians 3:28, 29)

From these verses, we can see that Jesus removed the distinction between Jew and Gentile and brought them together into a single flock, sharers all in the new covenant. This fact was prophesied by Caiaphas, not because he was a man of faith, but because of his position as high priest.

> But one of them, Caiaphas, who was high priest that year, said to them: "You do not know anything at all, and you have not reasoned that it is to your benefit for one man to die in behalf of the people rather than for the whole nation to be destroyed." He did not say this, however, of his own originality, but because he was high priest that year, he prophesied that Jesus was to die for the nation, **and not only for the nation but also to gather together into one the children of God who were scattered about**. (John 11:49-52)

"The nation" referred to Israel, but the "children of God who were scattered about" would indicate not all the Gentiles, but those within the non-Jewish world who were called to become God's children.

## Decoding John 10:16

Judge for yourself from the foregoing evidence which understanding makes the most sense and is most consistent with the rest of Scripture.

Would you accept that the other sheep are Gentiles brought into the Christian fold starting three and a half years after Jesus' death with the baptism of the Roman Centurion Cornelius and family?[8] Or does it seem more likely that Jesus had in mind a

---

8. Acts 10:1-48

## 7. Who Are the "Other Sheep"?

group of Christians who would not come onto the world scene for another 1,900 years? If you hold with the latter understanding promoted by the publications of the Society, then you have to resolve a number of sticky issues.

## Children of God or Just Friends

Since the JW Other Sheep are not anointed, they cannot be called children of God. So, *The Watchtower* clearly and unambiguously declares that the Other Sheep are declared righteous as *friends* of God.

> In 1985 it was understood that on the basis of Jesus' ransom sacrifice, other sheep are declared righteous as friends of God and with a view to surviving Armageddon.[9]

The problem with this view is that there are no scriptures to support it. One might think otherwise when reading declarations like the following *Watchtower* cranks out:

> "The things upon the earth" are Christ's other sheep, who have the hope of living forever on earth. To these also Jehovah's chosen Servant brings a righteous standing before Jehovah. Because they have faith in Christ's ransom sacrifice and thus "have washed their robes and made them white in the blood of the Lamb," Jehovah declares them righteous, not as spiritual sons, but as his friends, giving them the wonderful prospect of surviving "the great tribulation." (Rev. 7:9, 10, 14; Jas. 2:23)[10]

How do we know that "'the things upon the earth' are Christ's other sheep"? How do we know that they are declared righteous as God's friends? Let us examine the scriptures listed—Revelation 7:9, 10, 14 and James 2:23—that supposedly support these teachings.

> After this I saw, and look! a great crowd, which no man was able to number, out of all nations and tribes and peoples and tongues, standing before the throne and before the Lamb, dressed in white robes; and there were palm branches in their hands. And they keep shouting with a loud voice, saying: "Salvation we owe to our God, who is seated on the throne, and to the Lamb." (Revelation 7:9, 10)

---

9. it-1 p. 606; w95 7/1 p. 15 par. 5
10. w09 1/15 pp. 28-29 par. 16

> So right away I said to him: "My lord, you are the one who knows." And he said to me: "These are the ones who come out of the great tribulation, and they have washed their robes and made them white in the blood of the Lamb. (Revelation 7:14)

> ...and the scripture was fulfilled that says: "Abraham put faith in Jehovah, and it was counted to him as righteousness," and he came to be called Jehovah's friend. (James 2:23)

Do you see any support here for what they are saying in the article? I don't. Abraham was called God's friend, but **Abraham wasn't a Christian**!

It appears the Governing Body is relying on the credulity of Witnesses, and the fact that they rarely look up so-called corroborating scriptural citations with a critical eye.

The lack of Scriptural evidence leads to only one conclusion: *There is no basis for calling the other sheep, God's friends.*

If you enter "friends of God" or "God's friends" into the Watchtower Library program, you get zero hits in the Bible. On the other hand, entering "children of God" in it, yields 8 hits in the Christian Scriptures; "God's children," 3 hits; "sons of God," 3 hits; and "God's sons," 1 hit—ample proof that Christians are rightly referred to as the children of God.

In addition to this, is there any hint of exclusion, any implication of a limited number, provided by these words:

> However, **as many as did receive him**, to them he gave authority to become God's children, because they were exercising faith in his name; and they were born, not from blood or from a fleshly will or from man's will, but from God. (John 1:12, 13)

## The New Covenant: In or Out?

The New Covenant is God's promise to make his anointed Children kings and priests to rule with Jesus in the Kingdom of the heavens. This hope is not open to the Other Sheep according to Watch Tower theology.

> Are all Christians included in this new covenant? No. Some, like the apostles who drank of that cup that evening, are participants in the new covenant. Jesus made another covenant with them to rule together with him in his Kingdom. (Luke 22:28-30) They will share with Jesus in his Kingdom.—Luke 22:15, 16.

What of those who will live on earth under his Kingdom? They are beneficiaries of the new covenant. (Gal. 3:8, 9)[11]

The irony here is that this quote is taken from an article titled, "One Flock, One Shepherd," yet the purpose of the article is to paint a portrait of two very distinct flocks, one that rules and one that serves. This is a classic example of the eisegetical technique known as *cherry picking*, which relies on the student or reader to accept certain assumptions and ignore the context.

If you have ever watched a TV show or movie depicting a court case, you will surely have heard a lawyer cry out, "Objection, your honor! Assumes facts not in evidence." This is just such an instance. *The Watchtower* article has yet to provide Bible evidence for a class of Christian who will live on the earth as subjects of the Kingdom, but assuming this to be the case, they draw the further conclusion that such Christians will not be in the New Covenant. Yet no proof is given. There is no scripture that makes such a distinction, assigning some Christians as participants in the New Covenant, and others as merely beneficiaries of it.

The reference in paragraph 14 of the article to Galatians 3:8, 9 as support is cherry picking a verse to make it support an ideology while ignoring the context that actually teaches the opposite of what the Governing Body wants its followers to believe.

Let's start with the reference from Galatians 3:8, 9.

> Now the scripture, foreseeing that God would declare people of the nations righteous through faith, declared the good news beforehand to Abraham, namely: "By means of you all the nations will be blessed." So those who adhere to faith are being blessed together with Abraham, who had faith. (Galatians 3:8, 9)

*The Watchtower* would have us accept that those nations being blessed are the Other Sheep who are not participants in the new covenant but only beneficiaries of it. This is not what the context teaches. Paul is writing to the Galatians who are being persuaded by Judaizers to embrace the law of Moses for salvation rather than faith in Christ. He starts off with a harsh rebuke: "O senseless Galatians! Who has brought you under this evil influence…?"[12]

---

11. w10 3/15 pp. 26-27 pars. 13-14 "One Flock, One Shepherd"
12. Galatians 3:1

The Galatians were Gentiles, people of the nations. So, when Paul writes in verses 8 and 9 that "God would declare people of the nations righteous through faith" and about Abraham that, "by means of you all the nations will be blessed," was he speaking about the Galatians and other Gentiles like them, or about an earthly class of Christian some nineteen centuries in their future? We don't need to guess, because the context makes it clear that the Galatians specifically, and Gentiles in general, were the Christians he was referring to.

> This was so that the blessing of Abraham would come to the nations by means of Christ Jesus, so that we might receive the promised spirit through our faith. ...Now the promises were spoken to Abraham and to his offspring. It does not say, "and to your descendants," in the sense of many. Rather, it says, "and to your offspring," in the sense of one, who is Christ. ...the Law became our guardian leading to Christ, so that we might be declared righteous through faith. ...You are all, in fact, sons of God through your faith in Christ Jesus. For all of you who were baptized into Christ have put on Christ. **There is neither Jew nor Greek**, there is neither slave nor freeman, there is neither male nor female, for **you are all one in union with Christ Jesus. Moreover, if you belong to Christ, you are really Abraham's offspring, heirs with reference to a promise.** (Galatians 3:14, 16, 24-29)

Paul is not referencing any secondary class of Christian with an earthly hope that is outside of the New Covenant arrangement. He is speaking to the Galatians who are Gentiles and whom he properly refers to as both children of God and offspring of Abraham.

So, the Organization's use of this passage to try to support the idea of an earthly Other Sheep class of Christian outside the New Covenant is entirely bogus.

## Jesus as Our Mediator

I've found that whenever I told one of my Witness friends that Jesus is not their mediator, they're shocked and assumed I was wrong, until I showed them the proof from *Insight on the Scriptures*:

> **Those for Whom Christ Is Mediator.** The apostle Paul declares that there is "one mediator between God and men, a man, Christ Jesus, who gave himself a corresponding ransom for all"—for both Jews and Gentiles. (1Ti 2:5, 6) He mediates the new covenant

between God and those taken into the new covenant, the congregation of spiritual Israel.[13]

It makes sense that Jesus mediates between the Father and those in the New Covenant. What doesn't make sense is that this number is arbitrarily cut off at 144,000. Consider that the original covenant was made through Moses with the whole nation of Israel. If they had obeyed the voice of Jehovah, they would have become a kingdom of priests.[14] Jehovah made no mention of limiting that number to just 144,000. Likewise, when Jesus introduced the new covenant to replace the one the Jews failed to keep, he again made no mention of a limited number. Surely, if such a limitation existed, it would be misleading for Paul to write under inspiration that the invitation was extended to all men. He says to Timothy that there is only one mediator between God and men, not God and some men, not God and a tiny fraction of men, but *all men*.[15]

## Born Again: Just for Some Christians?

According to Watch Tower doctrine, since only 144,000 are spirit anointed, only that number is "born again."

> There is a difference, though, as Jesus indicated to Nicodemus even before he spoke of everlasting life. He said: "Unless anyone is **born again**, he cannot see the kingdom of God." (John 3:3-5) So a spiritual rebirth is experienced by those baptized Christians whom God calls to be joint heirs with Jesus in his Kingdom. (1 Corinthians 1:9, 26-30) The "other sheep" do not need any such rebirth, for their goal is life everlasting in the restored earthly Paradise as subjects of the Kingdom.—Matthew 25:34, 46b; Luke 23:42, 43.[16]

Before looking at what the Bible actually teaches us about being born again, let's examine the so-called proof text of Matthew 25:34 used by the Organization to show that the Other Sheep have a goal of being kingdom subjects in an earthly paradise.

---

13. it-2 p. 362 "Mediator"
14. Exodus 19:3-6
15. 1 Timothy 2:5, 6
16. w86 2/15 p. 14 par. 16

> Then the King will say to those on his right: "Come, you who have been blessed by my Father, inherit the Kingdom prepared for you from the founding of the world." (Matthew 25:34)

What a gross misapplication of Scripture this is! First of all, subjects don't inherit the kingdom, only the children of the king do. To inherit something is to own it and have a say over how it is run. Further, the phrase "the Kingdom prepared for you from the founding of the world" applies to the anointed children of God, not some non-anointed subject class. Paul makes this clear at Ephesians 1:4, 5 where he says, "just as he chose us in union with him before the founding of the world, that we should be holy and without blemish before him in love. For he foreordained us to the adoption through Jesus Christ as sons to himself."

The word used at John 3:3 often translated "born again" is γεννηθῇ ἄνωθεν [transliteration: *gennēthē anōthen*]. It literally means "born from above" which carries the idea of being born of God. In this context, John again uses it in his first letter:

> Beloved ones, let us continue loving one another, because love is from God, and everyone who loves has been **born from God** and gains the knowledge of God. (1 John 4:7)

> Everyone believing that Jesus is the Christ **has been born from God**, and everyone who loves the one that caused to be born loves him who has been born from that one. By this we gain the knowledge that we are loving the children of God, when we are loving God and doing his commandments. For this is what the love of God means, that we observe his commandments; and yet his commandments are not burdensome, because everything that **has been born from God** conquers the world. And this is the conquest that has conquered the world, our faith. (1 John 5:1-4)

I know that those Jehovah's Witnesses who consider themselves to be Other Sheep also believe they love God. So how can they not be born again or born from above, if *all who love God are born of God*, or born from above, as John says? Likewise, JW Other Sheep believe Jesus is the Christ, so again, according to John, they are born again.

There is nothing in Scripture that restricts the number of born-again Christians to only 144,000.

## Resurrected to Eternal Life or to Just a Chance at Life?

Jesus says that all those who did good things are resurrected to life, and all those who did vile things are resurrected to judgment.

Paul refers to a resurrection of the righteous and another, of the unrighteous.[17]

At Revelation 20:4-6, we learn that the resurrection to life is the first resurrection and that those who are resurrected in it are granted eternal life and can't die, for the second death has no power over them. This is not the case with the second resurrection of the unrighteous to judgment.

The resurrection to life is for the righteous. If you're declared righteous by God, who can change that? Your life is guaranteed by Jehovah God, who can never misjudge or make a mistake. Notice how Paul confirms this:

> However, when the kindness and the love for man on the part of our Savior, God, was manifested, owing to no works in righteousness that we had performed, but according to his mercy he saved us through the bath that brought us to life and through the making of us new by holy spirit. This [spirit] he poured out richly upon us through Jesus Christ our Savior, that, **after being declared righteous by virtue of the undeserved kindness of that one, we might become heirs according to a hope of everlasting life**. (Titus 3:4-7)

> Now we know that God makes all his works cooperate together for the good of those who love God, those who are the ones called according to his purpose; because those whom he gave his first recognition he also foreordained to be patterned after the image of his Son, that he might be the firstborn among many brothers. Moreover, those whom he foreordained are the ones he also called; and those whom he called are the ones he also declared to be righteous. **Finally those whom he declared righteous are the ones he also glorified**. (Romans 8:28-30)

There is nothing in Scripture to support the concept of a third resurrection, one in which humans are declared righteous, yet are still sinners and can still die the second death if they don't remain faithful throughout the thousand years. Just like the Catholic Church had to invent a purgatory as a third option for those who weren't good enough to go to heaven nor bad enough to go directly to hell, Witness leadership has had to invent a third type of resurrection, one which isn't to judgment with the unrighteous, yet which isn't to life with the anointed. This has

---

17.  John 5:28, 29; Acts 24:15

resulted in some rather bizarre speculation as evinced by this 1951 *Watchtower*.

> But for those who survive Armageddon and for those who will be resurrected from the memorial tombs, the **physical healing will be gradual until human perfection is reached, at the latest by the end of the thousand years**. This gradual progress in physical health will depend upon their progress in the way of righteousness under Christ's millennial rule.[18]

"Gradual physical healing"! What nonsense! If you're missing a leg, will it grow back slowly over the course of ten centuries?! When Jesus healed people, the change was instantaneous. The only "gradual healing," if you an even call it that, was when he healed the blind man in two stages so as to allow him to get accustomed to the light.[19] Things haven't changed much since the 1950s as this 2008 *Watchtower* shows:

> A thousand years of peace will follow, during which all who respond to God's love will be **progressively restored to the perfection** of life that Adam lost.[20]

So, while the little flock of Christians get sinless perfection immediately upon their resurrection, Witnesses contend that the Other Sheep have to struggle with their imperfect sinful state for upwards of another thousand years.

Further, you can't be progressively restored to perfection or sinlessness. Just as a woman cannot be a little bit pregnant, so a person cannot be a little bit sinful. Adam committed a single sin and was condemned to death for it.

There really is no difference for the JW Other Sheep and the unrighteous of the world, other than what some might call a head start. Since both are resurrected in a state of sin, both will have to persevere to be granted life at the end of the thousand years. This demonstrates yet another contradiction which this doctrine creates. When God declares someone as righteous, that judgment is irreversible. To suggest otherwise, is to suggest that God can get it wrong, that his judgment is faulty. So, if he declares the Other Sheep righteous as his friends as *The Watchtower* alleges,[21]

---

18. w51 5/15 pp. 308-309 par. 9
19. Matthew 8:22-25
20. w08 3/1 p. 9
21. it-1 p. 606

## 7. Who Are the "Other Sheep"?

it makes no sense that they would be resurrected in a state of sin. The children of God are also declared righteous and resurrected to immortal life. Jehovah God does not have a double standard of righteousness.

Watch Tower doctrine also requires that the faithful men of pre-Christian times be denied the reward promised to them in the Mosaic covenant, the original covenant.[22] Here is how *The Watchtower* of 1981 tries to explain it:

> That is Paul's comment on the matter. **Doubtless** that expression refers to the established government of God by the 'seed of Abraham,' under which government those three patriarchs will live on earth and gain human perfection by the end of the thousand years.[23]

"Doubtless" is one of those buzzwords you have to look out for in Watch Tower publications. It really means "here be speculation."

Are we to believe that men of such legendary faith like Job, Abraham, Jeremiah and Daniel will still have to *gradually progress to perfection* over the course of a thousand years, while men like J.F. Rutherford, Freddy Franz, and Stephen Lett are to be granted instantaneous perfection and immortality?

## Watch Tower's Two "Proofs" for the Other Sheep

The astute Bible student will have noticed the absence of scriptural proof for each and every assertion the publications make regarding the Other Sheep.

- They are friends of God, not His children.
- They are not in the New Covenant.
- They do not have the heavenly hope.
- They are not going to be kings and priests with Jesus.
- They are going to be earthly subjects of the Kingdom.
- They will live as sinners in the New World.
- They are not spirit anointed.
- They are not born again.
- They are not part of the body of Christ.
- They are not allowed to partake of the emblems.

---

22. Exodus 19:3-6
23. w81 3/15 p. 30

All of these doctrines are taught repeatedly and aggressively from both the publications and the platform. It appears that the basis for belief in these teachings is utter confidence in the Governing Body as God's channel. Of course, even die-hard Jehovah's Witnesses have to believe that such things are founded in Scripture. What scriptural passages does the Organization use to lay a foundation for all these teachings?

They have used two passages from the Bible to do this. We will analyze the logic behind both.

### First "Proof": Romans 8:16, A Special Token?

Jehovah's Witnesses are taught that to partake you must get a *special invitation or token* from Jehovah. The 2016 *Watchtower* reads:

> [9] But how does a person know that he has the heavenly calling, that he has, in fact, received this **special token**? The answer is clearly seen in Paul's words to the anointed brothers in Rome, who were "called to be holy ones." He told them: "You did not receive a spirit of slavery causing fear again, but you received a spirit of adoption as sons, by which spirit we cry out: 'Abba, Father!' The spirit itself bears witness with our spirit that we are God's children." (Rom. 1:7; 8:15, 16) Simply put, by means of his holy spirit, **God makes it clear to that person that he is invited** to become a future heir in the Kingdom arrangement.—1 Thess. 2:12.
>
> [10] Those who have received **this special invitation from God** do not need another witness from any other source....[24]

There you have it! The Governing Body's entire line of reasoning hinges on a very particular and self-serving interpretation of *a single Bible verse*. All Romans 8:16 actually says is that God's spirit informs the Christian that he has been accepted as one of God's children. Do not all Christians have Jehovah's holy spirit? Even Watch Tower publications admit that they do.

> **...the holy spirit is available** both to Christ's "little flock" and **to his "other sheep."**[25]

---

24. w16 January p. 19 "The Spirit Bears Witness With Our Spirit"
25. w11 12/15 p. 25 par. 12

## 7. Who Are the "Other Sheep"?

> They do not believe that they necessarily have **more holy spirit than** their companions of **the "other sheep" have**.[26]
>
> The **other sheep must also allow God's Word and his holy spirit** to purify, or sanctify, them.[27]
>
> Fundamentally, the answer is, yes, **faithful brothers and sisters of the other sheep class can share equally with anointed ones in receiving God's holy spirit**.[28]

Given that, let's examine this alleged "special token." What is it according to Scripture? In three places, the *New World Translation* speaks of a token, though it is never qualified as special in any way.

> But the one who guarantees that you and we belong to Christ and the one who anointed us is God. He has also put his seal on us and has given us the **token** of what is to come, that is, **the spirit**, in our hearts. (2 Corinthians 1:21, 22)
>
> Now the one who prepared us for this very thing is God, who gave us **the spirit as a token** of what is to come. (2 Corinthians 5:5)
>
> After you believed, you were sealed by means of him with the promised **holy spirit**, which is **a token** in advance of our inheritance, for the purpose of releasing God's own possession by a ransom, to his glorious praise. (Ephesians 1:14)

According to the dictionary, a token is:
1. a thing serving as a visible or tangible representation of a fact, quality, feeling, etc.
2. a voucher that can be exchanged for goods or services

So, the holy spirit is a token of our inheritance, which is eternal life as a Child of God.

For the holy spirit to be not just an ordinary token, but a *special token* as the Organization claims it is, it must be special holy spirit, but there's no such thing in Scripture. There is nothing to indicate that some Christians get the holy spirit (as a token) and others get special holy spirit (as a special token).

When we run all three of the NWT references to "token" through the 45 Bible versions available on biblehub.com, we find not a single one which renders the Greek word *arrabón* as "token." The

---

26. w09 6/15 p. 23 par. 15
27. w02 2/1 p. 21 par. 11
28. w96 6/15 p. 31

word can mean pledge, guarantee, or down payment. This guarantee or advance payment made by God is the holy spirit, which all Christians get. There is no special holy spirit, no special invitation advanced to some, but not others. The entire thing is a made-up teaching.

*Cherry Picking Romans 8:16*

Witnesses criticize Trinitarians for trying to support their doctrine by cherry picking ambiguous verses that seem to support their belief while ignoring the surrounding context. Is the Governing Body guilty of doing the same thing here? Let's find out. Let's read the context.

In the verses leading up to Romans 8:16, Paul makes a black-versus-white comparison between the flesh and the spirit. Let's read the context from Romans 8:5-13 and as we do, ask yourself how many options is Paul presenting to Christians?

> For those who are in accord with the flesh set their minds on the things of the flesh, but those in accord with the spirit on the things of the spirit. For **the minding of the flesh means death, but the minding of the spirit means life and peace**; because the minding of the flesh means enmity with God, for it is not under subjection to the law of God, nor, in fact, can it be. So those who are in harmony with the flesh cannot please God.
>
> However, YOU **are in harmony, not with the flesh, but with the spirit**, if God's spirit truly dwells in YOU. But if anyone does not have Christ's spirit, this one does not belong to him. But if Christ is in union with YOU, the body indeed is dead on account of sin, but the spirit is life on account of righteousness. If, now, the spirit of him that raised up Jesus from the dead dwells in YOU, he that raised up Christ Jesus from the dead will also make YOUR mortal bodies alive through his spirit that resides in YOU. So, then, brothers, we are under obligation, not to the flesh to live in accord with the flesh; for **if YOU live in accord with the flesh YOU are sure to die**; but **if YOU put the practices of the body to death by the spirit, YOU will live**. (Romans 8:5-13)

This is the power of exegesis—letting the Bible speak for itself. Here we see Paul offering two choices: Follow the leading of the flesh and die, or follow the leading of the spirit and live. Verse 9 makes it clear that those with the spirit belong to Christ, and in John 10:16, Jesus already told us that the other sheep belong to him. Since the holy spirit dwells in all Christians who are not minding the flesh, it is that spirit which verse 14 refers to when it drives the last nail into the coffin of Watch Tower reasoning:

> **For all who are led by God's spirit, these are God's sons.** (Romans 8:14)

*The Watchtower* (1987) claims that the Other Sheep are not God's sons, but only his friends.[29] It does this while acknowledging that they are led by God's spirit.

> Like David of old, elders, whether of the anointed or the "other sheep," pray to Jehovah: "Your spirit is good; may it lead me in the land of uprightness." (Psalm 143:10) And Jehovah hears their prayer. By means of his Son, **He grants them His spirit**, and Jesus uses this means actively to lead his disciples on earth.[30]

According to Paul in Romans, any Christian (which would include all members of the Other Sheep) who does not follow the spirit is following the flesh which leads to death. So, Other Sheep must be God's sons, because God's spirit leads them. There is no mention in any of Paul's writings of Other Sheep being called God's friends.

This distinction given to the Other Sheep is an invention of the Organization, going back to the days of Russell who believed they were a secondary heavenly class, which morphed into an non-anointed earthly class in Rutherford's day.[31]

## *More Evidence of Cherry-Picking Verses*

Evidence of the Organization's willingness to twist Scripture can be seen in the final part of paragraph 10 from the foregoing *Watchtower* reference:

> [10] ... He further states: "As for you, the anointing that you received from him remains in you, and **you do not need anyone to be teaching you**; but **the anointing from him is teaching you about all things** and is true and is no lie. Just as it has taught you, remain in union with him." (1 John 2:20, 27) **These ones need spiritual instruction just like everyone else.** But they do not

---

29. w12 7/15 p. 28 par. 7
30. w87 8/1 p. 19 par. 14
31. See "Rutherford Creates a Clergy Class" on page 232.

need anyone to validate their anointing. The most powerful force in the universe has given them this conviction!³²

It is astonishing how brazenly the publications can contradict Scripture. Here it is done from one sentence to the next. The Bible clearly says that the spirit anointing a Christian receives means that he has no need of being *taught by anyone,* but rather it is the spirit which teaches the Christian *all things*! Not some things, but *all things.*

However, the Governing Body denies this, writing that "these ones need spiritual instruction." Really? From whom? Other anointed ones?

I remember being told by a Circuit Overseer regarding direction from the Canada branch: "Remember, we don't instruct them. They instruct us!"

Thus, they would have us believe that when John tells us that the spirit anointing we receive as Christians *is teaching us all things*, what it really means is that it is validating our anointing. How does "teaching you about all things" devolve into one thing, the validation of our anointing?

Again, by cherry picking one verse, ignoring the context, and relying on us to be credulous enough to not read and ponder the context, they managed to convince us that their interpretation was valid. Consider now, the actual context from 1 John 2:18-27:

> Young children, it is the last hour, and, just as YOU have heard that antichrist is coming, even now there have come to be many antichrists; from which fact we gain the knowledge that it is the last hour. They went out from us, but they were not of our sort; for if they had been of our sort, they would have remained with us. But [they went out] that it might be shown up that not all are of our sort. And YOU have an anointing from the holy one; **all of YOU have knowledge**. I write YOU, not because YOU do not know the truth, but because YOU know it, and because no lie originates with the truth.
>
> Who is the liar if it is not the one that denies that Jesus is the Christ? This is the antichrist, the one that denies the Father and the Son. Everyone that denies the Son does not have the Father either. He that confesses the Son has the Father also. As for YOU, let that which YOU have heard from [the] beginning remain in YOU. If that which YOU have heard from [the] beginning remains

---

32. w16 January p. 19 par. 10b

in YOU, YOU will also abide in union with the Son and in union with the Father. Furthermore, this is the promised thing that he himself promised us, the life everlasting.
**These things I write YOU about those who are trying to mislead YOU.** And as for YOU, the anointing that YOU received from him remains in YOU, and YOU do not need anyone to be teaching YOU; but, as the anointing from him is teaching YOU about all things, and is true and is no lie, and just as it has taught YOU, remain in union with him. (1 John 2:18-27)

The validity of the spirit anointing is not in question here. What is of concern are the false teachings of the antichrist, but John assures his audience that they have the knowledge which was imparted to them by the spirit just as Jesus told them.

I have many things yet to say to YOU, but YOU are not able to bear them at present. However, when that one arrives, **the spirit of the truth, he will guide YOU into all the truth**, for he will not speak of his own impulse, but what things he hears he will speak, and he will declare to YOU the things coming. (John 16:12, 13)

So again, the Organization is ignoring the context, cherry picking a verse, and then giving it a peculiar interpretation that supports a false doctrine and relying on the trust of the JW community to take what they teach at face value, and not to verify as the Beroeans of Paul's day did, to see "whether these things were so."

### Shouldn't the Governing Body Be Instructing the Flock?

I know that some will counter here that we all need teachers, and that the Bible says that God gives some men the gift of teaching.[33] True, but Jesus also told us, "do not you be called Rabbi, for one is your Teacher, and all of you are brothers."[34]

How do we balance these two apparently contradictory statements? This is a topic we deal with in greater detail in "Chapter 13 Who Is the Faithful and Discreet Slave?"

However, to touch on it briefly, we all teach one another. I have some small reputation as a teacher, yet I am taught constantly by others who do not, in any way, consider themselves to be experienced teachers. We all have opportunities to help others to

---

33. Ephesians 4:11
34. Matthew 23:8

understand things, but in the end, it is the spirit that leads us to truth and protects us from falsehood. John warned the flock in his day against the antichrist[35]—likely gnostic teachers trying to infiltrate the Christian community with ideas that were pagan in origin. The protection the congregation had was that "all of you have knowledge."[36] The congregation acting as a whole, as the body of Christ, guided by the spirit into all the knowledge of God was able to protect itself from *false anointed ones*.

I was one of Jehovah's Witnesses into my sixth decade of life and I thought I had God's spirit, but it wasn't until I put down the publications of the Watch Tower Society and prayerfully started to read Scripture by itself that things started to slowly make sense. The Bible opened up to me, and I began to find answers to questions that had plagued me all my life. Others helped me to reason at times, but they too were speaking by spirit, so that the truth continued to unfold. When those who did not have the spirit tried to teach me, they eventually "went out from us" because "they were not of our sort," and I could see that what they taught was a lie.[37]

## Second "Proof": Matthew 25, The Sheep and Goats

Jesus gave his disciples several parables to prepare them for his impending departure to heaven. These are recorded in chapters 24 and 25 of the book of Matthew. The final parable is the famous one of the Sheep and Goats found at Matthew 25:31-46 which the Organization hijacks as a proof of the Other Sheep class.

There are three groups mentioned in this parable: 1) Jesus' brothers, 2) the sheep, and 3) the goats. The Governing Body interprets the identity of these three groups as follows:

- Jesus' brothers = anointed Jehovah's Witnesses
- The sheep = JW Other Sheep
- The goats = All non-JWs the world over.

---

35. It is noteworthy that Aramaic source manuscripts never say "antichrist," but rather "false anointed."
36. Ibid
37. 1 John 2:19

This interpretation makes the Other Sheep beholden to anointed Jehovah's Witnesses for their salvation as this 2012 *Watchtower* study article states:

> The other sheep should never forget that **their salvation depends on their active support of Christ's anointed "brothers" still on earth**. (Matt. 25:34-40) The anointed will enter into their reward, but the hope of the other sheep will just as certainly be fulfilled.[38]

According to the parable, the sheep are saved because of the acts of mercy they perform to alleviate the sufferings of Jesus' brothers. Therefore, the easy conclusion is that the sheep cannot be anointed brothers of Jesus and must therefore belong to a different non-anointed class of Christian.

There are a number of problems with this conclusion. The first is that it is inconsistent with the rest of Scripture. Nowhere in the Bible do we find a secondary group of Christians who are not anointed with holy spirit; who are depicted as outside of the New Covenant; who are excluded from the first resurrection; who are beholden to anointed Christians for their salvation; and who are not God's children, but only his friends.

Another problem with this interpretation is that it does not fit with what we know about our heavenly Father, Jehovah. Jesus is the perfect reflection of God's glory, the very image of his being.[39] Through his teaching and conduct while living as a human, Jesus revealed to us that God is love.[40] How does that square with the *Watchtower's* interpretation of who the goats are?

> The rest of mankind who did not respond favorably to the preaching work and offered no aid to those who carried the Kingdom message would be classed as "goats" and would go, not into a temporary death, but into "everlasting cutting-off" at the time when judgment is executed.[41]

It is one thing to kill those who actively oppose God and war against his people, but what the Organization is saying here is that everyone, even children and infants, will die eternally because they didn't respond favorably to the preaching work of

---

38. w12 3/15 p. 20 par. 2
39. Hebrews 1:3
40. 1 John 4:8, 16
41. w65 9/15 pp. 575-576

Jehovah's Witnesses. What about the hundreds of millions who have never even spoken with one of Jehovah's Witnesses?

One of the criticisms which Witnesses level against those who promote hellfire is that it blasphemes God's name by painting him as a monster who tortures people for all eternity just because they chose not to worship him. It appears that we can now paint Jehovah's Witnesses with the very same brush: Blasphemers who denigrate God's good name by claiming he kills people for all eternity, just because they don't respond to a message that many of them never even get.

**Parable or Prophecy?**

We must bear in mind that this is a parable, not a prophecy. A parable is defined as "a usually short fictitious story that illustrates a moral attitude or a religious principle."[42]

The mistake which countless religious scholars have made is to treat this particular parable as if it were a prophecy. A "short *fictitious* story" is not a prophecy. True, a parable may relate to some prophetic event, but its purpose isn't to foretell specifics about future events, but rather to teach us a valuable moral lesson relating to those events. The Organization has found it convenient to overlook that fact. By converting this into a prophecy, they seek to find scriptural support for their Other Sheep doctrine. But as we'll see, such support is entirely lacking.

As a result of their efforts to interpret it prophetically instead of morally, they have been forced to make multiple changes to their interpretation of this parable over its 140-year history.[43]

Because a parable is a means to illustrate a truth, it doesn't have to strictly conform to real world events. For instance, there are four parables listed consecutively right after Jesus finishes speaking of his coming presence or advent. These are:

- The parable of the Faithful and Evil Slaves
- The parable of the Talents
- The parable of the Ten Virgins
- The parable of the Sheep and Goats

---

42. Merriam-Webster
43. dx86-17 "Sheep and Goats (Illustration)" lists changes in these years: 1881, 1884, 1925, and 1995.

All these parables are given within the context of Jesus' prophecy regarding his future arrival as the Messianic King. So, each teaches us some moral lesson or Bible principle pertaining to his return as King. A clue to identifying the three groups depicted in the Sheep and Goats parable can be found by examining two other parables in this list.

## The Faithful and Discreet Slave and the Evil Slave

There are three groups depicted in this parable: 1) the faithful slave, 2) the evil slave, and 3) the domestics. Nevertheless, all three groups refer to Jesus' disciples from different points of view: The faithful and discreet slave represents all the disciples who faithfully feed each other with nourishment from Christ's teachings. The evil slave represents the disciples who abuse their place in the congregation and take advantage of their fellow Christians. The domestics represent all the disciples collectively.[44]

The moral of this parable is that to win the prize, one must labor on behalf of one's brothers and sisters feeding them spiritual food "at the proper time," meaning they must provide spiritual support when needed. This ties in with the message behind the Sheep and Goats parable as we'll soon see.

## The Ten Virgins

In the days of Jesus, an Israelite bridegroom would go to the home of his bride's parents with a bridal procession and then conduct her from there to his house. Because this was done at night, and since there was no street lighting in those days, virgins would be waiting for the procession with lamps to light the way. They couldn't know when the bride and bridegroom would arrive, so they had to be prepared with enough oil to keep their lamps burning far into the night.

In this parable, there are five virgins who were wise and had enough oil to keep their lamps burning, and five who were foolish and didn't bring enough oil. The foolish virgins were caught unawares when the bride and bridegroom finally showed up, and so had to leave to purchase more oil, and by the time they

---

44. For the parable of the Faithful and Discreet Slave, see Matthew 24:45-51 and Luke 12:41-48. For a full discussion of this parable, see Chapter 12, "Who Is the Faithful and Discreet Slave?" on page 293.

got back, the doors were closed, and they weren't allowed into the bridal celebration.

So, the point is a moral one. Jesus' disciples have to be prepared and alert and keep their senses about them, because they can't know when he will return to marry his bride which is the anointed Christian congregation.[45]

We have no problem with this as a parable, but if we try to turn it into a prophecy, as Witnesses do with the Sheep and Goats parable, we get into problems. The bride in the bridal procession is made up of Jesus' disciples, or his brothers. So how can the virgins also be his disciples? That makes no sense. But as a parable, this is not a problem, since it's only relating to being spiritually awake and waiting for Jesus to arrive.

## Making Sense of the Sheep and Goats Parable

The two parables we've covered so far are meant for you and me personally. When Jesus arrives, will he call you one of his faithful and discreet slaves, or will he dismiss you from his household as an evil slave? When Jesus comes to marry his bride, will you be awake and prepared and so be able to enter the feast, or will you be caught unawares and miss out? Each group depicted in each parable refers to Jesus' disciples, but you and I can only be in one group individually, so which group will we be in? That's the moral lesson our Lord is teaching us.

These parables recorded by Matthew in chapter 24 and 25 all follow a similar pattern, so let's consider the final parable—the Sheep and Goats—within that contextual pattern.

The faithful and evil slaves both come from within the disciples of Christ. In other words, both groups start out as Christ's brothers but only one group remains as his brothers in the end. The choices they make determine whether they win the reward of life.

Similarly, the five wise virgins, the five foolish virgins, and the bride of Christ are also made up of Christ's brothers. The bride is made up of Christ's brothers who are represented as having won the reward. So, the bride is not mentioned in the parable, but only implied. The parable is about getting to be that bride and

---

45. 2 Corinthians 11:2; Ephesians 5:22-27; Revelation 21:2, 9

winning life in the Kingdom of God. The ten virgins represent all Christians—Christ's brothers—but the choices they make determine whether they win the reward or are left out in the cold.

In a similar way, could the brothers of Christ in the parable of the Sheep and Goats represent all Christians who win the reward, just as the bride in the parable of the Ten Virgins represents the brothers of Christ after they've won the reward of life?

If the five foolish virgins start out as Christ's brothers and lose their reward of being with him in the Kingdom by the choices they make, could not the goats also start out as Christ's brothers and lose out on life by making similar bad choices?

And if the five wise virgins start out as Christ's brothers and remain so, winning the reward of life by making good choices, could not the sheep do the same?

In the parable of the Ten Virgins, the moral is that if you want to win the reward of life, you have to stay awake, alert, and guard your oil—the thing that allows you to shine as luminaries in the darkness of this world.

In the parable of the Sheep and Goats, the moral is that if you want to get everlasting life, you have to be merciful.

If we accept that reasoning, then we can resolve all the problems that the JW interpretation of the Sheep and Goats creates and which the publications choose to ignore. What problems are these?

Let's begin with verse 34 which reads:

> Then the King will say to those on his right: 'Come, you who have been blessed by my Father, inherit the Kingdom **prepared for you from the founding of the world**. (Matthew 25:34)

According to the theology of the Watch Tower, the sheep are subjects of the Kingdom. Subjects do not inherit the Kingdom. Only the kings and princes, i.e., royalty, inherit the Kingdom. That is why Jesus rebuked Peter for his impulsive answer in the affirmative to the question, "Does YOUR teacher not pay the two drachmas [tax]?"[46] In his answer, Jesus clarifies something important for us to understand when we consider who really *inherits* the Kingdom.

---

46. Matthew 17:24

However, when he entered the house Jesus got ahead of him by saying: "What do you think, Simon? From whom do the kings of the earth receive duties or head tax? From their sons or from the strangers?" When he said: "From the strangers," Jesus said to him: "Really, then, the sons are tax-free." (Matthew 17:25, 26)

The sons of the King inherit the kingdom, but not his subjects, nor his friends. Yet, the Organization teaches that the Other Sheep inherit the kingdom as God's friends, not his sons.

There is more.

The phrase Jesus uses in Matthew 25:34 referring to the sheep is: "Inherit the Kingdom prepared for you from *the founding of the world.*"

Where else do we find that phraseology in Scripture? It is telling that the *New World Translation* of 2013 has removed all the cross references to this verse found in the 1984 version, many of which point not to any Other Sheep class, but to the Children of God. Even in that older version, the key reference which would shed light on who is being referred to as sheep is missing. Here it is:

> Blessed be the God and Father of our Lord Jesus Christ, for he has blessed us with every spiritual blessing in the heavenly places in union with Christ, 4 just as **he chose us in union with him before the founding of the world**, that we should be holy and without blemish before him in love. For **he foreordained us to the adoption through Jesus Christ as sons** to himself..." (Ephesians 1:3-5)

"He chose us...before the founding of the world," and "he foreordained us to the adoption...as sons." See how nicely that ties in with "inherit the Kingdom prepared for you from the founding of the world"?

*The Watchtower* of 2010 makes the claim that the Other Sheep do inherit the Kingdom as shown here:

> Christ's "other sheep," who are striving to receive a blessing for themselves by means of Abraham's seed, will delight to hear Him say: "Come, you who have been blessed by my Father, inherit the kingdom prepared for you from the founding of the world."[47]

The Governing Body provides no scriptural evidence to back this up. How can we act like the ancient Beroeans and check to see if these things are so if they don't give us the scriptures to do

---

47. w10 9/15 p. 11 par. 18

that?[48] Well, we can see what the Scriptures actually say about inheritance. For example, these words of Paul to the Romans:

> **If, then, we are children, we are also heirs**: heirs indeed of God, but joint heirs with Christ, provided we suffer together that we may also be glorified together." (Romans 8:17)

Christ inherits the Kingdom. His brothers, as Children of God, are his joint heirs. The sheep of the parable inherit the Kingdom. Ergo, the sheep are Christ's brothers. Further evidence comes from Paul's statement to the Corinthians:

> However, this I say, brothers, that **flesh and blood cannot inherit God's kingdom**, neither does corruption inherit incorruption. (1 Corinthians 15:50)

If the sheep of the Sheep and Goats parable are the Other Sheep which Jehovah's Witnesses claim live as human subjects of the Kingdom, then they cannot inherit the Kingdom, because they are of flesh and blood.

Notice also that verse 46 says that these sheep inherit everlasting life. The JW Other Sheep do not inherit everlasting life according to Watch Tower theology. All they get is a chance at life, a chance they could still lose if they don't maintain their faith throughout the thousand-year reign of Christ.[49]

So far, nothing about this parable fits with the Witness interpretation; and there is still more to consider.

## The Basis for Judgment

Before we get any deeper into this analysis, we need to review what criteria the King uses to judge the sheep and goats. Each individual is judged on whether he or she:

- gave food to the hungry,
- gave water to the thirsty,
- showed hospitality to a stranger,
- clothed the naked,
- cared for the sick,
- comforted those in prison.

---

48. Acts 17:11
49. w51 5/15 pp. 308-309 par. 9

Each of these is an act of mercy, a means to alleviate the suffering of a fellow human being.

During the latter half of the 20th century, the number of those claiming to be anointed Jehovah's Witnesses hovered at just over 10,000. How could a population of billions possibly have any opportunity of showing mercy to one of the anointed Witnesses when their number was so low and when they were clustered geographically within English-speaking nations? The publications try to get around that problem by claiming these six elements represent the response people show to the preaching work.

Let's see if there is any basis to accept this understanding.

According to a 2015 *Watchtower*:

> The Watch Tower of October 15, 1923...presented **sound Scriptural arguments** that limited the identity of Christ's brothers to those who would rule with him in heaven, and it described the sheep as those who hope to live on earth under the rule of Christ's Kingdom.[50]

One has to wonder why these "sound Scriptural arguments" are not reproduced in this 2015 article. Alas, the October 15, 1923 issue of *The Watchtower* has not been included in the *Watchtower Library* program, and Kingdom Halls were ordered to remove all old publications many years ago, so there is no way for the average Jehovah's Witness to verify what these "sound Scriptural arguments" are unless he or she wishes to flout the direction of the Governing Body and go on the internet to research this. But a love of truth will not be intimidated by prohibitions which some men throw up to hide the truth. The old publications of the Organization have been converted to electronic files and are readily available on the internet for download.[51] So let's have a look at the 1923 *Watchtower* to read these "sound Scriptural arguments" for ourselves:

> To whom, then, do the symbols sheep and goats apply? We answer: Sheep represent all the peoples of the nations, not spirit-begotten but disposed toward righteousness, who mentally acknowledge Jesus Christ as the Lord and who are looking for and hoping for a better time under his reign. Goats represent all that class who

---

50. w15 03/15 p. 26 par. 5
51. One useful resource for public and private Watch Tower Society publications and documentation is avoidjw.org.

claim to be Christians, but who do not acknowledge Christ as the great Redeemer and King of Mankind, but claim that the present evil order of things on this earth constitutes Christ's kingdom.[52]

One would suppose that "sound Scriptural arguments" would include…I don't know…scriptures? Apparently not. Perhaps this is merely the result of slipshod research and overconfidence by the writer of the 2015 article. Or perhaps it is indicative of something more disturbing. Whatever the case, there is no excuse for misleading eight million faithful readers by telling them that one's teaching is based on the Bible when, in fact, it is not.

Of course, when that October 1923 issue of *The Watchtower* was first published, the Bible Students were being misled by Judge Rutherford—the then-foremost member of the Faithful and Discreet Slave according to the current doctrine—into believing that the end would come just two years later in 1925 starting with the resurrection of "ancient worthies" like Abraham, Moses, and King David. This was all part of the infamous "Millions Now Living Will Never Die!" preaching campaign.[53] So the pedigree of this *Watchtower*'s "sound scriptural reasoning" was never very high.

Paragraph 7 of the aforementioned March 2015 issue of *The Watchtower* goes on to assure the rank and file: "Today, we have a clear understanding of the illustration of the sheep and the goats."

A truly clear understanding of the parable would address all the issues we've just reviewed and provide credible, logical, and above all, scriptural answers to each and every one. This is not the case.

As further evidence of this, consider how the Organization interprets the six acts of mercy Jesus speaks of. How do the JW

---

52. w1923, page 309, par. 24
53. "Based upon the argument heretofore set forth, then, that the old order of things, the old world, is ending and is therefore passing away, and that the new order is coming in, and that 1925 shall mark the resurrection of the faithful worthies of old and the beginning of reconstruction, if is reasonable to conclude that millions of people now on the earth will still be on the earth in 1925. Then, based upon the promises set forth in the divine Word, we must reach the positive and indisputable conclusion that millions now living will never die." *Millions Now Living Will Never Die!* p. 97

Other Sheep provide for anointed Jehovah's Witnesses by quenching their thirst, feeding them when they are hungry, sheltering them when they are alone, clothing them when they are naked, nursing them when sick, and supporting them in prison? Bear in mind that these six acts of mercy apply to all so-called anointed Jehovah's Witnesses.

The answer the Organization provides is:

> The growing number of prospective sheep count it a privilege to support Christ's brothers not only in the preaching work but also in other practical ways. For example, they give financial contributions and help to build Kingdom Halls, Assembly Halls, and branch facilities, and they loyally obey those appointed by "the faithful and discreet slave" to take the lead.[54]

This means that—again, according to the teaching of the Organization—billions of humans are going to die forever, judged as goats by Jesus because they never supported the preaching work of Jehovah's Witnesses. Since there are currently hundreds of millions, if not billions, who have never been exposed to the preaching work of Jehovah's Witnesses, doesn't that make Jesus into a cruel and heartless judge?

**Mercy Triumphs Over Judgment**

Rather than put a spin on the six acts of mercy that Jesus lists, why not take them at face value? He is speaking about acts of kindness, actions intended to lighten the suffering of another. What is the basis for judgment according to Scripture? James tells us:

> For the one that does not practice mercy will have [his] judgment without mercy. **Mercy exults triumphantly over judgment**. (James 2:13)

The goats of the parable have access to the brothers of Christ (their fellow Christians) and yet do not extend mercy to them. Therefore, their judgment will be carried out without mercy.

None of us can be declared innocent by being righteous within ourselves. We have all fallen short of the standard. We have to receive grace from God—Witnesses call it, "undeserved

---

54. w15 03/15 p. 29 par. 17

kindness"—which the Lord will extend if we have acted mercifully to others. Thus, "mercy exults triumphantly over judgment."

This is the moral lesson of the parable. **It has nothing to do with preaching the good news of the Watch Tower Corporation.**

## What Is the Moral Lesson of the Sheep and Goats Parable?

There is one more element that helps us to see how we can personally benefit from the moral lesson of this parable. It is the most important aspect of the parable, and it is vital for us to understand it because our salvation depends on making the right choice. Jesus rewards the sheep because, as he says:

> For I became hungry and you gave me something to eat; I was thirsty and you gave me something to drink. I was a stranger and you received me hospitably; naked and you clothed me. I fell sick and you looked after me. I was in prison and you visited me... (Matthew 25:35, 36)

He then condemns the goats for failing to act mercifully toward him:

> For I became hungry, but you gave me nothing to eat; and I was thirsty, but you gave me nothing to drink. I was a stranger, but you did not receive me hospitably; naked, but you did not clothe me; sick and in prison, but you did not look after me.' (Matthew 25:42, 43)

Both groups respond to these words by asking Jesus when it was that they ever saw him hungry, or thirsty, or homeless, or naked, or sick, or imprisoned?

His answer is that an act of mercy to one of his brothers is tantamount to an act of mercy toward him, and a failure to be merciful to one of his brothers is the same as if he were the one in need.

The fact that both the sheep and the goats know who Jesus is indicates that, like the other three parables in Matthew's account, we are dealing with Christians, not the unbelieving world. Additionally, Christians in all denominations are well aware of this parable. Jehovah's Witnesses certainly know it well.

So why would it come as such a shock to the righteous sheep and the unrighteous goats to learn that they were helping—or failing to help—Jesus' brothers? They all know the parable, and they all know who Jesus' brothers are...or do they?

The answer to that question comes from yet another parable of our Lord, the parable of the Wheat and Weeds found at Matthew 13:24-30 and 36-43. According to what Jesus says there, it is impossible even for God's holy angels to distinguish a righteous Christian from a false one until the time of the harvest. The wheat are Jesus' brothers whom he gathers into his storehouse after first gathering, bundling, and then burning, the weeds— false Christians.

With this knowledge, let's take one last look at the parable of the Sheep and Goats. What Jesus is rewarding are acts of mercy given willingly out of love for one's fellow, without even knowing whether there will be any compensation. There are more than two billion people on earth today claiming to be Christian. Some are strands of wheat, but a far greater number are weeds.[55] When we show mercy, it is not done out of motivated self-interest, because we don't know whether the one we are helping is considered by our Lord to be one of his brothers or not. James tells Christians:

> Of what benefit is it, my brothers, if a certain one says he has faith but he does not have works? That faith cannot save him, can it? If a brother or a sister is in a naked state and lacking the food sufficient for the day, yet a certain one of YOU says to them: "Go in peace, keep warm and well fed," but YOU do not give them the necessities for [their] body, of what benefit is it? Thus, too, faith, if it does not have works, is dead in itself. (James 2:14-17)

Am I suggesting that we only have to be kind and merciful to people who claim to be Christian? No. Christians are told to love even their enemies.[56] One of the foremost enemies of early Christianity was the Pharisee known as Saul of Tarsus. Jesus knew his heart and even while he was a persecutor of the Christian congregation, Jesus called him, and he was born of God.

> After that he [Jesus] appeared to James, then to all the apostles; but last of all he appeared also to me as if to **one born prematurely**. For I am the least of the apostles, and I am not fit to be called an apostle, because **I persecuted the congregation of God**. But by God's undeserved kindness I am what I am. And his undeserved kindness that was toward me did not prove to be in vain, but I

---

55. Matthew 7:13, 14
56. Matthew 5:44-48

labored in excess of them all, yet not I but the undeserved kindness of God that is with me. (1 Corinthians 15:7-10)

In short, we don't know, nor can we know, who are the Children of God, the brothers of Christ, so our mercy can't be constrained, just as God's mercy isn't restrained. We must imitate our heavenly Father who has set the bar for us saying:

> For, indeed, **while we were still weak, Christ died for ungodly men** at the appointed time. For hardly would anyone die for a righteous man; though perhaps for a good man someone may dare to die. But **God recommends his own love to us in that, while we were yet sinners, Christ died for us**. Much more, then, since we have now been declared righteous by his blood, will we be saved through him from wrath. For if **when we were enemies we became reconciled to God** through the death of his Son, how much more we will be saved by his life, now that we have become reconciled. (Romans 5:6-10)

If such mercy has been shown to us, how can we turn our backs on anyone suffering who is also in need of some little help? Water, when thirsty; food, when hungry; warm clothing, when naked; shelter, when homeless; tender care, when sick; emotional support, when imprisoned.

This same message is echoed in the letter to the Hebrews:

> Let YOUR brotherly love continue. Do not forget hospitality, for through it **some, unknown to themselves, entertained angels**. Keep in mind those in prison bonds as though YOU have been bound with them, and those being ill-treated, since YOU yourselves also are still in a body. (Hebrews 13:1-3)

This was the mindset of Christians in the first century. When Paul went to Jerusalem to consult with the apostles and elders of the congregation there, he came away with the following mandate:

> James and Cephas and John, the ones who seemed to be pillars, gave me and Barnabas the right hand of sharing together, that we should go to the nations, but they to those who are circumcised. **Only we should keep the poor in mind.** This very thing I have also earnestly endeavored to do. (Galatians 2:9, 10)

Paul and Barnabas were to preach to the Gentiles while those other men would attend to the Jews. But they had this in common as Paul writes: *"Only we should keep the poor in mind."* There is evidence that this is precisely what they did. We know that the congregations made it part of their worship to care for widows and orphans.[57]

Such charitable works aren't part of the formal worship of Jehovah's Witnesses. I know from firsthand experience that congregations are counseled not to make formal arrangements for caring for the needy in their congregation, and those who are individually contributing time and money to local charitable activities outside of the congregation are discouraged from doing so.[58]

## Applying the Sheep and Goats Parable to Our Salvation

The message of the parable of the Sheep and Goats has nothing to do with the preaching work of Jehovah's Witnesses. It has everything to do with your salvation and mine because our being considered by Jesus as one of his sheep depends on our acts of mercy toward his brothers, our fellow Christians. If we are not merciful, then our judgment will be made without mercy. None of us truly wants that.

This is how the parable is meant to be applied: Since the sheep go off into eternal life inheriting the Kingdom the same as Christ's brothers, the sheep must also be Christ's brothers. As in the parable of the Ten Virgins, we are looking at Christ's brothers from two points of view. The five wise virgins are Christ's brothers before the marriage, and the bride of Christ are his brothers after getting their reward. Similarly, the sheep are Christ's brothers who have shown mercy to others while on this earth, and "Christ's brothers" in the Sheep and Goats parable, are Christians having received their reward. Same group, but from two different viewpoints.

Each of the four parables Matthew relates have to do with the time of Christ's arrival to settle accounts.

If we are to be considered as one of Christ's brothers, then our distinctive characteristic must be love, and mercy is a outward manifestation of love.

---

57. 1 Timothy 5:8-10; James 1:27
58. If there are needy ones in the congregation, it's okay for individuals to help out, but the elder body is not allowed to formalize the help at the congregation level. Such monies can only be managed by the Organization.

In fact, mercy combines the four cardinal qualities of God: Love, Wisdom, Justice, and Power.

An act of mercy is a response to the suffering of another. Love motivates us to act. Our wisdom guides us on how best to act. Our sense of justice keeps us from acting in a way that violates God's law. Our power provides the means to act.

## One Last Word

There is one final revelation to be extracted from this parable: It can only work if there is no such thing as an "approved" religion. The wheat—the children of God—are to be found growing everywhere in the field which is the world.[59] If there were a true religion, then the parable of the Wheat and Weeds would make no sense, since the angels would know well beforehand who are the wheat. They would be the members of the religion that Jesus approves of. Neither of the two parables—the Wheat and Weeds, and the Sheep and Goats—can work if Jesus has already declared a particular organized religion to be approved. Both parables depend on the element of anonymity. Only the Lord knows who his brothers are.

The message Christ is communicating to us in the parable of the Sheep and Goats is that if we want to get everlasting life, we must show love to those in need. Mercy is love in action—a response to need and suffering. It is an effort made to alleviate the pain of another. The Organization of Jehovah's Witnesses has highjacked this beautiful message to support their own theology that creates a fictitious secondary class of Christian with a lesser salvation hope. In doing so, they have also subverted the parables' fundamental message of mercy. Acts of mercy have been replaced with sacrifices made on behalf of the Organization. Ask yourself, if you are or were one of Jehovah's Witnesses, how many times have you bypassed the home of a JW widow, or a needy family, or a sick publisher, so that you could get your monthly quota of service time? The preaching work takes first place over helping the widows and orphans that James speaks of.[60] Donating to the Organization takes first place over any local charitable works.

---

59. Matthew 13:36-38
60. James 1:27

## What the Truth About the Other Sheep Means for You

I think it is very clear to any reasonable Bible student that the other sheep of John 10:16 does not refer to a secondary class of Christian made up of non-anointed Jehovah's Witnesses. Jesus was clearly referring to the Gentiles who would also join the Christian flock only three and a half years after his death.

My ancestry is a mix of part Scots and part Irish making me a Gentile. In other words, I'm a member of the other sheep that Jesus referred to. When I first learned that I could be one of the other sheep and at the same time accept the offer of the holy spirit to become an adopted Child of God, I rejoiced. When I shared this information with my late wife, Reta, her reaction was different. To my surprise, she broke down into tears. She had dreamed of spending eternity with me on the paradise earth that the Organization had promised her would be her reward for a lifetime of faithful service. She'd envisioned our life together, returning to youth and physical perfection and raising a family of our own. Now that was all gone. Or was it?

Does being the first fruits bought from Mankind as Revelation 14:4 says mean we miss out on being human? Are we giving up on precious things to be part of the first resurrection to life?[61] Before jumping to conclusions, bear in mind that if the Organization can be wrong about the hope of the other sheep, they hardly have the credentials to speak with authority on the hope of the Children of God. In fact, as we are about to see in the next chapter, they've got it all wrong.

---

61. Revelation 20:4-15

# 8

# The Salvation Hope of the 144,000 and the Great Crowd

> *So, if any one of YOU is lacking in wisdom, let him keep on asking God, for he gives generously to all and without reproaching; and it will be given him. 6 But let him keep on asking in faith, not doubting at all, for he who doubts is like a wave of the sea driven by the wind and blown about.*
> *(James 1:5, 6)*

Before proceeding further, we should pause and do our best to address the roadblocks to this discussion which are bound to come up due to years of steady indoctrination from meeting parts and convention talks. Any discussion with Jehovah's Witnesses about the resurrection always seems to end up focusing on location. Most churches teach that the good go to heaven and the bad go to hell. In contrast with this traditional view, Jehovah's Witnesses are taught that only 144,000 go to heaven while everyone else, both righteous and unrighteous will live on earth. They have been trained to look forward to living on a paradise earth, frolicking with lions and tigers, and occupying the mansions of rich people who will have been destroyed at Armageddon.

I can't count the number of times someone in a car group out in the preaching work has commented on the beauty of a home they had just visited and remarked how they'd love to live there after Armageddon. The irony is that the Organization constantly counsels Witnesses to avoid the snare of materialism. It does this while invoking images of a material paradise. It can be argued that Jehovah's Witnesses can be just as materialistic as everyone else, but their materialism is one of delayed gratification.

On the one hand, they are taught that anointed Jehovah's Witnesses will go to heaven when they die, never to be seen again, while the majority of Witnesses will either survive Armageddon, or if they die before the end, will be resurrected to live as humans on earth with their youth and vitality restored, and their bodies freed from every defect. With such a view, they really have no desire to be part of the first resurrection, to be with Jesus, to serve as kings and priests for the restoration of humankind. If you contrast the cold unknown of life as a spirit far off in heaven with the warm embrace of a paradise earth with all the pleasures a human can enjoy, it is only natural that they would find no appeal to the offer of being one of the anointed.

## Salvation Is Not About Location

If we are going to do justice to the provision God has made to Christians through His Son, we have to rid ourselves of all such notions. We can't assume the anointed go off into heaven never to be seen again. We can't even assume the earth will be a paradise during the thousand-year reign of Christ. We must allow the Bible to reveal all things to us in due course as we study its words, letting it unfold truth at a pace we can absorb. I am reminded of Jesus' parting words to his disciples shortly before ascending to heaven himself: "I still have many things to say to you, but you are not able to bear them now."[1]

One thing we should bear in mind as we move forward with this study is that our heavenly Father loves us. He has wondrous things in store for those whom he loves. The Bible tells us that,

> For the creation is waiting with eager expectation for the revealing of the sons of God. For the creation was subjected to futility, not by its own will, but through the one who subjected it, on the basis of hope that **the creation itself will also be set free from enslavement to corruption and have the glorious freedom of the children of God.** (Romans 8:19-21)

---

1. John 16:12

Whatever our loving Father has in store for us will surely surpass anything we can imagine.

## 144,000 – Literal or Symbolic?

According to Jehovah's Witnesses, only 144,000 will inherit the kingdom of the heavens. That means a different hope must exist for all the rest. They believe that when Jesus spoke of giving the kingdom to a *little flock* at Luke 12:32, he was speaking about the literal number of 144,000. Since the Bible doesn't specify that this number is literal and since the book of Revelation contains a series of symbol-filled visions given to the Apostle John, on what basis does the Governing Body claim that this particular number is literal and not also symbolic?

According to a "Questions From Readers" article in the September 1, 2004 issue of *The Watchtower*, there are two reasons for assuming the number is literal: The first from paragraph 5 of the article is that not all numbers in Revelation are symbolic. Some are literal. For instance, Revelation 21:14 speaks of "the twelve names of the twelve apostles of the Lamb." We know there were only twelve apostles, so we know that number must be literal.

This is a strawman argument. No one is suggesting that every number in Revelation is symbolic. Proving that one number is literal doesn't grant anyone the authority to simply pick a different number and claim it is also literal. What is our basis for determining that the number 12 used at Revelation 21:14 is not symbolic? That is simple to answer. We know it is a literal number because we can look elsewhere in Scripture and find the number of the apostles represented literally. At Matthew 10:2-4 we are not only given the number, but the names of all twelve as well.[2]

Such shallow reasoning doesn't bode well for the scholarship of the Governing Body as we consider the second reason *The Watchtower* puts forward for belief in a literal number of anointed.

---

2. When Judas betrayed Jesus and then committed suicide, he lost his office as an apostle, but the number 12 was completed again when Matthias was named to his office. (Acts 1:15-26)

> Note, however, the contrast that John draws between verses 4 and 9 of Revelation chapter 7. He states that the first group, "those who were sealed," has a definite number. However, the second group, "a great crowd," is without a definite number. With that in mind, it is logical to take the number 144,000 to be literal. If the number 144,000 were symbolic and referred to a group that is actually numberless, the force of the contrast between those two verses would be lost. Thus, the context strongly indicates that the number 144,000 must be taken literally.[3]

It all boils down to this: The number must be literal, otherwise "the force of the contrast between those two verses [4 and 9] would be lost." Really!?

What if the contrast between the two groups isn't meant to be about number?

Did you notice in reading this passage in Revelation that John doesn't *see* the 144,000? He only hears their number.

> [4]And I **heard** the number of those who were sealed, 144,000, sealed out of every tribe of the sons of Israel:
>
> [9]After this I **saw**, and look! a great crowd, which no man was able to number, out of all nations and tribes and peoples and tongues, standing before the throne and before the Lamb, dressed in white robes; and there were palm branches in their hands. (Revelation 7:4, 9)

Could it be that these two groups depicted in verses 4 and then again in 9 are actually the same group presented from two different points of view? Could it be that he hears a number that symbolizes the governing character of the great crowd? According to the *Insight* book, "twelve ...seems to represent a complete, balanced, divinely constituted arrangement."[4] Before we explore this possibility, it would serve us well if we could establish scripturally that the number of those sealed is not a literal 144,000. Is there scriptural evidence to indicate that this number is symbolic? Indeed, there is.

## Bible Proof that 144,000 Is a Symbolic Number

Perhaps you've watched a police procedural on TV where the officers focus on one suspect and get tunnel vision. They are so sure

---

3. w04 9/1 p. 30 "Questions From Readers"
4. it-2 p. 513

## 8. The Salvation Hope of the 144,000 and the Great Crowd 187

they have the bad guy in their sights that they don't look elsewhere, ignoring exculpatory evidence that he is innocent and leaving the real perpetrator free to commit more crimes.

I was so trusting in the weak logic that Watch Tower publications employ to convince the flock that only 144,000 can hope to be anointed by God, that I failed to consider all the evidence. There is, in fact, one passage of Scripture that makes the idea of a literal number ridiculous. We find it in the book of Galatians.

> Tell me, you who want to be under law, Do you not hear the Law? For example, it is written that Abraham had two sons, one by the servant girl and one by the free woman; but the one by the servant girl was actually born through natural descent and the other by the free woman through a promise. **These things may be taken as a symbolic drama**; for these women mean **two covenants**, the one from Mount Sinai, which bears children for slavery and which is Hagar. Now Hagar means Sinai, a mountain in Arabia, and she corresponds with the Jerusalem today, for she is in slavery with her children. But the Jerusalem above is free, and she is our mother. (Galatians 4:21-26)

The free woman was Sarah, Abraham's wife, who gave birth to Isaac when she was 90 years old and well past child-bearing age. That miraculous birth was how Jehovah fulfilled his promise to Abraham that his descendants would be many and that through his seed or offspring, the nations would be blessed.[5]

This is a symbolic drama or to put it in JW parlance, a prophetic antitype. Paul knew, of course, that the Jews were descended from Sarah, not Hagar, but he is writing here in metaphor. Hagar was Sarah's Egyptian maidservant—the slave girl. Because Sarah was barren, she gave Hagar to Abraham as a wife so that he could have a son, and the slave girl bore him Ishmael.[6] Sarah's children came into a covenant relationship with God when Moses freed them from slavery in Egypt. Under that covenant, they could have become a kingdom of priests. If they had kept that covenant, they would have ruled with Jesus in the Messianic Kingdom to restore all humankind back into the family of God.[7]

---

5. Genesis 22:17, 18
6. Genesis 16:11
7. Exodus 19:3; Revelation 5:10; 22:1-5

But they didn't keep it and so belonged to the physical city of Jerusalem, being slaves of sin.

So, in this symbolic drama, Hagar the slave girl typified Jerusalem, and in a spiritual or symbolic sense, her children were the Israelites who rejected Jesus as the Messiah.

In contrast, the Jews and Gentiles who accepted Jesus and were anointed with holy spirit were free of sin. They belonged to the Jerusalem above. This is evident from this passage, but it is also the understanding put forward in the publications of the Organization:

> Yet the name Jerusalem continued to be used as symbolic of something greater than the earthly city. The apostle Paul, by divine inspiration, revealed that there is a "Jerusalem above," which he speaks of as **the "mother" of anointed Christians**. (it-2 p. 49 Jerusalem)

Now consider what Paul says next:

> For it is written: "Be glad, you barren woman who does not give birth; break into joyful shouting, you woman who does not have birth pains; **for the children of the desolate woman are more numerous than those of her who has the husband**." Now you, brothers, are children of the promise the same as Isaac was." (Galatians 4:27, 28)

The children of the desolate woman, Sarah, are anointed Christians. The children of the slave girl, Hagar, are the millions of Jews who rejected Jesus.

All of this is supported by the publications of Jehovah's Witnesses, so how is it that I overlooked the obvious contradiction this presents with the teaching that there can only be 144,000 anointed Christians? How can the children of the desolate woman be more numerous than the millions of Jews who were children of slavery if the number is limited to 144,000? The only way that makes sense is if we consider that 144,000 is a symbolic number.

## Enormous Consequences for a Literal Number

J. F. Rutherford taught that the 144,000 was a literal number. By taking this number to be literal, Rutherford, who was essentially a one-man governing body, created the current Other Sheep

## 8. The Salvation Hope of the 144,000 and the Great Crowd

doctrine back in 1934.[8] In other words, the entire reason for creating a secondary class of Christian with an earthly hope having none of the benefits of the first resurrection[9] was to account for the growing number of adherents who were exceeding the literal number of 144,000. If Rutherford had been led by holy spirit, then he'd have humbly acknowledged he'd got it wrong and, bowing to the evidence before him, would have abandoned his belief in a literal number. Instead, he did what false prophets do. He compounded his lie with an even bigger one, weaving an increasingly complex web of misinformation and false interpretations until we now have within the ranks of Jehovah's Witnesses, millions who willingly deny themselves access to the life-saving flesh and blood of our Lord symbolized by the emblems of bread and wine.

By supporting Rutherford's conclusion that the number is literal, the Governing Body of Jehovah's Witnesses continues to deny millions the salvation hope that Jesus offered to all those putting faith in him—the authority to become children of God and inherit the Kingdom of the heavens.[10] How closely the current Governing Body parallels the governing body of Israel about whom Jesus said:

> "Woe to you, scribes and Pharisees, hypocrites! because you shut up the Kingdom of the heavens before men; for you yourselves do not go in, neither do you permit those on their way in to go in." (Matthew 23:13)

It was for good reason that Jehovah tells his servants: "Do not put your trust in princes, nor in a son of man, who cannot bring salvation."[11]

If you continue to subscribe to the Other Sheep hope of Jehovah's Witnesses, you are putting your trust not in God, but in the interpretations of men, or more specifically, in one man: J. F. Rutherford, a man who seized power away from the Board of Directors of the Watch Tower Society in 1917 using tactics having

---

8. For a full analysis of the foundation for the Other Sheep doctrine, see Chapter 7, "Who Are the "Other Sheep"?" on page 143.
9. Revelation 20:4-6
10. John 1:12, 13
11. Psalm 146:3

nothing to do with the Christian personality, but everything in common with today's corporate world.[12]

## The Flaw in the Watch Tower Society's Logic

The reason that the logic put forward in the 2004 *Watchtower* is flawed is that it is based on several false premises. These are the interpretation the Organization gives to: 1) The identity of the great crowd, 2) the location of the great crowd, and 3) the meaning of the great tribulation.

One can hardly be expected to draw a sound conclusion when basing it on faulty assumptions. Let's not do that. Let's instead read the context. I would invite you to read the entire seventh chapter of Revelation, and it would be good to have an interlinear at hand. If you have access to the web, might I suggest you use a resource like biblehub.com as they provide hyperlinks to an interlinear translation as well as several recognized Bible lexicons.

Notice that in Revelation 7:4, John says: "And *I heard* the number of those who were sealed..." but in verse 9 he says, "After this I saw, and look! a great crowd..." John didn't see 144,000. He only heard the number called out to him. When he turned to look, he saw an innumerable great crowd. Now, if we assume the number of 144,000 to be literal, it follows that the great crowd refers to a different group. But we've just seen from Paul's words to the Galatians that it cannot be literal. So, we come into this discussion with a scriptural fact: The number must be symbolic.

The Watch Tower Society acknowledges that there is only one heavenly hope. Far more important than that, the Bible establishes this without ambiguity:

> One body there is, and one spirit, just as you were called to **the one hope** of your calling; one Lord, one faith, one baptism; one God and Father of all, who is over all and through all and in all. (Ephesians 4:4-6)

Given that, if we can show that the great crowd are in heaven together with the 144,000, then we can deduce that we are

---

12. This is no empty assertion. The book, *Rutherford's Coup: The Watch Tower Succession Crisis of 1917 and Its Aftermath* (available on Amazon) provides overwhelming documented evidence that the takeover by Rutherford and his cronies was literally a corporate *coup de etat*.

reading about the same group, but from two different points of view.

## Identifying the Great Crowd

The publications refer to the "great crowd of other sheep" often, with this exact phrase appearing more than 300 times in their pages. It will likely surprise the average Witness to learn that not only does the phrase *never* occur in the Bible but that neither is there any scripture linking the other sheep of John 10:16 with the great crowd of Revelation 7:9. The relationship is entirely a construct of the Organization.

By linking the two groups together in this way, the publications have to explain how a crowd in heaven has no heavenly hope, but an earthly one. To do this, they explain that their appearance in heaven before the throne of God must be taken figuratively. Is there a basis for doing so?

Revelation 7:9, 10 depicts the throne of God, together with the Lamb [Jesus], the angels, the 24 elders, and the 4 living creatures. The publications do not argue that these ones are literally in heaven, literally before, around, and in the midst of the throne of God. Does that not make it likely that the great crowd is also literally there with the rest? But there is more. Verse 15 says that "they are rendering him sacred service day and night in his temple." The word rendered "temple" is *naos* in Greek. *Strong's Concordance* explains that this is "that part of the temple where God himself resides."[13] *Thayer's Greek Lexicon* agrees, stating it is "used of the temple at Jerusalem, but only of the sacred edifice (or sanctuary) itself, consisting of the Holy place and the Holy of holies (in classical Greek used of the sanctuary or cell of a temple , where the image of the god was placed...which is to be distinguished from...the whole temple, the entire consecrated enclosure; this distinction is observed also in the Bible."[14]

The Organization has an enormous investment in the teaching of the Other Sheep, making it virtually impossible for them to abandon it, even in the face of overwhelming scriptural evidence. Since the "great crowd of other sheep" is not considered

---

13. *Strong's Concordance*, #3485
14. biblehub.com/greek/3485.htm

to be a priestly class like the anointed are, the Governing Body must explain how these individuals can be depicted in the sanctuary where only the Levite priests were allowed to go. Their efforts to get around this very inconvenient fact say much about their true motivations. For instance, the *Revelation Climax* book states:

> The 24 elders and the anointed group of 144,000 are described as being "round about the throne" of Jehovah and "upon the [heavenly] Mount Zion." (Revelation 4:4; 14:1) The **great crowd is not a priestly class** and does not attain to that exalted position. True, it is later described at Revelation 7:15 as serving God "in his temple." But this temple does not refer to the inner sanctuary, the Most Holy. Rather, it is the earthly courtyard of God's spiritual temple. The Greek word *na·os'*, here translated "temple," **often conveys the broad sense of the entire edifice erected for Jehovah's worship**. Today, this is a spiritual structure that embraces both heaven and earth.[15]

The astute reader will quickly recognize that the sweeping statement that *naos* "often conveys...the entire edifice" of the temple with its courtyards is given without any references to support it. They are counting on the trusting credulity of the rank and file to accept this as gospel, but as we've just seen, this statement is patently false. There was a time they could and did get away with making such false statements, because few had the time to spend doing research in dusty libraries rummaging through volumes of printed matter in search of that one morsel of truth. That all changed by the turn of the century when the internet brought Bible research tools into the living rooms of the average person, together with search engines which could expose relevant facts within microseconds in response to just a few clicks of a mouse. Just as the printing press exposed many falsehoods taught in the Catholic Church by making the Bible readily available to the common Man, the internet has changed the playing field for the more studious among Jehovah's Witnesses who, in this instance, were not buying into the foregoing assertion from the 1988 edition of the book, *Revelation—Its Grand Climax at Hand*!

---

15. *Revelation Climax*, chap. 20 p. 124 par. 14

As we moved forward into the 21st century, studious JWs were forcing the Organization to revisit the issue, something they attempted to do in the May 1, 2002 issue of *The Watchtower*:

> Questions From Readers
>
> When John saw the "great crowd" rendering sacred service in Jehovah's temple, in which part of the temple were they doing this?—Revelation 7:9-15.
>
> It is reasonable to say that the great crowd worships Jehovah in one of the earthly courtyards of his great spiritual temple, specifically the one that corresponds with the outer courtyard of Solomon's temple.[16]

The article never goes on to explain why "it is reasonable to say that the great crowd worships Jehovah in one of the earthly courtyards." The rest of the article discusses the various courtyards of the various temples, apparently in an effort to cloud the issue and confuse the reader, because none of that is relevant to the question of what the "temple," *naos*, refers to. At one point, the article even states"

> In contrast, the Greek word (na·os') translated "temple" in John's vision of the great crowd is more specific. In the context of the Jerusalem temple, it usually refers to the Holy of Holies, the temple building, or the temple precincts. It is sometimes rendered "sanctuary."—Matthew 27:5, 51; Luke 1:9, 21; John 2:20.[17]

It is interesting that even the three scriptural references provided with that definition support the understanding that the "temple" of Revelation 7:15 refers to the Holy and Most Holy chambers, but not the temple courtyards.

Yet, the writer of the article ignores this evidence. He doesn't even attempt to explain it away. He simply restates the official position of the Organization, closing with a fabricated antitypical application to try to dodge the evidence that the great crowd are serving in a priestly capacity in God's temple.

> Members of the great crowd...are declared righteous with a view to becoming friends of God and of surviving the great tribulation. (James 2:23, 25) In many ways, they are like proselytes in Israel who submitted to the Law covenant and worshiped along with the Israelites.

---

16. w02 5/1 pp. 30-31 "Questions From Readers"
17. Ibid

> Of course, those proselytes did not serve in the inner courtyard, where the priests performed their duties. And members of the great crowd are not in the inner courtyard of Jehovah's great spiritual temple, which courtyard represents the condition of perfect, righteous human sonship of the members of Jehovah's "holy priesthood" while they are on earth. (1 Peter 2:5) But as the heavenly elder said to John, the great crowd really is in the temple, not outside the temple area in a kind of spiritual Court of the Gentiles. What a privilege that is! And how it highlights the need for each one to maintain spiritual and moral purity at all times![18]

Can you follow that? The question boils down to this: "Are members of the Great Crowd serving in the Holy of Holies where God resides and where only the priests can enter?"

By closing with a thought fog of irrelevant suppositions, the writer hopes the reader will think the Organization has won the argument and miss the fact that it never actually answered its "Question From Readers."

Given such evident duplicity, should we really be fixing our salvation hope on the interpretation of J. F. Rutherford and the current Governing Body as to the hope of the other sheep?

## Who Are the Great Crowd?

Since the Bible clearly places the *great crowd* in heaven, it is easy to assume that they are comprised of the anointed Children of God, those making up the first resurrection who will rule with Christ as kings and priests.[19] However, there's always a danger that we fail to consider whether the whole of the context supports any conclusion we might be drawing. Exegesis requires us to examine all the evidence and ensure that it all conforms to any understanding we might draw from Scripture. So, let's do that now by considering the context of Revelation 7:9-15 regarding the identity of the great crowd.

> After this I saw, and look! a great crowd, which no man was able to number, out of all nations and tribes and peoples and tongues, standing before the throne and before the Lamb, dressed in white robes; and there were palm branches in their hands. And they keep shouting with a loud voice, saying: "Salvation we owe

---

18. Ibid
19. Revelation 20:4-6; 5:10

## 8. The Salvation Hope of the 144,000 and the Great Crowd

to our God, who is seated on the throne, and to the Lamb....In response one of the elders said to me: "These who are dressed in the white robes, who are they and where did they come from?" So right away I said to him: "My lord, you are the one who knows." And he said to me: **"These are the ones who come out of the great tribulation**, and they have washed their robes and made them white in the blood of the Lamb. That is why they are before the throne of God, and they are rendering him sacred service day and night in his temple; and the One seated on the throne will spread his tent over them. (Revelation 7:9-15)

Let's examine the individual elements of this vision. These are people from all nations and tribes who are:
- Shouting they owe their salvation to God and Jesus,
- Holding palm branches,
- Standing before the throne,
- Dressed in white robes washed in the Lamb's blood,
- Coming out of the great tribulation,
- Rendering service in God's temple.

How would John have understood what he was seeing? To John, who was himself a Jew, "people out of all nations" would mean non-Jews or Gentiles, whereas people from every tribe could include the Jews who were divided into 13 tribes.[20]

What is the significance of the white robes? They are only mentioned in one other place in Revelation.

And when he opened the fifth seal, I saw underneath the altar the souls of those slaughtered because of the word of God and because of the witness work that they used to have. And they cried with a loud voice, saying: "Until when, Sovereign Lord holy and true, are you refraining from judging and avenging our blood upon those who dwell on the earth?" And **a white robe was given to each of them**; and they were told to rest a little while longer, until the number was filled also of their fellow slaves and their brothers who were about to be killed as they also had been. (Revelation 6:9-11)

These verses refer to the anointed children of God who are martyred for bearing witness about the Lord. Based on both accounts, it would appear that the white robes signify an approved

---

20. The thirteenth tribe was Levi, which received no allotment of land.

standing before God. They are justified for eternal life by God's grace.

As for the significance of the palm branches, the only other reference is found at John 12:12, 13 where the crowd is praising Jesus as the King of Israel who comes in God's name. The great crowd recognize Jesus as their King.

As we have already seen under previous subheadings, this great crowd is not only standing before the throne of God which is in heaven, but its members are depicted rendering God "sacred service day and night in his temple," representing the inner sanctuary or Most Holy chamber. Only the chosen ones, the children of God, are given the privilege to serve with Christ as both kings and priests before the throne of God in the heavens. Revelation 5:10 says of these ones that the Lord makes them into "a kingdom and priests to serve our God, and they will reign upon the earth."[21]

## Unifying the 144,000 with the Great Crowd

The Organization acknowledges that the 12 tribes listed in Revelation 7:5-8 are figurative or symbolic. For instance, there was no tribe of Joseph in Israel, as depicted in verse 8. The tribes of Dan and Ephraim are missing from the list, and the 13th tribe of Levi is included. So this is a symbolic listing. Out of each symbolic tribe, a symbolic number of individuals is extracted, exactly 12,000 from each tribe. Not a person more nor a person less; 12,000 on the nose. All this is obviously symbolic. Yet, for the Watch Tower Society, somehow when you add up these twelve symbolic numbers taken from twelve symbolic tribes, they suddenly morph into a literal number. What is the logic behind that?

We've already shown that the number 144,000 is symbolic, but why is Jesus using it here? As we read earlier, the number 12,

---

21. This rendering is from the *Berean Study Bible*. Virtually every translation on biblehub.com renders the Greek word *epi* as "on" or "upon". It appears that the *New World Translation* rendering of "over" might be in support of JW doctrine which does not consider the possibility that Jesus and the anointed will be physically present on earth during the millennium.

## 8. The Salvation Hope of the 144,000 and the Great Crowd

and multiples thereof, represent a complete, balanced, divinely constituted governmental arrangement.[22]

By summing up 12 symbolic numbers of 12,000 each, we must arrive at an equally symbolic number: 144,000, representing a large number of individuals participating in a "complete, balanced, divinely constituted governmental arrangement." What if John hears the symbolic number representing God's divine administration under Christ, but when he turns, he sees the reality, that this administration is made up of people out of "all nations and tribes [including the literal tribes of Israel] and peoples and tongues"?

Since the 144,000 are in heaven and the great crowd are also in heaven, and since there is only one heavenly hope, it follows that these verses are referring to the same group. In the first instance, the number John hears, but doesn't see, is how the Lord is demonstrating that this group is divinely arranged and is drawn from Jehovah's faithful servants. We know this because the body of Christ, the Christian congregation, is also called the "Israel of God."[23] By accepting Christ, both Jews and Gentiles become descendants of Abraham, spiritual Jews born of the free woman.

> You are all, in fact, sons of God through your faith in Christ Jesus. For all of you who were baptized into Christ have put on Christ. There is neither Jew nor Greek, there is neither slave nor freeman, there is neither male nor female, for you are all one in union with Christ Jesus. (Galatians 3:26-28)

Notice that the symbolic number of 12,000 is drawn from each of the 12 tribes. That means that only a small number are called out of each tribe. Not all claiming to be Christians are called to be priests and kings with Christ. This parallels what happened in Israel before Christ came. At Romans 9:27, Paul quoted from Isaiah saying, "Although the number of the sons of Israel may be as the sand of the sea, only the remnant will be saved." Likewise, while the billions who claim to be Christian are as the sands of the sea, only a remnant are called to be the Children of God. These are likened to wheat growing among the weeds.[24]

---

22. it-2 p. 513
23. Galatians 6:16
24. 1 John 3:1; Matthew 13:24-30, 36-43

So, throughout time, our heavenly Father has been drawing from out of Christendom or spiritual Israel, which is largely as apostate as was ancient Israel, a small group of humans the true sum of whom cannot be known; these are represented by a symbolic number of 144,000 indicating a large, balanced and divinely constituted administrative arrangement or government.

## JW.org Shuts up the Kingdom to Abraham, Isaac, Jacob, and the Prophets

We've just seen scriptural evidence to support the idea that the great crowd are anointed Children of God; but is their number limited to Christians, or does it include faithful pre-Christian servants of God dating all the way back to Abel?

That certainly would create problems for JW doctrine which contends that only 144,000 Christians are Children of God. How so? Because including pre-Christian servants of God would easily overwhelm the 144,000 limit!

It's difficult enough to imagine that less than 144,000 faithful Christian men and women were chosen and sealed by God during the first century of Christianity, let alone the intervening 1,900 years leading up to the formation of Jehovah's Witnesses in 1931. But to now think that in the thousands of years before Christ, there weren't enough faithful servants of God to fill and surpass that number is simply ludicrous.

So, to protect this teaching, the Governing Body has to get their flock to believe that none of the faithful men and women of old—including such towering figures as Moses, Deborah, and Daniel—share in the heavenly hope offered to Christians. To accomplish that task, they again press eisegesis into service by misapplying Jesus' expression at Matthew 11:11. Quoting from the JW publication, *Jesus—The Way* (2015):

> When John's disciples leave, Jesus assures the crowd that John is more than a prophet. He is "the messenger" of Jehovah prophesied about at Malachi 3:1. He is also the prophet Elijah, as foretold at Malachi 4:5, 6. Jesus explains: "Truly I say to you, among those born of women, there has not been raised up anyone greater than John the Baptist, but **a lesser person in the Kingdom of the heavens is greater than he is**."—Matthew 11:11.
>
> By saying that a lesser one in the Kingdom of the heavens is greater than John, **Jesus is showing that John will not be in the heavenly Kingdom.** John prepared the way for Jesus but dies

before Christ opens the way to heaven. (Hebrews 10:19, 20) **John is, though, a faithful prophet of God and will be an earthly subject of God's Kingdom.**[25]

Did you notice that Jesus doesn't specify what he meant when he spoke of "a lesser person in the Kingdom of the heavens" being greater than John the Baptist? Based on this verse alone, his words are open to interpretation. Anytime that the meaning of a passage of Scripture is unclear or ambiguous, we have to go elsewhere to resolve its meaning. But that doesn't work if you have an agenda, so the Governing Body simply makes the following categorical assertions.

> **Faithful servants of God in pre-Christian times, though not begotten as spiritual sons of God with heavenly hopes**, had God's spirit. (Judg. 6:34; 11:29; 14:6; 2 Sam. 23:2; 2 Tim. 3:16) John the Baptist, for example, was "filled with holy spirit"; yet he did not go to heaven, for Jesus said of him: "A lesser one in the kingdom of the heavens is greater than he is."—Matt. 11:11.[26]

> These princes will include all the men of faith from Abel on to John the Baptist. **Will none of these be in heaven? No.**[27]

These excerpts are yet another example of eisegesis—imposing one's interpretation onto a Bible verse, rather than letting the Bible speak for itself. You will recall from earlier chapters that we learned that the first rule when trying to determine the meaning of an ambiguous or cryptic verse is to discard any interpretation that conflicts with other parts of the Bible.

The Governing Body's interpretation of Matthew 11:11 is wrong, because we have clear proof that John the Baptist and other faithful prophets of old will be in the Kingdom of the Heavens from Jesus' words in Luke's gospel:

> There is where your weeping and the gnashing of your teeth will be, **when you see Abraham, Isaac, Jacob, and all the prophets in the Kingdom of God**, but you yourselves thrown outside. Furthermore, **people** will come from east and west and from north and south, and **will recline at the table in the Kingdom of God**. And look! there are those last who will be first, and there are those first who will be last." (Luke 13:28-30)

---

25. jy chap. 38 p. 96 pars. 6-7
26. g74 8/22 p. 28
27. g73 5/8 p. 7

Would the Governing Body agree that the reference to "the Kingdom of God" here refers to the heavenly hope of anointed Christians? Yes! Reading from *The Watchtower:*

> "Many" refers to people who begged to be let in after a door was shut and locked. These were "workers of unrighteousness" who did not qualify to be with **"Abraham and Isaac and Jacob and all the prophets in the kingdom of God."** The "many" had thought they would be first "in the kingdom of God," but they actually would be last, evidently meaning that they would not be in it at all.—Luke 13:18-30.
>
> **The context shows that Jesus was dealing with entry into God's heavenly Kingdom.** Jewish leaders back then had long enjoyed a privileged position, with access to God's Word. They felt that they were spiritually rich and were righteous in God's sight, in contrast with the common people, whom they held in low esteem. (John 9:24-34) Yet, Jesus said that tax collectors and harlots who accepted his message and repented could have God's approval.—Compare Matthew 21:23-32; Luke 16:14-31.
>
> **Common people who became Jesus' disciples were in line to be accepted as spiritual sons when the heavenly calling did open up at Pentecost 33 C.E.** (Hebrews 10:19, 20) Though vast multitudes heard Jesus, those who accepted him and later gained the **heavenly hope** were few.[28]

You might be scratching your head right now, wondering how they can say on the one hand that men like Abraham, Isaac, and Jacob, along with all the prophets don't have the heavenly hope, while on the other hand, admitting that Luke 12:32 refers to the heavenly hope when speaking of the Kingdom of God? If the Kingdom of God is the heavenly hope and "Abraham and Isaac and Jacob and all the prophets [are] in the kingdom of God," then "Abraham and Isaac and Jacob and all the prophets" have the heavenly hope. How can they get around that obvious conclusion? This is where eisegetical Bible research makes a mockery of itself and of all those who have naively trusted in the men teaching them *The Truth*.

The foregoing "Questions From Readers" concludes with:

> But **the little flock of spirit-begotten humans** receiving that reward **could be compared to Jacob** reclining at a table in heaven

---

28. w90 3/15 p. 31 "Questions From Readers"

## 8. The Salvation Hope of the 144,000 and the Great Crowd

with Jehovah (the Greater Abraham) and his Son (pictured by Isaac).

Do you see how they've twisted Scripture to cover over the plain truth being stated? If it is not readily obvious, let's look again at the verse they're trying to explain:

> There is where your weeping and the gnashing of your teeth will be, **when you see Abraham, Isaac, Jacob, and all the prophets in the Kingdom of God**, but you yourselves thrown outside. (Luke 13:28)

This verse has Jesus rebuking the Jewish leaders who think themselves righteous, but who will be thrown outside the Kingdom of God. But who will they see in the Kingdom of God? They will see all the prophets of old. What does *The Watchtower* say about that?

Nothing!

They make no attempt to explain how all the prophets of old can be seen in the Kingdom of God, which they acknowledge refers to the heavenly hope bestowed upon "the little flock of spirit-begotten humans." How can they say that when elsewhere they have categorically stated that the prophets before Christ only have an earthly hope? They can't! So, they choose to ignore it, and hope Jehovah's Witnesses will ignore it too.

But they still have to explain how Abraham, Isaac, and Jacob are in the Kingdom of God, when their official teaching is that those men do not have a heavenly hope.

This is where things get really silly.

Jesus doesn't mention that the wicked Jewish leaders will see a "little flock of spirit-begotten humans" as *The Watchtower* claims. He only mentions Abraham, Isaac, and Jacob, and of course, all the prophets. So, they now press an old standby into service: types and antitypes. They say that when Jesus says "Abraham," he really means "Jehovah," and when he says, "Isaac," he really means himself, and when he says "Jacob," he really means his "little flock of spirit-begotten humans"!? Huh?

Jesus Christ isn't speaking these words to Jehovah's Witnesses, but to the Jewish leaders who were opposing him. Those leaders believed the scripture that promised that the forefathers of the nation of Israel would make it into the Kingdom of God as would the faithful prophets. That Kingdom was promised to them for keeping the covenant God made with them through Moses.

Then Moses went up to the true God, and Jehovah called to him from the mountain, saying: "This is what you are to say to the house of Jacob and to tell the Israelites, 'You have seen for yourselves what I did to the Egyptians, in order to carry you on wings of eagles and bring you to myself. Now if you will strictly obey my voice and keep my covenant, you will certainly become my special property out of all peoples, for the whole earth belongs to me. **You will become to me a kingdom of priests and a holy nation.**' These are the words that you are to say to the Israelites." (Exodus 19:3-6)

This is the old covenant, the covenant that Jehovah made with the Israelites. If they had kept that covenant, then Jehovah would have kept his promise. They would have become a kingdom of priests. Was what Jehovah promised any different than the promise made through Christ for the new covenant which replaced the old? Peter shows that it wasn't. Quoting from Moses' words, but applying them to the Christian congregation, he writes:

> But you are "**a chosen race, a royal priesthood, a holy nation**, a people for special possession, that you should declare abroad the excellencies" of the One who called you out of darkness into his wonderful light. For you were once not a people, but now you are God's people; once you had not been shown mercy, but now you have received mercy. (1 Peter 2:9, 10)

The difference between the two covenants is the inclusion of the Gentiles. While the nation of Israel as a whole failed to keep the old covenant, a number of faithful men and women did keep it.[29] Jehovah is faithful and keeps his promises, so those faithful servants have the reward assured.

This is the message of Hebrews chapter 11:

> And yet all of these, although they received a favorable witness because of their faith, did not obtain the fulfillment of the

---

29. Jehovah did not make a covenant that was impossible for the Israelites to keep. Moses declares: "Now this commandment that I am commanding you today is not too difficult for you, nor is it beyond your reach. It is not in the heavens, so that you have to say, 'Who will ascend to the heavens and get it for us, so that we may hear it and observe it?' Nor is it on the other side of the sea, so that you have to say, 'Who will cross over to the other side of the sea and get it for us, so that we may hear it and observe it?' For the word is very near you, in your own mouth and in your own heart, so that you may do it." (Deuteronomy 30:11-14)

promise, because God had foreseen something better for us, **so that they might not be made perfect <u>apart from us</u>**. (Hebrews 11:39, 40)

This shows that the faithful pre-Christian servants gain the same reward—because they individually kept the covenant—as Christians receive.

Returning to the Watch Tower Society's attempt to support their 144,000 literal number, we are treated to an explanation that is completely nonsensical within the context of Jesus' prophetic pronouncement at Luke 13:28 to those wicked men, the Pharisees.

What can be said about teachers of the word of God who would go to such extremes to twist scripture to support their personal interpretation rather than let the Bible mean what it says?

Such preposterous reasoning is now so obvious to me that I wonder how I missed it for so long. There is a saying that goes: "Fool me once, shame on you. Fool me twice, shame on me." But what can be said about being fooled hundreds and thousands of times for years and years?!

All I can say is praise the Lord for his mercy in finally helping me, poor fool that I was, to see the light of truth!

## What Did Jesus Mean About John the Baptist Being a Lesser One?

Now that we have the powerful Bible research tool that is exegesis and now that we are open to the spirit and not bound to support the dogma of men, let us re-examine the context of Jesus' words concerning John the Baptist:

> While these were on their way, Jesus began to speak to the crowds about John: "What did you go out into the wilderness to see? A reed being tossed by the wind? What, then, did you go out to see? A man dressed in soft garments? Why, those wearing soft garments are in the houses of kings. Really, then, why did you go out? **To see a prophet? Yes, I tell you, and far more than a prophet**. This is the one about whom it is written: 'Look! I am sending **my messenger** ahead of you, **who will prepare your way ahead of you!**' Truly I say to you, among those born of women, there has not been raised up anyone greater than John the Baptist, but a lesser person in the Kingdom of the heavens is greater than he is. From the days of John the Baptist until now, the Kingdom of the heavens is the goal toward which men press, and those pressing forward are seizing it. For all, the Prophets and the Law,

prophesied until John; and if you are willing to accept it, he is 'Elijah who is to come.' Let the one who has ears listen. (Matthew 11:7-15)

Jesus ends his counsel regarding John by exhorting his listeners to listen, to pay attention, to discern the significance of what he has said, because it affects them. He opens in the first three verses by asking them what they went out into the wilderness to find. They saw John as a prophet, but now Jesus tells them he is much more than a prophet. He is God's messenger. So it is within that context that his next words must be taken. When he says that "there has not been raised up anyone greater than John the Baptist," he is putting John above all other prophets, including the greatest of them, Moses! That must have been a stunning declaration for his Jewish listeners to hear.

How could John be greater than Moses, who was used to lead the people to freedom out of Egypt, bringing forth the ten plagues, and splitting the Red Sea by the power of God working through him? The answer was because something greater than Moses and all the prophets had arrived. The Son of God had come, and John was the messenger preparing the way for him. John introduced the King of the Kingdom of God. In verse 12, Jesus says that all before him has been pressing forward toward the goal which is the Kingdom, but now the Kingdom had arrived.

So it is within that context that we must view his words that "a lesser person in the Kingdom of the heavens is greater than" John. Nothing in the context speaks to John's salvation hope, but rather his role as both the prophet and the messenger announcing the Messianic King.

> The next day he beheld Jesus coming toward him, and he said: **"See, the Lamb of God that takes away the sin of the world!** This is the one about whom I said, Behind me there comes a man who has advanced in front of me, because he existed before me. Even I did not know him, but **the reason why I came baptizing in water was that he might be made manifest to Israel."** (John 1:29-31)

How is it then that this great prophet, John the Baptist, is less than the least one of those in the Kingdom of the heavens? Consider his own words for our answer:

> Whoever has the bride is the bridegroom. But the friend of the bridegroom, when he stands and hears him, has a great deal of joy on account of the voice of the bridegroom. So my joy has been

## 8. The Salvation Hope of the 144,000 and the Great Crowd

made complete. **That one must keep on increasing, but I must keep on decreasing.**" (John 3:29, 30)

Is the friend of the bridegroom greater or even equal to the Bride? Remember, within the context of Jesus' words at Matthew 11:7-15, we are not speaking of salvation, but of the work each one does. John prophesied, which in Greek means to speak forth God's words. But he did not preach the Kingdom. Jesus preached the Kingdom, and his followers after him. John preached the King. He introduced the King and then he decreased while Jesus increased.

Jesus did greater works than John.

> But **I have the witness greater than that of John,** for the very works that my Father assigned me to accomplish, the works themselves that I am doing, bear witness about me that the Father dispatched me. (John 5:36)

But Jesus' followers would do greater works even than Jesus:

> Most truly I say to YOU, He that exercises faith in me, that one also will do the works that I do; and **he will do works greater than these**, because I am going my way to the Father. (John 14:12)

So, the chain of logic is evident: The prophets of old were surpassed by John not because he had a different salvation hope as the Organization claims, but because his work as a prophet surpassed theirs. He announced the King of God's Kingdom. They didn't. But that King, Jesus, did works greater than John because he preached the Kingdom of God. Jesus' disciples also preached the Kingdom and surpassed Jesus, according to his own words. Therefore, the lesser one in the Kingdom of the heavens does greater works than John.

It is wrong to teach, as the Governing Body does, that Jesus' words about John the Baptist relate to his salvation hope, and that of all pre-Christian men and women of faith. If John being less than a lesser one in the Kingdom of the heavens means he gets a lesser salvation hope, then what salvation hope does Moses, for instance, get since he is less than John according to Jesus' words. Is there a third-level resurrection hope? You see, if we are to apply the silly logic of the Organization, we have to take it to its silly illogical extreme.

Now that we've established a more plausible understanding of who the 144,000 and the great crowd represent, we are better prepared to tackle the question of what the great tribulation is.

# 9

# Is the Great Tribulation a Single Event?

*For though the tribulation is momentary and light, it works out for us a glory that is of more and more surpassing weight and is everlasting. (2 Corinthians 4:17)*

We've now established that the 144,000 (Revelation 7:4) is a symbolic number that represents the role that the great crowd of God's Children will play in the Kingdom of the heavens.

> After this I saw, and look! **a great crowd**, which no man was able to number, out of all nations and tribes and peoples and tongues, standing before the throne and before the Lamb, dressed in white robes; and there were palm branches in their hands. (Revelation 7:9)

With that new understanding, we can now examine Revelation 7:14 which introduces the *great tribulation*. The great crowd is shown as coming out of the great tribulation.

> "**These are the ones [the great crowd] who come out of the great tribulation**, and they have washed their robes and made them white in the blood of the Lamb. (Revelation 7:14b)

The majority of Christendom's churches—including Jehovah's Witnesses—consider the great tribulation to be an apocalyptic, end-of-the-world event. Does that interpretation fit with the facts we've uncovered about the real identity of the 144,000 and the great crowd? Remember that with exegesis, all the Bible facts must harmonize.

Now that we understand that it is the children of God who come out of the great tribulation, we are more prepared to determine what it refers to. Let's start with the word in Greek, *thlipsis*, rendered "tribulation" in the NWT and most other Bible versions. *Strong's Concordance* defines it as "persecution, affliction, distress, tribulation." You will notice it is not used as a synonym for "destruction."

According to *Strong's*, the word for "destruction" is *apóleia* which is used to describe "destruction, ruin, loss, perishing; eternal ruin." *HELPS Word-studies* provides more details:

> Cognate: 684 apóleia (from 622 /apóllymi, "cut off") – destruction, causing someone (something) to be completely severed – cut off (entirely) from what could or should have been. (Note the force of the prefix, apo.) See 622 (apollymi).

The word *apóleia* (destruction) certainly fits with the definition that the churches of Christendom and the Organization of Jehovah's Witnesses give to the *great tribulation*. But the Bible doesn't say "great destruction" (*apóleia*), but rather, "great tribulation (*thlipsis*). So, let's go with what the Bible says, shall we?

"Tribulation," (*thlipsis*) occurs 45 times in the Christian Scriptures according to biblehub.com.[1] A scan throughout the Christian Scriptures reveals that the word is almost invariably applied to Christians and the context is one of persecution, pain, distress, trials, and testing, not destruction. In fact, it becomes apparent that tribulation is the means by which Christians are proven and refined. For instance:

> And not only that, but let us exult while in **tribulations**, since we know that tribulation produces endurance; endurance, in turn, an approved condition; the approved condition, in turn, hope, and the hope does not lead to disappointment; because the love of God has been poured out into our hearts through the holy spirit, which was given us. (Romans 5:3-5)

> Who will separate us from the love of the Christ? Will **tribulation or distress or persecution** or hunger or nakedness or danger or sword? (Romans 8:35)

---

1. https://biblehub.com/greek/2347.htm

> Blessed be the God and Father of our Lord Jesus Christ, the Father of tender mercies and the God of all comfort, who comforts us in **all our tribulation**, that we may be able to comfort those in any sort of tribulation through the comfort with which we ourselves are being comforted by God. (2 Corinthians 1:3, 4)
>
> For though **the tribulation is momentary and light**, it works out for us a glory that is of more and more surpassing weight and is everlasting; while we keep our eyes, not on the things seen, but on the things unseen. For the things seen are temporary, but the things unseen are everlasting. (2 Corinthians 4:17, 18)

The persecution, affliction, distress, and tribulation upon the Children of God began shortly after Pentecost in 33 CE and has continued unabated ever since. It is only by enduring that tribulation and coming out the other side with your integrity intact that you get the white robe denoting an approved standing before God.[2]

For the last two thousand years, faithful Christians have endured constant tribulation and testing, often from their own brothers who claim to be true Christians themselves, though their works belie that claim. In the Middle Ages, it was often the priests of the Catholic Church that persecuted and killed the chosen ones for bearing witness to the truth. During the reformation, many new Christian denominations sprang into being, but over time they also took up the mantle of the Catholic Church by persecuting the true disciples of Christ. This is in line with the parable of the Wheat and Weeds, where the wheat grows together with the weeds and is only separated at the harvest.[3] Jehovah's Witnesses see their entire Organization as wheat and like to view themselves as victims of persecution, when in fact it is Witnesses who are actually persecuting true Christians by disfellowshipping and shunning them for having the courage to stand up and show the contradictions of the Governing Body's teachings.

It is noteworthy that the word "persecution" (Greek: *diōkō*), which is closely linked to "tribulation" in Scripture, comes from a word relating to the pursuit of a hunter for his prey. *HELPS Word-studies* provides this definition:

---

2. Revelation 6:9; 7:15
3. Matthew 13:24-30; 36-43

1377 diṓkō – properly, aggressively chase, like a hunter pursuing a catch (prize). 1377 (diṓkō) is used positively ("earnestly pursue") and negatively ("zealously persecute, hunt down"). In each case, 1377 (diṓkō) means pursue with all haste ("chasing" after), earnestly desiring to overtake (apprehend).

While Jehovah's Witnesses will balk at the suggestion that they are persecuting anyone, all you have to do to prove that this is precisely the case is question any doctrine of the Governing Body. You will quickly find the elders, who may not have called you for months, suddenly very eager to meet with you and becoming quite aggressive if you refuse to do so. In this situation, they immediately and zealously take on the role of hunters, chasing after you. They are fulfilling Scripture which says:

> In fact, all those desiring to live with godly devotion in association with Christ Jesus **will also be persecuted**. (2 Timothy 3:12)

No Christian religion would like to think of itself as being part of a great millennia-long tribulation/persecution upon Jesus' disciples, but that is exactly what the facts of history reveal.

While the phrase *great tribulation* occurs in three other places in the *New World Translation*, each refers to a situation completely apart and unrelated from that described in Revelation 7:14.[4] So to assert that it refers to a worldwide apocalyptic event of destruction upon mankind at the end of this system of things is to assume facts not in evidence. All we know for sure is that this testing, trial, or tribulation is great and comes upon those making up the great crowd.

Now that we've determined that the great crowd are the Children of God—the body of Christ, the Christian congregation—it becomes easier to determine what the *great tribulation* is.

However, the 2020 *Watchtower* claims it is *a specific event preceding* Armageddon. They even go so far as to claim it is divided into two parts, though the Bible makes no such declaration:

> ...the nations supporting the UN destroy the institutions of false religion. This marks **the opening phase of the great tribulation**.

---

4. Matthew 24:21 refers to the tribulation that befell the nation of Israel during the war with Rome in the first century. Acts 7:11 refers to a famine in Egypt and Canaan in the time of Joseph. Revelation 2:22 refers to God's punishment on adulterers within the congregation of Thyatira.

That tribulation will end with the destruction of the entire world system at Armageddon.[5]

Witnesses are taught that the great tribulation is a two-phase event: Phase one is the attack on false religion which Witnesses gleefully believe they are excluded from. Phase two is Armageddon, which is the great war of God the Almighty against Satan's world.

The "great crowd of other sheep" is the group of Jehovah's Witnesses who will survive all this destruction, according to Watch Tower theology.

But the Bible doesn't talk about Christians surviving Armageddon. Where does it say that? What it does say is that Jesus' true disciples alive at the time of his presence will be removed from danger.

> For this is what we tell you by Jehovah's word, that **we the living who survive to the presence of the Lord** will in no way precede those who have fallen asleep in death; because the Lord himself will descend from heaven with a commanding call, with an archangel's voice and with God's trumpet, and those who are dead in union with Christ will rise first. Afterward **we the living who are surviving will, together with them, be caught away in clouds to meet the Lord in the air**; and thus we will always be with the Lord. (1 Thessalonians 4:15-17)

No Christian can be "caught away in clouds to meet the Lord" unless first he or she has been tested as our Lord himself was.[6]

Are we really expected to believe that the only Christians who need to be tested by some end-of-times great tribulation are those who happen to be alive when Jesus returns? Is that reasonable? Why should their testing be any different from those faithful Christians who have lived down through the centuries?

But should we limit our scope to just Christians, God's servants since the time of Christ?

Revelation 6:9 speaks of "the souls of those slaughtered because of the word of God and because of the witness work that they used to have." Is that speaking only of Christians? Did the great tribulation or great time of testing start with Christ, or has it been going on since the beginning?

---

5.   w20 May p. 11
6.   Hebrews 5:8, 9

Consider carefully this denunciation from our Lord:

> "Serpents, offspring of vipers, how will you flee from the judgment of Gehenna? For this reason, I am sending to you prophets and wise men and public instructors. Some of them you will kill and execute on stakes, and some of them you will scourge in your synagogues and persecute from city to city, so that there may come upon you all the righteous blood spilled on earth, **from the blood of righteous Abel to the blood of Zechariah son of Barachiah**, whom you murdered between the sanctuary and the altar. Truly I say to you, all these things will come upon this generation. "Jerusalem, Jerusalem, the killer of the prophets and stoner of those sent to her—how often I wanted to gather your children together the way a hen gathers her chicks under her wings! But you did not want it. **Look! Your house is abandoned to you.** (Matthew 23:33-38)

Our Lord Jesus is just and fair. His judgment is faultless. Yet, here he condemns the religious leaders of his day for killing righteous men who were born hundreds and even thousands of years before them. Abel, Adam's son, was killed by Cain long before the nation of Israel came into being. What Jesus is recognizing is the contest between good and evil represented in the enmity between the serpent's seed and the seed of the woman.

> And I shall put enmity between you and the woman and between your seed and her seed. He will bruise you in the head and you will bruise him in the heel. (Genesis 3:15)

The religious leaders thought they were righteous, part of the seed or offspring that would crush the head of the serpent, Satan. But they were deceiving themselves. They were the Devil's offspring, his seed, as Jesus told them:

> YOU **are from** YOUR **father the Devil**, and YOU wish to do the desires of YOUR father. That one was a manslayer when he began, and he did not stand fast in the truth, because truth is not in him. When he speaks the lie, he speaks according to his own disposition, because he is a liar and **the father of [the lie]**. Because I, on the other hand, tell the truth, YOU do not believe me. Who of YOU convicts me of sin? If I speak truth, why is it YOU do not believe me? He that is from God listens to the sayings of God. This is why YOU do not listen, because YOU are not from God." (John 8:44-47)

By contrast, the seed of the woman starts with Abel and continues on to Christ and those who become Children of God. It follows then that this great tribulation refers to the testing of the seed of the woman, "the souls of those slaughtered because of the word of God and because of the witness work that they used to have," which would include individuals from righteous Abel, down to our present time and onward until the glorious manifestation of Jesus during his presence.[7] When that time comes, there won't be a great tribulation or testing, but something far more severe, a time of destruction (*apóleia*).

> Then, indeed, the lawless one will be revealed, whom the Lord Jesus will do away with by the spirit of his mouth and **bring to nothing by the manifestation of his presence**. But the lawless one's presence is according to the operation of Satan with every powerful work and lying signs and portents and with every unrighteous deception **for those who are perishing, as a retribution because they did not accept the love of the truth that they might be saved**. So that is why God lets an operation of error go to them, that they may get to believing the lie, in order that they all may be judged because they did not believe the truth but took pleasure in unrighteousness. (2 Thessalonians 2:8-12)

I don't know if the judgment described by Paul to the Thessalonians comes at the beginning of Christ's presence at the start of the thousand years, or during the thousand years of his reign, or after that reign has ended. What I do know is that whenever it comes, it will be final. Going back to Jesus' words to the religious leaders, he gave the nation no option for escape, but said at Matthew 23:38, "Look! Your house is abandoned to you."

And so it was. The destruction of the nation with its capital city and holy temple was written in stone, and it was utterly destroyed in 70 CE. Why did that happen? Why will it happen again to Christendom? Jesus says at Luke 19:44, "because you did not discern the time of your being inspected."

In summary, the prophesied destruction upon Babylon the great and the great war of God Almighty (Armageddon) is not *the great tribulation* spoken of at Revelation 7:14. That *great tribulation* is the testing that all faithful servants of God have had to endure throughout their lives as the means for their refinement, to perfect them for the task of serving with Christ as Kings and Priests.

As Peter relates:

---

7.   Revelation 6:9; 2 Thessalonians 2:8

Because of this you are greatly rejoicing, though for a short time, if it must be, you have been **distressed by various trials**, in order that **the tested quality** of your faith, of much greater value than gold that perishes despite its being tested by fire, may be found a cause for praise and glory and honor at the revelation of Jesus Christ. (1 Peter 1:6, 7)

Beloved ones, do not be puzzled at the **burning** among YOU, which is happening to YOU for a **trial**, as though a strange thing were befalling YOU. On the contrary, go on rejoicing forasmuch as YOU are sharers in the **sufferings** of the Christ, that YOU may rejoice and be overjoyed also during the revelation of his glory. If YOU are being reproached for the name of Christ, YOU are happy, because the [spirit] of glory, even the spirit of God, is resting upon YOU. (1 Peter 4:12-14)

Paul adds:

We must enter into the kingdom of God through **many tribulations**. (Acts 14:22)

## Hebrews Explains Why Christians Undergo Tribulation

This is a very important question for us to consider. I would go so far as to say that understanding why we must suffer tribulation is vital to our salvation. We find an excellent explanation for why we undergo this type of trial and testing in the 12th chapter of Hebrews, but before we get into that, I have to do some damage control. You see, the Organization has misappropriated a key verse in this chapter of Hebrews to justify one of its more egregious policies. In so doing, they have subverted the real message being communicated to us here. The verse they have cherry-picked is Hebrews 12:6. Here it is in its immediate context:

And you have entirely forgotten the exhortation that addresses you as sons: "My son, do not belittle the discipline from Jehovah, nor give up when you are corrected by him; ⁶ **for those whom Jehovah loves he disciplines**, in fact, he scourges everyone whom he receives as a son." (Hebrews 12:5, 6)

The Governing Body uses this scripture to justify the disfellowshipping policy they enforce for anyone who violates God's law as defined by them. But it has nothing to do with disfellowshipping as we'll soon see.

## 9. Is the Great Tribulation a Single Event?

Before going further, I need to clarify one thing: I accept the need to remove an unrepentant sinner from fellowship within the Christian congregation. Jesus gave us the loving three-step procedure recorded at Matthew 18[8] that concentrates on winning back the sinner, while still protecting the purity of the congregation. Paul and John both give us direction on how to deal with specific situations.[9] However, the Organization of Jehovah's Witnesses has gone way beyond what is written by creating a very complex and legalistic judicial system. A full exposé of the JW judicial system is beyond the scope of this book, though it is my hope to deal with it in a future volume. For now, I wish to focus on how they cherry-pick Hebrews 12:6, misapplying that verse to support their policy, and in doing so, hide a vital truth from Jehovah's Witnesses.

Here is an example of how they misapply Hebrews 12:6 taken from the 2021 *Watchtower*:

CAN FIRM DISCIPLINE BE MERCIFUL?

When we hear an announcement made at a Christian meeting that someone we know and love "is no longer one of Jehovah's Witnesses," we are deeply saddened. We may wonder if it was necessary to disfellowship our loved one. Is disfellowshipping really an expression of mercy? Yes, it is. **To withhold discipline from someone who needs it is not wise, merciful, or loving.** (Prov. 13:24) Can getting disfellowshipped help an unrepentant sinner change his course? It can. Many who have fallen into serious sin have found that the firm action the elders took gave them the very jolt they needed to come to their senses, change their course of action, and return to Jehovah's warm embrace.—**Read Hebrews 12:5, 6.**[10]

You will notice that after reading this paragraph in the congregation Watchtower Study, the conductor has someone read

---

8. "Moreover, if your brother commits a sin, go and reveal his fault between you and him alone. If he listens to you, you have gained your brother. But if he does not listen, take along with you one or two more, so that on the testimony of two or three witnesses every matter may be established. If he does not listen to them, speak to the congregation. If he does not listen even to the congregation, let him be to you just as a man of the nations and as a tax collector." (Matthew 18:15-17)
9. 1 Corinthians 5:1-5; 2 Corinthians 2:6-11; 2 Thessalonians 3:14, 15; 2 John 7-11
10. w21 October p. 10 "We Serve the God Who Is 'Rich in Mercy'"

Hebrews 12:5, 6. This is used to justify the disfellowshipping policy of Jehovah's Witnesses which is a total ostracism, a complete shunning of the individual. It is a humiliating policy, because even if the sinner repents, he or she must wait a minimum of a year—and often much longer—to be reinstated. All the time, they must attend all meetings, sit at the back, and endure the disdain of the entire congregation. This demeaning procedure is presented as a "wise, loving, and merciful" provision of Jehovah God based on their misapplication of Hebrews 6. It is bad enough to belittle and harm the little one, but to then blame Jehovah for it?! Shocking!

Once again, we see the wickedness that can result from studying the Bible eisegetically!

What is the real message of Hebrews 12:5, 6? To determine this we must let the Bible speak for itself and we do this by reading the full context. Here it is:

> In your struggle against that sin, you have never yet resisted to the point of having your blood shed. And you have entirely forgotten the exhortation that **addresses you as sons**: "My son, do not belittle the discipline from Jehovah, nor give up when you are corrected by him; for those whom Jehovah loves he disciplines, in fact, he scourges everyone whom he receives **as a son**." You need to endure as part of your discipline. **God is treating you as sons.** For what son is not disciplined by his father? But **if you have not all shared in receiving this discipline, you are really illegitimate children, and not sons**. Furthermore, our human fathers used to discipline us, and we gave them respect. Should we not more readily submit ourselves to the Father of our spiritual life and live? For they disciplined us for a short time according to what seemed good to them, but he does so for our benefit so that we may partake of his holiness. True, no discipline seems for the present to be joyous, but it is painful; yet afterward, **it yields the peaceable fruit of righteousness to those who have been trained by it**. (Hebrews 12:4-11)

Can you see now how ridiculous the Organization's application of Hebrews 12:6 really is?

First of all, it can't apply to the JW Other Sheep because the entire passage deals with the way Jehovah disciplines those who are *His sons*. The Other Sheep are told they are not God's sons, but only his friends. A father disciplines his sons. He doesn't discipline his friends. That's just silly. But the silliness continues.

## 9. Is the Great Tribulation a Single Event?

If Hebrews 12:6 applies to disfellowshipping as the Governing Body contends, then verse 8 must also apply to disfellowshipping. It reads: "if you have not all shared in receiving this discipline, you are really illegitimate children, and not sons."

So, if we follow the logic of the *Watchtower*, all Jehovah's Witnesses have to be disfellowshipped at some point in time. That would include especially all members of the Governing Body! Why? Because if they are not disciplined by Jehovah—remember, this passage is applied to the discipline one receives by being disfellowshipped—then they are illegitimate children, and not God's sons.

### What Does Hebrews 12:4-11 Really Mean?

By subverting the message of Hebrews 12:6 to their own ends, the Governing Body hides a vital truth from Jehovah's Witnesses. That truth is that if a Christian is not disciplined by God—we are not talking disfellowshipping now—then he or she is illegitimate, not a Child of God. Only the Children of God inherit life. There is no secondary inheritance, no consolation prize. If you want eternal life, you have to be adopted by God as one of His children.

When a man dies, his children inherit. If he has illegitimate children, they aren't entitled to the inheritance. The Children of God inherit everlasting life. Any human not adopted as His child is considered illegitimate and so gets *no inheritance.*

### Why We Suffer Tribulation

The answer to the question of why we must suffer trials and tribulation is now clear. It is because our heavenly Father loves us. The love referred to in Hebrews 12 is *agape*, which is a Greek word for love that refers to the type of love that always seeks what is best for its object. We are the object of God's love. But our heavenly Father doesn't mollycoddle us. He strengthens us because he is preparing us for a monumental work: The restoration of all humans back into His family. To do that work, we have to prove ourselves up to the task.

To understand better why that is, we turn again to the book of Hebrews where we find this scripture:

> During his life on earth, Christ offered up supplications and also petitions, with strong outcries and tears, to the One who was

able to save him out of death, and he was favorably heard for his godly fear. Although he was a son, **he learned obedience from the things he suffered**. And after **he had been made perfect**, he became responsible for everlasting salvation to all those obeying him, because he has been designated by God a high priest in the manner of Melchizedek. (Hebrews 5:7-10)

If our Lord had to learn obedience through the things he suffered, how are we to expect anything less for ourselves. Indeed, we welcome the discipline of our heavenly Father. It is something to be desired because it makes us acceptable. It is how we win the prize of everlasting life. Paul assures us of this:

For though the tribulation is momentary and light, it works out for us a glory that is of more and more surpassing weight and is everlasting. (2 Corinthians 4:17)

So, the great tribulation isn't an end-of-the-world event, but a millennia long refining process to prepare the Children of God for the work ahead. We thank and praise our Father in heaven that he should love us so much that he should bestow upon us this discipline.

## Why Do the Churches and JW.org Teach that the Great Tribulation Is a Final Test?

Given the foregoing, why do so many religions, Jehovah's Witnesses included, promote the idea that the great tribulation is some final test that all Christians have to prepare for, something above and beyond the trials and tribulations that real Christians have to face everyday? Could it be yet another means of control, of spiritual subjugation?

Let's start by looking at how Jehovah's Witnesses present their version of the great tribulation. We will soon see that though theirs varies from that taught by other churches, the motivation behind it all is basically the same.

Again, the Organization divides the great tribulation into two phases: Phase one is when false religion is attacked. Of course, for Jehovah's Witnesses, false religion is *everybody else but them*. Now, if you are one of Jehovah's Witnesses, you know that

## 9. Is the Great Tribulation a Single Event?

to survive this attack, you have to be inside the Organization, like Noah and his family had to be inside the Ark to survive the flood.[11]

Phase two is Armageddon. It will begin with an all-out assault on Jehovah's Witnesses. Loyal Witnesses will gather together for this final test, and Jesus will stand up for them to defeat the enemies of God's Kingdom. *The Watchtower* has this to say about the *coming great tribulation*:

> So, what can we expect will happen during the coming great tribulation? Jehovah will "cut short" the attack of the United Nations on false religion, not allowing true religion to be destroyed with the false. This will ensure that God's people will be saved.
>
> What happens after the initial part of the great tribulation has passed? Jesus' words indicate that there will be a period of time that will last until the start of Armageddon. What events will occur during that interval? The answer is recorded at Ezekiel 38:14-16 and Matthew 24:29-31.[12]

Is this a scripturally accurate portrait of our future, or just another method to get people to become compliant and obedient to the commands of men? Obedience to God is important, but the method Jehovah uses to get his children to obey him is reason, logic, and most of all, love. Satan and his ministers cannot avail themselves of such methods, so they use deception, fear, and intimidation.[13]

Consider this *Watchtower* excerpt which is typical of the Governing Body's thinking on the matter:

> Any who hope to be considered by God's Judge as "sheep" to be spared must prove themselves to be "righteous ones," **actively aiding Christ's anointed "brothers," who form the "faithful and discreet slave" class [aka the Governing Body]**. ...The only ones to whom the Bible extends hope of surviving the "great tribulation" are Christ's "brothers," or "chosen ones," and the "great crowd" of "sheep"...[14]

---

11. "Just as Noah and his God-fearing family were preserved in the ark, survival of individuals today depends on their faith and their loyal association with the earthly part of Jehovah's universal organization." (w06 5/15 p. 22 par. 8)
12. w13 7/15 p. 5 pars. 7-8
13. 2 Corinthians 11:14, 15
14. w82 4/1 pp. 30-31 par. 18

But we know there is no single, one-time, end-of-days tribulation that we have to prepare for. Our trial, our tribulation, is our Christian way of life. Jesus told us: "whoever does not accept his torture stake[15] and follow after me is not worthy of me."[16]

Jesus wasn't saying that we have to die a martyr's death to win the reward of life, though some have done so. Rather, he's referring to what death on a stake (or a cross) represented in those days. The manner of Jesus' death was the most shameful way there was to die. The condemned person was stripped of all his belongings—even his clothing—and made to parade before the crowd, all of whom shunned him and considered him to be a pariah. Today, Jehovah's Witnesses don't execute true Christians, but they mimic the shame of Jesus' death by publicly and privately shunning any dissenter.[17]

Jesus endured an ignominious and painful death, but he considered it as nothing for the joy of gaining the approval of his God and Father. That is why the Bible says he "despised shame."[18] If you despise something, it has no value to you. In fact, it has a negative value. You would pay money to get rid of it as we do with our garbage.

More than anything else, the tribulation Christians have faced and continue to face is the same as that which Christ confronted and conquered. Our love for him must be greater than any shame, dishonor, or hatred which the world, and even our closest friends and family members, might heap upon us. Only in this way can we win the reward that our heavenly Father is offering to us. That is why Jesus tells us:

> Everyone, then, who acknowledges me before men, I will also acknowledge him before my Father who is in the heavens. But whoever disowns me before men, I will also disown him before my Father who is in the heavens. (Matthew 10:32, 33)

---

15. Witnesses are taught that Jesus didn't die on a cross but rather on post or stake.
16. Matthew 10:38
17. Even if someone is not engaging in any sin, merely resigning from the Organization of Jehovah's Witnesses results in family and friends being required to shun and completely ostracise the one leaving.
18. Hebrews 12:2

## Surviving Armageddon and Our Final Destination

While the foregoing may have altered our understanding of what the great tribulation represents, there is still the issue of Armageddon, the great war of God the Almighty. That's definitely a one-time, end-of-days event. Don't the Children of God have to prepare for that? It may surprise you to learn that we do not. How is that possible? We will deal with that thoroughly in Chapter 11, "Is the Governing Body a False Prophet?" on page 249.

Another worrisome issue that arises is the question of our final destination. Witnesses are conditioned to think of eternal life in an earthly paradise, and the idea of going off to heaven never to return to see their loved ones again holds little appeal. But where do they get that idea from? The Bible doesn't teach that. It comes from the same men who've taught them about the overlapping generation, 1914, and a non-existent secondary salvation hope for the JW Other Sheep. While we can't have all the answers yet—our heavenly Father still has many surprises for us—we can draw some reasonable conclusions based on the evidence from Scripture. We'll do that in Chapter 14, "Should I Partake of the Bread and Wine?" on page 305.

But we are not finished with our examination of the Other Sheep doctrine. It is crucial that we examine its origin because that examination will tell us all we need to know about the spirit that has been guiding the Organization of Jehovah's Witnesses for the past 100 years.

# 10

# J. F. Rutherford Invents the Salvation Hope of the "Other Sheep"

*For, as it is, if someone comes and preaches a Jesus other than the one we preached, or YOU receive a spirit other than what YOU received, or good news other than what YOU accepted, YOU easily put up [with him].*
*(2 Corinthians 11:4)*

There is much to be learned by looking into the origin of the JW Other Sheep doctrine. Let us begin by establishing who is responsible for virtually all doctrines unique to the community of Jehovah's Witnesses.

On Friday, August 14, 2015, Governing Body member, Geoffrey Jackson was testifying under oath before the *Australia Royal Commission into Institutional Responses to Child Sexual Abuse.* As part of his testimony, he explained the role of the Governing Body within the community of Jehovah's Witnesses. On August 14, 2015, he stated that the Governing Body is:

> "...a spiritual group of men who are the **guardians of our doctrine**, and **as guardians of the doctrine, look at things that**

**need to be decided based on our doctrines,** which are based on the constitution of the Bible."¹

Of course, there is no scriptural basis for any group of men to assume the moniker of Guardians of Doctrine—a rather poor choice of words as it leads to the unfortunate acronym, GOD. When I first heard it, I immediately thought of Paul's words to the Thessalonians:

> Let no one seduce YOU in any manner, because it will not come unless the apostasy comes first and **the man of lawlessness gets revealed, the son of destruction. He is set in opposition and lifts himself up over everyone who is called "GOD"** or an object of reverence, so that **he sits down in the temple of The God, publicly showing himself to be a GOD.** Do YOU not remember that, while I was yet with YOU, I used to tell YOU these things? (2 Thessalonians 2:3-5) [Uppercase added for emphasis.]

In the July 15, 2013 issue of *The Watchtower*, in an article titled "Who Really Is the Faithful and Discreet Slave?" it was explained that in 1919, capable brothers such as those who today make up the Governing Body *were named by Jesus* as his faithful and discreet slave.

> "The faithful and discreet slave": A small group of anointed brothers who are directly involved in preparing and dispensing spiritual food during Christ's presence. **Today, these anointed brothers make up the Governing Body.**

> "Appointed over his domestics": In 1919, Jesus selected capable anointed brothers to be his faithful and discreet slave.²

In 1919, the foremost member of this faithful slave—some would argue that he became the only member—was J. F. Rutherford, a man who promoted himself as the "Generalissimo of the Bible Students' Organizations."³

---

1. ARC Case Study 29 (Day 155) Transcript 14 August 2015 (https://beroeans.net/arc-jackson-transcript/)
2. w13 7/15 p. 25 (box)
3. *The Messenger*, Tuesday, July 19, 1927.

# 10. Rutherford Invents the "Other Sheep"

Figure 17. "Generalissimo of the Bible Students' Organizations", *The Messenger*, Tuesday, July 19, 1927.

## Rutherford Talks Directly to God

Most of the doctrinal teachings of Jehovah's Witnesses which we have reviewed in this book can trace their roots back to the theology of J. F. Rutherford. This is especially true of:
- the 1914 presence of Christ,
- the 1919 appointment of the faithful and discreet slave,
- the 1918 resurrection of the anointed,
- the invention of the Other Sheep class.

From what source did Rutherford get those teachings? Was he led by holy spirit, or was a different spirit at work in him?

The current Governing Body claims that Rutherford was guided by the holy spirit. They also claim that he was appointed by Jesus in 1919 as part of the Faithful and Discreet Slave. But we need more than their word before we can believe any of that to be true. We need proof. Jesus tells us what to look for:

> But the helper, the holy spirit, which the Father will send in my name, that one will teach YOU all things and bring back to YOUR minds all the things I told YOU. (John 14:26)

> However, when that one comes, the spirit of the truth, he will guide you into all the truth, for he will not speak of his own initiative, but what he hears he will speak, and he will declare to you the things to come. (John 16:13)

If Rutherford were truly being led by God's holy spirit, then all his teachings would be true. Since we've just seen abundant scriptural proof that his teachings were anything but true, you may be wondering just where the Judge got his ideas. Well, you don't have to wonder, because Rutherford himself gives us the answer. In a 1930 *Watchtower* article, we find the Judge referring to himself in the third person as "the servant," writing:

> If the holy spirit as a helper were directing the work, then there would be no good reason for employing the angels ... the Scriptures seem clearly to teach that the Lord directs his angels what to do and they act under the supervision of the Lord in directing the remnant on earth concerning the course of action to take.
>
> It would seem there would be no necessity for the **'servant'** [Rutherford] to have an advocate such as the holy spirit because the 'servant' is in **direct communication with Jehovah and as Jehovah's instrument**, and Christ Jesus acts for the entire body.[4]

What a remarkable claim! Rutherford states unabashedly that he is in "direct communication with Jehovah" and is "Jehovah's instrument"! He states that this communication is not through holy spirit, but by means of angelic messengers! Apparently, God and the Judge were talking, and the holy angels are carrying the messages back and forth.

A year after making this sweeping assertion, Rutherford, *the servant*, picked the name "Jehovah's Witnesses," claiming it was by divine providence. Now, we know that the name "Christian" was given to the disciples by divine providence, because Acts 11:26 tells us so:

---

4. w30 9/1 p. 263

## 10. Rutherford Invents the "Other Sheep"

> It was first in Antioch that the disciples were by divine providence called Christians. (Acts 11:26b)

But what evidence do we have that Jehovah was communicating a new name to Judge Rutherford?

Would it surprise you to learn that this Rutherford teaching—that angels and not holy spirit are being used to carry messages from God to the Governing Body—is still current today within the Organization?

This interpretation is tied to the belief that the first resurrection has already occurred. In an article in the January 1, 2007 issue of *The Watchtower* titled "The First Resurrection"—Now Under Way!" we are told:

> What, then, can we deduce from the fact that one of the 24 elders identifies the great crowd to John? **It seems that resurrected ones of the 24-elders group may be involved in the communicating of divine truths today.** Why is that important? Because the correct identity of the great crowd was revealed to God's anointed servants on earth in 1935. If one of the 24 elders was used to convey that important truth, he would have had to be resurrected to heaven by 1935 at the latest. That would indicate that the first resurrection began sometime between 1914 and 1935. Can we be more precise?[5]

Can you follow the chain of logic? According to Witnesses, Jesus returned in 1914. Since he is back, there was no longer any need for the holy spirit, which was only sent in his absence.

> But because I have spoken these things to YOU grief has filled YOUR hearts. Nevertheless, I am telling YOU the truth, It is for YOUR benefit I am going away. **For if I do not go away, the helper will by no means come to YOU; but if I do go my way, I will send him to YOU.** (John 16:6, 7)

So now that he is back, Jehovah talks directly with "his servant" by means of angels and resurrected humans. Odd that, with Jesus back, it is Jehovah talking. What is Jesus doing? Sitting on his hands?

Now let's consider the ramifications of Rutherford's statement that he was not being directed by holy spirit, but by angels, which is based on the belief that the holy spirit was no longer needed

---

5. w07 1/1 p. 28 par. 11

because Christ had returned in 1914, something we now know to be false.

If angels ["messengers" in Greek], not holy spirit, were communicating with Rutherford, then from what source did these spirit messengers spring? When speaking to the Galatians, Paul warned them about a false or perverted good news:

> ...only there are **certain ones** who are causing YOU trouble and **wanting to pervert the good news** about the Christ. However, even if we or **an angel out of heaven** were to declare to YOU as good news something beyond what we declared to YOU as good news, **let him be accursed**. As we have said above, I also now say again, Whoever it is that is declaring to YOU as good news something beyond what YOU accepted, **let him be accursed**. (Galatians 1:7-9)

Let's examine some of Rutherford's teachings to see if they originated with God or from *a different* source.

## Rutherford's Gangrenous Teaching

According to this newly self-appointed Faithful and Discreet Slave aka the Governing Body, the first resurrection began in 1918.

> After 1914, during Jesus' "presence" in Kingdom power, he, as the archangel, issues the heavenly command for those "in union with Christ" to assemble. In the case of such anointed ones "asleep in death," this trumpetlike summons calls for their spiritual resurrection into the heavens. **The Watchtower has long presented the view that this resurrection of anointed Christians from death commenced in the year 1918.**[6]

The January 1, 2007 issue of *The Watchtower* confirms that this teaching is still current.

> Could it, then, be reasoned that since Jesus was enthroned in the fall of 1914, the resurrection of his faithful anointed followers began three and a half years later, **in the spring of 1918**? That is an interesting possibility. Although this cannot be directly confirmed in the Bible, it is not out of harmony with other scriptures that indicate that the first resurrection got under way soon after Christ's presence began.

---

6. w86 10/1 pp. 13-14 par. 18

For example, Paul wrote: "We the living who survive to the presence of the Lord [not, to the *end* of his presence] shall in no way precede those who have fallen asleep in death; because the Lord himself will descend from heaven with a commanding call, with an archangel's voice and with God's trumpet, and those who are dead in union with Christ will rise first. Afterward we the living who are surviving will, **together with them**, be caught away in clouds to meet the Lord in the air; and thus we shall always be with the Lord." (1 Thessalonians 4:15-17) Therefore, anointed Christians who died before Christ's presence were raised to heavenly life ahead of those who were still alive during Christ's presence. This means that the first resurrection must have begun early in Christ's presence, and it continues "during his presence."[7]

According to 1 Thessalonians 4:17, those alive at the presence of Christ will be caught away in the clouds "together with them," meaning *at the same time* those rise "who are dead in union with Christ." A parallel account is found in Paul's first letter to the Corinthians.

> Look! I tell YOU a sacred secret: We shall not all fall asleep [in death], but **we shall all be changed, in a moment, in the twinkling of an eye**, during the last trumpet. For the trumpet will sound, and the dead will be raised up incorruptible, and we shall be changed. (1 Corinthians 15:51, 52)

According to the publications, there were thousands of Bible Students associated with the Watchtower Bible & Tract Society in 1918, all of whom were anointed. Yet there are no reports from that year concerning the sudden disappearance of thousands of Christians off the face of the earth. How can they contend that the resurrection has already occurred when there is no evidence that Bible prophecy was fulfilled?

This is not the first time that Christians have been persuaded that the first resurrection has already occurred. Paul warns us about this very thing:

> Do your utmost to present yourself approved to God, a workman with nothing to be ashamed of, handling the word of the truth aright. But shun empty speeches that violate what is holy; for they will advance to more and more ungodliness, and **their word will spread like gangrene. Hymenaeus and Philetus are of that number. These very [men] have deviated from the truth,**

---

7. w07 1/1 p. 28 pars. 12-13 "'The First Resurrection'—Now Under Way!"

saying that the resurrection has already occurred; and they are subverting the faith of some. (2 Timothy 2:15-18)

Gangrene refers to the death of body tissue from infection or lack of blood flow. If the infected limb is not surgically removed, it will kill the whole body. A gangrenous teaching cuts off the blood flow of the Holy Spirit to the body of Christ. If not excised quickly, the entire body will die.

I have learned from personal experience that to ignore even the subtlest of warnings from Scripture is a great way to ruin your life. When the Lord gives us a warning, he expects us to heed it. Failing to do so always results in tragedy and loss, even if we can't see what the big deal it is at the time. This is a case in point.

Some will reason: What harm could there really be from believing the resurrection has already occurred? What difference could it make whether the anointed were resurrected over 100 years ago, or are still awaiting their release from death?

Let us follow the chain of events to see how God's warnings are not to be taken lightly. We will see that the gangrene Paul predicted in his day is just as threatening today as it was then.

## Angelic Messengers Talk to Rutherford

What messages did these angels impart to *the servant*, Judge Rutherford, in the 1930s? First, to rename the Bible Students as Jehovah's Witnesses. Then to inform Jehovah's Witnesses that the majority of them were in the Other Sheep class. Next, to tie the Great Crowd of Revelation 7:9-15 to the Other Sheep class. This changed the nature of the good news that Jehovah's Witnesses preached. Essentially, the message is now that by becoming a baptized member of Jehovah's Witnesses, an individual has the opportunity of being part of the great crowd of Armageddon survivors or of being resurrected to an earthly paradise. Either way, he or she is still not but not yet free of sin.

As we just read above, the Apostle Paul warned us about messages involving the good news that come from angelic sources.

> "However, even if we or **an angel out of heaven** were to declare to you as good news something beyond the good news we declared to you, let him be accursed." (Galatians 1:8)

Let's recap. Paul warned us that those teaching that the resurrection has already occurred were violating what is holy and that

## 10. Rutherford Invents the "Other Sheep"

their teaching would spread like gangrene. Rutherford taught that the resurrection had already occurred in 1918. That belief led directly to the belief that the holy spirit was no longer being used to guide Christians to "all the truth." Instead, angels and possibly resurrected Jehovah's Witnesses were now communicating truth from Jehovah God. Rutherford believed that "an angel out of heaven" had declared to him a version of the good news that involved a secondary class of Christian, a group he called the *Jonadabs*, who corresponded to the other sheep of John 10:16.

Of course, if this understanding is wrong, if it wasn't an angel out of heaven, but an angel from *a far less reputable source* that revealed this "truth" to Rutherford, then the other part of Paul's warning comes into effect: "Let him be accursed!" Serious stuff to be sure.

The fact that the Organization goes out of its way to hide the true nature of the origin of the doctrine of the Other Sheep is testament in and of itself that the source of this doctrine is not divine.

As we saw in the above quote from the 2007 *Watchtower* article, the identity of the Great Crowd was revealed in 1935. But the identity of the Great Crowd as belonging to the Other Sheep class is meaningless unless we can also identify who or what the Other Sheep are. According to JW theology, the Other Sheep are split into two groups: 1) the Great Crowd of Armageddon survivors; 2) those who are part of the earthly resurrection of the righteous.

The two publications indexes of the Organization cover all releases published over the past 92 years. These show dozens of references to discussion articles on the topic of the Great Crowd, with the landmark articles of 1935 clearly listed.[8] Given that the Great Crowd is merely a subset of the Other Sheep, one would think the Organization would be anxious to share the reference to the article wherein this *new light* of the identity of the Other Sheep was first revealed by one of the 24 elders resurrected in 1918. Yet that information is missing from the *Publications Index 1930-1985*. That "revelation," such as it is, came in the August 1 and 15, 1934 issues of *The Watchtower* in a two-part article titled "His Kindness."

---

8. w35 227-236, 243-252, 331-334

Why are they willing to tell us when the Great Crowd was identified, but never mention the more important article revealing who the Other Sheep are? It is not like there is a better, more complete discussion in a more recent publication. The earliest reference to any discussion of the Other Sheep in the *Watchtower Index* only goes back to the July 15, 1980 *Watchtower*. Yet, even scanning that and other discussion articles on the subject reveals no real discussion at all. Every reference you may care to look up only reveals the JW Other Sheep as a *fait accompli*, a given that needs no further explanation. The only real, detailed explanation to be found in the publications goes back to 1934 and given that it is entirely based on antitypical applications not found in Scripture, it is little wonder that the Organization fails to list it in the *Publications Index*. Nevertheless, despite a lack of Scriptural support, the Governing Body has never abandoned this teaching.

The question is: Why did Rutherford come up with it in the first place, and why were his angelic messengers so interested in communicating this idea to him?

## Rutherford Creates a Clergy Class

Only through a point-by-point analysis of the two articles in the August 1934 issue of *The Watchtower* can we really appreciate how the gangrene Paul warned about had spread to the point of endangering the life of that part of the body of Christ that dwells within the Organization of Jehovah's Witnesses.[9] Let us begin that analysis now. Buckle your seat belt. It's going to be a wild ride.

### "His Kindness," Part 1

In ancient Israel, there were six cities of refuges. These were designated places to which a manslayer—an Israelite who had accidentally killed another—could flee to escape death from the avenger of blood—usually, a close relative of the deceased.

---

9. The body of Christ are all the chosen ones, the Children of God. These individuals are like wheat growing among the weeds in all the religions making up Christendom.

## 10. Rutherford Invents the "Other Sheep"

In this article from the August 1, 1934 issue of *The Watchtower*, Rutherford looks to the Israelite cities of refuge as the basis for the Other Sheep doctrine.

> Christ Jesus, the Vindicator, will destroy the wicked; but the kindness of Jehovah has provided a place of refuge for those who now turn their hearts toward righteousness, seeking to join themselves unto Jehovah's organization. Such are known as the Jonadab class, because Jonadab foreshadowed them.[10]

Notice first that this place of refuge isn't for the anointed, but for a secondary class known as "the Jonadabs." This is the first of many antitypical applications that Rutherford makes to support his new doctrine. Jonadab was a Gentile who supported the Israelite, Jehu.[11] The cities of refuge were made for Israelites, not Gentiles, so Rutherford's antitype is broken before it even gets off the ground.

> This loving provision made by Jehovah being announced at the time of making of the covenant of faithfulness shows that the cities of refuge foreshadow God's loving-kindness for the protection of the people of good will during Armageddon...
> 
> **"God having now made known to his people** that the word spoken by him, as recorded in Deuteronomy, applies since the coming of Christ Jesus to the temple, [circa 1918] we may expect to find that the provision for the cities of refuge, as set down in the prophecies, have an antitypical fulfilment in close proximity to the time of taking the faithful followers of Christ Jesus into the covenant for the kingdom."[12]

Here the claim is made in print that Jehovah God is making known to his people (through angelic communication to Rutherford, presumably)[13] that the cities of refuge have an antitypical fulfillment in our day. As we will continue to see throughout our consideration of this two-part *Watchtower* article series, every conclusion is based on some type/antitype relationship which "God [has] made known to his people."

But was it Jehovah God who made these things known to "his people" through Rutherford? The Judge thought so, but the facts

---

10. w34 8/1 p. 228 par. 3
11. 2 Kings 10:15-17
12. w34 8/1 p. 228 pars. 4, 5
13. See "Rutherford Talks Directly to God" on page 225.

reveal that these spirit messengers were not coming from God. We know this because of what this recent *Watchtower* reveals:

> ...the March 15, 2015, issue of The Watchtower explained why our recent publications seldom mention prophetic types and antitypes: "Where the Scriptures teach that an individual, an event, or an object is typical of something else, we accept it as such. Otherwise, we ought to be reluctant to assign an antitypical application to a certain person or account if there is no specific Scriptural basis for doing so." Because **the Scriptures are silent regarding any antitypical significance of the cities of refuge**, this article and the next one emphasize instead the lessons Christians can learn from this arrangement.[14]

Let us be very clear on this. The organization is now *specifically denying that any antitypical fulfillment exists with regard to the cities of refuge.* Since the entire premise of Rutherford's argument in support of the Other Sheep as a separate class of Christian with a secondary earthly hope is based on an antitypical fulfillment *not supported in Scripture and specifically denied by the current Governing Body*, the foundation for the current Other Sheep doctrine of the Organization is gone. Vanished into thin air!

If you scan through the *Watchtower Library* online or use the *Publications Indexes* in search of scriptural support for the Other Sheep doctrine to replace Rutherford's now defunct explanation you will find nothing. You will find bold assertions. You will find deductive reasoning. But it all amounts to a hill of beans since it is not built on a solid foundation of Scripture.

Of course, the making of bold, unsupported assertions is nothing new in the publications. Rutherford continues:

> The setting up of the cities of refuge was notice to those who should have need therefor that God had made provision for their protection and refuge in time of distress. That was a part of the prophecy, and, being a prophecy, it must have its fulfilment at some later day and at the coming of the Greater Moses.[15]

What a wonderful example of circular reasoning this presents! The cities of refuge were prophetic because they have a prophetic application, which we know because they were prophetic.

---

14. w17/11 p. 10 Box
15. w34 8/1 p. 228 par. 7

## 10. Rutherford Invents the "Other Sheep"

Rutherford then goes on without breaking stride to say in the very next sentence:

> On the 24th day of February, A.D. 1918, by the Lord's grace and manifestly by his overruling providence and his direction, there was delivered, at Los Angeles, for the first time the message "The World has Ended—Millions Now Living Will Never Die", and thereafter that message was proclaimed by word of mouth and by printed publication throughout "Christendom". No one of God's people understood fully the matter at that time; but since being brought into the temple they see and understand that those on the earth who may live and not die are the ones who now 'get into the chariot', as Jonadab at the invitation of Jehu got into the chariot with Jehu.[16]

One can't help but be amazed at the unmitigated gall of the man to take one of his greatest humiliations[17] and turn it into a triumph. The 1918 speech he is referring to as being delivered by the 'manifest direction' of God was a prophetic fiasco rivaling that of 1975. It was built on the premise that 1925 would see the resurrection of the ancient worthies—men like King David, Moses, and Abraham—and the start of Armageddon. Now, almost a decade after that embarrassing failure, he is still spouting the claim that it came from God.

Rutherford even finds an antitypical application to support the making of monetary donations to the Watch Tower Society.

> Jehovah's commandment was that there should be given to the Levites forty-eight cities and suburbs. This shows that the peoples of "Christendom" have no right to crowd Jehovah's servants, and particularly his anointed witnesses, out of the land, but must allow them freedom of activity and a reasonable amount for their maintenance. This also supports the conclusion that those who obtain literature… should contribute something to defray the expense of publication.[18]

Of course, Rutherford's interest in financial support wasn't confined to keeping the printing presses going. The man maintained a 10-bedroom mansion in San Diego called Beth Sarim,

---

16. Ibid
17. Rutherford eventually admitted to A.H. Macmillan of the 1925 fiasco that "he had made an ass of himself." – *Apocalaypse Delayed: The Story of Jehovah's Witnesses* 2nd ed. by James M. Penton, p. 57
18. w34 8/1 p. 228 par. 8

built originally to house the ancient worthies who were to appear in 1925 but missed the boat. He also maintained a residence in Staten Island and had not one, but two, 16-cylinder Cadillacs, one on each coast of the United States.[19]

His conclusion that the members of Christendom's churches "must allow a reasonable amount" for the maintenance of the JW priestly class may seem gutsy to some, but it also suggests a troubling disconnect with reality. Moreover, it exposes a common danger with contrived typical-antitypical relationships: Where does one stop? If there is a real relationship between A and B, then why not between B and C? And if C, then why not D, and on and on *ad absurdum*? This is precisely what Rutherford proceeds to do in the following paragraphs.

In paragraph 9, we are told that there were six cities of refuge. Since six symbolizes imperfection in the Bible, that number here represents "God's provision for refuge while imperfect conditions still exist on the earth."

Then in paragraph 11, we are told why the Israelite cities of refuge represent the Organization of Jehovah's Witnesses.

> These cities of protection symbolized the organization of those who are wholly devoted to God and his temple service. There was no other place that the manslayer could find refuge or safety. This is **strong proof** that the Jonadab class who seek refuge against the day of vengeance must find it only in Jehu's chariot, that is to say, in the organization of Jehovah, of which organization Christ Jesus is the Head and great High Priest.[20]

Jonadab never used a city of refuge, but the Jonadab class does need them. Jonadab climbed into Jehu's chariot at his invitation, not because he was a manslayer. Still, Jehu's chariot is a type for the antitypical Organization of Jehovah's Witnesses. The

---

19. "To place the value of this automobile in perspective, a new Ford in 1931 cost approximately 600 dollars. A 16-cylinder Cadillac cost between 5400 and 9200 dollars, depending on style... both cars were used exclusively by Judge Rutherford." (Leonard & Marjorie Chretien, in *Witnesses of Jehovah* (Eugene, Or.: Harvest House, 1988), pp. 45, 46). Auto historians tell more about the V-16: "Naturally, it was the very rich — and often as not, the famous — who made up the limited clientele of the V-16. Among the owners of the first-generation cars was Al Jolson... Robert Montgomery...Marlene Dietrich...." (*Special Interest Autos*, April 1986, p. 21).
20. w34 8/1 p. 229 par. 11

## 10. Rutherford Invents the "Other Sheep"     237

*The Judge Starting on His 700 Mile Trip to Detroit Convention*

**Figure 18. "The Judge Starting on His 700 Mile Trip to Detroit Convention".**

Jonadab class, however, does double duty as both the antitypical Jonadab and the antitypical manslayer. All of this Scripturally unsupported supposition is "strong proof"? Please!

Rutherford is now on a roll:

> The cities of refuge would be set up after the Israelites reached Canaan...This would seem to correspond to the time when the Elisha-Jehu work begins....In 1918 Jesus brought his faithful remnant then on earth across the **antitypical Jordan river** and into the "land", or kingdom condition...The priests bearing the ark of the covenant were the first ones to enter the waters of the Jordan, and stood firm on the dry ground in the river until the people had crossed. (Josh 3:7, 8, 15, 17) Before the Israelites crossed the Jordan river, Moses, by the direction of Jehovah, appointed three cities of refuge on the east side of the river. Likewise also before the remnant were gathered into the temple the Lord caused to be delivered his message "Millions Now Living Will Never Die", meaning, of course, that they must be subject to the conditions announced by the Lord. There also began an announcement that the **Elijah work had ended**. It was a period of transition from the

Elijah to the **Elisha work** performed by the faithful followers of Christ Jesus.[21]

There is a virtual legion of antitypes in this one paragraph. We have an antitypical Elijah-Jehu work beginning, an antitypical Elijah work ending, and an antitypical Elisha work beginning concurrent with an antitypical Jehu work. There is also an antitypical Jordan river and an antitype to the priests carrying the ark and pausing in the river to dry it up. There is something antitypical about the three cities of refuge on the east side of the river as opposed to the other three on the west side. Some of this ties in with the antitype which became the "Millions Now Living Will Never Die" campaign message.

Is your head spinning yet?

*Getting to the Heart of the Matter*

From paragraph 13 thru 16, Rutherford starts to make his main point. The ones who fled to the cities of refuge were unwitting manslayers. They fled to escape the wrath of the avenger of blood—usually a close relative of the deceased who had the legal right to kill the manslayer outside of the city of refuge. In the modern-day application, those who are unwitting manslayers are those who have supported the political and religious elements of the earth in their bloodletting.

> Among both the Jews and "Christendom" there have been those who have had no sympathy with such wrongdoing, yet by reason of circumstances have been forced into participating in and supporting these wrongdoers, to some degree at least, and are thus of the class that unwittingly or unawares are guilty of shedding blood.
> These unwitting manslayers must have an antitypical means of escape corresponding to the cities of refuge in Israel, and "Jehovah in his loving-kindness has made just such a provision as is needed for their escape.[22]

Of course, if there is an antitypical manslayer in need of an antitypical city of refuge, there must also be an antitypical "avenger." Paragraph 18 opens with the words: "Who is "the

---

21. Ibid. par. 12
22. Ibid. pars. 15, 16

## 10. Rutherford Invents the "Other Sheep"

avenger," or the one who executes vengeance antitypically upon such wrongdoers?"

Paragraph 19 answers: "The great kinsman of the human race by birth is Jesus...hence he was the kinsman of the Israelites."

Paragraph 20 adds: "Jesus Christ, the great Executioner, will certainly meet or overtake all the bloodguilty ones at Armageddon and will slay all such as are not in the cities of refuge."

Then paragraph 21 nails down the lid on what are the antitypical cities of refuge by saying, "Those...who would now escape to the city of refuge, must hasten thereto. They must get away from the Devil's organization and take their place with the Lord God's organization and remain there."

(If, at this point, you're recalling Hebrews 2:3 and 5:9 and saying, "I thought Jesus was God's loving provision for escape and salvation," well, you're obviously just not following. Please try to keep up.)

In an article which points not to Jesus, but to a religious organization as the means for mankind's salvation, we find a rare and definitely ironic moment of prophetic insight at the end of paragraph 23:

> The plain declaration of the Lord is that "organized religion", which has so greatly defamed this name, and those therein who have participated in the persecution of his faithful people and have defamed God's name, shall be destroyed without mercy.[23]

### A Distinction Is Made

Paragraph 29 makes a clear distinction between two classes of Christians each expecting a different form of salvation.

> It does not appear from the Scriptures that the cities of refuge have any reference to those who become members of the body of Christ. There does not seem to be any reason why they should. There is a **wide distinction** between such and those who become of the class known as the 'millions that will not die', meaning those people of good will who obey the Lord God now but who are not accepted as a part of the sacrifice of Christ Jesus.[24]

---

23. Ibid. par. 23
24. Ibid. par. 29

The claim is that there is a "wide distinction" between the "body of Christ" and *"people of good will...who are not accepted as a part of the sacrifice of Christ Jesus."* Further, the claim is that this "wide distinction" is scriptural. However, the careful reader will note that no scriptures are provided to support this claim.

In the final paragraph of the study, it is reasoned—again, without any scriptural support *whatsoever*—that there is a correspondence or a typical-antitypical relationship at work. The typical part was the order of things in that, first the covenant at Mount Horeb was put in place, then years later when the Israelites settled in the land of Canaan, the cities of refuge were set up. The antitypical part was the completion of all members making up the new covenant which began when Jesus came to his temple in 1918. This method of salvation ended, and then the antitypical cities of refuge were put in place. The latter is the provision for the unanointed people of good will—the Jonadab class—to be saved from the avenger, Christ. The reason they are called Jonadabs is that the original Jonadab was a non-Israelite, (corresponding to unanointed Christians) but was invited into the chariot (Jehovah's Organization) driven by Jehu, an Israelite (an anointed Christian aka spiritual Israelite) to work with him.

Of course, the idea of a non-anointed Christian is a ridiculous contradiction in terms. Christian comes from Greek *christos* which means "anointed one". Therefore, to say in Greek, "non-anointed Christian," is to say, "non-anointed anointed one."

Apparently, the bulk of Jehovah's Witnesses loyal to Rutherford in the 1930s were so conditioned to accepting types and antitypes that they couldn't see this for the pigswill of reasoning that it was. It's very clear now why the *Publications Index 1930-1985* makes no reference to this little gem of antitypical lunacy.

Is this all there is? Oh, no. Rutherford is just getting his second wind. We have yet to consider the next article of this two-part *Watchtower* series.

## "His Kindness," Part 2

The second article in this series was published in the August 15, 1934 issue of *The Watchtower*. It extends the cities-of-refuge antitype into the current JW doctrine of two distinct salvation hopes, one heavenly and one earthly.

## 10. Rutherford Invents the "Other Sheep"

Jesus Christ is God's provided way of life, but not all men who get life will become spirit creatures. There are Other Sheep which are not of the Little Flock.[25]

While the first class with a heavenly hope is saved by the blood of Jesus, the second class is saved by joining an organization or a specific denomination of organized religion: Jehovah's Witnesses.

> The antitype of the cities of refuge is Jehovah's Organization, and he has made provision for the protection of those who place themselves fully on the side of his organization..."[26]

The typical-antitypical parallels continue to abound in this second article. For example:

> It was the duty of the Levites in the cities of refuge to give information, aid and comfort to those seeking refuge. Likewise it is the duty of the antitypical Levites [anointed Christians] to give information, aid and comfort to those who now seek the Lord's organization.[27]

Then drawing yet another typical-antitypical parallel, Ezekiel 9:6 and Zephaniah 2:3 are invoked paralleling the "mark in the forehead" with the anointed "giving them [the Jonadabs] intelligent information...." Similar parallels are drawn in paragraph 8 between Deuteronomy 19:3; Joshua 20:3, 9; and Isaiah 62:10; to show that "the priestly class, meaning the anointed remnant now on earth, must minister unto the people...the Jonadabs".

Astoundingly, typical-antitypical parallels are even drawn from the ten plagues.

> In antitypical fulfillment of what happened in Egypt, notice and warning to the rulers of the world have already been given. Nine of the plagues have been antitypically fulfilled, and now, before the falling of the vengeance of God upon the firstborn and upon the whole world, foreshadowed by the tenth plague, the people must have instructions and warning. Such is the present work of Jehovah's witnesses.[28]

---

25. w34 8/15 p. 243 par. 1
26. Ibid. par. 3
27. Ibid. par. 5
28. Ibid. par. 9

Paragraph 11 illustrates the major problem that arises when men take it upon themselves to create a prophetic parallel where none was intended. It becomes impossible to make all the pieces fit.

> If the decision was that the slaying was without malice and was accidental or unwittingly committed, then the slayer should find protection in the city of refuge and must remain there until the death of the high priest.[29]

This simply doesn't fit antitypically. The evildoer hanged next to Jesus did not kill accidentally nor unwittingly, yet he was still forgiven. This application of Rutherford's only allows for unwitting sinners to enter, but we have the example of King David whose adultery and subsequent murder conspiracy were anything but unwitting, yet he too was forgiven. Jesus makes no distinction between degrees or types of sin. What matters to him is a broken heart and sincere repentance. Rutherford's antitypical applications now get even more bizarre:

> At the death of the high priest, the slayer might return with safety to his own place of residence. This would clearly seem to teach that the Jonadab class [aka the other sheep], having sought and found refuge with God's organization, must remain in the chariot or organization of the Lord with the Greater Jehu, and must continue in heart sympathy and harmony with the Lord and his organization and must prove their proper heart condition by cooperating with Jehovah's witnesses until the office of the high priest class yet on the earth be finished.[30]

This point is important enough that the Rutherford repeats it in paragraph 17:

> Such [Jonadabs/other sheep] do not come with the provisions of the new covenant, and life cannot be granted to them until the last member of the priestly class has finished his earthly course. "The death of the high priest" means the change of the last members of the royal priesthood from human to spirit organism, which follows Armageddon.[31]

---

29. Ibid. par. 11a
30. Ibid. par. 11b
31. Ibid. par. 17

## 10. Rutherford Invents the "Other Sheep"

Jesus is referred to in the Bible as our high priest.[32] Nowhere do we find anointed Christians referred to as a high priest class, especially while on the earth. When our high priest died, he opened the way for our salvation. However, Rutherford has a different idea for the salvation of the Other Sheep or Jonadab class. He is here creating a super-clergy class. This isn't your typical clergy *a la* Catholic church. No! This clergy is charged with your salvation. Only when they—not Jesus—have all passed away can the Other Sheep be saved, provided of course that they have remained in the antitypical city of refuge, the organized religion of Jehovah's Witnesses.

Here we encounter another problem with made-up prophetic antitypes: The need to twist scriptures to make them work. The Bible indicates that the anointed are taken to heaven before Armageddon. There is nothing in Scripture to indicate that some will survive Armageddon as humans.

> For this is what we tell YOU by Jehovah's word, that we the living who survive to the presence of the Lord shall in no way precede those who have fallen asleep [in death]; because the Lord himself will descend from heaven with a commanding call, with an archangel's voice and with God's trumpet, and those who are dead in union with Christ will rise first. Afterward we the living who are surviving will, together with them, be caught away in clouds to meet the Lord in the air; and thus we shall always be with [the] Lord. (1 Thessalonians 4:15-17)

> Look! I tell YOU a sacred secret: We shall not all fall asleep [in death], but we shall all be changed, in a moment, in the twinkling of an eye, during the last trumpet. For the trumpet will sound, and the dead will be raised up incorruptible, and we shall be changed. (1 Corinthians 15:51, 52)

So, if all the anointed die or are transformed prior to Armageddon, Rutherford's Other Sheep—the Jonadabs—don't have to remain inside the Organization, the antitypical city of refuge. They can leave before Armageddon, because they have been saved by the death of the high priest—the anointed.

---

32. Hebrews 2:17

## Rutherford's Real Agenda Is Revealed

Rutherford's true agenda was to create a clergy/laity class distinction and frighten the laity class into loyal obedience. How is this different from the Catholic model of organized religion with its creation of controlling such as the fires of Hell and the need to pay to escape purgatory?

> If after receiving these good things from the hand of the Lord any man is found exercising too much personal liberty, that is to say, not keeping with the bounds of Jehovah's merciful provision made for him at the present time; not taking into consideration that he does not yet possess the right to life [as the priestly class do]...he loses the protection which Jehovah has provided for him. He must continue to appreciate the certainty and nearness of Armageddon and also the fact that soon the priestly class will pass from the earth....[33]

> **Christ, the great [antitypical] Avenger and Executioner, will not spare any of the Jonadab company that get outside of Jehovah's safety arrangement made for them in connection with his organization.**[34]

Amazingly, Rutherford's quiver of type/antitype pairings is not yet empty. Continuing in paragraph 18, he draws next on the account of Solomon and Shimei. Solomon required Shimei to remain in the city of refuge for his sins against Solomon's father, David, or suffer death. Shimei disobeyed and was killed at Solomon's order. The antitype is Jesus, as the greater Solomon, and any of the Jonadab class who "now venture outside of their own haven of refuge" and "run ahead of Jehovah" are the antitypical Shimei.

## When Does the Antitypical City of Refuge Start?

The typical cities of refuge only came into being when the Israelites settled in the promised land. The antitypical promised land is the paradise to come, but that hardly works for Rutherford's purpose. Therefore, other timelines have to shift.

> Therefore it is after 1914, at which time God enthroned the great King and sent him forth to rule. It is then that the holy city, the

---

33. Ibid. par. 15
34. Ibid. par. 18

## 10. Rutherford Invents the "Other Sheep"

new Jerusalem, which is Jehovah God's organization, descends out of heaven. It is that holy city which is the abiding place of Jehovah. (Ps 132:13) The time is when "the tabernacle of God is with men, and he will dwell with them, and they shall be his people, and God himself shall be with them, and be their God". (Rev 21:2, 3)...The prophetic picture of the city of refuge could have no applications prior to the beginning of the reign of Christ in 1914.[35]

So, the tent of God depicted in Revelation 21:2, 3 has been with us for the past hundred years. It would appear that the whole "mourning, outcry, pain, and death will be no more" thing has been on back order for some time.

### The Other Sheep Identified

If any doubt remains as to the identity of the Other Sheep, it is removed in paragraph 28.

> Those people of good will, that is, the Jonadab class, are the sheep of the 'other flock' which Jesus mentioned, when he said: "And other sheep I have, which are not of this fold: them also I must bring, and they shall hear my voice; and there shall be one fold, and one shepherd." (John 10:16)[36]

Rutherford tells us that the doors have been closed to the heavenly hope. The only hope left is for life on earth as part of the Other Sheep or Jonadab class.

> The city of refuge was not for the anointed of God, but such city and loving provision made for those who should come to the Lord after the temple class is selected and anointed.[37]

In ancient Israel, if a priest or Levite were to become a manslayer, he too would have to take advantage of the provision of a city of refuge. Thus, they were not exempt from the provision, but that doesn't fit with Rutherford's application, so it is ignored. The antitypical cities of refuge are not for the priestly class of Jehovah's Witnesses.

---

35. Ibid. p. 248 par. 19
36. Ibid. p. 249 par. 28
37. Ibid. par. 29

*Finally, a Clergy/Laity Distinction Emerges*

To this day, Witness are told that there is no clergy/laity distinction in the Organization of Jehovah's Witnesses. However, this claim is not followed in practice. Rutherford's words bear out that it hasn't been true since they took the name *Jehovah's Witnesses*.

> Be it noted that the obligation is laid upon **the priestly class to do the leading or reading of the law of instruction to the people**. Therefore, where there is a company of Jehovah's witnesses...**the leader of a study should be selected from amongst the anointed**, and likewise those of the service committee should be taken from the anointed....Jonadab was there as one to learn, and not one who was to teach....The official organization of Jehovah on earth consists of his anointed remnant, and **the Jonadabs [other sheep] who walk with the anointed are to be taught, but not to be leaders**. This appearing to be God's arrangement, all should gladly abide thereby.[38]

It appears that all this ridiculous antitypical gobbledygook was written for one purpose: To exalt a clergy class over a more numerous laity class. It's an old story. Of course, things didn't work out as Rutherford anticipated. The end was not imminent. His clergy class was finite, having been limited by his own declaration that the numbers were now filled. As the number of Witnesses grew and the number of those professing to be anointed diminished, it became necessary to include "Jonadabs" among the clergy, so an ecclesiastical hierarchy was created that included zone overseers (formerly all overseers were called "servants"), branch overseers, district overseers (now gone), circuit overseers, and local elders.

Should someone argue that these do not constitute a clergy, it should be noted that, except for the local elders, all are supported financially, and more important, all have great power. The local elders can punish any publisher through disfellowshipping, which means the individual is cut off socially and often economically from family and friends. Disfellowshipping is total ostracism. A significant number of Witnesses and ex-Witnesses who have suffered this punishment have taken their own lives.

How do Jehovah's Witnesses avoid accepting blame when their unscriptural policy results in such tragic consequences? They

---

38. Ibid. p. 250 par. 32

blame the disfellowshipped one for being unstable, but they take no responsibility for such deaths. We hear some say that "the demons got them" and that is why they committed suicide. Such a dismissal of personal responsibility will carry no weight on Judgment Day.

## Rewriting History

The Organization cannot abandon this teaching. It is so fundamental to JW theology that to abandon it would tear the Organization apart. So, they treat it as a given. As one might say, "the sky is blue" without feeling the need to prove the point, so Witnesses teach that the Other Sheep are a class of Christian who are not anointed with God's spirit; who do not have a heavenly calling; who are not to partake of the emblems; who do not have Jesus as their mediator; who are not children of God; who only achieve an approved state before God at the end of the thousand years. They teach all this without ever feeling the need to explain the doctrine, or back it up with Scripture.

The real source of the doctrine is too embarrassing to reveal, so they make no reference to it in their publications. The landmark article series that gave birth to the whole doctrine has been all but excised from the collective memory of Jehovah's Witnesses. The Watchtower Library only goes back to publications printed since 1950. An edict went out years ago to all bodies of elders to remove all old publications from the Kingdom Hall library—the JW equivalent to a book burning. In my case, the elders suspected me of apostasy when they learned I had downloaded old *Watchtower* volumes. The Watch Tower Society seems to be terrified of its past and doing whatever it can to rewrite its history.

To hide your history from scrutiny while not correcting your false teachings would seem to fit perfectly with the condemnation found at Revelation 22:15.

> Outside are the dogs and those who practice spiritism and the fornicators and the murderers and the idolaters and **everyone liking and carrying on a lie**.

## A Final Word

I realize that some may be a little offput by my sardonic tone expressed throughout this book, and in this chapter in particular. Generally, an analytical work such as this strives for an emotionally detached consideration of the subject matter. However, I am not some detached observer. What I am is a lifelong victim of deception. Now, as I read the source of the doctrine that robbed me for most of my life of a proper relationship with my Lord Jesus and my Father, Jehovah, I am overwhelmed by the sheer idiocy of it all. That Freddy Franz and Nathan Knorr who lived through that era should have collaborated in perpetuating this ridiculous teaching seems unimaginable if they were truly men of God, humble servants of our Lord Jesus, led by holy spirit!

For those who are uncomfortable with my tone, my defence is that "sarcasm is a healthy response in the face of overwhelming stupidity." In this, I have no other than the apostle Paul to imitate. He used sarcasm often when dealing with the short-sighted stupidity of men. For example, to the Corinthians, he wrote:

> Are you already satisfied? Are you already rich? Have you begun ruling as kings without us? (1 Corinthians 4:8)

> But someone may ask, "How will the dead be raised? What kind of bodies will they have?" What a foolish question! When you put a seed into the ground, it doesn't grow into a plant unless it dies first. (1 Corinthians 15:35, 36 NLT)

> You gladly put up with fools since you are so wise! In fact, you even put up with anyone who enslaves you or exploits you or takes advantage of you or puts on airs or slaps you in the face. To my shame I admit that we were too weak for that! (2 Corinthians 11:19-21 NIV)

I think Rutherford's Other Sheep doctrine qualifies as overwhelmingly stupid, don't you? However, the Governing Body's attempt to cover it up and keep it from Jehovah's Witnesses is wicked. I say this because lies are wicked, and by Gerrit Lösch's own admission, keeping facts from someone who deserves to know the truth is a lie.[39]

---

39. See "Is the Governing Body Really Guilty of Lying?" on page 117.

# 11

# Is the Governing Body a False Prophet?

> *"If any prophet presumptuously speaks a word in my name that I did not command him to speak or speaks in the name of other gods, that prophet must die. However, you may say in your heart: 'How will we know that Jehovah has not spoken the word?' When the prophet speaks in the name of Jehovah and the word is not fulfilled or does not come true, then Jehovah did not speak that word. The prophet spoke it presumptuously. You should not fear him." (Deuteronomy 18:20-22)*

Jehovah's Witnesses are often accused of being false prophets because they are well known in Christendom as a group with multiple failed prophetic warnings about the coming end of the world. Yet the average Jehovah's Witness will deny the validity of such accusations by stating that the Governing Body has never claimed to be a prophet. This excerpt from the book, *Reasoning from the Scriptures*, is typical of that position.

> **Jehovah's Witnesses do not claim to be inspired prophets.** They have made mistakes. Like the apostles of Jesus Christ, they have at times had some wrong expectations.—Luke 19:11; Acts 1:6.[1]

If it walks like a duck, quacks like a duck, and swims like a duck, claiming it is really an ostrich won't fool anyone. In a now-infamous speech, President Richard Nixon claimed, "I am not a crook,"

---

1. *Reasoning from the Scriptures* p. 136 "False Prophets"

but the world soon learned otherwise. Is the Organization's claim that they have never acted like a false prophet valid, or is it a lie?

## False Prophets: The Watch Tower Definition

The book, *Reasoning from the Scriptures,* provides the following definition of what a false prophet is:

> **Definition:** Individuals and organizations proclaiming messages that they attribute to a superhuman source but that do not originate with the true God and are not in harmony with his revealed will.[2]

The book also quotes from the Bible to provide a scriptural definition:

> Deut. 18:18-20: "A prophet I shall raise up for them from the midst of their brothers, like you [like Moses]; and I shall indeed put my words in his mouth, and he will certainly speak to them all that I shall command him. And it must occur that the man who will not listen to my words that he will speak in my name, I shall myself require an account from him. However, the prophet who presumes to speak in my name a word that I have not commanded him to speak or who speaks in the name of other gods, that prophet must die." (Compare Jeremiah 14:14; 28:11, 15.)[3]

## What the *Reasoning* Book Omits

After reading the foregoing, the average Jehovah's Witness will conclude that the Organization doesn't fit the mold of a false prophet. As one of Jehovah's Witnesses, I too believed that the Governing Body had made mistakes, but that they had never claimed to be a prophet.

My confidence in their integrity caused me to trust what was written in the publications and not to look too deeply into the context of the verses they quoted from Scripture. If I had, perhaps I would have noticed that they failed to provide the full definition of a false prophet as revealed in Deuteronomy. That they are aware of this evidence is clear from the fact they quote part of it, but only the part that doesn't directly condemn them. They

---

2. Ibid. p. 132
3. Ibid. p. 133 par. 2

## 11. Is the Governing Body a False Prophet?

quoted Deuteronomy 18:18-20, but failed to include the next two verses which read:

> However, you may say in your heart: "How will we know that Jehovah has not spoken the word?" **When the prophet speaks in the name of Jehovah and the word is not fulfilled or does not come true, then Jehovah did not speak that word. The prophet spoke it presumptuously.** You should not fear him. (Deuteronomy 18:21, 22)

The omission of these two verses from the *Reasoning* book is very telling because based on Deuteronomy 18:21, 22, there are two aspects to determining whether a prophet speaks falsely or truthfully.

1. He claims to speak in the name of Jehovah.
2. The word he speaks does not come true.

As we read earlier, Jehovah's Witnesses say they are not inspired prophets, so they would claim this passage in Deuteronomy can't be applied to them. Is that a valid claim?

What does it mean to be an "inspired prophet"? *The Watchtower* states:

> This expression "inspired of God" translated the Greek phrase the·o'pneu·stos, meaning "God-breathed." By 'breathing' on faithful men, God caused his spirit, or active force, to become operative upon them and directed what he wanted recorded, for, as it is written, "prophecy was at no time brought by man's will, but men spoke from God as they were borne along by holy spirit."[4]

Paul, writing in the Greek language, used a word that literally means "God-breathed." The word "spirit" in Greek is *pneuma* which means "wind" or "breath," i.e., air in motion. Air is invisible but as wind or breath it can be felt and can affect material things. So it is with God's spirit. It cannot be seen but its effects can be felt and it can influence us.[5]

### Speaking in God's Name

Does the Governing Body claim to speak in the name of Jehovah? Yes, they do. According to the publications, the Governing Body is the Faithful and Discreet Slave and was formed as such in 1919

---

4. it-1 p. 309
5. w10 3/1 p. 4

with the then-president J. F. Rutherford as its principal member. Rutherford claimed to speak in God's name as we saw in the previous chapter.

In a 1930 *Watchtower* article, referring to himself as *the servant*, he claimed:

> It would seem there would be no necessity for the 'servant' [Rutherford] to have an advocate such as the holy spirit because the 'servant' is in **direct communication with Jehovah**...[6]

Judge Rutherford left no doubt in our minds that he meets the first qualification for someone claiming to be a prophet for he clearly states that he "speaks in the name of Jehovah."

That takes care of the first member of the Governing Body AKA Faithful and Discreet Slave. What about the modern Governing Body?

Let's allow them to answer that question for themselves as they do in these recent *Watchtower* articles:

> Surely there is ample evidence to show that **you can trust the channel that Jehovah has used for nearly a hundred years** now to lead us in the way of the truth.[7]

> "**That faithful slave is the channel** through which Jesus is feeding his true followers in this time of the end. It is vital that we recognize the faithful slave. Our spiritual health and our relationship with God depend on this channel."[8]

The modern Governing Body has linked itself with, as they put it, "the channel that Jehovah has used for nearly a hundred years." That is a clear reference to J. F. Rutherford.

Just to demonstrate that better, consider this: You and I can come up with an interpretation on any Bible subject, but we aren't claiming to be *the channel by which God speaks to his servants on earth*. The moment we claim to be God's channel, we are saying that he communicates through us to others. To put it another way, if God is using his spirit so as to have someone act as his channel of communication, then what they say must come from God. If it doesn't come from God, then they have no right to claim to be his channel of communication, isn't that so?

---

6. w30 9/1 p. 263
7. *The Watchtower*, July 2017, "Winning the Battle for Your Mind" p. 30
8. w13 7/15 p. 20 par. 2

# 11. Is the Governing Body a False Prophet?

You can't call yourself God's channel unless you are channeling God, right?

Peter warns us about this when he writes:

> For YOU know this first, that no prophecy of Scripture springs from **any private interpretation**. For prophecy was at no time brought by man's will, but men spoke from God as they were borne along by holy spirit. However, there also came to be false prophets among the people, as there will also be false teachers among YOU. (2 Peter 1:20-2:1)

If the Governing Body tells us that something is going to happen and it doesn't, then that prophecy was the result of "private interpretation."

## Punishing Heretics or Those Who Question

There is another factor to consider. When the Governing Body as God's channel publishes any prophetic interpretation, it will tolerate no challenge to its position. This was the attitude of the Catholic Church in centuries past. We are all familiar with the Catholic Inquisition, and how it dealt with heretics, with anyone who challenged or even questioned its authority as the channel of God.

Let's turn now to the teaching of the overlapping generation to see how the Governing Body deals with anyone who disagrees with it or simply questions it.

In the April 15, 2010 issue of *The Watchtower*, the Governing Body introduces what it likes to call *New Light* on its application of Jesus' use of "this generation" as recorded at Matthew 24:34.

Essentially, the teaching is that the individual lifespans of the generation of anointed Witnesses who were alive in 1914 will overlap with the lifespans of a different generation of anointed Witnesses who will be around to see Armageddon. These two separate and distinct generations overlap each other to form a sort of super generation or what is now referred to as the *overlapping generation.*

This change has been very disturbing to many thoughtful Jehovah's Witnesses for obvious reasons: It flies in the face of Scripture, common usage, and for that matter, simple logic. Nevertheless, should any Witness choose to disagree with this teaching, he or she will be accused of apostasy and face the threat of being disfellowshipped, which means being cut off from their entire social support system. In its heyday, the Catholic Church could torture dissenters and even execute them, sometimes by burning them while bound to a stake. Often, those Church officials justified such horrendous acts by claiming they were acting out of love, and a concern to save those *heretics* from the fires of Hell.

Fortunately, all the modern Organization of Jehovah's Witnesses can do is to execute dissenters socially, as they don't have the support of the secular courts as did the Catholic Church in medieval times. Yet, that is still no trivial thing. In fact, it causes so much emotional distress that a shocking number have committed suicide as a result. I have received many communications from viewers of my channels telling tragic stories of suicide by those who have been dealt with egregiously by JW elders claiming to be acting out of love.

As we think about the similarities between the power structure of the Catholic Church and that of the Governing Body of Jehovah's Witnesses, it is important for us to grasp that the purpose of a false prophet, as explained in Deuteronomy 18:22, is to instill fear in his followers. Jehovah tells his people: "You should not fear him." Why? Because a false prophet aims to control others so as to enrich and empower himself by convincing them he is privy to special life-saving knowledge, and that his listeners must follow him and do as he says or suffer the dire consequences. The false prophet must also convince his followers that their salvation depends on their obeying him. While he will claim he is speaking for God, the reality is that he has placed himself in the seat of God, in that he demands and gets the obedience and devotion which we should only give to the Almighty.

> Let no one seduce YOU in any manner, because it will not come unless the apostasy comes first and the man of lawlessness gets revealed, the son of destruction. He is set in opposition and lifts himself up over everyone who is called "god" or an object of reverence, so that he sits down in the temple of The God, publicly showing himself to be a god. Do YOU not remember that, while I was yet with YOU, I used to tell YOU these things? (2 Thessalonians 2:3-5)

In summary, the formula for identifying a false prophet is very simple. Anyone can apply it: If the prophet speaks in God's name as, say, his *channel of communication*, and then, if his prophecies turn out to be false, *he is a false prophet*. There are no excuses, no work arounds. He is a liar, and we are commanded by God not to fear him. If we were still under the law of Moses, we'd be required to put him to death! But under the Christian system of things, Jesus will take care of false prophets.

## The Failed Prophecy of 1914

To this day, Jehovah's Witnesses take great pride in what they consider a true fulfillment of prophecy proclaimed some 40 years in advance in the pages of *Zion's Watch Tower and Herald of Christ's Presence*:

> For some 40 years the Bible Students boldly proclaimed that the year 1914 would mark the end of the Gentile Times.[9]

> For 40 years before 1914, the Bible Students—as Jehovah's Witnesses were then called—had been announcing boldly that the times of the Gentiles would end in that year. The distressful events of 1914 proved them correct.[10]

These statements lead the reader to the conclusion that a true prophecy had been boldly proclaimed four decades before its 1914 fulfillment. We've already established that the gentile times didn't end in that year.[11] There is no scriptural proof to support their claim. For that matter, there is no empirical evidence supporting it either. What evidence is there historically to prove beyond any doubt when the gentile times of Luke 21:24 ended? Does the Bible say? Is it even important that we know? If so, why doesn't the Bible give us something to measure by?

But let's overlook that for the moment. Instead, let's focus on what else was boldly predicted during those forty years—predictions which the Watch Tower Society would prefer we forget about.

It will likely come as a shock to the majority of Jehovah's Witnesses to learn that one thing that wasn't predicted during those forty years was that 1914 was *the start of the invisible presence of Jesus Christ* as the Messianic King. *Zion's Watchtower* and other Watch Tower publications proclaimed that his presence

---

9. w89 4/15 pp. 6-7 par. 8
10. re chap. 21 p. 130 par. 4
11. See "Pulling the 1914 Doctrinal Lynchpin" on page 93.

had already begun in 1874.[12] What was predicted to start in 1914 was the great tribulation which Witnesses believe is the first phase of the end of the system of things, culminating in the war of Armageddon.

What follows is just a sampling, as there are literally hundreds of occurrences of 1914 predictions in the publications in the years leading up to that date.

From *Zion's Watch Tower*, August, 1880:

> "...the 40 years of trouble or "Day of wrath" ending with the times of the Gentiles in 1914, **when the kingdom of God** [soon to be *set up* or exalted to power] **will have broken in pieces and consumed all earthly kingdoms.**" (p. 124)

From *Zion's Watch Tower*, September 1883:

> "**As we find the forty years, from 1874 to 1914, A. D., prophetically marked out as the time for the change of earth's administration**, it would seem not unreasonable to suppose that the proper physical changes might occur during the same period. Not that we expect all changes to be completed in the specified forty years, but that by that time the new systems and arrangements will be thoroughly introduced, which will be gradually improving, **and will reach absolute perfection at the same time that mankind in general will reach absolute perfection by restitution**. Thus the perfect earth and its perfect lord (man) will both be prepared to enter upon the ceaseless ages of perfection into which shall never enter sin, death, pain or sorrow." (p. 534)

From *Zion's Watch Tower*, January 15, 1892:

> "The date of the close of that "battle" is **definitely marked in Scripture as October, 1914.**" (p. 1355)

From *Zion's Watch Tower*, August 1, 1892:

> "That the overthrow of the present nominal ecclesiastical systems shall precede the overthrow of the civil powers is thus indicated-the former continuing only until A. D. 1908 and the latter until A. D. 1914." (p. 1434)

From *Zion's Watch Tower*, July 15, 1894:

> "We see no reason for changing the figures—nor could we change them if we would. **They are, we believe, God's dates, not ours.**

---

12.   jv chap. 5 p. 47

## 11. Is the Governing Body a False Prophet?

But bear in mind that the end of 1914 is not the date for the *beginning*, but for the *end* of the time of the trouble. (p. 1677)

Can the Organization legitimately claim not to be acting as a prophet and speaking for God when it states: "They are...God's dates, not ours"? After forty years of beating this prophetic drum, it would be disingenuous in the extreme to assert that they weren't acting as a prophet in God's name. Yet, that is what the Watch Tower publications continue to claim.

## The Failed Prophecy of 1925

While the Governing Body may try to distance itself from the prophetic failures of Russell, they have nailed their colors to the mast when it comes to the predictions of J. F. Rutherford. This is so because the official teaching out of Watch Tower publications is that Jesus appointed prominent Watch Tower leaders as his Faithful and Discreet Slave in 1919 to feed his flock.[13] The first of those leaders was Judge Rutherford, who became president in 1917 and held on to the post until his death in 1942. He authored many books and articles during that time, becoming the chief source of the "spiritual food" being dispensed to the flock.

Shortly after the death of C. T. Russell in 1916, Rutherford began to preach that millions then living would never die, prophesying that the beginning of the end would come by 1925.

> **That period of time beginning 1575 before A. D. 1 of necessity would end in the fall of the year 1925**, at which time the type ends and the great antitype must begin. What, then, should we expect to take place? In the type there must be a full restoration; therefore the great antitype must mark the beginning of restoration of all things. The chief thing to be restored is the human race to life; and since other Scriptures definitely fix the fact that there will be a resurrection of Abraham, Isaac, Jacob and other faithful ones of old, and that these will have the first favor, **we may expect 1925 to witness the return of these faithful men of Israel** from the condition of death, being resurrected and fully restored to perfect humanity and made the visible, legal representatives of the new order of things on earth.[14]

---

13. w17 February pp. 25-26 par. 10
14. *Millions Now Living Will Never Die* (1920), p. 88

## EARTHLY RULERS

As we have heretofore stated, the great jubilee cycle is due to begin in 1925. At that time the earthly phase of the kingdom shall be recognized. The Apostle Paul in the eleventh chapter of Hebrews names a long list of faithful men who died before the crucifixion of the Lord and before the beginning of the selection of the church. These can never be a part of the heavenly class; they had no heavenly hopes; but God has in store something good for them. They are to be resurrected as perfect men and constitute the princes or rulers in the earth, according to his promise. (Psalm 45:16; Isaiah 32:1; Matthew 8:11) Therefore we may confidently expect that 1925 will mark the return of Abraham, Isaac, Jacob and the faithful prophets of old, particularly those named by the Apostle in Hebrews chapter eleven, to the condition of human perfection.[15]

The 1921 edition of *The Harp of God* made this bold assertion on its front cover: "Conclusive proof that millions now living will never die."[16]

That his readers took this as a reliable prophetic interpretation is evident by the incredibly rapid growth in the number of partakers at the memorial in the years leading up to "the date," as reported in the book, *Jehovah's Witnesses in the Divine Purpose*.[17]

- 1922 – 32,661 partakers.
- 1923 – 42,000 partakers.
- 1924 – 62,696 partakers.
- 1925 – 90,434 partakers.

This is an excellent example of the power of false prophecy to motivate people. If they come to believe the prophecy, fear of the consequences for ignoring the prophetic warning will ensure their compliance. It is surely for this very reason that Jehovah has not revealed the day nor the hour that Christ will return because He doesn't want us to serve Him out of fear or selfishness. He wants us to obey Him out of faith—faith that He is good and that He will keep his word no matter how long it may take.[18]

---

15. Ibid. p. 89, 90
16. See "Appendix D: The Harp of God Cover and Canvassing Script" on page 363
17. Page 110
18. Matthew 24:36; 2 Peter 3:9

## 11. Is the Governing Body a False Prophet?

What happens inevitably when a prophecy fails to come true? We can look to history for the answer. As a consequence of the failure of Rutherford's millions-now-living prediction, the number of Watch Tower adherents dropped from 90,434 in 1925 to a mere 17,380 by 1928.[19] Rutherford's failed prediction caused about 75% of all the Bible Student groups previously affiliated with the Watch Tower Society to break away!

At this point, it is worthwhile that we again reference the book, *Reasoning from the Scriptures*, which tells us:

> True prophets and the false can be recognized **by the fruitage** manifest in their lives and the lives of those who follow them[20]

So, a false prophet can be "recognized by the fruitage manifest in [his life]." What fruitage did Rutherford manifest in his life?

We can start with the fact that he seized control of the Watch Tower corporations by employing the tactics of a corporate raider.[21] He then used that position of power to promote his prediction that the end would come by 1925. When that failed, Rutherford never apologized in the publications for misleading his followers. Instead, he just attempted to adjust their expectations. In 1929, still pushing his end-of-the-world prediction, Rutherford used donated funds to acquire a 10-room Spanish-style mansion in San Diego, naming it "Beth Sarim" which means "House of the Princes." The justification for this enormous expenditure was that it was intended to house men like King David, Abraham, Isaac, and Jacob, upon their impending resurrection.

In the meantime, it was an excellent place for Rutherford to winter, and to house one of his two 16-cylinder Cadillacs—hugely expensive cars to own and run at a time when the country was going through the worst economic depression in its history and faithful colporteurs (now called pioneers) were living off the meagre profits from their sale of Rutherford's books.

As for the "fruitage manifest" in the lives of his followers, the rapid decline in the number of partakers still affiliated with Rutherford's theology tells the all-to-familiar tale of disillusionment and loss of faith experienced by those who put their trust in

---

19. *Jehovah's Witnesses in the Divine Purpose*, p. 312, 313.
20. rs p. 135 "False Prophets"
21. *Rutherford's Coup: The Watch Tower Succession Crisis of 1917 and Its Aftermath* (ISBN-13 978-1778143014) by Rud Persson.

men and their predictions. How many *little ones* were stumbled by Rutherford's folly?

Causing Christians to lose faith is a very serious sin. It is one that Jesus said is so bad that it would be preferable for the stumbler to have a massive stone chained to his neck and to be tossed into the deep, blue sea, rather than face the full punishment due him.[22] Yet, Jesus' warning goes unheeded by Witnesses who are trained to easily excuse something as egregious as the failed 1925 prediction, claiming it to be merely the result of human imperfection.

But is that what the Scriptures teach us to do? Do they tell us that if a Christian makes a mistake that affects the faith of his fellow Christians, then he has no need to acknowledge how he has harmed others, to apologize, to ask for forgiveness, and to make amends? Have we seen evidence that the leaders of the Organization have acted that way following their numerous prophetic failures?

A false prophet is essentially a liar, and we know that inveterate liars will try to cover their tracks by making up new lies to support the old ones.

Can we excuse such a huge prophetic fiasco as the 1925 millions-now-living-will-never-die campaign as just the mistake of one imperfect but well-intentioned man? Remember, the Governing Body claims Rutherford as one of their own, part of the Faithful and Discreet Slave named by Jesus to feed his flock since 1919. Therefore, by their own teaching, and by Rutherford's own claim to be in direct communication with Jehovah,[23] he was the channel God was using to communicate with his faithful people. Given that, are we not being indefensibly naïve to say that he wasn't engaged in perpetuating a false prophecy, but simply made a mistake?

## The Failed Prophecy of 1975

My late wife recalled a discussion that ensued among some brothers and sisters following the release of the October 15, 1966

---

22. Matthew 18:6
23. w30 9/1 p. 263

## 11. Is the Governing Body a False Prophet?

*Watchtower* covering the convention of that year and the release of a new book.

Here's what got them so excited.

> "To give aid today in this critical time to prospective sons of God," announced President Knorr, "a new book in English, entitled 'Life Everlasting—in Freedom of the Sons of God,' has been published." At all assembly points where it was released, the book was received enthusiastically. Crowds gathered around stands and soon supplies of the book were depleted. Immediately its contents were examined. It did not take the brothers very long to find the chart beginning on page 31, showing that 6,000 years of man's existence end in 1975. **Discussion of 1975 overshadowed about everything else.**[24]

I was just 17 when the *Life Everlasting* book was released.[25] I recall studying it in our Tuesday night Congregation Book Study, and I vividly remember the fervor it caused among the brothers and sisters. There is no mystery as to what got the community of Jehovah's Witnesses so excited. How else was a group of Christians, already primed to expect Armageddon at any moment, going to react at reading the following excerpt from the newly released book:

> The published timetable resulting from this independent study gives the date of man's creation as 4026 B.C.E. According to this **trustworthy Bible chronology six thousand years from man's creation will end in 1975, and the seventh period of a thousand years of human history will begin in the fall of 1975 C.E.** So six thousand years of man's existence on earth will soon be up, yes, **within this generation**... So in not many years within our own generation we are reaching what Jehovah God could view as the seventh day of man's existence. **How appropriate it would be for Jehovah God to make of this coming seventh period of a thousand years a sabbath period of rest and release**, a great Jubilee sabbath for the proclaiming of liberty throughout the earth to all its inhabitants! This would be most timely for mankind. It would also be most fitting on God's part, for, remember, mankind has yet ahead of it what the last book of the Holy Bible speaks of as the reign of Jesus Christ over earth for a thousand years, the millennial reign of Christ... **It would not be by mere chance or accident but would be according to the loving**

---

24. w66 10/15 pp. 628-629
25. See "Appendix C: Life Everlasting Book Inside Cover" on page 362.

purpose of Jehovah God for the reign of Jesus Christ, the 'Lord of the Sabbath,' to run parallel with the seventh millennium of man's existence.[26]

The Organization continued to feed the fever their publication had created. At every semi-annual circuit assembly and annual district convention, we heard talks referring to 1975. I'm sure the incentive to promote the year via convention discourses happened because of the implicit endorsement given at the 1966 Baltimore convention by vice president, Fred Franz, and later reproduced in *The Watchtower* for the worldwide JW community to read:

THE YEAR 1975

At the Baltimore assembly Brother Franz in his closing remarks made some interesting comments regarding the year **1975**. He began casually by saying, "Just before I got on the platform a young man came to me and said, 'Say, what does this **1975** mean? Does it mean this, that or any other thing?'" In part, Brother Franz went on to say: 'You have noticed the chart [on pages 31-35 in the book Life Everlasting—in Freedom of the Sons of God]. **It shows that 6,000 years of human experience will end in 1975, about nine years from now.** What does that mean? Does it mean that God's rest day began 4026 BCE? It could have. The Life Everlasting book does not say it did not. The book merely presents the chronology. You can accept it or reject it. If that is the case, what does that mean to us? [He then went into some length showing the feasibility of the 4026 BCE date as being the beginning of God's rest day.]

What about the year **1975**? What is it going to mean, dear friends?' asked Brother Franz. 'Does it mean that Armageddon is going to be finished, with Satan bound, by **1975**? It could! It could! All things are possible with God. Does it mean that Babylon the Great is going to go down by **1975**? It could. Does it mean that the attack of Gog of Magog is going to be made on Jehovah's witnesses to wipe them out, then Gog himself will be put out of action? It could. But we are not saying. All things are possible with God. But we are not saying. And don't any of you be specific in saying anything that is going to happen between now and **1975**. But the big point of it all is this, dear friends: Time is short. Time is running out, no question about that.

---

26. *Life Everlasting in Freedom of the Sons of God* (1966) pp.26-30

## 11. Is the Governing Body a False Prophet?

When we were approaching the end of the Gentile Times in 1914, there was no sign that the Gentile Times were going to end. Conditions on earth gave us no hint of what was to come, even as late as June of that year. Then suddenly there was a murder. World War I broke out. You know the rest. Famines, earthquakes and pestilences followed, as Jesus foretold would happen.

But what do we have today as we approach **1975**? Conditions have not been peaceful. We've been having world wars, famines, earthquakes, pestilences and we have these conditions still as we approach **1975**. Do these things mean something? These things mean that we're in the "time of the end." And the end has to come sometime. Jesus said: "As these things start to occur, raise yourselves erect and lift your heads up, because your deliverance is getting near." (Luke 21:28) **So we know that as we come to 1975 our deliverance is that much nearer.**[27]

Circuit and district overseers alike fanned the flames of speculation. I remember being at a district convention in Florida in 1972 and hearing District Overseer Charles Sinutko sounding forth on the topic. I was very impressed by his speaking ability. Here is an excerpt from a talk he gave in 1967 at the district convention in Sheboygan, Wisconsin:

As Jehovah's Witnesses, as runners, even though some of us have become a little weary, it almost seems as though Jehovah has provided meat in due season, because He's held up before all of us a new goal: a new year; something to reach out for, and it just seems it's given all of us so much more energy and power in this final burst of speed for the finish line, and that's the year, 1975. As one brother put it: **"Stay alive to 75"**[28]

I remember convention programs where the speaker actually counted down the months to the finish line.[29] These prominent Watch Tower leaders surely felt the backing of the Organization in speaking so strongly in support of this teaching. Indeed, Fred Franz continued to promote his pet theory that 6,000 years of man's existence would end in 1975 with huge ramifications for

---

27. w66 10/15 p. 631
28. A recording of this talk can be found by a simple google search.
29. One example of this is a talk given by District Overseer Duggan at the Pampa, Texas Assembly in November 1968 where he claimed that "not really a full 83 months remains".

the world right to the bitter end in 1975.[30] He is documented as still promoting the year from the platform at a Los Angeles assembly as late as February 10, 1975:

> And then if we turn to page 35 we are starting to see the year **nineteen hundred and seventy five**, where we actually are. And, what does it say with regard to **1975**? It says, the end, now notice this, the end of the six one thousand year day of man's existence in early autumn. And then it carries us beyond that, beyond this year, the next date is 2975. So you see, **we haven't much left till this year 1975**. It is going to end at sundown of September the 5th, and that **immediately after September the the 5th, why the millennial kingdom of the Lord Jesus Christ must begin in order to fulfil the final thousand years of God's great seven creative days**, and they're expecting the great tribulation to occur and the destruction of Babylon the Great and the annihilation of all the political systems of this world and then the binding of Satan and his demons and their abyssing to occur before this year is ended, this year **nineteen hundred and seventy five**, and immediately thereafter the thousand year reign of the Lord Jesus Christ to begin. Now that is all it says about the year **1975**. (Audience applauses.)[31]

He kept the theme alive that year while delivering a graduation talk to the Gilead class of missionaries, as reported by the May 1975 Watchtower:

> Another speaker, F. W. Franz, the Society's vice-president, forcefully impressed on the audience the urgency of the Christian preaching work. He stressed that, according to dependable Bible chronology, 6,000 years of human history will end this coming September according to the lunar calendar. This coincides with a time when "the human species [is] about to starve itself to death," as well as its being faced with poisoning by pollution and destruction by nuclear weapons. Franz added: "There's no basis for believing that mankind, faced with what it now faces, can exist for the seventh thousand-year period" under the present system of things.
>
> Does this mean that we know exactly when God will destroy this old system and establish a new one? Franz showed that we do

---

30. There is credible Bible chronology showing that Franz's "trustworthy" calculations were off by about 650 years. For details, visit https://beroeans.net/?p=15824
31. Transcript of a recording: jwfacts.com/watchtower/1975.php

## 11. Is the Governing Body a False Prophet?

not, for we do not know how short was the time interval between Adam's creation and the creation of Eve, at which point God's rest day of seven thousand years began. (Heb. 4:3, 4) But, he pointed out, **"we should not think that this year of 1975 is of no significance to us,"** for the Bible proves that Jehovah is **"the greatest chronologist"** and **"we have the anchor date, 1914, marking the end of the Gentile Times."** So, he continued, "we are filled with anticipation for the near future, for our generation."[32]

It would be ridiculously naïve to imagine that the leadership of an Organization as tightly controlled as that of Jehovah's Witnesses would be unaware of the growing anticipation spreading through the rank-and-file of that time period. Should anyone still doubt that, we have the evidence from the Society's own publications to consider.

> Just think, brothers, **there are only about ninety months left** before 6,000 years of man's existence on earth is completed. Do you remember what we learned at the assemblies last summer? The majority of people living today will probably be alive when Armageddon breaks out, and there are no resurrection hopes for those that are destroyed then.[33]

> The immediate future is certain to be filled with climactic events, for this old system is nearing its complete end. **Within a few years at most the final parts of Bible prophecy relative to these "last days" will undergo fulfilment.**[34]

There are far too many references from the Society's publications on this subject to list here, but I will provide a smattering and encourage you to look them up to view the context:

> So whatever the date for the end of this system, it is clear that the time left is reduced, **with only approximately six years left** until the end of 6,000 years of human history.[35]

> If you are a young person, you also need to face the fact that **you will never grow old** in this present system of things.[36]

> The fact that fifty-four years of the period called the "last days" have already gone by is highly significant. **It means that only a**

---

32. w75 5/1 p.285
33. *Kingdom Ministry*, March 1968, p. 4
34. w68 5/1 p. 272 par. 7 "Making Wise Use of the Remaining Time"
35. w70 5/1 p. 273
36. g69 5/22 p. 15

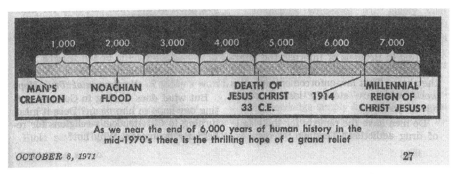

Figure 19. The *Awake!* of October 8, 1971 provided this timeline with the caption, "As we near the end of 6,000 years of human history in the mid-1970's there is the thrilling hope of a grand relief".

> **few years, at most, remain** before the corrupt system of things dominating the earth is destroyed by God.[37]
>
> Are we to assume from this study that the battle of Armageddon will be all over by the autumn of 1975, and the long-looked-for thousand-year reign of Christ will begin by then?... **It may involve only a difference of weeks or months, not years.**[38]

Just in case the message wasn't clear enough, the October 8, 1971 issue of *Awake!* even provided the graphical timeline shown in Figure 19.

It seems silly as we sit here some 50 years later that such an attitude of expectation should have been so prevalent among the worldwide community of Jehovah's Witnesses, but most of us were guilty of it. We got caught up in the hype and didn't want to contemplate that the end might drag on. I was among that crowd. I remember sitting with a friend during the year-end holidays as 1970 drew to a close and contemplating the number of years left for us in this system of things.

That friend is still alive and still expecting that the end will come imminently. I, however, have realised how foolish I was not to take to heart Jesus' warning to his disciples that "no man knows the day or hour." You might be wondering yourself why Jehovah's Witnesses, who claim to be such avid Bible students, didn't pick up on that warning of our Lord back at the time?

---

37. g68 10/8 p. 13
38. w68 8/15 p. 499

## 11. Is the Governing Body a False Prophet?

Well, the Organization had its own special way of dealing with naysayers back then as we see in this 1968 *Watchtower* article:

> One thing is absolutely certain, Bible chronology reinforced with fulfilled Bible prophecy shows that six thousand years of man's existence will soon be up, yes, within this generation! (Matt. 24:34) This is, therefore, no time to be indifferent and complacent. **This is not the time to be toying with the words of Jesus that "concerning that day and hour nobody knows, neither the angels of the heavens nor the Son, but only the Father." (Matt. 24:36)** To the contrary, it is a time when one should be keenly aware that the end of this system of things is rapidly coming to its violent end. Make no mistake, it is sufficient that the Father himself knows both the "day and hour"!
>
> Even if one cannot see beyond 1975, is this any reason to be less active? The apostles could not see even this far; they knew nothing about 1975.[39]

Would a true prophet, one who—by the Organization's own criteria—speaks in "harmony with God's word and promotes true worship"[40] ever suggest that applying a clear and unambiguous warning from our Lord would be "toying with his words"? That sounds more like the actions of a false prophet, doesn't it?

## The Aftermath of the 1975 Prophetic Fiasco

I know that the tendency for many Jehovah's Witnesses will be to dismiss the whole 1975 fiasco as the result of imperfect men getting a little carried away in their zeal to prepare for the end. They will believe that there was no bad intent. I can state that with confidence, because I used to feel that way. I know that my willingness to excuse them back then had more to do with my need to preserve the fortress of my faith than anything else. That was undoubtedly the attitude of many at that time, though there was a significant number who were not so forgiving and ended up leaving the Organization.

Nevertheless, the whole episode continued to bother me for years. The problem for me and many others wasn't the prophetic failure—though in hindsight, it should have been—but

---

39. w68 8/15 pp. 500-501 pars. 35-36 "Why Are You Looking Forward to 1975?"
40. it-2 p. 696

the leadership's unwillingness to take responsibility for it. The leadership of the Organization was wholly responsible for promoting 1975 from the convention platform as well as through the publications.

Faithful Jehovah's Witnesses had put their trust in men who claimed to be God's channel of communication. Many made great changes in their lives, sacrificing jobs, education, and even the prospect of having a family. The Governing Body was aware of these sacrifices as the following quotes indicate:

> Reports are heard of brothers **selling their homes** and property and planning to finish out the rest of their days in this old system in the pioneer service. **Certainly this is a fine way to spend the short time remaining before the wicked world's end.**[41]

> Today there is a great crowd of people who are confident that a destruction of even greater magnitude is now imminent. The evidence is that Jesus' prophecy will shortly have a major fulfilment, upon this entire system of things. **This has been a major factor in influencing many couples to decide not to have children at this time.**[42]

In my case, my father took early retirement and moved our family to Cali, Colombia to serve where "the need was greater." He took my sister out of high school, leaving her with only a grade 10 education. I decided to forego a university education because the end was so near, though I had wanted to study electronics. When the money ran out, my dad was forced to live on a meagre half-pension. Both my parents died in the 1980s, never seeing the end which the Organization had promised would surely have come by then.

Given all those unnecessary sacrifices, one would think a sincere apology would not be too much to ask for. Yet, in 1976, what we got was a rebuke in *The Watchtower* that shifted the blame onto the rank-and-file Jehovah's Witness.

> "[11] **It may be that some who have been serving God have planned their lives according to a mistaken view of just what was to happen on a certain date or in a certain year.** They may have, for this reason, put off or neglected things that they otherwise would have cared for. But they have missed the point of the

---

41. *Kingdom Ministry* May 1974 p. 3
42. *Awake!* 1974 Nov 8 p.11

Bible's warnings concerning the end of this system of things, thinking that Bible chronology reveals the specific date. ...

¹³ **Did Jesus mean that we should adjust our financial and secular affairs so that our resources would just carry us to a certain date that we might think marks the end?** If our house is suffering serious deterioration, should we let it go, on the assumption that we would need it only a few months longer? Or, if someone in the family possibly needs special medical care, should we say, 'Well, we'll put it off because the time is so near for this system of things to go'? This is not the kind of thinking that Jesus advised...

¹⁵ **But it is not advisable for us to set our sights on a certain date**, neglecting everyday things we would ordinarily care for as Christians, such as things that we and our families really need. We may be forgetting that, when the "day" comes, it will not change the principle that Christians must at all times take care of all their responsibilities. If anyone has been disappointed through not following this line of thought, he should now concentrate on adjusting his viewpoint, seeing that it was not the word of God that failed or deceived him and brought disappointment, **but that his own understanding was based on wrong premises.**⁴³

This makes it sound like the "wrong premises" were the work of the congregation publishers who were setting their "sights on a certain date." The *wrong premises* were published and repeatedly hyped, both through the publications and by prominent members of headquarters.

What happens today if you choose to call some teaching in a publication a *wrong premise*? You'll find yourself in the back room of the Kingdom Hall facing a couple of elders faster than you can say "apostate."

They then go on to add insult to injury with this:

¹⁷ The Scriptures repeatedly tell us that the end will come as a complete surprise upon the world. The apostle spoke of this, saying: "You yourselves know quite well that Jehovah's day [for judgment] is coming exactly as a thief in the night." (1 Thess. 5:2) So that true Christians would not be 'overtaken as thieves,' Jesus said even to his disciples back there, and to us today: "Keep on the watch, therefore, because **you do not know on what day your Lord is coming**." Thereafter he said: "Prove yourselves ready,

---

43. w76 7/15 pp. 440, 441

because at an hour that you do not think to be it, the Son of man is coming." (Matt. 24:42-44) **These clear statements of Jesus indicate that God's servants will never be given the date of Christ's "coming" for judgment until it actually takes place.** In fact, it will come at what appears to them an 'unlikely' time.—Luke 12:39, 40.[44]

They actually had the unmitigated gall to counsel the worldwide community of Jehovah's Witnesses on applying Matthew 24:36—you know, the words of Jesus they had previously told us *not to toy with*!?[45]

They refer to this warning as "clear statements of Jesus." Why were these statements so clear in 1976, yet just a few years earlier they had criticized any Witness invoking the warning behind these "clear statements" as someone who was "toying" with the Lord's words?

There is a level of brazenness and hypocrisy about that which caused a far amount of commotion among the brotherhood. The recoil forced the Governing Body to take stock of their situation, and eventually take some steps to appease the flock. Nevertheless, in true fashion for a false prophet whose back is against the wall, instead of an abject apology and sincere repentance, what we got was this lame attempt made in the March 1980 *Watchtower*, some five years after the fact. Just a single sentence, written in passive tense that barely acknowledges there might be some blame for them to share with the rank-and-file. It is a stretch to call it an apology at all.

> With the appearance of the book Life Everlasting—in Freedom of the Sons of God, and its comments as to how appropriate it would be for the millennial reign of Christ to parallel the seventh millennium of man's existence, considerable expectation was aroused regarding the year 1975. There were statements made then, and thereafter, stressing that this was only a possibility. Unfortunately, however, along with such cautionary information, **there were other statements published that implied that such realization of hopes by that year was more of a probability than a mere possibility.** It is to be regretted that these latter

---

44. Ibid. p. 441 par. 17 "A Solid Basis for Confidence"
45. w68 8/15 pp. 500-501 pars. 35-36

## 11. Is the Governing Body a False Prophet?

statements apparently overshadowed the cautionary ones and contributed to a buildup of the expectation already initiated.[46]

This is as close as they have come to actually accepting responsibility for misleading millions. Notice that it isn't an apology. At best, this is a half-hearted attempt to placate the masses.

"There were other statements published..."!? Who made these other statements?

"It is to be regretted..."!? Once again, Watch Tower leaders fall back on the passive tense to avoid responsibility. Why not write: "We regret that we published statements that far and away overshadowed the few-and-far-between cautionary ones."

Apparently, there was such a hue and cry from the rank-and-file over this blatant shifting of blame that the fellows at headquarters had to issue a retraction, but as seems to be par for the course, they couldn't quite bring themselves to admit guilt. There is none of the repentant candor one reads in Scripture by guilt-ridden kings, like King David, imploring God for forgiveness. What we got in this same article in the March 1980 *Watchtower* was this:

> In its issue of July 15, 1976, *The Watchtower*, commenting on the inadvisability of setting our sights on a certain date, stated: "If anyone has been disappointed through not following this line of thought, he should now concentrate on adjusting his viewpoint, seeing that it was not the word of God that failed or deceived him and brought disappointment, **but that his own understanding was based on wrong premises**." In saying "anyone," *The Watchtower* included all disappointed ones of Jehovah's Witnesses, hence *including persons having to do with the publication of the information* that contributed to the buildup of hopes centered on that date. [Italics in copy][47]

It took them five years to build up the courage to issue this tepid response. Yet again, they failed to apologize. Instead, they are playing the victim. "We were just as disappointed as the rest of you."

Oh, well, I guess that makes it alright then, doesn't it?

One consistent characteristic of any false prophet is an unwillingness to apologize and make amends.

---

46. w80 3/15 p. 17 par. 5 "Choosing the Best Way of Life"
47. w80 3/15 pp. 17-18 par. 6

One of the more galling statements in this 1980 issue of *The Watchtower* is written in paragraph 7.

> It is day-to-day living on the part of the Christian that is important. He must not live a single day without having in mind that he is under Jehovah's loving care and direction and must submit himself thereto, **keeping also in mind that *he* must account for his acts**.[48]

*The Watchtower* writers could not even bring themselves to be included. It is not "we must account for our acts," but rather it is he—the poor misguided, trusting congregation publisher who loyally *listened, obeyed, but was not blessed*—who must account for his acts.

## Why Should the 1975 Failure Concern Us Now?

You might be tempted to think this is all ancient history, that it shouldn't really concern us now. All the members of the Governing Body who promoted this failed prophecy are gone and none of the current Governing Body members were directly involved. The reality of the situation is quite another thing though.

If the current Governing Body members want us to consider them to be true prophets, then they must live up to the standards they themselves have set. To list the two criteria that we considered at the start of this chapter, as taken from the *Insight* book,[49] a true prophet:

- Speaks in harmony with God's Word and promotes true worship,
- Advocates righteousness and expresses the mind of God.

Therefore, a true prophet wouldn't cover over wrongdoing, nor would he blame the innocent for the sins of another. A true prophet doesn't distort the facts, nor does he lie. He is humble, loves righteousness, exercises justice and is guided by the mind of God.[50]

With those two principles in mind, consider what the current Governing Body did at the 2017 regional convention in the drama,

---

48. Ibid. p. 18 par. 7
49. it-2 p. 696
50. Micah 6:8

## 11. Is the Governing Body a False Prophet?

*Don't Give Up*, to tie themselves to the sins of their predecessors. The lead character in the drama makes this confession:

> I never thought this system would last so long, and I certainly never thought I would be a grandfather. ... when I was about your age, I had just become a new father. ... years later another test came our way, you see, back then some were looking to a certain date as signifying the end of this old system of things....A few went so far as selling their homes and quitting their jobs.

He then explains how he overcame this test of his faith.

> **Both at meetings and in my personal study**, I was reminded of what Jesus said: "Nobody knows the day or hour." I was dedicated to Jehovah, not a date.

Anyone who didn't live through that era, as I did, would conclude from this that the test came about because some were running ahead of the direction from the Organization. No one would conclude, based on what is presented in this convention drama, that the Governing Body members were the ones responsible for Witnesses "looking to a certain date as signifying the end of the old system of things." Additionally, the protagonist in this drama claims he was saved from discouragement by going to meetings and engaging in personal study. What nonsense! Going to meetings and studying the publications were the things that kept us in expectation of 1975. They were the things which fueled our fever of anticipation.

The final point is a bald-faced lie! We were not reminded of what Jesus said: "Nobody knows the day or hour." Rather, we were counselled "not to toy with those words."

There was no apparent reason for the current Governing Body to even resurrect this painful episode from the history of Jehovah's Witnesses. Why they would do this instead of letting sleeping dogs lie is a matter of speculation, but the fact that they did so in this way, attempting to exonerate their predecessors by misrepresenting the facts of history and actually lying about the past clearly identifies them as false prophets. How could we see it otherwise?

As we read earlier, the word "prophet" in Greek is *prophétés* which means more than predicting the future. According to *Strong's Concordance*, it means "a prophet (an interpreter or forth-teller of the divine will)" and is used of "a prophet, poet; **a person gifted at expositing divine truth.**"

That is why the Samaritan woman said to Jesus at John 4:19, "Sir, I perceive you are a prophet," even though Jesus had not foretold the future, but revealed events of her past.

The Organization foretold that 1975 would mark the end of 6,000 years of human history. It also foretold that the end of the current system of things would come on or close to that year. This episode represents the greatest prophetic failure of the modern Organization of Jehovah's Witnesses. Yet, the current Governing Body, instead of "expositing divine truth" and admitting to the sin of the former Governing Body, chose to cover it up in a video presentation at the 2017 regional convention, that included lying about the historical facts.

We all know what happened to Ananias and Sapphira when they lied about keeping back some of the money they claimed to have received and donated from the sale of their property. That was a lie that harmed no one directly, yet they were executed by God for it. How much worse will be the judgment for those whose lies have harmed the lives of millions, whose false teachings have caused the *little ones* to lose faith and miss out on salvation, and who to this day have failed to repent?[51]

## The Danger Persists

False prophets are very dangerous. Their desire is to seduce us away from our Lord Jesus and our God Jehovah by getting us to follow their advice, their rules, and their interpretation of Scripture. This is nothing new. The prophet Nehemiah encountered just such a false prophet and could have lost his good standing with God had he not identified the man for what he really was.

> Then I went to the house of Shemaiah the son of Delaiah the son of Mehetabel while he was confined there. He said: "Let us set a time to meet at the house of the true God, within the temple, and let us close the doors of the temple, for they are coming to kill you. They are coming to kill you by night." But I said: "Should a man like me run away? Can a man like me go into the temple and live? I will not go in!" Then I realized that God had not sent him, but that Tobiah and Sanballat had hired him to speak this prophecy against me. He had been hired to frighten me and to cause me to

---

51. Acts 5:1-11; Luke 17:1, 2

## 11. Is the Governing Body a False Prophet?

sin, so that they would have grounds to damage my reputation in order to reproach me. Do remember, O my God, Tobiah and Sanballat and these deeds, and also Noadiah the prophetess and the rest of the prophets who were constantly trying to frighten me. So the wall was completed on the 25th day of Elul, in 52 days. (Nehemiah 6:10-15 NWT 2013)

Nehemiah realized that this prophet had not been sent by God, but was hired to frighten him, and so cause him to sin.

Are Jehovah's Witnesses in a position like that of Nehemiah? Is there a chance that the Governing Body might again lead them astray as they did in the past with 1914, 1925, or 1975? Has the Governing Body finally learned its lesson and given up making prophetic predictions? Apparently not! As recently as April of 2022, we have this proclamation to ponder:

**15. Why do we need to trust Jehovah's direction now more than ever before?**

15 As the end of this system of things draws near, we need to trust in Jehovah's way of doing things as never before. Why? During the great tribulation, **we may receive instructions that seem strange, impractical, or illogical. Of course, Jehovah will not speak to us personally. He will likely provide direction through his appointed representatives. That will hardly be the time to second-guess the direction or to view it with skepticism, wondering, 'Is this really coming from Jehovah, or are the responsible brothers acting on their own?' How will you fare during that crucial time in human history?** The answer might be indicated by how you view theocratic direction now. If you trust the direction we receive today and readily obey, you will likely do the same during the great tribulation.—Luke 16:10.[52]

This prophetic warning is reinforced by means of this dramatic scene depicting faithful Jehovah's Witnesses hiding in a basement during the JW version of the great tribulation, supposedly receiving instructions from Jehovah via his appointed channel, the Governing Body working through the local elders. These will be instructions they must follow faithfully if they want to be saved, yet they are told that this divine direction may seem "strange, impractical, or illogical."

---

52. w22 February p. 6 par. 15

How can they make such a claim as this without also acknowledging that they are acting as prophets? The idea being conveyed is that blind obedience will be required for salvation. "Listen, obey, and be blessed" is the refrain being sung.[53] Any doubting will lead to death. If this prophecy is true, then we must obey to survive; but if it is false, then we must obey the Bible which tells us not to fear the false prophet. We are dealing with a life-and-death decision here. How are we to know whether the prophet is true or false? Jehovah does not leave us in doubt. The formula is simple. Let's again read from Deuteronomy about the false prophet doing a little paraphrasing, applying it to JW.org.

> When the [Governing Body] speaks in the name of Jehovah and the word is not fulfilled or does not come true, then Jehovah did not speak that word. The [Governing Body] spoke it presumptuously. **You should not fear [the Governing Body].** (Deuteronomy 18:22)

Should Jehovah's Witnesses fear the prophet of JW.org, the Governing Body? Before answering, let us examine some historical examples of divine salvation.

## Escape from Sodom and Gomorrah

Before Jehovah brought down fire from heaven upon the cities of Sodom and Gomorrah, he sent two angels who warned Lot and his family of the coming destruction. They prophesied that the city would be destroyed the following day, and that Lot and his family had to flee to be saved. How did Lot know he was listening to a true prophet? The angels performed a miraculous salvation when a crowd of homosexual rapists attacked the house where they were staying. In other words, the prophets had credentials that were undeniable.

## Escape from Slavery in Egypt

When Pharoah would not let Israel leave the country, Jehovah brought a tenth plague on the nation in which the firstborn male of every family was killed. The Israelite firstborn were spared by following the directions given to them by Jehovah through the

---

53. dx86-17 DVDs (Digital Videodiscs); yb14 p. 21 "Vietnam: Little ones enjoying the jw.org video Listen, Obey, and Be Blessed;" sjj song 89

## 11. Is the Governing Body a False Prophet?

Figure 20. Artwork from *The Watchtower* depicting events during the "Great Tribulation".

prophet Moses. How did the Israelites know that Moses' prophecy concerning the tenth plague was going to come true? They knew he was a true prophet because Jehovah provided three miraculous signs for them to see, as recorded in Exodus 4:1-9. And if that weren't enough, they had the other plagues that preceded the tenth to go by. Moses' credentials as a prophet were impeccable.

### Escape from Jerusalem

In 66 CE, when the Roman army surrounded Jerusalem, the Christians in that city knew exactly what to do to escape the destruction that would soon come upon the nation. They knew because Jesus had foretold exactly what to look for, and what to do when they saw it. These Christians would include many who had witnessed the numerous miracles performed by Jesus, and so the credentials of God's foremost prophet were beyond question.

### Escape from Armageddon

In each of the three preceding situations, God's servants knew exactly what to do beforehand because one of his prophets had revealed that information to them. But this isn't the case with the Other Sheep of Jehovah's Witnesses theology. They are given no advance knowledge about what they must do to escape the destruction of Armageddon. All they are told is that when the time comes, the necessary information will be given to them by the Governing Body.

Can the Governing Body lay claim to the prophetic credentials of the angels visiting Lot, of Moses in Egypt, of Jesus in the first century? Can the Governing Body point to even a single prophetic prediction which has come true?

## Be Like Nehemiah and You Will Be Saved

Nehemiah was not fooled by the false prophet who was hired to deceive him. The Governing Body claims that when the time comes, the Other Sheep of the Jehovah's Witnesses community must wait for their "strange, impractical, and illogical" instructions to be saved, but the path to salvation has been in place and recorded for all to read since the first century.

> Moreover, brothers, we do not want YOU to be ignorant concerning those who are sleeping [in death]; that YOU may not sorrow just as the rest also do who have no hope. For if our faith is that Jesus died and rose again, so, too, those who have fallen asleep [in death] through Jesus God will bring with him. For this is what we tell YOU by Jehovah's word, that we the living who survive to the presence of the Lord shall in no way precede those who have fallen asleep [in death]; because **the Lord himself will descend from heaven with a commanding call**, with an archangel's voice and with God's trumpet, and those who are dead in union with Christ will rise first. Afterward **we the living who are surviving will, together with them, be caught away in clouds to meet the Lord in the air**; and thus we shall always be with [the] Lord. Consequently keep comforting one another with these words. (1 Thessalonians 4:13-18)

The reason that Jehovah's servants today—the Children of God—don't have to take some specific action to escape Armageddon as Lot did, and the Israelites in Egypt did, and as the Christians in Jerusalem did, is because our salvation is in the hands of our Lord. We just have to stay awake and remain faithful.

But the Governing Body of the Watch Tower Organization doesn't want you to believe that. They claim the Other Sheep have a different hope and a different path to salvation, one that depends on supporting them and obeying them.

## 11. Is the Governing Body a False Prophet?

The other sheep should never forget that **their salvation depends on their active support of Christ's anointed "brothers" still on earth.**[54]

There is nothing in Scripture to support this teaching—nothing that tells Christians to wait for a Governing Body of self-appointed men to provide direction at the last minute. Like Nehemiah's false prophet, the leadership of the Watch Tower Society want the Other Sheep to believe these words and fear them, yet their record of prophetic failures clearly identifies them as a false prophet. The wise course is therefore to follow the inspired word found at Deuteronomy 18:22 – "The prophet spoke it presumptuously. **You should not fear him.**"

---

54. w12 3/15 p. 20 par. 2

# 12

# Was There a First-Century Governing Body?

> *"Then the apostles and the elders, together with the whole congregation, decided to send chosen men from among them to Antioch..." (Acts 15:22)*

Growing up, I don't recall ever hearing about a governing body directing the work of Jehovah's Witnesses. We were led to believe that men like Russell, Rutherford, and Nathan Knorr, all presidents of the Watch Tower Bible & Tract Society of Pennsylvania, were in charge. It wasn't until the early 1970s, when the elder arrangement was introduced, that I first remember learning about a governing body with a rotating chairman.

In my youth, I used to take pride in the belief that the brothers "taking the lead" in the Organization were not seeking prominence. We had no Pope, no Archbishop, no Pastor. When the *Proclaimers* book[1] came out in the early 1990s, all that started to change.

Reta, my wife, was greatly disturbed when she saw all the pictures of the then-members of the Governing Body. She felt it was very inappropriate that they should be drawing attention

---

1. *Jehovah's Witnesses—Proclaimers of God's Kingdom* (1993)

to themselves. I believe that book marked a significant change in the character of the Governing Body. It now claims to be the Faithful and Discreet Slave of Matthew 24:45, named as such by Jesus Christ since 1919. They justify their exalted status as those who govern the Organization of Jehovah's Witnesses based in part on the belief that there was a first-century governing body. If that is true, then there would be a substantial basis to claim that Jehovah God has again commissioned a body of men to govern the congregation. But let's not jump to any conclusions. Instead, let's turn to Scripture for the answer.

## Was There Really a Governing Body in the First Century?

To justify itself, the Governing Body of Jehovah's Witnesses claims that Jehovah has always had an organization, even though the word "organization," which appears almost 20,000 times in Watch Tower publications, never appears in the Bible. Obviously, an organization needs to be governed, so it is important that Witnesses believe the fallacy that the early Christian congregation was organized and centrally governed along the lines of the modern Organization of Jehovah's Witnesses. To accomplish that, they must convince the rank and file that the apostles and early elders in Jerusalem constituted a first-century governing body. *Insight on the Scriptures* explains:

> **Organization of the Christian Congregation.** While Christian congregations of God were established in various places, **they did not function independently of one another. Instead, they all recognized the authority of the Christian governing body at Jerusalem**. This governing body was comprised of the apostles and older men of the Jerusalem congregation, there being no rival bodies elsewhere seeking to supervise the congregation. It was to the faithful Christian governing body of the first century C.E. that the issue of circumcision was submitted for consideration. When the governing body made its decision, as directed by the holy spirit, that decision was accepted and became binding upon all Christian congregations, these willingly submitting to it.—Ac 15:22-31.[2]

---

2. it-1 pp. 498-499

## 12. Was There a First-Century Governing Body?

This all sounds plausible until you start to check it out for yourself, at which point, you will find, as I did, that there is no evidence in the Christian Scriptures to support the statement that the congregations "did not function independently" and that "they all recognized the authority of the Christian governing body at Jerusalem."

The only example of the congregations in the first century obeying instructions from the original congregation formed in Jerusalem is found in Acts chapter 15, but a careful analysis of those verses does not support the idea of a centralized governing body directing the worldwide work in the first century.

### The Circumcision Issue

According to Acts chapter 15, a problem arose when "some men came down from Judea and began to teach the brothers: 'Unless you get circumcised according to the custom of Moses, you cannot be saved.'" This resulted in "quite a bit of dissension and disputing by Paul and Barnabas with them," so "it was arranged for Paul, Barnabas, and some of the others to go up to the apostles and elders in Jerusalem regarding this issue."[3]

Did the congregation of Antioch send Paul, Barnabas, and some others to Jerusalem because they recognized that the elders in Jerusalem constituted a centralized governing body? No. They sent them to Jerusalem because the troublemakers had come from there. In other words, they were sent to where the troublemakers had come from—they went to the source of the problem to resolve it.

Further evidence that there was no small group of men—a governing body—making all the decisions can be gleaned from the way the final decision on the circumcision issue was made:

> Then the apostles and the elders, **together with the whole congregation**, decided to send chosen men from among them to Antioch, along with Paul and Barnabas; they sent Judas who was called Barsabbas and Silas, who were leading men among the brothers. (Acts 15:22)

The entire congregation at Jerusalem was involved in making the decision, which means that the entire congregation heard all

---

3. Acts 15:1, 2

the facts and reached a decision guided by holy spirit. In contrast, when the Governing Body of Jehovah's Witnesses meets, it does so behind closed doors and the rulings come only from the men appointed to that body.[4] The only place in Scripture where such a governing body is to be found meeting behind closed doors and making unilateral decisions is the Jewish Sanhedrin that judged and condemned our Lord Jesus Christ.

## No Bible Proof of a First-Century Governing Body

The only arrow that the Governing Body has in its quiver to support its contention that they have a first-century counterpart is the account on the circumcision issue which we've just covered and dismissed as real proof. That's it!

If you scan through the articles in *The Watchtower* over the past few decades, could there be any doubt in your mind that the Organization of Jehovah's Witnesses is utterly controlled by a governing body, now centered at Warwick, New York? Of course not. The term "governing body" appears over three thousand times in Watch Tower publications based on a keyword search in the *Watchtower Library* program. Yet, it never occurs in the text of the Bible. Why would Bible writers like Peter, James, and Paul make no mention of it?

When the first "elder" appointment was made, it was to fill the post vacated by the treachery of Judas. Did the apostles act as the Governing Body of today acts, deciding for themselves whom to appoint? No. The entire congregation was involved. At Acts 1:15, we read of Peter speaking to the whole body of believers, a crowd of approximately 120 persons.[5] It was the congregation that selected two candidates:

> So they put up two, Joseph called Barsabbas, who was surnamed Justus, and Matthias. And they prayed and said: "You, O Jehovah, who know the hearts of all, designate which one of these two men you have chosen, to take the place of this ministry and

---

4. At the time of this writing, only eight individuals comprise the Governing Body of Jehovah's Witnesses: Kenneth Cook, Samuel Herd, Geoffrey Jackson, Stephen Lett, Gerrit Lösch, Anthony Morris, Mark Sanderson, and David Splane.
5. Acts 1:15

## 12. Was There a First-Century Governing Body?

apostleship, from which Judas deviated to go to his own place." So **they cast lots over them**, and the lot fell upon Matthias; and he was reckoned along with the eleven apostles." (Acts 1:23-26)

The next appointments were of the first ministerial servants. Again, the selection was not made by a central governing authority, nor even by the 12 apostles, but by the entire congregation.

> So the twelve called **the multitude of the disciples** to them and said: "It is not pleasing for us to leave the word of God to distribute [food] to tables. So, **brothers, search out for yourselves seven certified men from among YOU**, full of spirit and wisdom, that we may appoint them over this necessary business; but we shall devote ourselves to prayer and to the ministry of the word." And **the thing spoken was pleasing to the whole multitude, and they selected Stephen**, a man full of faith and holy spirit, and Philip and Prochorus and Nicanor and Timon and Parmenas and Nicolaus, a proselyte of Antioch; and **they placed them before the apostles**, and, after having prayed, these laid their hands upon them." (Acts 6:2-6)

Of course, it was the apostles who laid their hands on them, because they had been chosen by Jesus and the holy spirit was conferred by them through the laying on of hands, but the apostles did not choose those men. Instead, they accepted the selection made by the multitude of the disciples.

### More Bible Evidence of a Lack of Centralized Control

Today, the Governing Body controls everything. Missionaries are designated, assigned and funded by the Watch Tower Society's various corporate entities all under the control of the Governing Body. The name "Jehovah's Witnesses" was chosen by the Governing Body under the leadership of J. F. Rutherford. Reports are all sent into the Governing Body from around the world.

The current Governing Body of Jehovah's Witnesses teaches that first-century congregations "did not function independently of one another, but instead...all recognized the authority of the Christian governing body at Jerusalem."[6] Is there evidence that the Jerusalem congregation sent out missionaries? Did reports from all congregations funnel back to Jerusalem? Was it

---

6. it-1 p. 498

from Jerusalem that the edict went forth that henceforth all the disciples should be known as Christians?

No, no, and no!

Paul went on three lengthy and costly missionary tours, all originating from and funded by the Gentile congregation of Antioch. Why wasn't the so-called governing body in Jerusalem directing and funding this historic series of missionary tours? The answer is that the congregations back then did indeed "function independently of one another."

If there truly was a governing body in Jerusalem, then why didn't God reveal the name "Christian" to them and have them dispatch letters to all the congregations telling them of this new name? Instead, Acts 11:26 reveals that "it was first in Antioch that the disciples were by divine providence called Christians."

J. F. Rutherford chose the name "Jehovah's Witnesses" all by himself in 1931 and forced all the Bible Student Groups that were affiliated with the Watch Tower Society to accept it. If all the first-century congregations "recognized the authority of the Christian governing body at Jerusalem," then how do we account for the fact that they had nothing to do with the name that continues to identify Jesus' disciples down to this day?

If Jehovah God was using a governing body to exercise centralized control in the first century so that no congregation acted independently, then how do we explain Paul's apparent disdain for men claiming authority over the congregation?

> But when God, who separated me from my mother's womb and called [me] through his undeserved kindness, thought good to reveal his Son in connection with me, that I might declare the good news about him to the nations, **I did not go at once into conference with flesh and blood. Neither did I go up to Jerusalem** to those who were apostles previous to me, but I went off into Arabia, and I came back again to Damascus. Then three years later I went up to Jerusalem to visit Cephas, and I stayed with him for fifteen days. But **I saw no one else of the apostles**, only James the brother of the Lord. (Galatians 1:15-19)

After an absence of 14 years, Paul returns to Jerusalem and has this to say about the visit:

> But on the part of those who seemed to be something—whatever sort of men they formerly were makes no difference to me—God does not go by a man's outward appearance—to me, in fact, **those outstanding men imparted nothing new**. (Galatians 2:6)

## 12. Was There a First-Century Governing Body?

Can you imagine a circuit or branch overseer of Jehovah's Witnesses treating the Governing Body's direction this way, as of no relevance to his preaching work?

How could he go for fourteen years and then return to the governing body that Jehovah was using to direct the worldwide work and find that they had nothing new to impart?! The elders of today can hardly go a month without an update from Warwick imparting some new directive.

Why is there no record in historical Christian writings from the first and second centuries of a centralized governing body? Why is there no indication of a new location for a governing body following the destruction of Jerusalem in 70 CE? Eventually, the Christian congregation did have a governing body. In fact, there were two. For the Eastern Church, there came to be a governing body exercising centralized control in Constantinople. For the Western Church, the governing body was in Rome under the control of the Pope and Cardinals. In other words, governing bodies and ecclesiastical hierarchies only came into being when the apostasy set in just as Paul predicted would happen.

> And now you know what is acting as a restraint, so that **he will be revealed in his own due time**. True, the mystery of this lawlessness is already at work, but only until the one who is right now acting as a restraint is out of the way. (2 Thessalonians 2:6, 7)

### Is a First-Century Governing Body Even Feasible?

It doesn't take much thought for us to realize that the idea of a centralized authority directing the preaching work in the first century is ridiculous. How would a governing body located in Jerusalem communicate with congregations hundreds and even thousands of miles away at a time when there was no reliable mail service and when communications could take weeks to arrive, assuming they did arrive at all? We only need to look at the travels of the apostle Paul to see how arduous and dangerous travel was in those days.[7]

The Organization of Jehovah's Witnesses chooses to ignore these facts and continues to promote the fantasy that a governing body controlled the first century congregation through

---

7.   2 Corinthians 11:23-27

the appointment of travelling overseers, much like today's circuit overseers. For example:

> Serious questions that could not be handled by local elders were referred to **mature traveling overseers, such as Paul. Vital doctrinal matters were referred to a central governing body located in Jerusalem.** The governing body was initially made up of the apostles of Jesus Christ but was later extended to include older men of the congregation in Jerusalem. Each congregation recognized **the God-given authority of the governing body** and its representatives to organize the ministry, appoint men to positions of service, and make decisions on doctrinal matters. When an issue was settled by the governing body, the congregations accepted the decision and "rejoiced over the encouragement."[8]

There was indeed a centralized authority controlling the congregations in the first century, and there is ample evidence in the Bible to establish that truth, but that centralized authority was not a group of men governing from Jerusalem, but rather our Lord Jesus.

The apostle Paul was not appointed by any so-called governing body in Jerusalem. He was appointed directly by Jesus Christ.[9] When he appointed overseers in the congregations he established, he did so under the direction of holy spirit, not by any communication with the elders in Jerusalem. Apollos and Timothy received the holy spirit while preaching among the Gentiles, not from Jerusalem. Any authority they had was from Jesus through holy spirit and the laying on of hands from the *local brothers*.[10] Paul had decided to go into Bithynia to preach, but the spirit of Jesus blocked him and instead directed him to preach in Macedonia.[11]

Despite all that evidence, Jehovah's Witnesses—or members of any of the mainstream Christian religions today—will argue that we don't have the direct intervention of holy spirit anymore and that to control and unify millions of people and manage assets worth billions of dollars, we need to have someone in charge operating through some form of authority structure—an

---

8. w00 1/1 p. 31 "We Need Jehovah's Organization"
9. Acts 26:12-18
10. Acts 18:24-28; 1 Corinthians 16:10-12
11. Acts 16:9, 10

*ecclesiastical hierarchy* as Governing Body member Gerrit Lösch explained in an affidavit.[12]

That is true if you accept the premise that Jehovah God needs an organization to get the good news preached and to gather in the chosen ones—the Children of God.[13] But what if that premise is wrong? Are we allowing eisegetical thinking to guide us? Shouldn't we first look for evidence in Scripture to see how Jehovah God has managed and governed his people in the past?

## Why a Governing Body Is a Bad Thing

I believe, based on my study of Scripture, that any type of governing body controlling the Christian congregation will ultimately corrupt it. But let's see what the Bible has to say.

We know very little about the pre-flood world. What we do know is restricted to a mere nine chapters in the book of Genesis. A mere nine chapters to cover over 16 centuries of history!

It appears that Jehovah God left humanity to itself, protecting only a few selected individuals who remained faithful to him and who would constitute the lineage of the seed or offspring of the woman prophesied to bring salvation.[14] It was only in the post-flood world that God undertook to create a nation for His name, which He did through the faithful man Abraham. The purpose of that nation was to prepare the way for the Messiah who would be the means by which humankind was saved from sin and death.[15]

The Organization of Jehovah's Witnesses likes to claim that ancient Israel was the first earthly organization of Jehovah God. They do this in an attempt to establish a scriptural foundation for their teaching that they are now the modern earthly organization of God. This is all based on the premise that God has a heavenly and earthly organization and that only through an organization can God's purpose be accomplished.[16]

---

12. See "Appendix E: Gerrit Lösch's Declaration" on page 365.
13. Matthew 28:19; 24:31
14. Genesis 3:15
15. Galatians 3:24; Romans 5:12-21
16. "Jehovah God has a visible earthly organization accomplishing his purpose." (w68 8/1 p. 455)

While it is true that Jehovah God has a "people for his name" and that both Israel and the Christian congregation are referred to as a nation, nowhere in the Bible is the term "organization" used.[17] Why do Jehovah's Witnesses prefer to refer to themselves as an organization?

Is it not to emphasize the organized nature of their form of worship? An organization must be governed to maintain its unity by means of rules stressing conformity. This is why many worldly organizations employ insignia and even uniforms. The Organization does the same in its way. There is no scriptural reason for all Christian men to go clean shaven, and dress in suit and tie, nor for women to avoid pant suits, even in frigid winter weather. It is a uniform used to enforce conformity. Is this the way Jehovah God wants us to worship him? Let us examine the so-called first earthly organization to see if it was organized and if so, how.

The Bible book of Judges covers a period of over 300 years starting with the conquest of the land of Canaan and ending just before the Israelite monarchy was established. This one verse best describes how the nation of Israel was "organized."

> In those days there was no king in Israel. As for everybody, what was right in his own eyes he was accustomed to do. (Judges 17:6)

They had the law of God to follow. They had the priesthood to reconcile themselves with God when they sinned, but there was no central ruling authority. The family heads ruled and did what they thought was right according to their understanding of God's law. Did they always do the right thing? Of course not. We're talking about sinful humans after all. But this was the best arrangement possible at that time.

It is true that God appointed judges, but their job was not to rule the nation. They were there to resolve disputes between families. The judges were also used to save Israel by leading them in war against foreign enemies who enslaved them.[18] But once that job was accomplished, things went back to the way they were, with each man doing what was right in his own eyes.

However, the Israelites foolishly wanted to abandon this way of life and to be like the nations around them who all were ruled

---

17. Acts 15:14; Matthew 21:43
18. Judges 2:10-16; 3:15

## 12. Was There a First-Century Governing Body?

by kings. God warned them against this choice and told them that things would go badly for them if He appointed a king over them; but they stubbornly insisted, and so the royal lineage of Israelite kings came into being. Here is Jehovah's warning. See if it doesn't have a familiar ring to it:

> So Samuel told the people who were asking him for a king all the words of Jehovah. He said: "This is what the king who rules over you will have the right to demand: He will take your sons and put them in his chariots and make them his horsemen, and some will have to run before his chariots. And **he will appoint for himself chiefs over thousands and chiefs over fifties**, and some will do his plowing, reap his harvest, and make his weapons of war and equipment for his chariots. He will take your daughters to be ointment mixers, cooks, and bakers. **He will take the best of your fields, your vineyards, and your olive groves, and he will give them to his servants**. He will take the tenth of your grainfields and your vineyards, and he will give it to his court officials and his servants. And he will take your male and female servants, your best herds, and your donkeys, and he will use them for his work. He will take the tenth of your flocks, and you will become his servants. **The day will come when you will cry out because of the king you have chosen for yourselves, but Jehovah will not answer you in that day**." (1 Samuel 8:10-18)

So here we have it from God's own mouth. A human king, governor, or ruler will not bring blessings, but trouble. Did Jehovah change his mind when he abandoned the nation of Israel for "a nation producing its fruits"—the Christian congregation?[19] Of course not. There is nothing in Scripture indicating that there was to be a group of men governing the Christian congregation. We have only to look at the evidence of history to see where ecclesiastical rulership has led. Is there even one religion that has truly benefitted from having men tell other men and women what to do?[20]

But didn't Jesus appoint a faithful and discreet slave to rule over his domestics? Doesn't that mean that the Christian congregation needs to be organized under the direction of a Governing Body to accomplish the mission of preaching the good news to the world?

---

19. Matthew 21:43
20. Ecclesiastes 8:9

Virtually every Christian denomination has seized on the parable of the Faithful and Discreet Slave to find scriptural support for the authority of a clergy class. But is that what Jesus was trying to tell us with that parable?

The next chapter will analyze not only Matthew's account of the faithful and discreet slave, but also the more extensive one that Luke presents.

# 13

# Who Is the Faithful and Discreet Slave?

*"Who really is the faithful and discreet slave whom his master appointed over his domestics, to give them their food at the proper time?" (Matthew 24:45)*

At Matthew 24:45-51, Jesus gave us a parable about two slaves. One slave proved to be faithful and discreet (or wise) while the other turned to evil. Throughout my life as one of Jehovah's Witnesses, I was taught to believe that the faithful and discreet slave was a class comprised of all the anointed Jehovah's Witnesses alive on earth at any given time. We used to refer to them as "the remnant."

The parable also referred to other slaves—*domestics*—who were understood to refer to anointed Christians as individuals. The food at the proper time referred to the spiritual nourishment that was provided by the anointed through the publications of the Watch Tower Society. The belongings were all of Christ's possessions which included the monies, property, buildings, and all other assets used in support of the preaching work. These belongings also included all the Other Sheep—a class of Christian who Witnesses claim is not anointed with holy spirit and which has an earthly salvation hope. The slave class was supposedly appointed over all the master's belongings in 1918.[1]

All of that changed suddenly in October 2012 when David Splane of the Governing Body revealed *new light* at the annual meeting of the Watch Tower Society. Apparently, Jehovah God had revealed to the Governing Body that, after a century of getting it wrong, they alone were the embodiment of the faithful and discreet slave. No proof, scriptural or otherwise, was provided for this doctrinal change. The Witness community was just expected to accept it because their leaders said it was so. In effect, the Governing Body was bearing witness about itself that it had been appointed by Jesus Christ in 1919 as his Faithful and Discreet Slave.

Jesus tells us: "If I alone bear witness about myself, my witness is not true."[2] If that applies to Jesus, how much more so must it apply to sinful humans?

In the previous chapter, we saw that there was no scriptural support for the idea that there was a governing body controlling the preaching work and congregations in the first century. However, the current Governing Body of Jehovah's Witnesses is not concerned about that. They used to talk about the first-century governing body a lot in years past, but since 2020, they've all but forgotten about it. The reason, apparently, is due to a June 2020 video on JW.org titled *The "Slave" Is Not 1900 Years Old (Matt. 24:45)* given by David H. Splane of the Governing Body.

In that video, Splane tries to explain why they now believe there was no faithful and discreet slave appointed by Jesus for the past 1,900 years, and why it only came into existence in 1919.[3] He provides no scriptural evidence to support this outrageous claim. But we'll waste no time trying to disprove unsubstantiated and self-serving human speculation. Instead, let's learn what we can from the Bible itself.

There are two accounts of the parable of the Faithful and Discreet Slave. The Watch Tower publications focus almost

---

1. w52 2/1 pp. 77-78; w90 3/15 pp. 10-14 pars. 3, 4, 14; w98 3/15 p. 20 par. 9; w01 1/15 p. 29; w06 2/15 p. 28 par. 11; w09 10/15 p. 5 par. 10; w09 6/15 p. 24 par. 18; w09 6/15 p. 24 par. 16; w09 6/15 p. 22 par. 11; w09 2/15 p. 28 par. 17; w10 9/15 p. 23 par. 8; w10 7/15 p. 23 par. 10
2. John 5:31
3. *Morning Worship Video* dated June 15, 2020

## 13. Who Is the Faithful and Discreet Slave?

exclusively on what Matthew recorded, but Luke's account is more detailed and merits our attention. You may be wondering why the publications don't emphasize the more detailed account of the parable that Luke delivers. The answer to that question is provided under our next subheading.

## Why Does the Governing Body Ignore Luke's Account of the Faithful Steward?

Since our analysis will not be a self-serving eisegetical interpretation, we'll start by including the wider context. Jesus is speaking by way of parables or illustrations. He says:

> Be dressed and ready and have your lamps burning, and you should be like men waiting for their master to return from the marriage, so when he comes and knocks, they may at once open to him. **Happy are those slaves whom the master on coming finds watching!** Truly I say to you, he will dress himself for service and have them recline at the table and will come alongside and minister to them. And if he comes in the second watch, even if in the third, and finds them ready, happy are they! But know this, if the householder had known at what hour the thief would come, he would not have let his house be broken into. **You also, keep ready, because at an hour that you do not think likely, the Son of man is coming.** (Luke 12:35-40)

There are clearly defined elements to this parable or illustration. The master of the slaves is absent. The slaves must remain awake to find favor in the master's eyes upon his return. The slaves have no way of knowing when the master will return.

Reading the master's final warning that he would return at a time his disciples would "not think likely" makes me wonder what Russell and associates were thinking when they predicted Jesus would return in October 1914 to bring the end and restore Israel! The Lord tells us, "I'm coming at a time you think unlikely," but Russell says, "Ah, no, Lord. You've got it all wrong. We've already nailed the year and the month."

Luke makes no mention of the faithful and discreet slave or steward in the verses we've just read, yet they are linked to the parable of the faithful and discreet slave or steward. How do we know that? By the context. Right after hearing Jesus' words at

Luke 12:35-40, Peter is prompted to ask in verse 41, "Lord, are you telling this illustration just to us or also to everyone"[4]

Peter wants to know if this warning applies only to those present, or to all his disciples, or to all the Jews. Instead of giving him a direct answer, Jesus launches into the famous parable of the Faithful Slave or Steward.

> And the Lord said: "Who really is **the faithful steward**, the discreet one, whom his master will appoint over his body of attendants to keep giving them their measure of food supplies at the proper time? Happy is that slave if his master on coming finds him doing so! I tell you truthfully, he will appoint him over all his belongings. But if ever that slave should say in his heart, 'My master delays coming,' and starts to beat the male and female servants and to eat and drink and get drunk, the **master of that slave** will come on a day that he is not expecting him and at an hour that he does not know, and he will punish him with the greatest severity and assign him a part with the unfaithful ones. Then **that slave who understood the will of his master** but did not get ready or do what he asked will be beaten with many strokes. But **the one who did not understand** and yet did things deserving of strokes will be beaten with few. Indeed, everyone to whom much was given, much will be demanded of him, and the one who was put in charge of much will have more than usual demanded of him." (Luke 12:42-48)

In the illustration that prompted Peter's question (vs. 35-40), Jesus focuses only on the need for the slaves to remain awake and prepared. However, in the answer he provides to Peter's question, he explains *why* they must be prepared and awake. *He again emphasizes the unexpected nature of the master's return*, but he also explains the need for the slave to do his job in the master's absence. The job is a simple one: To feed his fellow slaves their food as needed, "at the proper time."

Again, the application the Governing Body gives to the parable of the faithful slave or steward makes a mockery of Jesus' warning. Jesus says in Luke 12:40 that he will come at a time that his disciples think unlikely, and then again in verse 46, Jesus, addressing the evil slave specifically, tells us that he will "come on a day that he is not expecting him and at an hour that he does not know."

---

4. Luke 12:41

## 13. Who Is the Faithful and Discreet Slave?

Given this double warning, how can the Governing Body keep a straight face while claiming they knew down to the year and month (October 1914) when Jesus would return? Are they mocking the words of our Lord? It would appear so, but as we've seen already in this book and will now see again, the joke's on them.

But that isn't the only flaw in the reasoning behind the Watch Tower doctrine of the Faithful and Discreet Slave. We've barely scratched the surface.

You will notice that the master in the parable doesn't appoint a faithful and discreet slave! He frames it as a question. He appoints a slave which he *hopes will prove* to be faithful and discreet, but the outcome of that slave is not predetermined. In other words, he is not appointed because he is faithful and discreet. He is appointed in the hope that *he will prove to be* faithful and discreet. Can you see the difference?

Luke's account demonstrates this by showing that while there is a faithful and discreet slave, there is also an evil one. In addition, there are two more slaves. Verse 47 speaks of a slave who understood what the will of the master was but failed to comply with the master's wishes. That slave is beaten with many strokes or lashes. There is another slave in verse 48 who also did not comply with the master's wishes, but his failure was due to ignorance. Apparently, he did not know what was really required of him, likely because he didn't read the master's own words, but relied on others to interpret them for him. Nevertheless, he is still punished, though not so severely as the slave who knowingly disobeyed.

If we accept the Governing Body's interpretation that a small group of individuals is being referenced, then we must also accept that the other three slaves are represented by other small groups of individuals. This does not play well within the theology of Jehovah's Witnesses. If the Faithful and Discreet Slave was appointed in 1919, then who was the Evil Slave at that point in time? And who, in 1919, was the slave that didn't do the master's will knowingly and how was he beaten with many strokes? Also, who comprises the slave that failed to do the master's will out of ignorance, and how is he punished with a few strokes?

The Organization tries to get around this by ignoring the other two slaves and focusing only on Matthew's account which just mentions two slaves: One faithful slave and one evil slave. They then discount the evil slave by claiming he isn't a real person, but just a metaphorical warning. In other words, the faithful slave is a literal appointment, but the evil slave is a figurative warning. We can see this from this excerpt from the 2015 *Watchtower*:

> In the illustration of the faithful and discreet slave, Jesus spoke of an evil slave who beat his fellow slaves. Jesus was not there foretelling that an evil slave class would arise. Rather, he was warning the faithful slave not to display the traits of an evil slave.[5]

That's quite a stretch, but it would be impossible to extend it to explain about the *other two slaves* Luke speaks of which is why there is virtually no mention nor explanation given to Luke 12:47, 48 in the last 70 years of Watch Tower publications.

## Examining Luke's Account Exegetically

If you go back and read Luke 12:35-40 concerning the need for the slaves to be awake, do you see any reason to conclude that Jesus is referring to a small group of slaves, one appointed with oversight over the entire congregation? No, it's obvious that those words of warning are made to all Christians, because all Christians are servants of the Master, our Lord Jesus Christ. All of us must remain awake and keep our figurative lamps burning.

Why then would anyone consider that the amplified explanation given in answer to Peter's question in Luke 12:41 would suddenly refer to a small group of individuals? Some have drawn that conclusion because this slave is appointed to feed his fellow slaves. This leads to the conclusion that this slave is in a position of oversight. But I ask you, who feeds this slave who feeds the others? Notice that Jesus makes this appointment because he has left and is not around to do the feeding himself. So, this slave does the job of feeding his fellow slaves, but who feeds him?

The Bible answers that at Colossians 3:16 which reads: "Let the word of Christ richly dwell within you as you *teach and admonish one another with all wisdom...*"

We all feed—*teach and admonish*—one another at various times as the need arises. Sometimes we feed others and sometimes we are the ones needing to be fed. That is why Jesus adds the phrase "at the proper time." Each of us needs spiritual food to be strong when we are facing various trials. Even the strongest

---

5. w15 3/15 pp. 23-24 par. 15

of us can weaken at times. Was there ever anyone stronger than Jesus Christ himself? And yet even he needed support in his most difficult hour, and he received that help from his heavenly Father who sent him an angel to minister to him and strengthen him—to feed him spiritually.[6]

If our Lord needed to be fed at a moment like that, how much more so do we, miserable and weak humans that we are, need the support of others at various times in our life? The Bible tells us that "as iron sharpens iron, so one man sharpens his friend."[7]

The Governing Body's error is to take this parable and turn it into a prophecy. They do this because they need to find some scriptural foundation to justify their assumption of power and control over the entire congregation of Jehovah's Witnesses with its billions of dollars in funds and assets. They have assumed the role of leaders even though Jesus told us that no one should be our leader, and they also assume the role of teachers, even though Jesus told us that he alone is our teacher. He warned us all:

> But YOU, do not YOU be called Rabbi, for one is YOUR teacher, whereas all YOU are brothers. Moreover, do not call anyone YOUR father on earth, for one is YOUR Father, the heavenly One. Neither be called 'leaders,' for YOUR Leader is one, the Christ. But the greatest one among YOU must be YOUR minister. **Whoever exalts himself will be humbled, and whoever humbles himself will be exalted.** (Matthew 23:8-12)

In these verses, Jesus is not saying that no one should teach another, nor is he denying the need for someone to take the lead in any particular endeavor. What he is saying is that no one should replace him as our leader, because he alone can tell us what to do and what not to do with our life. Likewise, no one should replace him as our teacher. Anyone teaching another is merely relaying the teaching of Christ and not coming up with his own interpretation. To come up with one's own interpretation and force it on the flock means a person—or group of persons—is presuming to replace Jesus as *The Teacher.*

As he said, we are all brothers, but if a group wants to become more than our brothers, if there is a group of men who wishes

---

6.  Luke 22:43
7.  Proverbs 27:17

to become our governors or rulers, then they need to find some basis in Scripture for this. There is no basis for that, so they have to make one up. The men of the Governing Body have exploited the parable of the Faithful and Discreet Slave for that purpose. In doing so, they have exalted themselves. They fail to heed the counsel of Jesus that we just read: "Whoever exalts himself will be humbled, and whoever humbles himself will be exalted."

## Identifying the Four Slaves

Once we understand that the parable of the Faithful Slave applies to all the Children of God, we can start to make sense of it. A good way to accomplish that is to reverse engineer the parable; that is, to work backward from its conclusion.

### The Faithful and Discreet Slave

The faithful slave is the only one of the four who gets appointed over all the Lord's belongings. How is that fulfilled?

We know that Jesus has been appointed over all things in heaven and earth.[8] We know that his Kingdom will endure for a thousand years and that together with him, the Children of God will rule as kings for that same period of time.[9] The Bible tells us that Christ belongs to God, and that the Children of God belong to Christ, *and that all things belong to the Children of God.*[10] We also know that the Children of God include both men and women.[11] What that means is that all faithful Christians, male and female, will be appointed over the Lord's belongings as kings and priests, because all things will belong to them.

This single fact disproves the Governing Body's claim that they alone are the Faithful and Discreet Slave, a slave they claim only came into existence since 1919. If we accept the Governing Body's interpretation, then we must conclude that the original twelve apostles don't make up the slave and so will not be appointed over all of Christ's belongings. Such a conclusion is simply preposterous!

---

8. Matthew 28:18
9. Revelation 20:4-6
10. 1 Corinthians 3:21-23
11. Galatians 3:26-28; 1 Peter 3:7

This bears repeating: There is only one slave whom Jesus Christ appoints over all his belongings: The Faithful and Discreet Slave. If that slave is confined to the Governing Body since 1919, then men like J. F. Rutherford, Fred Franz, and Stephen Lett are expecting to be presiding over all things in heaven and earth, while the apostles, like Peter, John, and Paul stand on the sidelines looking on.

What outrageous nonsense these men would have you believe!

We all are fed spiritually by others, and we all have the opportunity to return the favor when someone else is in need of spiritual nourishment.

I have been meeting online with faithful Christians, true Children of God, for some years now. While you might think I have some considerable knowledge of Scripture, I can assure you that not a week goes by that I don't learn something new at our meetings. What a refreshing change that has been after enduring decades of boring, repetitious meetings in the Kingdom Hall.

This is not because these online meetings are filled with Bible scholars and learned experts. Quite the opposite. What we have is a group of spirit-filled people of mostly humble backgrounds. The difference is that the spirit speaks through them all in an atmosphere that promotes freedom of expression. Thus, everyone has a role in feeding the domestics, the household servants of our Lord. If you should wish to experience these online Bible study groups for yourself, the schedule is posted on beroeans.net/events/.

## The Evil Slave

All of us, as slaves of Jesus have the potential to be declared faithful and discreet by our Lord at his future presence. By the same token, if we tire of waiting and become selfish and self-indulgent, "eating and drinking and getting drunk," and begin to mistreat our fellow slaves, we run the risk of being declared evil. One doesn't have to be a member of the clergy to qualify as someone who beats his fellow slaves. Just as any one of us can qualify as a faithful slave by feeding our companion slaves spiritual food when they need it, any one of us can become abusive of our fellow slaves.

The Organization makes for a good object lesson in this regard. On my YouTube channel, I've had occasion to publish recordings of judicial hearings where the victim is accused of apostasy simply for wanting to feed his fellow slaves with the truth from God's word. The Governing Body decrees that such ones must be dealt with judicially. The local branch instructs the circuit overseers to educate the local elders on the proper procedures to administer what they like to call "discipline." But the local elders do not need to comply. They do not need to beat their fellow slaves.

There is no reason for us to conclude that the evil slave is restricted to men who are appointed to official positions in a church or congregation, like local priests or elders. All men and women in the congregation can act in the manner depicted in this parable. If brothers and sisters engage in false and harmful gossip and readily support the policies of the church, cheering on the priest as he burns the heretic at the stake, or complying with the shunning policies of an organization, can they escape the judgment of the evil slave? As to his punishment, we read that Jesus "will punish him with the greatest severity and will assign him his place with the hypocrites. There is where his weeping and the gnashing of his teeth will be."[12]

## The Two Slaves That Get Beaten

While Matthew only speaks of two slaves, Luke mentions four, the last two of which are beaten for being disobedient:

> Then that slave who understood the will of his master but did not get ready or do what he asked **will be beaten with many strokes**. But the one who did not understand and yet did things deserving of strokes **will be beaten with few**. (Luke 12:47, 48)

The remaining two are punished but not to the same degree as the evil slave. The evil slave is thrown out of the master's household and assigned the same fate as the hypocrites and faithless ones. That is not a fate any one of us would desire.

The other two slaves are not thrown out but are punished. They lose out on being appointed over the master's belongings, meaning they will not share in the Kingdom of the Heavens as kings and priests. Still, they will live. This implies a part in the resurrection of the unrighteous.[13]

---

12. Matthew 24:51; Luke 12:46
13. Acts 24:15; John 5:28, 29

## 13. Who Is the Faithful and Discreet Slave?

There are Christians who know what the will of the Christ is, yet they choose not to do it. They don't harm fellow Christians in that they don't participate in beating them as the evil slave does. Perhaps they've grown tolerant of wrongdoing, like those in the congregation of Thyatira[14] who tolerated the woman Jezebel who called herself a prophetess and misled some Christians to commit fornication. Perhaps they've merely grown apathetic as the members of the Laodicean congregation[15] were, becoming comfortable in their wealth.

Knowing what Christ demands of us and yet failing to do his will results in being beaten with many strokes. On the other hand, there are many Christians who believe they're doing Christ's will, obeying all his commands and leading a good Christian life. These are Christians who are being misled by seductive false teachings. The majority of Christians, Jehovah's Witnesses included, truly believe they're serving God. Witnesses who obey their leaders and shun someone for speaking the truth, believe they're doing this out of love and faithful obedience to God, even as Jesus predicted:

> Men will expel YOU from the synagogue [or Kingdom Hall]. In fact, the hour is coming when everyone that kills YOU [or shuns you] **will imagine he has rendered a sacred service to God**. (John 16:2)

Failing to do the will of the Lord is no excuse, even if one is acting out of ignorance. However, the punishment is less for such ones. They will be beaten with a few strokes. Exactly what form this punishment will take is not defined. Does it matter? Do any of us want to find out the hard way? I think not! Better to be counted by Christ as faithful and discreet, wouldn't you agree?

---

14. Revelation 2:20
15. Revelation 3:14-18

# 14

# Should I Partake of the Bread and Wine?

*For you did not receive a spirit of slavery causing fear again, but you received a spirit of adoption as sons, by which spirit we cry out: "Abba, Father!" (Romans 8:15)*

The Bible tells us at John 1:12 that to "all who did receive him, he [Jesus] gave authority to become God's children because they were exercising faith in his name." This means anybody who puts faith in Jesus is given the right to become a Child of God. We learned that in our scriptural analysis of the Other Sheep doctrine of Jehovah's Witnesses.[1]

If you have always believed you are of the Other Sheep class, learning that the other sheep are actually anointed Christians of Gentile origin (non-Jews) means you must have the heavenly hope and should be partaking of the emblems. That is a huge step for many Jehovah's Witnesses to take. My guess is that after years of idyllic *Watchtower* illustrations and moving regional convention videos depicting everlasting life in an earthly paradise, the heavenly hope is just not appealing to you.

On top of that there comes the feeling of unworthiness which has been inculcated into Jehovah's Witnesses through the

---

1. See also Chapter 7, *"Who Are the "Other Sheep"?"* on page 143.

misapplication of Romans 8:15 as this excerpt from the 2016 *Watchtower* illustrates:

> But how does a person know that he has the heavenly calling, that he has, in fact, received **this special token**? The answer is clearly seen in Paul's words to the anointed brothers in Rome, who were "called to be holy ones." He told them: "You did not receive a spirit of slavery causing fear again, but you received a spirit of adoption as sons, by which spirit we cry out: 'Abba, Father!' The spirit itself bears witness with our spirit that we are God's children." (Rom. 1:7; 8:15, 16) Simply put, by means of his holy spirit, God makes it clear to that person that he is invited to become a future heir in the Kingdom arrangement.—1 Thess. 2:12.
>
> Those who have received **this special invitation from God** do not need another witness from any other source. They do not need someone else to verify what has happened to them.[2]

I will explain why this *special token* or *special invitation* is not scriptural later in this chapter. For now, we need to understand that all Witnesses are baptised as one of the Other Sheep. You are told that you only get to be one of the anointed if God calls you, but why would he call you if he has thousands of long-time faithful Jehovah's Witnesses to choose from? In addition, since the manner of this *calling* is never explained, how can you be sure you have been called and are not just experiencing a psychotic episode or suffering from delusions of grandeur? Since the Bible says nothing about "this special invitation," you have nothing to go on. Thus, to start partaking carries with it a stigma.

I began partaking a couple of years before I was removed as an elder. However, I did so privately with my wife and some close friends. The reason I didn't partake at the annual memorial of Jehovah's Witnesses was because I knew I would be stigmatized. My fellow elders would think I was getting above myself, acting presumptuously. However, after I was removed, I became less concerned with such stigmatization and felt it might be a means to open dialogue with some of my friends. That didn't turn out to be the case.

What did result from the first time I partook in the Kingdom Hall was an effort on the part of some elders to have me brought before a committee. They viewed my partaking as further evidence of what they considered to be apostate thinking. Let's

---

2.  w16 January p. 19 pars. 9-10 "The Spirit Bears Witness With Our Spirit"

pause for a moment to take that in. Here you have a Christian acting on the basis of his conscience to obey a command of Jesus Christ, and the reaction of the elders is to charge him with apostasy. It was for this reason that my wife declined to partake with me at the Kingdom Hall. She realized that the two of us partaking together would offend many and cause us problems. She was right, of course.

There was a congregation in Miami, Florida where a small group—more than a dozen publishers—all began to partake together. I was informed by my sister, who lives nearby, that HQ sent down a representative to investigate. Imagine! Christians accepting Jesus' offer for everlasting life and blatantly doing so in public! The horror of it all! Send in the troops!

> So Jesus said to them: "Most truly I say to you, **unless you eat the flesh of the Son of man and drink his blood, you have no life in yourselves.** Whoever feeds on my flesh and drinks my blood has everlasting life, and I will resurrect him on the last day; for my flesh is true food and my blood is true drink. Whoever feeds on my flesh and drinks my blood remains in union with me, and I in union with him. Just as the living Father sent me and I live because of the Father, so also the one who feeds on me will live because of me. This is the bread that came down from heaven. It is not as when your forefathers ate and yet died. **Whoever feeds on this bread will live forever.**" (John 6:53-58)

## "But I Don't Want to Go to Heaven!"

This is a common objection I hear from Jehovah's Witnesses, one I felt myself when I first realized the hope that was being extended to me. But I drew comfort from these verses:

> "Eye has not seen and ear has not heard, nor have there been conceived in the heart of man the things that God has prepared for those who love him." For it is to us God has revealed them through his spirit, for the spirit searches into all things, even the deep things of God. (1 Corinthians 2:9, 10)

> You open your hand And **satisfy the desire of every living thing**. Jehovah is righteous in all his ways And loyal in all that he does. (Psalm 145:16, 17)

When I first started to partake in obedience to Jesus' command that all Christians should do so "in remembrance of me," I still accepted the JW teaching that the anointed go to heaven never to return to life on earth. I didn't know what it would be like to live in heaven, but I realized that for those passages we've just read to be true, it would have to be every bit as good, if not better, than living on earth. Then, as time went by, I began to wonder if I was again allowing myself to be influenced by JW indoctrination.

Does the Bible actually say that Christians go to heaven? I decided that it would be foolish to blindly accept such reasoning, which I might add is hardly exclusive to Witnesses. Both Catholics and Protestants also believe that faithful Christians go to heaven. The main difference is that they don't limit the number to a mere 144,000 as Witnesses do.

**Location! Location! Location!**

While location may be the most important thing when it comes to real estate, should it really factor into your salvation?

The reward we get isn't about where we live, but what we get to do. However, if we focus on location, as we are prone to do due to the influence of Watch Tower publications, we can easily misinterpret Scripture. For example, if you ask a Jehovah's Witness, "Where is the Kingdom of God?" he will undoubtedly reply, "In heaven." Yet, if you enter the phrases, "kingdom *in* the heavens" and "kingdom *in* heaven," into the Watchtower Library program, you will get zero hits in the Bible. On the other hand, the phrase "kingdom *of* the heavens" does appear some 33 times in the *New World Translation*, though only in the book of Matthew.

There is a significant difference between "of the heavens" and "in the heavens." One speaks of origin while the other speaks of location. In the Bible, the word "heaven" is *ouranos*. Regarding how it is used, *Strong's Concordance* lists: "heaven, (a) the visible heavens: the atmosphere, the sky, the starry heavens, (b) the spiritual heavens." *HELPS Word-studies* has this to say about it:

> 3772 ouranós – heaven (singular), and nearly as often used in the plural ("heavens"). "The singular and plural have distinct overtones and therefore should be distinguished in translation (though unfortunately they rarely are)" (G. Archer).

An exhaustive analysis of the word *ouranós* is beyond the scope of this book. However, one thing is clear: The majority of times the word is used, especially in the plural, it isn't referring to the physical location of God. In fact, even considering God to have a physical location is a human precept, an attempt to try to

## 14. Should I Partake of the Bread and Wine?

understand that which is infinite and beyond our comprehension. At times, this need to anthropomorphize God has led men to outrageous stupidities, such as this one from the 1928 book, *Reconciliation*, by J.F. Rutherford:

> The constellation of the seven stars forming **the Pleiades** appears to be the crowning center around which the known systems of the planets revolve even as our sun's planets obey the sun and travel in their respective orbits. It has been suggested, and with much weight, that **one of the stars of that group is the dwelling-place of Jehovah** and the place of the highest heavens; that it is the place to which the inspired writer referred when he said: "Hear thou from thy dwelling place, even from heaven" (2 Chron. 6 : 21) ; and that it is the place to which Job referred when under inspiration he wrote: "Canst thou bind the sweet influences of Pleiades, or loose the bands of Orion?"-Job 33:31.
>
> The constellation of the Pleiades is a small one compared with others which scientific instruments disclose to the wondering eyes of man. But the greatness in size of other stars or planets is small when compared with the Pleiades in importance, because **the Pleiades is the place of the eternal throne of God**.[3]

The idea that an entity capable of creating a universe containing billions of galaxies and trillions of stars should decide to take up residence in one lone star system within our modest Milky Way galaxy is just plain silly.

The fact is that even when the word "heaven" is used to speak of "God's dwelling place," as 2 Chronicles 6:21 does, it is not referring to a physical place, but rather somewhere that is beyond human comprehension—somewhere out there. Even the word "somewhere" is misleading because it still implies a place.

We live in a physical world. Our language expresses physicality. We find it difficult, if not impossible, to think in terms that exceed the four dimensions that we know: Length, width, depth, and time. But Jehovah God is outside of and above all such things. We just lack the terminology to express what He is and where He is—if there even is such a thing as "what" (God's nature) and "where" (God's location) when it comes to the Almighty.

We have to start looking at "heaven" as the term is expressed in Scripture. It is used most frequently in the plural, usually to express that which is over or above us. Even in English, we say

---

3. *Reconciliation* (1928) p. 14

heavens to mean the sky or air. If I say, "there are birds flying in the heavens," you would know I meant the sky.

When Matthew refers to "the kingdom of the heavens," he is speaking of the origin of the Kingdom's authority.[4] Thus, phrases like "the kingdom of God"[5] and "the kingdom of Christ"[6] are synonymous with Matthew's "the kingdom of the heavens." None of those terms refers to location, but instead to the source and authority of the Kingdom's rulership.

When Christians think about their salvation, they wonder about where it will be and what it will be like. These are normal concerns. We are, after all, only human.

Alas, the Bible has very little to say on the subject, and with good reason. God isn't tempting us with goodies. He wants us to listen to him and be guided by him because we have faith in his goodness and love.

## What Do We Know About Our Salvation Hope?

The Bible tells us that the anointed of God dwell in the New Jerusalem. Where is that?

> The one who conquers—I will make him a pillar in the temple of my God, and he will by no means go out from it anymore, and I will write upon him the name of my God and the name of the city of my God, **the New Jerusalem that descends out of heaven from my God**, and my own new name. (Revelation 3:12, 13)

> And I saw a new heaven and a new earth; for the former heaven and the former earth had passed away, and the sea is no more. I also saw the holy city, **New Jerusalem, coming down out of heaven from God** and prepared as a bride adorned for her husband. With that I heard a loud voice from the throne say: "Look! **The tent of God is with mankind, and he will reside with them**, and they will be his people. And God himself will be with them. And he will wipe out every tear from their eyes, and death will be

---

4. There is a school of thought that explains why only Matthew uses the term "kingdom of the heavens" instead of "kingdom of God" as the other gospel writers do. He was catering to the superstitions of his particular audience who were uncomfortable even referencing God by title.
5. Matthew 12:28; Mark 4:11; Romans 14:17; 1 Corinthians 4:20
6. Ephesians 5:5; 2 Peter 1:11; Revelation 11:15

## 14. Should I Partake of the Bread and Wine?

no more, neither will mourning nor outcry nor pain be anymore. The former things have passed away. (Revelation 21:1-4)

The anointed live in the New Jerusalem which descends from heaven to be on the earth. The tent or tabernacle of God doesn't refer to a common tent, but to the tabernacle which existed for centuries from the Exodus to the time when King Solomon built the temple in Jerusalem that replaced it. The tabernacle contained the sanctuary (*naos* in Greek) where we see the great crowd of anointed kings standing in Revelation 7:15. Of course, all this imagery is symbolic, a metaphor to help us understand that God will be with us under the Messianic Kingdom.

Rather than going off to a distant heaven never to be seen again by their loved ones, and ruling from there, as the Organization would have us believe, the Bible has something different to convey. The Children of God have work to do on the earth. According to the Berean Study Bible, and just about every other English version in print, Revelation 5:10 reads:

> You have made them to be a kingdom and priests to serve our God, and they will reign **upon** the earth.

Virtually every modern translation renders this as either "upon" or "on." The Greek word is *epi* and *Strong's* gives only "on" or "upon" as its definition. For usage in Scripture, *Strong's* gives: "on, to, against, on the basis of, at."

Why does the *New World Translation* use "over" when translating *epi* in this instance? Could it be that it fits nicely with their theology which has the anointed governing from far away in heaven?

Just within the 5th chapter of Revelation, *epi* occurs six times:[7]

- Vs. 1: "...the One seated on [*epi*] the throne..."
- Vs. 3: "But no one in heaven or on [*epi*] earth..."
- Vs. 7: "...the One seated on [*epi*] the throne..."
- Vs. 10 "...and they will reign upon [*epi*] the earth."
- Vs. 13a "And I heard every creature in heaven and on [*epi*] earth..."
- Vs. 13b "To Him who sits on [*epi*] the throne..."

Further evidence that leans toward the conclusion that the anointed kings and priests will be *on* (not over) the earth can

---

7. Quotes taken from *Berean Study Bible*

be derived from the parable of the faithful and discreet slave in Matthew 24:45-51.

The master appoints the slave to feed his domestics **during his absence**. Upon his return he judges the performance of each slave. Why does the master appoint the slave to feed his domestics? Obviously, because he is not there to do it himself. Why was the holy spirit sent to reveal the truth to his disciples? Because Jesus was no longer there to do it.[8] Why is Jesus with us when two or three are gathered in his name? It's not because he physically returns every time a couple of Christians get together in his name, but because the spirit works through us to feed one another.[9] Why did Jesus speak of a second coming? If he can rule remotely from heaven, why does he have to come back to the earth?[10]

One of the first things Jesus does upon his return is to gather the anointed to him:

> Afterward we the living who are surviving will, together with them, be caught away in clouds to meet the Lord in the air; and thus we shall always be with [the] Lord. (1 Thessalonians 4:17)

"In clouds" and "in the air" are both metaphors that pertain to the vicinity of the earth, not far away in heaven. Additionally, the verb "to meet" is a special word in Greek used about a friendly encounter. *Strong's* explains *apantēsis* as "a meeting; the act of meeting, to meet (a phrase seemingly almost technical for *the reception of a newly arrived official*)." The idea being conveyed is that the newly arrived official—in this case, our Lord Jesus—is met on his way in by representatives of the place he is coming to.

Think about this: How did Jesus teach his disciples immediately following his resurrection? He took on human form, sat with them, ate with them, and talked with them. He was resurrected a spirit, but like the angels that visited Abraham, he could assume human form to communicate.[11]

This is the pattern that spirit creatures use to physically communicate with men. The faithful men of old entertained angels

---

8. John 16:7-13
9. Matthew 18:20
10. 2 Thessalonians 2:8-12
11. 1 Corinthians 14:45; Genesis 19:1

who took on the form of men.¹² When Gabriel visited Daniel, Zechariah, and Mary, he appears as a man because spirits cannot be seen by human eyes.¹³ Jesus, though resurrected as a life-giving spirit, took on human form to communicate with his disciples.¹⁴

While we cannot speak with absolute certainty, there seems to be a significant amount of evidence leading to the conclusion that for the Children of God to perform the dual tasks of ruling as kings and serving as priests for the reconciliation of humanity, we will have to follow the same pattern the angels have used and take on flesh so as to interact with those resurrected ones coming back as part of the resurrection of the unrighteous.¹⁵ This will require that we be physically present on the earth.

As to what our resurrected bodily form will be like, the Bible is notably vague. Even John could only add this:

> Beloved ones, now we are children of God, but as yet it has not been made manifest what we shall be. We do know that whenever he is made manifest **we shall be like him**, because we shall see him just as he is. (1 John 3:2)

"We will be like him"! Let's be reasonable here. We don't know exactly what our spiritual body¹⁶ will be like, but if we are going to be like Jesus, that should be good enough for any of us, shouldn't it?

## What It Means to Partake of the Bread and Wine

It must be a remarkable sight for people coming to a JW memorial from other Christian denominations to behold an entire congregation of faithful Christians publicly turning down the offer to share in the lifesaving flesh and blood of our Lord Jesus as represented by the bread and wine.

Make no mistake about it: There is no other path to salvation! Remember that Jesus said:

> **Unless YOU eat the flesh of the Son of man and drink his blood, YOU have no life in yourselves.** He that feeds on my flesh and

---

12. Hebrews 13:1; Genesis 18:2, 3; 19:1-3
13. Daniel 9:21; Luke 1:18-26; 24:39
14. 1 Corinthians 14:45; John 20:19-23; 21:4-24; Mark 16:12
15. John 5:28, 29; Acts 24:15
16. 1 Corinthians 15:50; 2 Corinthians 5:1, 4

drinks my blood has everlasting life, and I shall resurrect him at the last day; for my flesh is true food, and my blood is true drink. He that feeds on my flesh and drinks my blood remains in union with me, and I in union with him. Just as the living Father sent me forth and I live because of the Father, he also that feeds on me, even that one will live because of me. This is the bread that came down from heaven. It is not as when YOUR forefathers ate and yet died. **He that feeds on this bread will live forever.** (John 6:53-58)

Jesus provided no secondary path to salvation. If there were to be a secondary group of Christians who would be declared righteous as God's friends, but only if they actively refused to partake of the bread and wine, he would surely have said so. Clear instructions would have been provided since this is a matter of eternal life. Yet, we have no other instruction from our Lord other than what Paul relays to us:

> The cup of blessing which we bless, is it not a sharing in the blood of the Christ? The loaf which we break, is it not a sharing in the body of the Christ? Because there is one loaf, we, although many, are one body, for **we are all partaking of that one loaf**. (1 Corinthians 10:16, 17)

The evidence in Scripture for this understanding is overwhelming. For example, there is only one body of Christ. "We, although many, are one body...partaking of...one loaf." Do we see here any provision for a secondary, lesser body of worshippers?

Paul also told the Corinthians:

> For I received from the Lord that which I also handed on to YOU, that the Lord Jesus in the night in which he was going to be handed over took a loaf and, after giving thanks, he broke it and said: "This means my body which is in YOUR behalf. **Keep doing this** in remembrance of me." He did likewise respecting the cup also, after he had the evening meal, saying: "This cup means the new covenant by virtue of my blood. **Keep doing this**, as often as YOU drink it, in remembrance of me." For as often as YOU eat this loaf and drink this cup, YOU **keep proclaiming the death of the Lord**, until he arrives." (1 Corinthians 11:23-26)

Here we have a direct command from Jesus to "keep doing this."

How has the Governing Body managed to trick millions into believing that this simple and direct command doesn't apply to them? They've done so, in part, through word play. Notice this excerpt from *Insight on the Scriptures*:

## 14. Should I Partake of the Bread and Wine?

On the night before his death, Jesus instituted the Lord's Evening Meal, the Memorial of his death, and instructed his disciples to keep **observing** it. (Lu 22:19) This **observance** is to be kept "until he arrives." (1Co 11:26)[17]

Neither Jesus, nor the apostles, ever refer to the Lord's Evening Meal as an "observance." In English, the word means:

1. the action or practice of fulfilling or respecting the requirements of law, morality, or ritual. "strict observance of the rules"
2. the action of watching or noticing something.

You see how clever that is? The anointed can "observe" the memorial by "the action or practice of fulfilling...the requirements" to partake, and the Other Sheep can "observe" by the action of watching or noticing" what's going on without *actually taking part*. The Governing Body has convinced faithful Christians that they are obeying Jesus' command to "keep doing this," by the simple act of attending the memorial and looking on.

> The other sheep attend the Memorial, not as partakers, **but as observers**. In 1938, those with the earthly hope were for the first time specifically invited to attend the Memorial. The Watchtower of March 1, 1938, stated: "It will be entirely right and proper for the [other sheep] to be present at such meeting and observe what is done. . . . It should be and is a time of rejoicing for them also." Like invited guests who are happy to observe a wedding ceremony, the other sheep are happy to be **present as observers** at the Memorial.[18]

But our Lord did not tell us to "observe." He told us to *participate*. "Keep doing this in remembrance of me" is what he said. Doing what? Standing passively by, looking on? What were the disciples doing when he said those words? They were partaking of the bread and wine that Jesus passed among them.

What the Governing Body requires their Other Sheep class to do is even worse than passively looking on. The JW Other Sheep are required to take action, to make a definite choice. When the bread is offered to them, **they must refuse it**! When the Wine is passed to them, **they must turn it down**!

---

17. it-2 p. 344
18. w22 January p. 21 par. 6 "Why We Attend the Memorial"

Remarkable! Who would benefit from having millions of Jesus' disciples turn down the emblems that represent the offer made to them to become God's Children? Who has been warring with the remaining ones of the seed of the woman of Genesis 3:15 since he was cast down from heaven?[19] When trying to find the guilty party, we should always look at who benefits!

The Governing Body tells their Other Sheep not to partake. They tell them that their salvation doesn't depend on obeying this command of Jesus to eat of his flesh (represented by the bread) and drink of his blood (represented by the wine) even though this contradicts the express words of our Lord that "unless YOU eat the flesh of the Son of man and drink his blood, YOU have no life in yourselves."[20] Instead, they tell the Other Sheep that their salvation depends on ignoring Christ's command and instead on loyally supporting the men of the Governing Body:

> **The other sheep should never forget that their salvation depends on their active support of Christ's anointed "brothers" still on earth.**[21]

So, if you have always considered yourself as one of the Other Sheep as defined by the Watch Tower Society, you have a decision to make: Obey Christ, or obey the men of the Governing Body!

We've already seen that the number of anointed is not limited to 144,000.[22] We've also seen that Romans 8:16 does not represent some *special token* or *special invitation*.[23] I know that the impulse to obey the "direction of the faithful slave," as the Organization so often puts it, is very strong. But consider this: When you are standing before the judgment seat of the Lord, do you want your excuse to be: "I was just following orders"?

Jesus tells us that by partaking on a regular basis,[24] we are proclaiming his death. Why would the majority of Christians be prohibited from proclaiming the death of the Lord? It makes no sense. By partaking of the emblems, we are publicly expressing

---

19. Revelation 12:7-17
20. John 6:53
21. w12 3/15 p. 20 par. 2 "Rejoicing in Our Hope"
22. See "Bible Proof that 144,000 Is a Symbolic Number" on page 186.
23. See "First "Proof": Romans 8:16, A Special Token?" on page 160.
24. There is evidence that first-century Christians commemorated the Lord's death more than only once a year.

not only our faith, but also our acceptance of this life-saving provision. We are also acknowledging our acceptance of our adoption as God's children and our willingness to be part of the seed that will crush Satan and his demons.

What honest-hearted Christian wouldn't embrace that privilege and hope?

# 15

# How the Watch Tower Society Shuts Up the Kingdom of the Heavens

> *Woe to YOU, scribes and Pharisees, hypocrites! because YOU shut up the kingdom of the heavens before men; for YOU yourselves do not go in, neither do YOU permit those on their way in to go in. (Matthew 23:13)*

When Jesus walked the earth, Jehovah's nation (or organization, if you will) was Israel. They alone, out of all the nations on earth, had the law of God to guide them into the Kingdom of the Heavens. They alone were in a covenant relationship with the true God, Jehovah (YHWH). That covenant was for them to become a "kingdom of priests."

> And now if YOU will strictly obey my voice and will indeed **keep my covenant**, then YOU will certainly become my special property out of all [other] peoples, because the whole earth belongs to me. And YOU yourselves will become to me **a kingdom of priests and a holy nation**. (Exodus 19:5, 6)

Salvation from death and the hope for eternal life rested with the Jews. Jesus told the Samaritan woman that "salvation originates with the Jews."[1] The Savior that God would send to redeem us all from death would not go to Rome where the pagan god Jupiter or Jove was worshipped, nor would he be sent to the Greeks, who worshipped Zeus. Those false gods are gone, vanished into the mists of history.

It was only to the nation of Israel that Jehovah would send His only begotten Son, in one last attempt to turn them from their wicked course. But instead of taking a truly God-given opportunity and repenting, they murdered the Son of God. By this action, they broke their covenant, lost their chosen status, and condemned their nation.[2]

As a nation, they lost out on the reward that would have been theirs for keeping God's covenant. But some individuals, like the faithful men and women described in Hebrews chapter 11, did not miss out. Nevertheless, the New Covenant came into being.[3] This time, it would not be limited to the Jews, but would include people of all nations.

This was bad news for the Devil because from the very beginning in Eden, God foretold how Satan would meet his end.

> And I shall put enmity between you and the woman and between your seed and her seed. He will bruise you in the head and you will bruise him in the heel." (Genesis 3:15)

That seed or offspring of the woman[4] would spell doom for the Devil, so his goal has been to eliminate that seed. Ultimately, the seed of the woman would turn out to be Jesus, but it would not stop with Him. It would include an untold number of anointed humans: The Children of God. Satan, having failed to turn Jesus to his side, would now go after these ones. Revelation uses symbolic imagery to demonstrate this:

> Now when the dragon saw that it was hurled down to the earth, it persecuted the woman that gave birth to the male child. But the two wings of the great eagle were given the woman, that she might fly into the wilderness to her place; there is where she is fed for a time and times and half a time away from the face of the serpent. And the serpent disgorged water like a river from its

---

1. John 4:22
2. Jesus explains this by the parable at Matthew 21:33-41
3. Hebrews 8:13
4. Galatians 4:21-26

mouth after the woman, to cause her to be drowned by the river. But the earth came to the woman's help, and the earth opened its mouth and swallowed up the river that the dragon disgorged from its mouth. And the **dragon grew wrathful at the woman, and went off to wage war with the remaining ones of her seed**, who observe the commandments of God and have the work of bearing witness to Jesus. (Revelation 12:13-17)

As we learned earlier in this book, God's Children comprise a "great crowd" who are taken "out of all nations and tribes and peoples and tongues."[5] All Mankind has been waiting for these ones to be revealed:

> For the creation was subjected to futility, not by its own will but through him that subjected it, on the basis of hope that **the creation itself also will be set free from enslavement to corruption and have the glorious freedom of the children of God**. (Romans 8:20, 21)

Naturally, the Devil wages war with the remaining ones of the woman's seed, because when their number is complete, he is done for.[6] In Jesus' day, Satan had already been working very hard among Israelite leaders to block the development of the seed. Jesus pointed this out in no uncertain terms:

> Woe to YOU, scribes and Pharisees, hypocrites! because YOU **shut up the kingdom of the heavens** before men; for YOU yourselves do not go in, neither do YOU permit those on their way in to go in. "Woe to YOU, scribes and Pharisees, hypocrites! because YOU **traverse sea and dry land to make one proselyte**, and when he becomes one YOU make him a subject for Gehenna twice as much so as yourselves. (Matthew 23:13, 15)

Satan's war against the seed of the woman didn't stop when Israel was rejected by God because the Kingdom of God was given to another nation, as Jesus himself foretold:

> This is why I say to you, the Kingdom of God will be taken from you and be **given to a nation producing its fruits**. (Matthew 21:43)

That new nation wasn't situated between borders marked out on a map. Instead, these men and women were considered

---

5. Revelation 7:9
6. Revelation 12:17

"temporary residents"[7] because their citizenship is in the heavens.[8]

These are the strands of wheat planted by Jesus in the field of the world, but the Devil—ever the opposer and enemy—over sowed the field with false Christians, weeds.[9] His goal was to seduce men and women away from the Kingdom of God into a false hope, one based on false teachings.

In the 18th century, many sincere Bible students were breaking away from false religion. They were forming small, independent congregations based on the first century model. They were freeing themselves from religious hierarchies and the oppressive nature of the teachings and traditions of men.

> This people honor me with their lips, but their hearts are far removed from me. **It is in vain that they keep worshipping me, for they teach commands of men as doctrines.** (Matthew 15:8, 9)

These Bible students came to see that God dishonoring beliefs like hellfire were an invention of religious leaders intended to subjugate the flock.

However, Satan would not give up. Since the beginning, he has used lies and falsehoods to keep people away from the Kingdom of God. These lies are spread by means of his ministers.

In Israel, these were the religious leaders that Jesus condemned:

> YOU are from YOUR father the Devil, and YOU wish to do the desires of YOUR father. That one was a manslayer when he began, and he did not stand fast in the truth, because truth is not in him. When he speaks the lie, he speaks according to his own disposition, because he is a liar and the father of [the lie]. (John 8:44)

Once the Christian congregation got underway, Satan transferred his attention to those who were striving to become God's Children. But he has no new strategies. So, he fell back on the tried and true tactic of getting humans to put their trust in men.[10]

> For such men are false apostles, deceitful workers, transforming themselves into apostles of Christ. And no wonder, for Satan

---

7. 1 Peter 1:1
8. Philippians 3:20
9. Matthew 13:24-30, 36-43
10. Psalm 146:3

himself keeps transforming himself into an angel of light. It is therefore nothing great if **his ministers also keep transforming themselves into ministers of righteousness**. But their end shall be according to their works. (2 Corinthians 11:13-15)

## How Has Watch Tower Stolen Salvation from Jehovah's Witnesses?

The theme of this book is specific to the religion of Jehovah's Witnesses, but in principle applies to all Christian sects. So, we come back to the question: How has the Watch Tower Society stolen salvation from Jehovah's Witnesses?

I focus on the Watch Tower Society, because it predates the formation of the modern Governing Body, but ultimately, it all comes down to men: Specifically, the leaders of any religious movement. In Jesus' day, it was the scribes (legal scholars), Pharisees, and priests of Israel who shut up the Kingdom of God to the people by teaching falsehoods and inducing them to act wickedly by deceiving them into thinking they were serving God. At John 16:2, Jesus says that "the hour is coming when everyone that kills YOU will imagine he has rendered a sacred service to God."

The leaders of the Watch Tower Society—now the Governing Body of Jehovah's Witnesses—have also shut up the Kingdom of God by means of false teachings, and by inducing their flock to punish anyone who shines the light of truth onto their wicked deeds.

This began with Russell who got people to believe in a false presence of Christ. This lie has continued to form a major part of the preaching of the Good News spread by Jehovah's Witnesses. We learned from Paul that preaching a false Good News brings condemnation from God:

> I am amazed that you are so quickly turning away from the One who called you with Christ's undeserved kindness to another sort of good news. Not that there is another good news; but there are certain ones who are causing you trouble and wanting to distort the good news about the Christ. However, even if we or an angel out of heaven were to declare to you as good news something beyond the good news we declared to you, let him be accursed. As we have said before, I now say again, **Whoever is declaring to you as good news something beyond what you accepted, let him be accursed.** (Galatians 1:6-9)

You can hardly expect to get into the Kingdom of God if you are accursed by God, can you?

But Satan doesn't corrupt all at once. His influence is like leaven that slowly works to corrupt the entire mass of dough.[11] We saw how Rutherford formed the religion of Jehovah's Witnesses in 1931, and then just three years later, introduced what is possibly the worst teaching ever accepted by the community: **the earthly hope of the Other Sheep**. By this teaching, which is the major component of the Good News Witnesses preach, he induced millions to turn their nose up at the life-saving blood and flesh of our Lord represented by the symbols of the bread and wine.

If Jesus were here now, would he say of the Governing Body of Jehovah's Witnesses, like he said of their ancient counterparts, the scribes and Pharisees, that they have "shut up the kingdom of the heavens before men; for YOU yourselves do not go in, neither do YOU permit those on their way in to go in?"[12]

Ultimately, Jesus Christ will be the judge of that.[13] Our personal concern, yours and mine, should be to free ourselves and others from enslavement to the teachings of men so that we can find the glorious freedom of the Children of God and understand what it truly means to be part of the body of Christ.

Let no man nor group of men steal that hope from us ever again!

## Preparing Yourself to Become a Child of God

This is a very extensive subject. In fact, an entire book would not do it justice, but there is one important and relevant point that can be made here: Satan the Devil, by means of his crafty lie, brought about the fall of humankind. Therefore, what has happened is a crime against humanity and in all fairness, should be dealt with and judged by humans.

I am a Canadian by birth. However, if I travel to France and commit a crime there, I will be judged by a court in France, not Canada. That is as it should be. A criminal act is judged within the jurisdiction where it occurs.

---

11. Matthew 16:6-12
12. Matthew 23:13, 15
13. John 5:22

The justice of God is evident by the fact that he made an arrangement right at the start, right after the crime had been committed, to try the criminal in a court of the land. The Devil and his demons have all sinned against humanity. It will be humans who bring them to justice, try them, judge them, and sentence them to death. Paul told the Corinthians: "Do you not know that we will judge angels?"[14]

What happened in Eden was a human problem and it is not going to be fixed by outsiders, but by humans. The Devil and his demons have caused untold pain and suffering to the human race, and so they will be dealt with by us. That was one of the reasons why Jesus became a man.

> Keep this mental attitude in YOU that was also in Christ Jesus, who, although he was existing in God's form, gave no consideration to a seizure, namely, that he should be equal to God. No, but he emptied himself and took a slave's form and **came to be in the likeness of men**. More than that, when **he found himself in fashion as a man**, he humbled himself and became obedient as far as death. (Philippians 2:5-8)

> Because he has set a day in which he purposes **to judge the inhabited earth in righteousness by a man** whom he has appointed, and he has furnished a guarantee to all men in that he has resurrected him from the dead. (Acts 17:31)

Jesus' loyalty and obedience to God had never been put to the test. Before he could be given full authority, our heavenly Father had to ensure that His only begotten Son would not follow the same independent course which the Devil took. Hence, we read:

> In the days of his flesh [Christ] offered up supplications and also petitions to the One who was able to save him out of death, with strong outcries and tears, and he was favorably heard for his godly fear. Although he was a Son, **he learned obedience** from the things he suffered; and **after he had been made perfect** he became responsible for everlasting salvation to all those obeying him. (Hebrews 5:7-9)

If Jesus had to learn obedience by suffering, so as to be perfected or made complete for the task before him, could we expect anything less for those who are to serve alongside him as kings

---

14. 1 Corinthians 6:3

and priests?[15] It is for this reason that Jesus says, "whoever does not accept his torture stake and follow after me is not worthy of me."[16] The torture stake or cross (Romans used both though a cross was more common) was the most degrading and shameful form of execution of that time. The prisoner was stripped of all his belongings, even his outer garments. His family and friends turned their back on him. He was shunned by all. He was beaten and paraded through the streets for public humiliation. Finally, he was nailed to a stake or cross and died a slow, painful death.

Jesus wasn't telling us that to be worthy of him we have to die the painful death of a martyr—though, at times it has come to that. Rather, he was saying that we had to be willing to give up whatever we held to be precious; and more, we had to be willing to endure shame for his name's sake.

In an effort to encourage fellow Christians, the writer of Hebrews chapter 11 lists many cases of faithful pre-Christian servants and then sums his reasoning up with this faith-strengthening exhortation:

> Because we have so great a cloud of witnesses surrounding us, let us also put off every weight and the sin that easily entangles us, and let us run with endurance the race that is set before us, as we look intently at the Chief Agent and Perfecter of our faith, Jesus. For the joy that was set before him he endured a torture stake, **despising shame**, and has sat down at the right hand of the throne of God. Indeed, consider closely the one who has **endured such contrary talk by sinners against their own interests**, that YOU may not get tired and give out in YOUR souls. (Hebrews 12:1-3)

When you start to partake of the emblems because you recognize your true status as a Child of God, you will experience "contrary talk." Gossip will fly through the congregation. You will be slandered. Precious friendships and cherished family relations within the Organization will be lost. While you won't be disfellowshipped for partaking, you will be soft-shunned and stigmatized. Was Jesus ever concerned about gossip and slander? No, he despised shame. If you despise something, it does not mean nothing to you, it means *less than nothing* to you. That is the attitude you will have to acquire if you are to become a Child of God.

---

15. Revelation 20:4-6
16. Matthew 10:38

And why do you need to go through all that? Because, like Jesus, you will have to be refined and tested before our heavenly Father can trust you with the authority and power that goes with the position of co-ruler alongside his Son.

> Because of this you are greatly rejoicing, though for a short time, if it must be, you have been distressed by various trials, **in order that the tested quality of your faith, of much greater value than gold** that perishes despite its being tested by fire, may be found a cause for praise and glory and honor at the revelation of Jesus Christ. (1 Peter 1:6, 7)

# 16

## Can I Worship God Without Religion?

---

*...Nevertheless, the hour is coming, and it is now, when the true worshipers will worship the Father with spirit and truth, for, indeed, the Father is looking for suchlike ones to worship him. (John 4:23)*

---

Let's start with the Israelites of the prophet Samuel's day. They stubbornly insisted on having a human king appointed over them, even when God warned them that it would all go wrong.[1] Why were the Israelites so eager to give up their freedom and become enslaved to the whims of a king? What is it in human nature that seems to yearn for subjugation? Paul encountered the same attitude in the congregation at Corinth. He chided them for it, writing:

> Since you are so "reasonable," you gladly put up with the unreasonable ones. **In fact, you put up with whoever enslaves** you, whoever **devours** your possessions, whoever **grabs** what you have, whoever **exalts himself** over you, and whoever **strikes** you in the face. (2 Corinthians 11:19, 20 NWT 2013)

As I woke up to the reality of the Organization—to the realization that I had believed and promoted false doctrines of men all my life—I realized I had to leave. Yet, I resisted. What kept me

---

1. 1 Samuel 8:4-22

tethered was the belief that I had to belong to some religious organization to be saved. As it turns out, this is false.

Organized religion is a sure way to distance yourself from your Savior, Jesus Christ, and the one who sent him, Jehovah God. For this piece of wisdom, we have to thank Charles Taze Russell—ironically, the man the Governing Body claims to be the founder of Jehovah's Witnesses, a prominent organized religion. He had this to say about the dangers of religion:

> Surely all know that whenever they join any of these human organizations, accepting its Confession of Faith as theirs, they bind themselves to believe neither more nor less than that creed expresses on the subject. If, in spite of the bondage thus voluntarily yielded to, they should think for themselves, and receive light from other sources, in advance of the light enjoyed by the sect they have joined, they must either prove untrue to the sect and to their covenant with it, to believe nothing contrary to its Confession, or else they must honestly cast aside and repudiate the Confession which they have outgrown, and come out of such a sect. To do this requires grace and costs some effort, disrupting, as it often does, pleasant associations, and exposing the honest truth-seeker to the silly charges of being a "traitor" to his sect, a "turncoat," one "not established," etc. **When one joins a sect, his mind is supposed to be given up entirely to that sect, and henceforth not his own. The sect undertakes to decide for him what is truth and what is error; and he, to be a true, staunch, faithful member, must accept the decisions of his sect, future as well as past, on all religious matters, ignoring his own individual thought, and avoiding personal investigation, lest he grow in knowledge, and be lost as a member of such sect. This slavery of conscience to a sect and creed is often stated in so many words, when such a one declares that he "belongs" to such a sect.**[2]

Don't Russell's words eerily reflect the present-day situation of all Jehovah's Witnesses who choose to stand up for truth within the Organization that was formed in 1931 by Rutherford? After he took over from Russell, he created the very thing that Russell warned us about! Should Witnesses "think for themselves" and receive "light from other sources [like the Bible]" then choose to believe "contrary to [the Organization's] Confession," these

---

2. For the full context see *Studies in Scriptures*, vol. 3, pp. 181-187

## 16. Can I Worship God Without Religion?

"honest truth-seekers" are exposed to "silly charges of being a 'traitor' [an apostate]."

See now the impact of Russell's closing words as we consider the additional words of the Apostle Paul:

> **Russell:** "This slavery of conscience to a sect and creed is often stated in so many words, when such a one declares that **he "belongs" to such a sect.**"

> **Paul:** "Hence let no one be boasting in men; for all things belong to YOU, whether Paul or Apollos or Cephas or the world or life or death or things now here or things to come, all things belong to YOU; in turn YOU **belong to Christ**; Christ, in turn, belongs to God." (1 Corinthians 3:21-23)

If, by this point in our study, you have come to see yourself quite properly as a Child of God due to your faith in Jesus Christ, then you won't belong to an organization. You won't belong to men. You won't belong to a self-appointed Faithful and Discreet Slave in the form of the Governing Body of Jehovah's Witnesses. Indeed, as a qualifying characteristic of the Children of God, we belong to our Lord Jesus Christ and to each other. We will not follow any who set themselves up as religious leaders, nor do we seek to have people follow us. Instead, we must now consider ourselves as part of the Body of Christ, as members belonging to each under the headship of Christ.

> For just as the body is one but has many members, and all the members of that body, although being many, are one body, so also is the Christ. For truly by one spirit **we were all baptized into one body**, whether Jews or Greeks, whether slaves or free, and we were all made to drink one spirit. (1 Corinthians 12:12, 13)

> For just as we have in one body many members, but the members do not all have the same function, so we, although many, **are one body in union with Christ, but individually we are members belonging to one another**. (Romans 12:4, 5)

Can you see how these two scriptures undercut the entire basis of the baptism practiced by the Organization? If we are "all baptized into one body," then how can there be an anointed body of Christians, and another unanointed body of Other Sheep?

This is yet another example of what Russell was saying. We have to abandon what the Bible teaches and obey the interpretations of men if we want to remain in a religion. But we are no longer directed by a group of men claiming the spirit works through them. Instead, the spirit works through all of us. If only two or three are gathered in Jesus' name, he is there, and the spirit is guiding those few.[3] And if there are many, then the same spirit guides them, unifies them, and keeps them true to the course set for all of us by God.

This results in the most exalted condition imaginable for us because as Paul concludes, "all things belong to you." This is a difficult concept for Witnesses to accept who have been raised to view themselves as a secondary, subjugated class of Christian—just one of the Other Sheep.

To now hold the view that the hope open to us is that of serving with Christ as kings and priests, inheriting with him the Kingdom of God—well, that's pretty heady stuff, isn't it? This is the hope that the Governing Body has been denying Jehovah's Witnesses for decades. Let no man, nor group of men, take that away from us ever again!

## Jesus Explains the Difference Between Religion and Worship

On one occasion, Jesus sat alone at a well when a Samaritan woman came to get water. He engaged her in conversation, something Jews never did with Samaritans, for the two groups hated each other. In the course of the discussion, she comes to see that he is no ordinary man. John 4:19, 20 records her as saying, "Sir, I see that you are a prophet. Our forefathers worshipped on this mountain, but you people say that in Jerusalem is the place where people must worship."

Why would she go from acknowledging that he is a prophet straight into her implied query concerning worship? Her people claimed that worship must be performed on Mount Gerizim, which was sacred to them, but Jews claimed that only worship at the temple in Jerusalem was acceptable to God. Evidently, she wanted to worship God in an acceptable manner, but was confused about how to do it.

For all people of that time, worship was only valid if linked to some geographic location. For a Jew, the place was the holy temple in Jerusalem; for a Samaritan, it was the holy mountain.

---

3. Matthew 18:20

## 16. Can I Worship God Without Religion?

Not much has changed. Today, for Catholics, worship is performed in a building, an ornate church; for Jews, it's their local synagogue; for Jehovah's Witnesses, their Kingdom Hall. Or we can expand the geography figuratively: for Catholics, it's the Catholic Church with its rituals; for Jews, it's rabbinical Judaism with its traditions; for Jehovah's Witnesses, it's the Organization with its practices.

How did Jesus respond to the woman's implicit question? His answer was revolutionary!

> Believe me, woman, the hour is coming when **neither on this mountain nor in Jerusalem** will you worship the Father. You worship what you do not know; we worship what we know, because salvation begins with the Jews. Nevertheless, the hour is coming, and it is now, when the true worshippers will worship the Father with spirit and truth, for indeed, the Father is looking for ones like these to worship him. God is a Spirit, and those worshipping him must worship with spirit and truth. (John 4:21-24)

Jesus detaches worship from a geographical location, and in so doing, from a particular religious brand. No longer is God looking for people who belong to an organization or the brand of a religious denomination. According to our Lord, we need only two things to worship our heavenly Father: One is holy spirit, and the other is truth. These two are intertwined because you cannot get the holy spirit unless you are a sincere seeker for truth, and you cannot understand the truth unless the holy spirit resides in you.[4]

Jesus is saying, in other words, that ritualized worship—i.e., religion—was no longer the means to worship God. It is as Hebrew 7:19 says: "For the Law made nothing perfect, but the introduction of a better hope did, through which we are drawing near to God."

The worship of the nation of Israel was only a means by which Jehovah would bring the faithful to a proper understanding of their relationship with him as children. Worship of God isn't about ritual, rules, or works. When Jehovah created Adam and Eve, they were his children. He didn't institute anything ritualistic in their relationship with Him.

---

4. 1 John 2:26, 27; Romans 8:14

The word "worship" is greatly abused, misused and misunderstood today. In Greek, it is *proskuneó* and implies in the absolute sense—that is, with reference to God—*complete submission*. Worship isn't about ritual. It's about obedience; not the obedience of a fearful subject before a tyrannical king, but rather the willing obedience which a beloved son or daughter willingly gives to a loving Father.

When Jehovah brought the Jews out of Egypt, they were not spiritually advanced enough to grasp that truth. The Mosaic law gave them the foundation that would eventually guide them, like a tutor, to the way, and the truth, and the life in Christ.[5]

> Therefore, brothers, since we have boldness for the way of entry into the holy place by the blood of Jesus, which he opened up for us as a new and living way through the curtain, that is, his flesh, and since we have a great priest over the house of God, **let us approach with sincere hearts and complete faith**, [not by works of law] having had our hearts sprinkled clean from a wicked conscience and our bodies bathed with clean water. (Hebrews 10:19-22)

Jesus was telling the Samaritan woman, and through her, all of us, that he brought something new: Now, God was looking only for those who were willing to break free from such ritualized worship, because they were seeking His spirit and His truth through faith in Jesus Christ. These true worshippers were breaking free from religion that bound them to religious leaders and made them obedient to men. This was what Jesus promised when he said:

> If YOU remain in my word, YOU are really my disciples, and YOU will know the truth, and the truth will set YOU free. (John 8:31, 32)

We cannot remain in "his word," if we are required to obey church leaders, can we? Joining a religion or worshipping inside a church or a Kingdom Hall does not impart holy spirit nor truth. Quite the opposite.

I can hardly think of anything J. F. Rutherford came up with that I can agree with except for this one expression of his: "Religion is a snare and a racket."

---

5. Galatians 3:24; John 14:6

## Why Is Religion a Snare and a Racket?

For many, it will still be difficult to rid themselves of strongly entrenched concepts such as religion being the way to worship God. Jehovah's Witnesses are taught that all other religions are false, while theirs is the only true religion. Throughout this book, I've provided ample proof that that is not the case. Was Rutherford right? Is all religion a snare and a racket? What exactly is a racket?

One definition—the one Rutherford meant—is this: "A fraud or swindle; an illegal scheme for profit." From this we get the term, "racketeering" which is, "any act or threat involving murder, kidnapping, gambling, arson, robbery, bribery, extortion intended to rob or steal from a victim."

The Catholic church extorted money from parishioners by threatening them with purgatory or hellfire unless they obeyed church leaders. Televangelists get rich promising (bribery) prosperity from God if their viewers send in money.

How ironic it would be if Rutherford's condemnation were applicable to the very religion he founded in 1931!

To see if that's applicable, we need to go back to the beginning: We start with C. T. Russell founding a publishing company to preach the good news, heralding Christ's presence. We now know that he got it wrong, but one thing we can say in his favor is that he didn't start up a religion. There were many independent congregations and Bible student groups who subscribed to his writings, but they weren't controlled by a central authority. There was no ecclesiastical hierarchy governing all the Bible Student groups in those days. Rutherford was the one who set that up in 1931 by giving the small number of Bible Student groups still affiliated with the Watch Tower Society a distinct name. This is when a Christian religion really starts, when it brands itself as different from other Christians. But it still takes time for the rot to set in as it always does. (Of course, Rutherford's condemnation of religion was classic projection. He was condemning the very thing he was creating. Projection of this type is a slight-of-hand trick to get you to look elsewhere and not at the person doing the same thing he is criticizing others of doing.)

## Does the Organization of Jehovah's Witnesses Engage in Racketeering?

When I was a child living in Hamilton, Ontario, the local congregation built its first Kingdom Hall. Up until that time, we had been holding meetings in the Legion Hall which we rented. The new Hall was owned by the local congregation. I used to brag to my Bible studies when I was preaching in the Catholic land of Colombia that Witnesses were not about money; that our Kingdom Halls were modest and were owned by the local congregation, not by Headquarters in Brooklyn.

In 2008, that was still the case when we built the new Kingdom Hall in Alliston at a cost of more than one million Canadian dollars. I was one of the three trustees on the deed which listed the Alliston Congregation of Jehovah's Witnesses as the owner.

That all changed six years later. A letter dated March 29, 2014 was sent out to all the congregations under the innocuous subject line: "Re: Adjustment to financing Kingdom Hall and Assembly Hall construction worldwide."

The first page was to be read to the congregations and promised that a new arrangement was now in effect which cancelled all Kingdom and Assembly Hall loans. On the surface, that sounds wonderful, doesn't it?

The letter stated that "congregations will now be *asked* to pool their resources worldwide to support the construction of theocratic facilities" and promised that "all congregations will have the *opportunity* to support Kingdom Hall and Assembly Hall construction worldwide by resolving to make a monthly donation from congregation funds."[6]

That also sounds nice, doesn't it?

In Alliston, we still owed a few hundred thousand before our mortgage could be paid off, which we were doing at a rate of about $1,839 a month. So now, we'd be free of that onerous monthly cost.

They were cancelling all loans and *asking* (not demanding) for congregations to pool their resources and offering congregations the *opportunity* to make a monthly donation. When you are asked for something, you don't have to agree, do you? When you are

---

6. *Letter to all congregations*: 3/29/14-E (page 1) available on AvoidJW.org (https://accessjw.org/.php/lte-2014.php?download=20140329LTC_us.pdf)

## 16. Can I Worship God Without Religion?

given an opportunity to contribute funds, you don't have to avail yourself of the opportunity, do you? Only if some form of coercion were used could such *requests* and *opportunities* be considered racketeering—like when a couple of thugs go into a pizzeria and offer the owner the *opportunity* to contribute a monthly donation to be protected from damage to his or her establishment.

There were three pages to the letter which were not supposed to be read to the congregation publishers. On the second page, the elders were told:

> The elders in congregations currently making loan repayments would likely propose a resolution that is **at least** the same amount as the current monthly loan repayment... [Italics in original letter, boldface mine.][7]

Dutifully, the elders in the Alliston congregation (I was no longer serving then) read out a resolution for $1,800 a month. So, nothing really changed for the Alliston publishers. They still had to come up with the same amount as before, but with one notable exception: A loan will eventually be paid off and thus the financial load on the congregation will be lightened. However, a "voluntary" donation never goes away.

It should be noted that congregations without an outstanding loan were also expected to make a monthly donation (or pledge):

> The elders in congregations without loans...should take a confidential survey of all publishers to determine the amount of the new resolution.[8]

You will notice how the *ask* on page 1 has become *direction* to the elders on page 2.

The next paragraph directs that the "elders should review this resolution annually" every May.

Page 4 of the letter directs the elders to forward any surplus funds the congregation may have on hand for future renovations or construction into the branch office.

### Rutherford Was Right!

It took a little time, but the true nature of this scheme revealed itself as the months went by. Starting with the JW Broadcasting

---

7. Ibid. page 2
8. Ibid. page 2

episode of May 2015, we find Stephen Lett talking up the benefits of the new arrangements, claiming the monies are needed for many thousands of theocratic construction projects. The Organization, it would seem, was growing by leaps and bounds.

He made the following astonishing claim:

> For example, all congregations that had a Kingdom Hall or Assembly Hall loan to pay off were informed that their mortgages were cancelled. Now, if you think about that, it's amazing, isn't it? All their loans were cancelled. **Can you imagine a bank telling homeowners that all their loans were cancelled**, and that they should merely send into the bank whatever they can afford? Only in Jehovah's organization could such a thing happen. [9]

That does sound very laudable, but he wasn't telling us the whole story, which only emerged sometime later.[10]

You see, what Lett said about no bank doing what the Organization did, isn't true! If a bank held mortgages on billions of dollars worth of property, then it would never cancel all those loans *unless* it could make more money by doing so. To do that, it would need two things: It would need the power to control the people operating those properties, and it would need the title for all those properties to be passed to the bank. Now imagine we can go beyond that. Imagine that the bank can also get ownership of any property for which it has ever held a mortgage, even though those mortgages had been paid off years or decades before. Would you buy a house if you learned that at any time, the bank could seize ownership of your house, even long after you had paid off your mortgage and that it could sell your home at any time without your premission?

That is the situation with the new financing arrangement of the Organization. That is what Lett is so proud of announcing.

As I said, prior to this arrangement, the congregations owned their own hall.

When we built our hall in Alliston in 2008, we sold our old hall for over half a million dollars and the funds went into our congregation account. We used those funds to buy the land and to

---

9. See video excerpt here: https://youtu.be/qfPMCDEuoNQ
10. For a full accounting of this history, see this article: https://beroeans.net/2018/06/30/identifying-true-worship-part-11-the-unrighteous-riches/

## 16. Can I Worship God Without Religion?

put a down payment on the mortgage the branch office gave us. All that has changed. Congregations no longer can choose to sell a hall, but if the hall is sold, it is done directly by a committee controlled by the branch office. In that case, the funds don't return to the local publishers who built and financed their own hall, but go directly to the local branch office of the Society.

The Organization, through its various legal entities, now claims ownership of all Kingdom and Assembly Hall properties and has set up committees around the world to evaluate which Kingdom Halls or Assembly Hall are underused. Congregations which enjoyed the convenience of a local hall—a hall they built with their own hands and funded with their own money—have been shocked to learn that, without so much as a by-your-leave, their hall has been sold and they now must travel long distances to get to their meetings. When halls are sold in this manner, the monies disappear into the coffers of the Organization.

The Service Committee consisting of the congregation Coordinator, the Secretary, and the Service Overseer make up the trustees for any Kingdom hall. What happens if these local elders—these legal trustees—balk at the idea of their hall being sold? If any should resist the "direction" of the Organization, the Circuit Overseer is empowered to remove that elder, and place another more compliant elder to his office of oversight. Thus, full compliance is all but guaranteed.

The same goes for excess congregation funds. I know of one local congregation that had over $80,000 in a fund to repave their parking lot. The elders refused to send in the money to the branch. Over the course of several C.O. visits, they were finally "persuaded" to do so, if they wanted to remain as elders. Of course, if they refused, they would have been removed and others elevated to their places—others who would "see reason."

No longer content to allow the local congregations to determine what constitutes "surplus funds," a letter to the bodies of elders dated July 15, 2022 has now directed all congregations to close their bank accounts and transfer all monies to the local branch office. So, from September 1, 2022, it would appear that every cent contributed at the local level will go directly into the bank account of the Society, and the local branch will take charge of paying the utilities for each local congregation.

All this is done under the guise of religion, and the secular authorities are woefully reluctant to tamper with religions.

Nevertheless, what you have is a plot to take over billions of dollars worth of property and abscond with millions in financial reserves. If the local men object, they are replaced. If the congregation publishers object to their hall being sold, the congregation is disbanded and the local publishers are redistributed to various neighboring congregations. And of course, they back all this up by claiming their authority comes from Jehovah God. Talk about an intimidation tactic!

If any do resist—if any do speak out—they will be branded as a divisive apostate and shunned by all their family members and their friends.

Can anyone now truly claim that Rutherford wasn't *spot on* when he declared that "religion is a snare and a racket"?

## Learning to Worship Without Religion

It has been said that attempting the same thing over and over while expecting a different result is the definition of insanity.

Given that the course of any religion or religious brand has been the same since the beginning of time, we don't want to fall again into that snare.

> For such freedom Christ set us free. Therefore, stand firm, and **do not let yourselves be confined again in a yoke of slavery**. (Galatians 5:1)

I used to think that religion and worship were synonymous terms. I no longer think so. We say "organized religion" as if there were any other kind. By definition, religion is organized worship—enslavement to men. Religion is never simply worship of God, but always ends up as being worship of men, because in the end, you must worship *according to the rules, teachings, and interpretation of the men* making up the leadership of the religion.

Ask the average Jehovah's Witness which he would obey if given a choice between a Bible command or some direction from the Governing Body given through *The Watchtower* or a branch letter? You will quickly see who is actually being worshipped.

Jesus is freeing us from that. No need to go to the temple. No need to go to the mountain. No need to go to the Kingdom Hall. Let's never again allow ourselves to come under "a yoke of slavery."

We do worship in a temple, but the temple is the body of worshippers, the Body of Christ.

## 16. Can I Worship God Without Religion?

Do YOU not know that YOU people are God's temple, and that the spirit of God dwells in YOU? If anyone destroys the temple of God, God will destroy him; for the temple of God is holy, **which [temple] YOU people are**. (1 Corinthians 3:16, 17)

What! Do YOU not know that **the body of YOU people is [the] temple of the holy spirit within YOU**, which YOU have from God? Also, YOU do not belong to yourselves, for YOU were bought with a price. By all means, glorify God in the body of YOU people. (1 Corinthians 6:19, 20)

In union with him the whole building, being harmoniously joined together, is **growing into a holy temple for Jehovah**. In union with him YOU, too, are being built up together into a place for God to inhabit by spirit. (Ephesians 2:21, 22)

### *Meeting Together*

I am not suggesting that gathering together to worship God is equivalent to being part of an organized religion. What, then, is this holy temple that Paul is referring to? We can answer that by reading about how the first-century congregation worshipped:

> So those who gladly accepted his word were baptized, and on that day about 3,000 people were added. And they continued devoting themselves to **[1]** the teaching of the apostles, **[2]** to associating together, **[3]** to the taking of meals, **[4]** and to prayers. Indeed, fear began to fall upon everyone, and many wonders and signs began to occur through the apostles. All those who became believers were together and **[5]** had everything in common, and they were selling their possessions and properties and distributing the proceeds to all, according to what each one needed. And day after day they were in constant attendance in the temple with a united purpose, and **[6]** they took their meals in different homes and shared their food with great rejoicing and sincerity of heart, **[7]** praising God and finding favor with all the people. At the same time Jehovah continued to add to them daily those being saved. (Acts 2:41-47)

Can you imagine how different our worship would have been as Jehovah's Witnesses if we'd followed that pattern? The closest we ever came to it was the Book Study arrangement, but the Governing Body did away with that some years ago. Just imagine meeting once a week for a meal. That would make the meetings smaller and more numerous, again, like the Book Study arrangement used to be.

Imagine getting together in small groups of about 15 or 20, and [1] reading the Christian Scriptures together, and commenting freely on our understanding of the reading, and [2] associating together, and [3] enjoying a meal together, and [4] praying together.

I won't speak for other religions, but as Jehovah's Witnesses, we never went to the Kingdom Hall to share a meal, we never associated save for a few minutes before and after, we didn't study the Bible, but instead studied the publications of the Governing Body, and we didn't pray together. One man prayed formally to open the meeting and another to close it, but you never heard different ones offer prayers publicly. In fact, women weren't allowed to pray despite what the apostle Paul reveals at 1 Corinthians 11:5, 13.

As far as [5] sharing everything in common, what a laugh. But in the first century, they didn't have formal meetings and didn't have dedicated meeting halls, but instead [6] met at different homes. As you examine the various letters of Paul and other first-century Bible writers, you find they were often directed to the congregations meeting in the home of some Christian in the area. Meetings were times for sharing a meal and encouraging others. That is the thrust of the exhortation which the Organization often misuses to promote their five formalized and structured weekly meetings:

> And let us consider one another **to incite to love and fine works, not forsaking the gathering of ourselves together**, as some have the custom, but **encouraging one another**, and all the more so as YOU behold the day drawing near. (Hebrews 10:24, 25)

The writer of Hebrews was not thinking of answering preformatted questions and prepared answers in 30-second sound bites at *The Watchtower* Study when he told us to "incite to love and fine works" and to encourage one another.

As far as [7] goes, we cannot be praising God when the focus of our meetings is on obedience to the commands of men. If you are familiar with the meetings and worship of Jehovah's Witnesses, then these two scriptures speak for themselves:

> If any man seems to himself to be a formal worshiper and yet does not bridle his tongue, but goes on deceiving his own heart, this man's form of worship is futile. The form of worship that is clean and undefiled from the standpoint of our God and Father is

this: to look after orphans and widows in their tribulation, and to keep oneself without spot from the world. (James 1:26, 27)

This people honors me with their lips, yet their heart is far removed from me. It is in vain that they keep worshiping me, because they teach commands of men as doctrines. (Matthew 15:8, 9)

## Walking on Water

Can you imagine how hard it must have been for those thousands of Jewish converts to give up their form of worship for this new faith in the Messiah? The temple in Jerusalem was a marvel of the ancient world. A massive and impressive structure. Jesus' own disciples remarked on the magnificence of the building:

As he was going out of the temple, one of his disciples said to him: "Teacher, see! what wonderful stones and buildings!" (Mark 13:1)

Later, when some were speaking about the temple, how it was adorned with fine stones and dedicated things, (Luke 21:5)

Jesus had only just that day predicted the destruction of the temple and of the city of Jerusalem, and now in response to their remarks he told them:

Do you see these great buildings? By no means will a stone be left here upon a stone and not be thrown down. (Mark 13:2)

They were not to be misled by the illusion of permanence that such structures were meant to convey. There is comfort in tradition, a sense of security that comes from worshipping God within a well-established religious structure, but it is a false security. Less that forty years after the disciples marvelled at the temple, it lay in ruins, just as Jesus had prophesied.

There is a message for us in all of this. When I first realized that I hadn't been worshipping the Father in spirit and truth, but that I'd been unwittingly preaching falsehoods my entire life, I realized I had to make a change, but I couldn't see anywhere else to go. I was conditioned by long practice to equate membership in some religion as the means to salvation.[11] I hadn't yet grasped the full significance of Jesus' words to the Samaritan woman.

To use an analogy, I had viewed all other religions as ships loaded with passengers. These ships were all different sizes and speeds, but they had one thing in common: They were all sailing toward a waterfall. They were all doomed. They were all part of Babylon the Great, and their end was assured. My ship, however, was sailing to paradise and I was on it. To learn that the "good ship jw.org" was also heading for the waterfall left me in a quandary. There was no other ship I could hop onto to be saved. All the ships were heading in the same direction, toward destruction. Was I expected to jump overboard and swim for it?

Then I remembered that remarkable incident when Jesus came to the disciples walking on water. I realized that I didn't need a lifeboat or another ship to get to paradise. I just needed faith in Jesus Christ.

With that faith, we can walk on water. We don't need an organization. But even if, by faith, we can figuratively "walk on water," we still need to know where to go.

So, simply believing in Jesus is not enough. We need to understand God's love, and learn how to worship in both spirit and truth. That will be the subject of the final chapter.

> But you, beloved ones, build yourselves up on your most holy faith, and pray with holy spirit, in order to keep yourselves in God's love, while you await the mercy of our Lord Jesus Christ with everlasting life in view. (Jude 20, 21)

---

11. "Just as Noah and his God-fearing family were preserved in the ark, survival of individuals today depends on their faith and their loyal association with the earthly part of Jehovah's universal organization." (w06 5/15 p. 22 par. 8)

# 17

# "Where Do I Go from Here?" The Path Forward

*"...it is already the hour for you to awake from sleep, for now our salvation is nearer than at the time when we became believers." (Romans 13:11 NWT 2013)*

I won't sugar-coat this. The journey from darkness to light is not an easy one. Few things that are truly worthwhile are easy. As you begin your search for truth, bear in mind that Jesus is speaking to you when he says:

> The kingdom of the heavens is like a treasure hidden in the field, which a man found and hid; and for the joy he has he goes and sells what things he has and buys that field.
> Again the kingdom of the heavens is like a traveling merchant seeking fine pearls. Upon finding one pearl of high value, away he went and promptly sold all the things he had and bought it. (Matthew 13:44-46)

How valuable is the Kingdom of God to you? What would you be willing to give up to attain it?

If you are one of Jehovah's Witnesses, you'll know that just possessing a book like this will bring persecution in the form of rebukes by family and friends and most certainly the local elders.

You may recall that earlier in this book we discussed the meaning of the word "persecution" (*diōkō* in Greek) which means "to chase, like a hunter pursuing his prey." If you're one of Jehovah's Witnesses and have now decided that you are willing to give up everything for the prize of everlasting life serving with Jesus in the Kingdom of God, then you will be hunted down (persecuted).

It will probably start with gossip behind your back. In the Witness community, word spreads like wildfire, and anything you have said will soon become wildly distorted.

The elders will surely pull you aside to have a talk with you. They will threaten you with disfellowshipping, meaning you'll be shunned by all your former JW friends and even close JW family members. Jesus anticipated this when he warned us of the consequences of worshipping God in spirit and truth:

> Truly I say to YOU men, No one has left house or brothers or sisters or mother or father or children or fields for my sake and for the sake of the good news who will not get a hundredfold now in this period of time, houses and brothers and sisters and mothers and children and fields, with persecutions, and in the coming system of things everlasting life. (Mark 10:28-30)

That a Christian could be cut off from his social network and shunned by even intimate family members just for exercising his God-given right to free and independent thought must seem bizarre to outsiders, but it's a reality all Witnesses are painfully aware of. I have come to see that this form of shunning—not due to sin, but to punish anyone for challenging the rule of the Governing Body—is not just unscriptural, but Satanic—bearing in mind that "Satan" means "resister or opposer."

It is a lot to risk, so we shouldn't take this step blindly.

When I began to study on my own, my biggest concern was how to avoid being misled ever again. Perhaps you are thinking the same thing. You know the truth is out there, but how can you distinguish it from all the false interpretations spouting from the lips of the many costumed characters littering the religious landscape with their priestly frocks or Armani suits and gold Rolex watches?

## How I Rebuilt My Faith

No one builds a house with their bare hands. You need good tools to do the job, but you have to know how to use those tools correctly and where to start to build. It took me a while to find those tools when I first started down this road of discovery. The tools I speak of are not made of wood and metal, but are far more durable, and will serve you for the rest of your life. Paul teaches us that our foundation must be Christ, and how we build on that foundation will be revealed as if with fire.

> According to the undeserved kindness of God that was given to me, as a wise director of works I laid a foundation, but someone else is building on it. But let each one keep watching how he is building on it. **For no man can lay any other foundation than what is laid, which is Jesus Christ.** Now if anyone builds on the foundation gold, silver, precious stones, wood materials, hay, stubble, each one's work will become manifest, for the day will show it up, because it will be revealed by means of fire; and the fire itself will prove what sort of work each one's is. If anyone's work that he has built on it remains, he will receive a reward; if anyone's work is burned up, he will suffer loss, but he himself will be saved; yet, if so, [it will be] as through fire. (1 Corinthians 3:10-15)

Because I had been building my faith as a Jehovah's Witness on a fusion of Bible truth and Watch Tower dogma, my foundation was a mixture of gold, silver and precious stones combined with wood, hay, and stubble. When the fire came, the work I had built up over my lifetime was consumed and turned to ash, but thanks to the love of God, I was saved. The truths I had gleaned from years of Bible study, despite the corrupting influence of Watch Tower teachings, survived the fire and remained.

I had to rebuild, but now I knew how to avoid introducing more false teachings—more wood, hay, and stubble—into my understanding of God and my salvation. The method is simple: Accept no human interpretation as truth. Instead, go to Scripture and let the Bible speak for itself. Let me give you an example.

I have on several occasions had the opportunity to speak with Jehovah's Witnesses who have approached me in their preaching work. I do not argue with them, but I do ask them to read John 1:12, 13:

> However, to all who did receive him, **he gave authority to become God's children**, because they were exercising faith in his name. And they were born, not from blood or from a fleshly will or from man's will, but from God. (John 1:12, 13 NWT 2013)

I then ask them how they can say that there are other sheep who don't get the right to become God's children when this verse makes it very clear that **all** who receive Jesus and exercise faith in his name, get authority to become God's children.

They'll say they have to do some research and arrange a return visit, usually with one of the elders in tow. I simply let them expound their understanding, but ask them continually the same question: "Where does it say that?"

I have seen them time and again get increasingly frustrated, because they rely on the reasoning from the publications to prove their point but can't make their argument solely from Scripture. Soon, they will leave, never to return. That pattern has never changed.

If you want to rebuild your faith, make that question your mantra: *Where does it say that?*

If you can find something declared clearly in the Bible, an understanding that doesn't conflict with the rest of Scripture, then you are likely on the right path. But always enter every Bible reading and research session with a mind clear of bias and preconception (easier said than done) and be vigilant not to allow your ego, personal preferences, and life experiences to influence your understanding of any verse.

## Breaking Free from the Past

Were you raised as one of Jehovah's Witnesses like I was? If so, your task will be even more difficult than it is for someone who converted to the religion as an adult. A child implicitly trusts his parents and accepts what they say as absolute truth. He has not yet learned to evaluate new information critically. As adults, we are more likely to do this, at least at first. However, once we come to trust the person who is teaching us, we tend to suspend critical thought and just accept what is being taught as truth.

So here we are now—you and I—with years of beliefs stored in our brains, coloring our thinking processes and our reasoning ability. Some of these beliefs are bound to be true, but others are false. How do we distinguish one from the other? How do we avoid, as the saying goes, throwing the baby out with the bathwater?

We do this by acknowledging to ourselves that everything is on the table. There is no belief we may hold that is too dear or too precious to go unexamined. We have nothing to fear by critically and carefully examining any and all of our beliefs. If we are sincere, and if we are starting out without an agenda other than the goal to arrive at truth, then we will be rewarded. This is easy to say, but not so easy to do, because often a belief is buried so deep that we are not even aware of it.

## Learning from Jesus' Words to the Samaritan Woman

Fundamental doctrines are, by definition, the foundation of our belief system. They are the basement upon which our house of faith is built. We have to be willing to examine everything, no matter how solid and well-founded we may believe it to be. That was what Jesus was asking his disciples to do, and there is no better example of that than the account of Jesus at the well with the Samaritan woman.

> The woman said to him: "Sir, I perceive you are a prophet. Our forefathers **worshiped in this mountain**; but YOU people say that in **Jerusalem is the place where persons ought to worship**." Jesus said to her: "Believe me, woman, **The hour is coming when neither in this mountain nor in Jerusalem will YOU people worship** the Father. YOU worship what YOU do not know; we worship what we know, because salvation originates with the Jews. Nevertheless, the hour is coming, and it is now, when the true worshipers will worship the Father with spirit and truth, for, indeed, the Father is looking for suchlike ones to worship him. God is a Spirit, and those worshiping him must worship with spirit and truth." (John 4:19-24)

As a Jehovah's Witness, would you have ever gone to a Catholic Church to worship God? Of course not! Witnesses go to the Kingdom Hall to worship Jehovah God. Now imagine if Jesus came to you one day and told you that *the hour has come when neither in a Catholic Church nor in a Kingdom Hall will people worship God*. In other words, you don't need to belong to an organization to worship Jehovah. What you need is to worship in spirit and in truth.

How would you have reacted to Jesus' telling you that you don't need to go to the Kingdom Hall, because essentially, that is what he was telling the Samaritan woman and his Jewish disciples?

# No Regrets

I was into my sixties before I realized that the core teachings of the Organization of Jehovah's Witnesses were unscriptural. Yet, what to some would appear to have been a wasted life never caused me to doubt the existence of God, nor the value of Christianity. I do not view my decades as one of Jehovah's Witnesses to have been a waste since it got me to where I am now. To an atheist, a lifetime in what would seem a vain pursuit amounts to a total waste, but we are not atheists who think that this life is all there is. Paul told Timothy to "get a firm hold on everlasting life."[1] You cannot get hold of something which is not already present with you. Everlasting life is not something in our future. It is *now*. We can grasp hold of it *now*.

If I have spent the first 60 years of my life as a Christian, albeit a misguided one, what of it? As long as it led me to the real life that Paul speaks of, it was worth every second, because everlasting life is infinite life. Let me illustrate that: The average male in Canada lives for 80 years. Imagine a pie that represents that lifespan. Cut it into four equal slices each representing a quarter of that lifespan. An atheist looking at my life prior to my awakening to the truth would say that I'd already eaten three of those slices and had only one left—20 years. But a Christian, as a Child of God, measures life with an infinite ruler. If that pie represents everlasting life, just how thin would a piece be that measures out a mere 60 years? There is no knife sharp enough to cut a slice that thin.

If the past 60 years were necessary for me to awaken to the true hope of everlasting life, then it was time well spent. It is of no benefit to me to agonize on what might have been.

> Jesus said to him: "No man who has put his hand to a plow and looks at the things behind is well-suited for the Kingdom of God." (Luke 9:62 NWT 2013)

> Not that I have already obtained this or am already perfect, but I press on to make it my own, because Christ Jesus has made me his own. (Philippians 3:12 ESB)

Did I have to go through all this to be where I am now? Would I have become the believer I am now if I hadn't had the grounding in Scripture that I obtained from years of Bible study with Jehovah's Witnesses? I can't say for sure, but I doubt it.

I think of Saul of Tarsus who became the apostle Paul. Jesus saw in him something no one else could see. Why did Jesus wait

---

1. 1 Timothy 6:12, 19

until after Saul persecuted the disciples before appearing to him? Was it that Saul's heart was not yet ready? Would Saul have become the zealous evangelizer that he proved to be if Jesus had appeared to him earlier, say, following the stoning of Stephen? Was it the guilt Paul surely felt for his horrible persecution of innocent Christians that, at least in part, drove him to become such a key figure in the development of the Christian congregation?[2] Who can say? Jesus knows.

All we can know is that our heavenly Father knows the heart, and He calls each of us when we are ready and able to respond to the call. And even then, it can take multiple prompts from above before we respond. Jesus told Saul of Tarsus that he was "kicking against the goads."[3] So, the process can be quite a trial.

I write all this because I imagine that many of you who are reading this book have wondered about these same things. It is sad to say, but I'm sure that most Jehovah's Witnesses would recoil at even the sight of this book. I know of one sister—now awakened—who used to continually check out *Crisis of Conscience* from her local library. This is the book that ex-GB member Raymond Franz wrote after he left the Organization. She didn't check it out over and over so as to read it. Her goal was simply to keep it out of the hands of others so that it would not "poison" them.

Her mentality is common among Witnesses because they have been trained to think this way. It is not logical nor scriptural. It is the product of mind-numbing indoctrination. If there is a spiritual poison, it is to be found in the indoctrination that quashes independent and critical thinking.

Lies are spiritual poison, but the antidote to the poison of a lie is hard, cold truth. We see this in the life of Jesus, who wasn't afraid to talk to the Devil, the greatest apostate of all time. And why not? Because he had the truth on his side and so could conquer the Devil.[4] As his disciples, we imitate him in conquering the Devil, the father of the lie.

> I write you, young men, because **you are strong** and the word of God remains in you and you have **conquered the wicked one**. (1 John 2:14)

---

2. 1 Corinthians 15:8, 9
3. Acts 26:14
4. 1 John 5:2-6

> You originate with God, little children, and you have conquered them, because the one who is in union with you is greater than the one who is in union with the world. They originate with the world; that is why they speak what originates with the world and the world listens to them. We originate with God. **Whoever comes to know God listens to us; whoever does not originate with God does not listen to us.** By this we distinguish the inspired statement of truth from the inspired statement of error. (1 John 4:4-6)

If we "originate with God," then we listen to truth. In fact, we yearn for truth. When someone tells you not even to listen to another, it usually means that person has something they want to keep hidden from you.

Why would so many Jehovah's Witnesses fall for such a cheap trick? I think the fact of the matter is that they want to believe the fiction they are being fed on a weekly basis. They are afraid to put their own faith to the test because they are happy with the fake reality others have spun for them. I'm referring to the fiction fed to Witnesses that tells them they are special, an Organization that God has chosen to survive Armageddon while the rest of the world burns. They don't want to burst that fragile bubble of illusion by a close inspection of Scripture.

That you have read this far into the book shows that you value truth above all else. But we have only scratched the surface here. There are still many things to research. It takes time, but it is time worth investing.

It will also require sacrifice—for many, a very great personal sacrifice. Jesus spoke of the Kingdom by likening it to a pearl of great value. He spoke of a man who was willing to sell all he owned so as to purchase this one pearl. Would you give up everything you hold of value to possess the Kingdom of God? Peter did.

> Then Peter said to him in reply: "Look! We have left all things and followed you; what actually will there be for us?" Jesus said to them: "Truly I say to YOU, In the re-creation, when the Son of man sits down upon his glorious throne, YOU who have followed me will also yourselves sit upon twelve thrones, judging the twelve tribes of Israel. And everyone that has left houses or brothers or sisters or father or mother or children or lands for the sake of my name will receive many times more and will inherit everlasting life. (Matthew 19:27-29)

As I said earlier, when I realized that Witnesses were wrong about 1914, it shook my faith, but not to the point that I doubted that I was still "in the truth." After all, it wouldn't be the first time that the Governing Body got a prophetic interpretation wrong. What counted for me was the belief that only Jehovah's Witnesses understand the real salvation hope promised in Scripture. When my studies progressed and I came to see how wrong I was about that, I realized that to attain the real hope of the good news offered in Scripture, I would have to break free from all the implanted Watch Tower doctrinal bias that had kept me enslaved to men throughout my whole life.

In this book, we have only examined the teachings of Jehovah's Witnesses which are in some way related to the good news they preach. It is my desire to continue writing not only to expose false doctrine, but to help my brothers and sisters making up the body of Christ to come to a deeper and fuller understanding of the truth that sets us free.

For now, it is my hope that the information I've shared thus far has proven beneficial. For information on many topics pertaining not only to Jehovah's Witnesses but to other religious beliefs as well as pure Bible themes, please visit the *Beroean Pickets* web site (beroeans.net) as well as the *Beroean Pickets* YouTube channel (https://www.youtube.com/c/BeroeanPickets/videos).

What we are all seeking now is true freedom. This is not attainable through any worldly source, whether political, commercial, or religious, but only through Jesus Christ, our Lord and Mediator:

> For I put YOU on notice, brothers, that the good news which was declared by me as **good news is not something human**; for neither did I receive it from man, nor was I taught [it], except through revelation by Jesus Christ. (Galatians 1:11, 12)
>
> If YOU remain in my word, YOU are really my disciples, and YOU will know the truth, and **the truth will set YOU free**. (John 8:31, 32)

May our heavenly Father bless and guide you through his Son and our Savior, the Lord Jesus.

Your brother in Christ,

Eric Michael Wilson aka Meleti Vivlon

# Appendix A: My Letter to the Alliston Congregation

November 19, 2013
To the Body of Elders
Alliston Congregation

Dear Brothers,

There is a matter that has been concerning me for some time. I could remain silent, but I would be doing so out of fear alone. (1 Cor. 16:10) That would be cowardly and unloving. (Rev. 21:8)

As you know, I have laboured for almost ten years in this congregation. I've watched children grow into adults. I've watched brothers young in the truth mature, become ministerial servants, and even elders. They are my family, and you the elders I have considered my brothers-in-arms. So I feel a moral obligation to write.

(1 John 4:18) ...*There is no fear in love, but perfect love throws fear outside, because fear exercises a restraint. Indeed, he that is under fear has not been made perfect in love.*

The fear John refers to is not the reverential fear of God, but rather a fear that cripples, that stifles the expression of love. Love will move us to protect the little one. It will move us to do what is best for all concerned, both the individual and the collective. Fear of God will cause us to be obedient to the divine direction of his word. On the other hand, fear of man will nullify all the good that love might accomplish.

I want you to consider yourselves for a moment.

For many years, I would brag—I'm not ashamed to admit it—that this was simply the best body of elders I had ever served with in my forty-plus years as an overseer. We did not abuse the power of our office. We sought only to serve, but never to impose our personal conscience into the lives of the publishers. At times we failed to maintain this standard, but the fact is that for the most part we kept to it. I felt the reason for this was that we had all suffered ourselves under those who abused their power and presumed to judge others. Chris would talk about the difficulties he experienced in Orangeville. Dan was wounded emotionally by the harsh, insensitive treatment he and his son underwent in their former congregation. Doug had been severely hurt by the previous body of elders to the point of fleeing from Alliston to Orillia. Pat has known more abuse by authority figures than neither he nor I would care to relate. I also know of some of the injustices Bill and John have suffered in the past at the hands of supposedly well-meaning leaders. Gerry has seen such misconduct as has Frank. Perhaps only Rocco has been spared.

We have all endured our own share of tribulation, and I felt that this had given us a special empathy for the suffering of others. It produced among us a genuine sense of camaraderie, of cooperation, and of bonhomie. About two years ago that seemed to change. This past year has been particularly hard. Dissention almost tore us apart.

I do not feel the decision to remove me was an honorable one. However, based on what I observed at the meeting, I felt that any attempt to appeal would be futile. I also felt extremely discouraged by the lack of support from those whom I had supported in their hour of need. That I could be removed for adhering to a Bible principle such as that found at Acts 5:29 astonishes me still. I have researched what the publications and the Bible have to say about that verse and have found nothing that supports the way it was applied against me at that meeting.

Having said that, I take it no farther. I simply bring up the events leading to my removal to make a key point: I was removed because hypothetically—let's repeat that—because hypothetically I might disobey some future instruction of the Governing Body. No one could point to any occasion when I actually disobeyed direction from the Governing Body or the Canada branch, for that matter. It was all hypothetical.

Now contrast that with what happened to me in the weeks following that meeting. At the direction of the body of elders, I had to answer charges of apostasy on three occasions. Were these charges based on facts? Evidence? The testimony of two or more witnesses? No! By the admission of the brothers investigating me, the charges were hearsay. Those that were true were not valid charges at all. Those that could have been valid turned out to be lies and fabrications.

## Appendix A: My Letter to the Alliston Congregation

Remember, I was removed because of the *hypothetical possibility* of disobedience to the Governing Body. Now contrast that with what the body of elders has actually done.

The Governing Body tells us that two or more witnesses are required for judicial action.

> "There must be **two or three eyewitnesses,** not just people *repeating hearsay; no action can be taken if there is only one witness.*—Deut. 19:15, John 8:17" (KS 5:37) [Italics mine; boldface, theirs]

Notice that "people repeating hearsay" do not provide grounds for any action.

Even if there are serious questions raised, and apostasy is most serious, the accused still has the right to face those accusing him.

> "39. **If the accused denies the accusation,** the investigating elders should try to arrange a meeting with him and the accuser together..." (KS 5:39)

The Governing Body says that. Here's what Jehovah says:

> **(1 Timothy 5:19)** . . .*Do not admit* an accusation against an older man, *except* only on the evidence of *two or three witnesses.*

You are commanded by God not to "admit an accusation against an older man" except on "**evidence** of two or three witnesses." Brothers, you disobeyed this command. There was no evidence. What there was turned out to be falsehoods fabricated to make me out as something I am not. Even if you didn't know that at the time, you did know that it was all hearsay.

I was never allowed to face my accusers though I have a scriptural right to do that. (Prov. 18:17) I was not even allowed to know who they were, with the exception of [publisher name redacted] who was upset because he had been promised his name would be kept secret from me. One false accusation came from within the body of elders, but when I asked repeatedly with whom it had originated, I was told by those interviewing me that they couldn't remember. A serious accusation of apostate acts brought against an older man, and they couldn't remember who made it???

Brothers, you have disobeyed the direction of not only the Governing Body, but of Jehovah God. Why would you do this? One accusation that was brought against me was based on my having committed the oddly reprehensible act of downloading old Watchtower volumes. Apparently, some on the body have trouble distinguishing between apostasy and our 'rich spiritual heritage'. How could you even consider that as valid and bring it up to question my motives? Can you see how 'admitting an accusation against an older man' on such a silly premise undermines your credibility and the respect due your office of oversight?

It would seem that the mere mention of the "A" word throws reason out the window. Satan doesn't need to use apostates to undermine our faith and cause tribulation to the little one. He only has to get us so afraid of it that we'll do his job for him. Fear restrains love. Where there is no love, there is no defence against the evil one.

What is it that you are so afraid of that it would cause you to disregard the direction of the Governing Body and the commandment of Jehovah God? Perhaps it is this: When someone with a forceful personality or a superior office of oversight speaks, we may fear to dissent, preferring what you feel is the safe course of doing nothing, remaining silent. There is a truth in the saying that "silence grants consent". If you do not speak up when you feel something wrong is being done, you are consenting to it, and this before God.

"All evil needs to prosper is for good men to do nothing."

Consider that of all the sins that lead to the second death, the first one listed at Revelation 21:8 is cowardice. We can deceive ourselves with faulty reasoning, thinking that we need to have unity as a body, a oneness of mind. True, the Bible speaks of this, but in what context? Jesus said, "...in order that they may be one **just as we are one**." Of what value can it be if the entire body is of one mind, but that mind is not in unity with the mind of Christ? (John 17:11; 1 Cor. 2:16) When being asked to take a course of action, please remember that the Bible says, "You must not take up an untrue report....You must not follow after the crowd for evil ends." (Ex. 23:1,2)

Brothers, as a body (a crowd) you did indeed take up an untrue report against me. If some of you felt what was going on was wrong, but still supported the Body's decision, can it not be said you went after the crowd for evil ends?

Do not trivialize what you put me through nor think I am overreacting. Truly I tell you that the tribulation I have endured as a consequence of those 'investigations' is the most severe test of faith I have ever faced. That I have come through it is no credit to you—save one—nor to the circuit overseer. I mean no disrespect, but I do speak the truth.

When you fail to stand up to one who is pushing ahead, you are not showing love for the congregation nor for the man himself. Allowing a brother to follow a bold course of action in opposition to the direction from the Governing Body and from God will only embolden him further. This will lead to new problems. In fact, it already has, but to go into that here would be to reveal confidential matters. The fact is, I don't really need to, because I know you brothers are aware of those incidents where some have acted presumptuously. The question is, What are you prepared to do about it?

You are the protection Jesus has placed for his sheep. On behalf of us all, I ask you to please stand firm, and never remain silent in the face of wrongdoing that comes in the guise of 'protecting the congregation'. (James 3:1; Matthew 18:6; Revelation 21:8)

Your brother,

Eric Wilson

# Appendix B: My Letter to Headquarters and Reply

November 28, 1974

"Questions from Readers" Desk,
Watchtower, Bible and Tract Society,
Brooklyn, New York

Dear Brothers:

In the November 15, 1974 issue of "The Watchtower" on page 683, column 2, first paragraph, the statement is made that 'because Jehovah's "chosen ones" had fled the doomed city, He did not have to prolong the time of distress and could thereby spare some "flesh". Applying the rules of logic, if we put this in the conditional negative, we get: 'If Jehovah's "chosen ones" had not fled from the doomed city, He would have to have prolonged the time of distress and thereby some "flesh" would not have been saved.'

I do not understand how the fleeing of Jehovah's chosen ones allowed for the days to be cut short—as if their remaining in Jerusalem would conversely require the lengthening of those days. Also, I do not understand why jehovah would cut those days short on account of his chosen ones. They were far away in the mountains and would not be affected by those days whether they were short or long—leaving 97,000 alive or killing all the jews in the city. I would truly appreciate any help you can give me in clearing up these doubts.

Your brother,

Eric Wilson

Figure 21. My letter questioning the Watch Tower interpretation of Matthew 24:22.

# Appendix B: My Letter to Headquarters and Reply

**WATCHTOWER**
BIBLE AND TRACT SOCIETY
OF NEW YORK, INC.
117 ADAMS STREET, BROOKLYN, NEW YORK 11201, U.S.A.

TELEPHONE (212) 625-1240     CABLE WATCHTOWER

EG:ER     December 14, 1974

Mr. Eric Wilson
Calle 71A No 19-63
Apartado Aereo 51617
Castellana, Bogota
Colombia

Dear Brother Wilson:

    We have received your letter with regard to the application of Jesus' words at Matthew 24:21, 22.

    To a considerable extent we have to be guided by the way things actually worked out. When the tribulation on ancient Jerusalem began in 70 C.E., the Christian chosen ones were out of the city, so they were not in danger. When the tribulation began, it came swift and hard. It was not protracted over a very long period of time. You bring up as a possible question for consideration: What would have happened if the Jewish Christians were not in the city, whether the tribulation would not have been cut short, so to speak. But that is contrary to how things actually worked out and it would seem to be pointless to consider hypothetical cases that are contrary to fact and thus are contrary to the prophecy, for what Jesus prophesied was in accord with what occurred.

    Dealing with the fact of the matter, that the Jewish Christians were already out of the city, having fled when they saw the signal Jesus mentioned, the tribulation was not being cut short for their sake, as if they were going to benefit in some way because of its being cut short. Hence, its being cut short must have been on account of the chosen ones, on account of the fact that they were not there and would not be directly affected when Jehovah brought the destructive tribulation. With the actual fact of matters as it worked out in 70 C.E. in mind and the resulting understanding of Matthew 24:21, 22 in the first century C.E., we can conclude that the "great tribulation" in the future will be cut short, not for the sake of the chosen ones, but will come in a way not restricted in any way by the anointed, for they will already be out of the danger area, so to speak.

    We join with you in looking forward to the outworking of matters, knowing that the understanding of Bible prophecy is always the best after prophesied events have taken place.

                                        Your brothers and fellow servants,

                                          Watchtower B. & T. Society
                                              OF NEW YORK, INC.

**Figure 22. The Reply from the Service Desk in Brooklyn Headquarters.**

# Appendix C: *Life Everlasting* Book Inside Cover

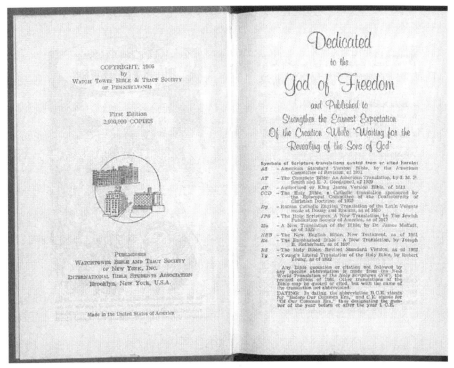

Figure 23. Inside cover of *Life Everlasting in the Freedom of the Sons of God*.

# Appendix D: *The Harp of God* Cover and Canvassing Script

Figure 24. This is the 1921 edition. The damning subtitle was removed in the 1925 edition.

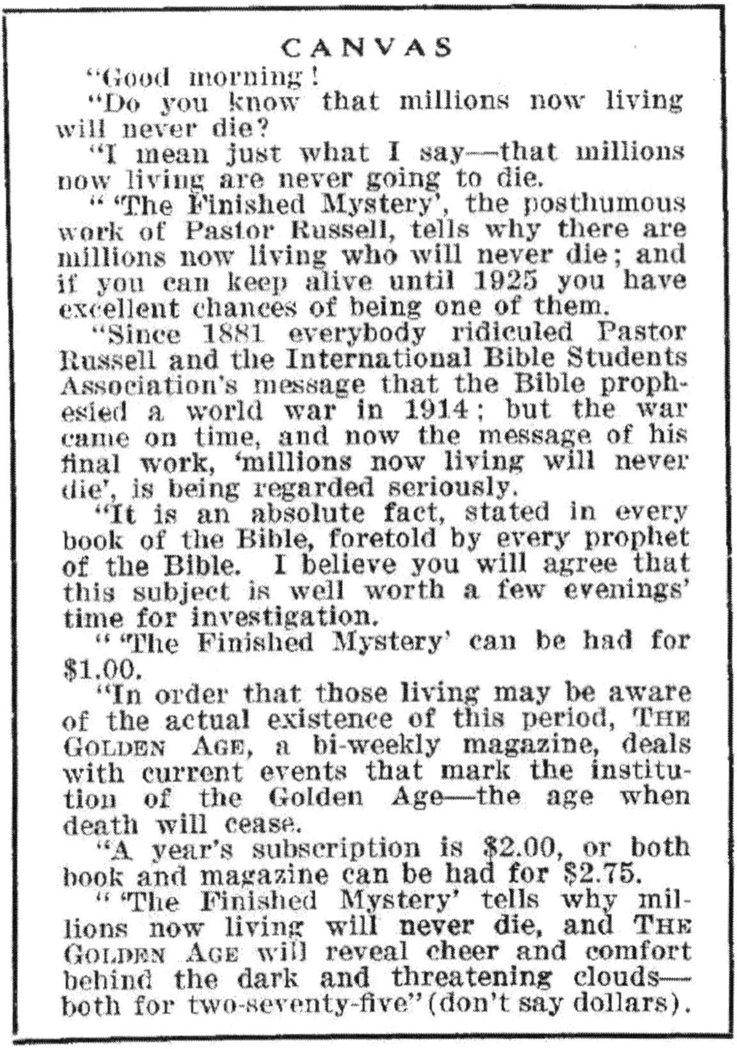

## CANVAS

"Good morning!

"Do you know that millions now living will never die?

"I mean just what I say—that millions now living are never going to die.

"'The Finished Mystery', the posthumous work of Pastor Russell, tells why there are millions now living who will never die; and if you can keep alive until 1925 you have excellent chances of being one of them.

"Since 1881 everybody ridiculed Pastor Russell and the International Bible Students Association's message that the Bible prophesied a world war in 1914; but the war came on time, and now the message of his final work, 'millions now living will never die', is being regarded seriously.

"It is an absolute fact, stated in every book of the Bible, foretold by every prophet of the Bible. I believe you will agree that this subject is well worth a few evenings' time for investigation.

"'The Finished Mystery' can be had for $1.00.

"In order that those living may be aware of the actual existence of this period, THE GOLDEN AGE, a bi-weekly magazine, deals with current events that mark the institution of the Golden Age—the age when death will cease.

"A year's subscription is $2.00, or both book and magazine can be had for $2.75.

"'The Finished Mystery' tells why millions now living will never die, and THE GOLDEN AGE will reveal cheer and comfort behind the dark and threatening clouds—both for two-seventy-five" (don't say dollars).

Figure 25. From October 1920 Kingdom Ministry, used in the door-to-door work.

# Appendix E: Gerrit Lösch's Declaration

```
                                                    F I L E D
                                                    Clerk of the Superior Court
                                                    FEB 0 5 2014

1  Megan S. Wynne, Esq., SBN 183707
   Ashley A. Escudero, Esq., SBN250473
2  MORRIS POLICH & PURDY LLP                        F I L E D
   One America Plaza                                Clerk of the Superior Court
3  600 West Broadway, Suite 500
   San Diego, California 92101                      '14 FEB 5    4:34
4  Tel: (619) 557-0404                                   FEB 0 5 2014
   Fax: (619) 557-0460
5                                                   By:_____ Deputy

   Donald T. Ridley, Esq.
6  Pro Hac Vice
   THE MANDEL LAW FIRM
7  370 Lexington Avenue, Suite 505
   New York, NY 10017
8  Tel: (212) 697-7383
   Fax: (212) 681-6157
9

10 Attorneys for Gerrit Lösch

11            SUPERIOR COURT OF THE STATE OF CALIFORNIA

12                        COUNTY OF SAN DIEGO

13 JOSE LOPEZ, an Individual,          CASE NO. 37-2012-00099849-CU-PO-CTL

14           Plaintiff,                DECLARATION OF GERRIT LÖSCH IN
                                       SUPPORT OF MOTION TO QUASH
15 v.                                  ORDER GRANTING PLAINTIFF'S
                                       MOTION TO COMPEL DEPOSITION OF
16 DOE 1, LINDA VISTA CHURCH;          GERRIT LÖSCH
   DOE 2, SUPERVISORY
17 ORGANIZATION; DOE 3,                Hearing Date:      TBD
   PERPETRATOR; and DOES 4 through     Time:              TBD
18 100, inclusive,                     Dept:              C-65
                                       Judge:             Joan M. Lewis
19           Defendants.               Complaint Filed:   June 29, 2012
                                       Trial Date:        June 27, 2014
20

21

22

23      I, Gerrit Lösch, declare as follows:

24      1.    I am over 18 years of age, of sound mind, and competent to make this Declaration.
25 I have personal knowledge of the matters contained herein, and they are all true and correct.
26      2.    I provide this Declaration to support the Motion to Quash Order Granting
27 Plaintiff's "Motion to Compel the Deposition of Gerrit Lösch and the Underlying Notice of
28
                                              1
                             DECLARATION OF GERRIT LOSCH
```

Figures 26, 27, and 28. The declaration to the State of California from Gerrit Lösch.

Taking the Deposition of Gerrit Lösch, with Production of Documents Required – Videorecorded for Use at Trial."

3. If called upon to testify in this civil action, I would provide the information contained in this Declaration.

4. I was not served with the Notice of Deposition, but I learned that Plaintiff vacated the original deposition date after Watchtower objected to the Notice.

5. I recently learned that this Court entered an Order compelling Watchtower Bible and Tract Society of New York, Inc. (sued as Doe 1; hereinafter referred to as "Watchtower") to produce me for deposition, but I have not been served with a copy of the Court's Order.

6. I am a member of the ecclesiastical Governing Body of Jehovah's Witnesses, having been appointed to serve in that capacity on July 1, 1994. I was not on the Governing Body in 1986 when the Plaintiff alleges he was abused by Gonzalo Campos.

7. The Governing Body of Jehovah's Witnesses is the highest ecclesiastical authority for the faith of Jehovah's Witnesses, and it exercises spiritual oversight for Jehovah's Witnesses worldwide.

8. I am not, and never have been, a corporate officer, director, managing agent, member, or employee of Watchtower. I do not direct, and have never directed, the day-to-day operations of Watchtower. I do not answer to Watchtower. I do not have, and never have had, any authority as an individual to make or determine corporate policy for Watchtower or any department of Watchtower.

9. Watchtower does not have, and never has had, any authority over me.

10. I have no personal knowledge of any facts or circumstances concerning the subject matter of this case because, among other things:

    (a) I do not supervise or work for, and I have never supervised or worked for, the Watchtower Legal Department or the U.S. Service Department.

    (b) I did not move to live in the United States until July, 1990.

    (c) Prior to July 1990, I resided in Austria.

    (d) I do not know and have never met the Plaintiff, Jose Lopez.

2
DECLARATION OF GERRIT LOSCH

(e) I do not know and have never met Leticia Lopez, the mother of Plaintiff Jose Lopez.

(f) I do not know and have never met the Defendant, Gonzalo Campos, who is sued as Doe 3.

11. I am a resident of the State of New York, as I live and work in Brooklyn where the world headquarters of Jehovah's Witnesses is located.

I declare under penalty of perjury under the laws of the State of California that the foregoing is true and correct, and that this Declaration is executed this 4th day of February 2014.

_____
Gerrit Lösch

# Appendix F: When Was Satan Cast Down?

Watch Tower publications claim that Revelation 12:7-12 was fulfilled in 1914:

> And war broke out in heaven: Michael and his angels battled with the dragon, and the dragon and its angels battled but it did not prevail, neither was a place found for them any longer in heaven. So **down the great dragon was hurled**, the original serpent, the one called Devil and Satan, who is misleading the entire inhabited earth; he was hurled down to the earth, and his angels were hurled down with him. And I heard a loud voice in heaven say: "Now have come to pass the salvation and the power and the kingdom of our God and the authority of his Christ, because the accuser of our brothers has been hurled down, who accuses them day and night before our God! And they conquered him because of the blood of the Lamb and because of the word of their witnessing, and they did not love their souls even in the face of death. On this account be glad, YOU heavens and YOU who reside in them! **Woe for the earth and for the sea, because the Devil has come down to YOU, having great anger**, knowing he has a short period of time." (Revelation 12:7-12)

Since 1914 has been shown to be a fiction of Watch Tower theology, there is no reason to suspect that Satan was cast out of heaven then. So, just when was he cast down?

While the Bible doesn't say, we can draw some conclusions from the following scriptures.

> Then the 70 returned with joy, saying: "Lord, even the demons are made subject to us by the use of your name." At that he said to them: "I see Satan already fallen like lightning from heaven." (Luke 10:17, 18)

Was our Lord speaking of events that would be two millennia in the future, or about something that would happen following his death and resurrection?

After his resurrection, we read:

## Appendix F: When Was Satan Cast Down?

> He was put to death in the flesh but made alive in the spirit. And in this state he went and preached to the spirits in prison, who had formerly been disobedient when God was patiently waiting in Noah's day, while the ark was being constructed, in which a few people, that is, eight souls, were carried safely through the water. (1 Peter 3:18-20)

What is the meaning behind this passage? The Organization teaches:

> Because he came off the victor through faithful endurance, the Son of God, as a spirit person, was able to proclaim a message of judgment against the "spirits in prison."[1]

But the question here is, why were these spirits in prison? Was it because the Devil and his demons had been cast down just as predicted in Revelation 12:9 and confined to the vicinity of the earth? That would seem to fit.

Once Jesus had died with his integrity unbroken, there was no more reason to tolerate the Devil and his demons. Any accusation they could make had been rendered moot by Jesus' faithful completion of his mission. Michael, the archangel could act and war with Satan, and throw him out of heaven. This could have happened the moment Jesus died.

Witnesses would disagree because they are taught that Jesus is the archangel Michael, but Hebrews makes it clear that Jesus is not, nor ever was, an angel.

> For example, to which one of the angels did he ever say: "You are my son; I, today, I have become your father"? And again: "I myself shall become his father, and he himself will become my son"? But when he again brings his Firstborn into the inhabited earth, he says: "And let all God's angels do obeisance to him." (Hebrews 1:5, 6)

Further, Satan crushes Jesus in the heel when he had him crucified, but Jesus crushes Satan in the head, when he destroys him for good.[2] There is no mention of a second, lesser crushing of Satan by the seed who turned out to be Jesus. Surely, such a crushing would fit if Jesus were Michael.

---

1. bw chap. 8 p. 126 par. 34
2. Genesis 3:15; Revelation 20:10

As to the "woe for the earth," we should bear in mind that the great apostasy set in not long after John's Revelation was penned, and following that began the "Dark Ages," one of the worst periods of human history.

Is there anything else in Scripture to help us to determine when Satan was cast out of heaven? Consider this passage:

> Now my soul is troubled, and what shall I say? Father, save me out of this hour. Nevertheless, this is why I have come to this hour. Father, glorify your name." Therefore a voice came out of heaven: "I both glorified [it] and will glorify [it] again." Hence the crowd that stood about and heard it began to say that it had thundered. Others began to say: "An angel has spoken to him." In answer Jesus said: "This voice has occurred, not for my sake, but for YOUR sakes. Now there is a judging of this world; **now the ruler of this world will be cast out.** (John 12:27-31)

Within this context, Satan is cast out. What context? Jesus is referring to the glorification he was about to receive for faithfully completing his mission on earth by dying with his integrity intact. This would result in a sanctification of God's name which the devil had been slandering since the original sin. Now there would be no reason to tolerate such slander anymore, so *the ruler of the world will be cast out*. This makes perfect sense within the context of Jesus' death and resurrection. Is there another time in history when the casting out of Satan would be more fitting?

Again, we can't say for sure, and Jehovah has not seen fit to give us the timetable, but one thing we can say: There is nothing scriptural that supports a 1914 ousting of the Devil and his demons.

# Appendix G: A Legacy of Shifting Years

Fixing the exact timing of organizational adjustments to the year marking the start of the Last Days and the beginning of the invisible presence of Christ can be a challenge. So as not to undermine its credibility, Watch Tower publications tend to hide these historical facts from the rank and file. Nevertheless, much can be gleaned from a review of the published evidence.

The November 1, 1922 Watchtower was a report of Rutherford's speech at the 1922 Cedar Point Convention where the Judge brought in a new idea that Jesus became King in 1914 rather than the previous view Barbour/Russell view of 1878 (not 1874). Rutherford said:

> Since 1914 the King of glory has taken his power and reigns. He has cleansed the lips of the temple class and sends them forth with the message. The importance of the message of the kingdom cannot be overstated. It is the message of all messages. It is the message of the hour. It is incumbent upon those who are the Lord's to declare it. The kingdom of heaven is at hand; the King reigns; Satan's empire is falling; millions now living will never die.
>
> Do you believe it? **Do you believe that the King of glory is present, and has been since 1874?** Do you believe that during that time he has conducted his harvest work? Do you believe that he has had during that time a faithful and wise servant through whom he directed his work and the feeding of the household of faith? Do you believe that the Lord is now in his temple, judging the nations of earth? Do you believe that the King of glory has begun his reign?
>
> Then back to the field, O ye sons of the most high God! Gird on your armor! Be sober, be vigilant, be active, be brave. Be faithful and true witnesses for the Lord. Go forward in the fight until every vestige of Babylon lies desolate. Herald the message far and wide. The world must know that Jehovah is God and that Jesus Christ is King of kings and Lord of lords. This is the day of all days. Behold, the King reigns! You are his publicity agents. Therefore **advertise, advertise, advertise, the King and his kingdom.**"[1]

---

1. *The Watch Tower*, November 1, 1922, p. 337

Compare this to how Watchtower depicts Rutherford's statement in the *Faith in Action* film or the *Our Kingdom Ministry* of August 2014 **where the 1874 reference is dropped**. The *Kingdom Ministry* says:

> "In 1922, J.F. Rutherford boldly proclaimed: 'Behold, the King reigns! ...Advertise, the King and his kingdom.' In this 100th year of Kingdom rule, his exclamation still fills us with excitement..."[2]

There are various steps in the switch to 1914—**The last days was changed from 1799 to 1914 in the December 1, 1929 *Watch Tower*** in an article called, "Locating the Time."

> Taking all these scriptures together, and knowing that they must be in exact harmony with one another, and taking the well known facts in connection therewith, it is easy to be seen that the definitely fixed "time of the end" was and is 1914 A.D. Nothing came to pass in 1799 that corresponds so well with these prophecies as did in 1914.[3]

Rutherford's book, *Light* Volume 1 (1930) says:

> The period of waiting for the Lord Jesus had come to an end and Jehovah sent forth his King and Judge, and he goes into action. *The Watch Tower* of March 1, 1925, commenting on Revelation 12, and the issue of September 15, 1925, commenting on Psalm 110, called attention to the beginning of the kingdom and the action of the King. The mighty One on the white horse wore a crown, denoting his authority and that he 'whose right it is to rule' had come. (See Ezekiel 21: 27.) The King is present. War between Christ and Satan was fought following 1914, to 1918, and Satan and his hosts were defeated and cast out of heaven. Thus Christ Jesus conquered, and he goes on to conquer at Armageddon.[4]

*The Golden Age* of April 30, 1930 has an article called, "Question and Answer." It says:

> This work of destruction began in 1914 and is proceeding rapidly and surely. The old order is to be dashed to pieces, and no human power can perpetuate it. Men perceive that the old order is collapsing, and in feverish excitement are forming leagues of nations, federations of churches, and giant mergers of business, as well as a giant international bank, hoping that by these

---

2. *Our Kingdom Ministry*, August 2014, p. 1
3. *The Watch Tower*, December 1, 1929, par. 12
4. *Light* Volume 1, pp. 73-74

expedients they can perpetuate the present order, with all its corruption and oppression. **If it is true that Jesus has been present since the year 1914, then it must be admitted that nobody has seen him with his natural eyes. The only way that He can be seen is by these signs or evidences, which Jesus declared would indicate His presence.**[5]

There is an interesting article in *The Golden Age* of March 14, 1934 titled "The Nobleman's Return." The article states:

> Prior to 1914 and years thereafter we thought that our Lord's return dated from 1874; and we took it for granted that the parousia or presence of our Lord dated from that time. An examination of the scriptures containing the word parousia shows that the presence of the Lord could not date prior to 1914...
> 
> Just so, when the disciples asked Jesus, "What shall be the sign of thy presence [parousia], and of the consummation of the age?" (Matthew 24:3) the Master gave unmistakable evidence of its proper application. **For some time now many have believed that the things mentioned in the great prophecy of Matthew twenty-four have application since 1914 and not before. It necessarily follows, then, that the presence or parousia of Christ, the "nobleman", could not be before 1914.**[6]

From this it is clear that the oft-repeated claim that *Zion's Watch Tower and Herald of Christ's Presence* was predicting Christ's enthronement as King in 1914 is a lie and that in reality, that understanding would not become official until some twenty years after 1914 had come and gone.

---

5. *The Golden Age*, April 30, 1930, p. 503
6. *The Golden Age*, March 14, 1934, pp. 380-381

# Appendix H: The One Man Who Is Really Responsible for 607 BCE

It is well established that archaeologists agree on 587 BCE as the year the temple in Jerusalem was destroyed by the Babylonians and the Jews were taken into captivity. However, Witnesses are taught that the real year this happened was 607 BCE. How do they arrive at that year? I was taught that it was because, following careful Bible research, they determined that the land of Israel had to lie totally desolate for a period of 70 years and since the year of the Jewish return to the land was known to be 537 BCE, the archaeologists had to be wrong, because the alternate was that the Bible was wrong, and that is unacceptable.

I agree, but what I failed to realize, and what my former JW friends still fail to realize, is that there is a third option. The Bible is right, and the archaeologists are right. What's wrong is the interpretation of the Organization. By misinterpreting the relevant texts, Jehovah's Witnesses are forced to accept a false date for the Jewish exile.

The question is: Who got it wrong initially? Who is responsible for the interpretation that has misled Jehovah's Witnesses for the past century and a half?

Indeed, who is responsible for the entire 1914 prophetic fiasco? Let's follow the evidence!

In the October 1876 *Bible Examiner*, C. T. Russell focuses on Leviticus 26 where Jehovah warns the nation of Israel that if they fail to keep his covenant, he will punish them "seven times." This phrase is repeated four times in that chapter. To Russell, this bore a correlation with the "seven times" of Nebuchadnezzar's madness.

Russell held the belief that when the gentile times ended in 1914, the "seven times" of Leviticus 26 would be fulfilled and the nation of Israel would be restored to its land.

Did Russell come up with this prophetic chronology on his own?

In the *Herald of the Morning* of March 1898, Nelson Barbour writes:

"C. T. Russell first became slightly interested by reading the HERALD OF THE MORNING, in 1875 [I believe this should be 1876],

## Appendix H: The Man Responsible for 607 BCE

but did not identify himself with the movement until the autumn and winter of 1876-1877, through listening to lectures which I delivered during the Centennial, at St. George's Hall Phila., and in other places. Both men [Barbour is writing about J. H. Paton and C. T. Russell] left the movement in 1878. C. T. Russell then, having been in the movement about eighteen months; felt competent to start a paper of his own. **Since which he has remained faithful to just what he learned from me**, prior to the 'midnight,' while we 'ALL slumbered and slept.'"

According to this article, Russell got all his 1914 end-of-the-gentile-times chronology from Nelson Barbour.

So we have Adventist[1] Pastor Nelson Barbour to blame for the erroneous date of 607 BCE.[2] Just how did he come up with it?

To answer that, we turn to an article he wrote in the Advent Christian denomination periodical, *The World's Crisis and Second Advent Messenger* of November 20, 1872. In his article titled, "Bible Chronology (Part II)" we read:

> Nearly all writers on chronology leave out the eleven years reign of Zedekiah, and commence the 'seventy years' with Jehoiakim's captivity. **As there is so much authority against me here, I will try and show very clearly why the seventy years captivity cannot begin until after Zedekiah's reign.**

The reasoning that Barbour uses is the same reasoning used by the Organization of Jehovah's Witnesses today. It is the same flawed reasoning which Carl Olof Jonsson exposed as such in his *Gentile Times Reconsidered*.[3]

What is remarkable about all this is that the source of the entire Invisible Presence of Christ and Last Days theology of Jehovah's Witnesses is a discredited Adventist preacher from the 19th century, and not Charles Taze Russell who simply failed to fact-check Barbour's chronology.

---

1. Not to be confused with Seventh Day Adventist. Barbour was an adventist in the generic sense. He was affiliated with the Advent Christian Church which published the periodical *The World's Crisis and Second Advent Messenger*.
2. Initially, Barbour used 606 BCE because of the belief there was a Zero year around the birth of Christ.
3. Currently in its fourth edition and available on Amazon.

# Glossary

**Christian Scriptures:** Also called the *New Testament* or the *Christian Greek Scriptures*, encompassing the Bible books from *Matthew* to *Revelation* in the traditional canon.

**Eisegesis:** "From outside in." A Bible study methodology where an outside interpretation is imposed onto a Bible text or passage of Scripture.

**Exegesis:** "From inside out." A Bible study methodology that allows Scripture to interpret itself, by looking for background from the context, harmony with the rest of Scripture, taking into consideration the historical context and the speaker's or writer's audience.

**Pre-Christian Scriptures:** Also called the *Old Testament* or the *Hebrew-Aramaic Scriptures*, encompassing the Bible Books from *Genesis* to *Malachi* in the traditional canon.

## List of Abbreviations

### Watchtower Publication Symbols

| | |
|---|---|
| bh | *What Does the Bible Really Teach?* |
| g | *Awake!*, formerly *Consolation, Golden Age* |
| it-1 | *Insight on the Scriptures*, Volume 1 |
| it-2 | *Insight on the Scriptures*, Volume 2 |
| jv | *Jehovah's Witnesses—Proclaimers of God's Kingdom* |
| re | *Revelation—Its Grand Climax at Hand!* |
| w | *The Watchtower*, formerly *Zion's Watch Tower and Herald of Christ's Presence* |

### Bible Version Symbols

| | |
|---|---|
| BSB | Berean Study Bible |
| HCSB | Holman Christian Standard Bible |
| LSV | Literal Standard Version |
| NIV | New International Version |

Printed in Poland
by Amazon Fulfillment
Poland Sp. z o.o., Wrocław

94857545R00231